Homeschooling In Wisconsin: At Home With Learning

Additional copies of this book are available from

Wisconsin Parents Association
Post Office Box 2502
Madison, WI 53701-2502
608.283.3131
www.homeschooling-wpa.org

Members of Wisconsin Parents Association receive a discount.
Contact us for information.

For ongoing information about homeschooling,
become a member of WPA. You will receive
the WPA newsletter and special bulletins as needed.

Homeschooling In Wisconsin: At Home With Learning

Sixth Edition

Wisconsin Parents Association
Madison, Wisconsin

Wisconsin Parents Association
Homeschooling in Wisconsin: at home with learning
p. cm.
Includes bibliographical references and index.
ISBN 0-9651864-2-3

1. Homeschooling—Curricula—Handbooks, manuals. 2. Non-formal education—Curricula—Handbooks, manuals. 3. Parenting.
Wisconsin Parents Association.

649.68
HO

 For information address:
Post Office Box 2502, Madison, WI 53701-2502.
608.283.3131
www.homeschooling-wpa.org

This edition printed in the United States
of America.

CONTENTS

Acknowledgments

This book would not have been possible without the work of many, many people. Among them:

• The homeschoolers who have created Wisconsin Parents Association (WPA) as a strong, effective grassroots organization and who have worked together through WPA to develop and maintain a favorable climate for homeschooling in Wisconsin. Some of the most obvious work has been done to gain and maintain a reasonable homeschooling law. But far more important, and requiring far more work, has been the growth and development of homeschools by thousands of families. These homeschooling families are reclaiming and reshaping a traditional approach to learning and showing the world that homeschooling works.

• All the homeschoolers who have stood up to school officials and others when they made unreasonable demands, tried to increase state regulation of homeschools, unfairly criticized homeschoolers, and intentionally or unintentionally gave out incorrect information about homeschooling. Through seemingly minor actions by thousands of people, we are reclaiming and maintaining our rights and responsibilities.

• The people who helped gather and develop the information in this book. Many people have read, thought, researched information, attended hearings, worked through support groups, and shared their experiences and stories, all of which has been distilled into the information presented here.

• Those who participated in the production of this book by researching, writing, editing, proofreading, laying out text and graphics, and coordinating production. A special thank you to the artist whose woodcut prints throughout this book convey the solidity, spirit, and down-to-earth nature of homeschooling.

• The cooperative and generous souls who willingly cooked meals, washed dishes, ran errands, and offered endless support so the people listed above could build WPA and work on this book.

• Most important, the children who have given their parents and their communities the opportunity to discover the wonder of homeschooling; to reclaim learning, family bonds, and whole lives; and to demonstrate that even in a complex, fast-paced, highly technological society, people can have fun learning together at a gentle pace. Without these children with their courageous spirits and enthusiasm for learning, neither homeschooling, nor WPA, nor this book would be possible. We give them our heartfelt thanks and our love.

Introduction

The book you are holding has the information you need to homeschool in Wisconsin. Homeschooling families have created it by living courageously, holding to our principles and beliefs, and daring to be different. Some of us are quoted here; more have contributed.

This book is our gift to you. We want to share some of what we've learned and support and encourage you. We want to tell you not to be afraid to homeschool, even if people close to you question you. Go for it, even if doubts threaten to overwhelm you. We know homeschooling isn't the only way, but we can assure you it's a good way. Only you can decide what's best for your family, but if you decide to homeschool, you can do it.

Families homeschool for many different reasons. Some want their children to have a conventional education while learning in their own way, at their own pace. Some want their children to pursue special interests. Other parents choose to share more of their beliefs and values than attending conventional school would allow. Some seek academic excellence, while others can't find an acceptable alternative. Some children cannot learn well in a conventional school. Other parents do not want their children trapped by the academic and social pressures of conventional schools. Some prefer to learn from life experience. Opportunities to build a stronger family draw others. And some want to take charge of their own lives rather than surrendering them to conventional schools.

Homeschooling encompasses all these reasons and more. Whatever your reasons, you are not alone.

Homeschooling families are amazing. In a society dominated by conventional schools, we are learning in our homes and communities, reveling in discovery, growing in confidence. We are contributing to our communities, doing important work, and having fun. We are living in the present as surely as we are preparing for the future.

Our lives make much needed statements:

• Families matter.
• Ordinary parents can raise children without relying on "experts."
• Children who are given love, support, and guidance are eager to learn and good at it.
• Everyone benefits when families learn and grow together, when parents consider raising their children a high enough priority to arrange income and career advancement around it.
• Even a small minority can work through a grassroots organization to maintain its rights and responsibilities in the face of continuing challenges from powerful interest groups.
• People can create and maintain a space where children and families are free to learn and live.

Today's homeschoolers walk in the footsteps of pioneers and provide the trail for those who will follow. Chapter 20 outlines Wisconsin homeschoolers' rich legacy that includes one of the most reasonable homeschooling laws in the country. Actions that will enable us to keep our freedoms and pass them on are discussed in Chapter 21. What you do will affect the way you and others, maybe even your children and grandchildren, can homeschool. Please act carefully, boldly, courageously, and wisely. Welcome to homeschooling in Wisconsin!

About This Book

Part One covers how to begin homeschooling.

Part Two discusses daily life: curriculums and learning resources, using the library and the Internet, homeschooling children with special needs, recognizing and evaluating learning, record keeping, high school at home, diplomas, socialization, support groups, parenting, problem solving, and secrets of experienced homeschoolers.

Part Three presents reasons homeschooling works, stories from homeschooling families, the history of homeschooling in Wisconsin, and the role of Wisconsin Parents Association (WPA).

Part Four explains why we must take responsibility for maintaining our freedoms. Reasons and strategies in Chapter 21 are followed by specific ways in which homeschoolers can work effectively individually and together.

Details about Wisconsin's homeschooling law and others affecting homeschoolers and ways of working with the Legislature are in **Part Five.**

"Homeschooling in a Non-Homeschooling World," **Part Six,** includes minimizing the chances a truant officer will contact you, responding if they do, working with public schools (if you want to), protecting your family's privacy, and current developments that affect homeschoolers,

Appendix A contains texts of important Wisconsin statutes. **Appendix B** describes WPA, who we are and what we do. WPA resolutions in **Appendix C** offer important perspectives on issues.

How You Can Use This Book

Read it straight through or choose the most important parts, whether you are a new homeschooler, a veteran seeking fresh perspectives, a teen developing your credentials, or a grandparent surprised that your grandchildren are homeschooling. Take it in the spirit in which it is offered: use the parts that fit your family and leave the rest. Read with pen in hand: underline, cross out, add your ideas. Insert tabs for quick reference. Make it your own.

To make information accessible, the book is formatted as a manual with lists of ideas, options, and suggestions plus cross references. Some repetition is inevitable as it presents, in linear form, ideas that are interconnected.

If you need information not in this book, call the WPA Voice Mail at 608-283-3131; visit the website at www.homeschooling-wpa.org; write to WPA, P. O. Box 2502, Madison, Wisconsin 53701-2502; or contact your WPA Regional Coordinator, listed in the WPA Newsletter and on the website.

May your family's homeschooling adventure be rich and rewarding!

Guide to Finding the Help You Need

For Information on Homeschooling

- → My children's current school situation has become intolerable. I need to begin homeschooling NOW, but I'm not sure how to begin. See pages 20 and 39.
- → I want to continue homeschooling, but I feel tired, overwhelmed, confused, and discouraged. See pages 39, 118, and 124.
- → I've just decided to homeschool our children, but I don't know what to do next. See pages 20 and 39.
- → How can I get a copy of form PI-1206 that homeschoolers are required to submit to the Department of Public Instruction (DPI)? See page 27.
- → Can I begin homeschooling in the middle of the school year or do I have to wait until next fall? See pages 27 and 33.
- → It is after the October 15th deadline to send form PI-1206 to the DPI. Can I still begin homeschooling? See pages 27 and 33.
- → Where do I get the books? See page 39.
- → I'm trying to decide whether our family should homeschool. See page 17.
- → I want to begin homeschooling. What is legally required? See page 23.
- → How old should my child be when I start sending in form PI-1206 for them? See page 32.
- → What is our family supposed to actually do to learn things when we start homeschooling? See pages See page 39.
- → How do I choose a curriculum? What choices do I have? Do I have to buy a whole curriculum? See page 44.
- → What qualifications do I need to homeschool our children? See page 18.
- → Can I homeschool my child with special needs even though I'm not trained in special education? See page 69.
- → Our children are already in high school. Is it too late to begin homeschooling? See page 89.
- → My teens don't like school work. How can I homeschool them? See page 89.
- → Can homeschoolers get good student discounts on auto insurance? See page 95.
- → How can homeschoolers get high school diplomas? See page 99.
- → How do homeschoolers get into college or technical school and get scholarships? See page 104.
- → Is there any way to get college credit without enrolling in college? See page 65.
- → What records do I have to keep? See page 82,

→ I'm not sure that our kids are learning enough of the right stuff. How should I evaluate their progress? Should I have them tested? See page 81.

→ What about socialization? See page 109.

→ Our child has trouble with reading (or whatever). What can I do? See page 119.

→ Our close friends, extended family, or neighbors are questioning our homeschooling. What can I do? See page 190.

→ As a homeschooling parent, I just don't have enough time for myself. See page 116.

→ A newspaper reporter has asked to interview our family about homeschooling. Should I agree to this? How do I prepare for the interview? See page 195.

→ How can I help our children prepare to enter or re-enter a conventional school after homeschooling? See page 240.

→ I am involved in a custody dispute with my ex-spouse. Can you help me? See page 122.

→ I want to hire an attorney for a case involving homeschooling. How can I find a good one? See page 178.

If a Public Official Contacts You

→ The school census taker is at the door (or on the phone, or has sent me a letter) requesting the names and ages of our children. See page 224.

→ A social service worker is at the door (or on the phone). See page 231.

→ A truant officer is at the door (or on the phone). See page 235.

→ The police have taken our homeschooled children into custody for being absent from school without a valid excuse. See page 236.

→ Someone at our children's school just told me that we should begin homeschooling. See page 34.

→ Our child has been diagnosed as "learning disabled," "hyperactive," as having "attention deficit hyperactivity disorder" (ADHD), or some similar label, and school officials are pressuring us to put him or her into special education. See pages 69 and 219.

→ I just received a letter telling me to bring in our 4 year old (or 3, 2, or 1 year old) for preschool screening. Should I go? Am I required by law to go? See page 219.

→ I have received a letter and a questionnaire from our local school district requesting information about our family because we are homeschooling. Should I fill it out and send it in? See page 226.

→ Should I get our children's school records from the time they attended public schools? How do I do this? See page 247.

→ Our children would like to take a course in the local public school. Is this possible? See page 242.

→ I would like my special needs child to get speech therapy or other services from the public school. Is this possible? How do I make the necessary arrangements? See page 242.

For Information about Homeschooling in Wisconsin

→ What does Wisconsin's homeschooling law require? See page 23.

→ How can I find out more about Wisconsin's homeschooling law and other laws that affect homeschoolers? See pages 201 and 206.

→ What was it like to homeschool in Wisconsin before the current law passed in 1984? See pages 133 and 143.

- → How many homeschoolers are there in Wisconsin? See page 185.
- → Are homeschools in Wisconsin private schools? See page 203.
- → I just heard (or read) that Wisconsin's homeschooling law is too lax. Is this true? Does the law hold parents accountable? See page 203.
- → Should the state require that homeschoolers take standardized tests? See page 184.
- → I want to be a responsible homeschooler. What should I be doing? See page 157.
- → Is it legal for homeschooling parents to homeschool children from another family along with their own children? See page 204.

For Questions about Policy and Practical Action

- → What can we do as parents to reclaim and maintain our rights and responsibilities? See page 157.
- → What issues do homeschoolers face today? See page 179.
- → Should homeschoolers get tax credits or other benefits from the state or federal government? See page 181.
- → What is the difference between compulsory attendance and compulsory education? Why does this matter? See page 166.
- → How can I get in touch with my legislators? See page 210.
- → How can I participate effectively in a legislative hearing? See page 213.
- → Do I need to worry about protecting my family's privacy? If so, what should I do? See page 251.
- → Should homeschoolers support legislation supposedly designed to protect parental rights? See page 257.
- → Should habitual truants or other "unqualified" people be prohibited from homeschooling? See page 187.
- → Why does Wisconsin have such a good homeschooling law? See page 141.
- → Should I have my question my children screened? See page 219.

For Questions Not Answered in This Book

- → Call the WPA Voice Mail at 608-283-3131.
- → Contact your WPA Regional Coordinator listed in the WPA Newsletter and on the website at www.homeschooling-wpa.org.
- → Visit the WPA website at www.homeschooling-wpa.org.
- → Write to WPA at P.O. Box 2502, Madison, Wisconsin 53701-2502

A Note on Quotes in This Book

Many homeschoolers have contributed to this book. Most of the quotes are anonymous to protect the privacy of the writers and their families. First names within quotes have also been changed. However, a few quotes are from the opening remarks given each year at the WPA conference. Because the speakers were identified both at the conference and when their remarks were published in the WPA newsletter, these quotes have been identified as "From Opening Remarks, WPA Conference, [year]." Speakers were: 1999 Carol Gutenberger, 2000 Cindy Duckert, 2002 Roy Underhill, 2004 Melanie Burgi, and 2005 Kathleen Plunkett-Black. (See the WPA website for the complete texts of their remarks.) Thank you to them and to all the other people who contributed to this book.

PART ONE

STARTING HOMESCHOOLING

Chapter 1

Deciding to Homeschool

The decision to begin homeschooling involves much more than where children will learn to read and do long division. Homeschooling is a big responsibility with far-reaching consequences. It is also an adventure.

People decide to homeschool for many reasons and in many ways. Some make an intellectual decision that it will provide the best education for their children. Others are lead through prayer or feel in their hearts that it is right for them. There are parents who reluctantly choose homeschooling as the best alternative despite a lack of confidence in their own abilities. Whatever your reasons for homeschooling, you are not alone.

Parents' feelings about homeschooling vary, too. Many embrace homeschooling joyfully and truly love it. Some begin out of a sense of duty and find they like it better than they had expected, while others persist mainly because they are convinced it is best for their children.

Questions to Consider

Many parents consider questions such as the following when deciding whether to homeschool:

• What effect would homeschooling have on our children? In what ways would homeschooling benefit them? Are there any ways might it be detrimental?

• How would having more time together and sharing more experiences strengthen our family and the relationships we have with each other?

• How would homeschooling affect:

—our family budget?

—our children's relationships with their friends?

—our relationships with people outside the family?

—the work being done by adults in the family?

• Would homeschooling or attending a conventional school be a better way for our children to learn each of the following:

—basic academic skills?

—how to learn?

—religious and moral values?

—how to get along with peers?
—how to get along with people older and younger than they are?
—how to be responsible members of a group?
—how to master skills that interest them?
—how to assume responsibility and get a job done?
—appreciation of natural beauty and the arts?
(Add other skills, qualities, etc. that you consider important.)

• Would homeschooling or attending a conventional school give our children a better opportunity to learn at their own pace, according to the learning style that suits them? Which would give them a better chance to pursue topics that especially interest them?

• What stresses and tensions would our children face in attending a conventional school? In homeschooling? Which would they be better able to handle? Where would they get the most support? Where would they have the best opportunity to mature socially?

• What are my biggest concerns or worries about homeschooling? With whom could I discuss them?

Reassuring Information for Parents Considering Homeschooling

• Many parents find that it is easier to parent children when they are homeschooling than when they are attending a conventional school. The time that homeschooling families spend together is more relaxed and enjoyable than the limited time before and after school, on weekends, and during school vacations. (See Chapters 15, 16, and 17.)

• Most parents find that life as a homeschooling parent is different from what they imagined before they started homeschooling. It is certainly different from the lives of parents whose children attend conventional schools. It is better, according to the vast majority of homeschooling parents. Since they have more control over their time, space, and energy, the inevitable problems and frustrations are more manageable. Homeschooling is a big responsibility and can be a lot of work, but most parents find they gain more than they give.

• Homeschooling does not need to be expensive. Many homeschoolers rely on libraries and other sources of free and inexpensive learning materials.

• Meeting the requirements of Wisconsin's reasonable homeschooling law is not difficult. (See Chapter 3.)

• A decision to homeschool does not have to be a lifetime commitment. Many homeschooled children have entered or re-entered conventional schools without difficulty, richer for the homeschooling experiences they have had.

Am I Qualified to Homeschool My Children?

Yes! How can that statement be made so definitely? For a number of reasons, including the following:

• You are a parent who cares enough about your children to consider homeschooling. (It is important to realize that homeschooling, or even considering homeschooling, is obviously not the only way parents show that they care deeply about their children. But parents who homeschool obviously care about their children.) Parents who care about their children, are committed to doing the best they can for them, and love them are well prepared to homeschool.

• If you are considering homeschooling, there's a good chance that your children have already learned to walk and talk. Think about that. They've learned two of the most complicated human skills. To walk they've learned about balance, using muscles, choosing a direction, and more. Somehow, from all the sounds they've heard, your children have selected the ones that are part of our language, figured out what they mean, and learned to make them. With your help and support, your children have learned all this! Of course you can homeschool.

• Doubts don't mean you shouldn't homeschool. Conscientious parents have doubts and feel concerned at times, whether they send their kids to conventional or alternative schools or homeschool.
• Homeschooling parents sometimes make mistakes as they are parenting and helping their children learn. That's okay. One of the big advantages to homeschooling is that it gives families time to make mistakes, learn from them, make amends, and proceed.
• You are a person who seeks out information and resources for things you are considering doing. If you weren't, you wouldn't be reading this book. So you not only know how to find resources; you use them once you've found them. People who are willing to admit that more information would help and have some idea of how to find it, and who listen to other people's experiences and use what will work for their families, are obviously prepared to get the information and support they need to homeschool.

At the same time, getting a pile of information is not difficult. People today are surrounded by information, overloaded by it. The problem is finding accurate information that can be trusted. People who choose this book are choosing information from experienced homeschoolers who have worked hard to reclaim and maintain families' rights to homeschool, and who have helped develop a climate of public opinion favorable to homeschooling. Information from other homeschoolers in the state where you live is more reliable and useful than is information from school officials, the Department of Public Instruction (DPI), publishers trying to market homeschooling curriculums, or national homeschooling organizations that have limited knowledge of and commitment to homeschooling laws and practices in individual states. It is far superior to information from professionals and experts in education who know very little about homeschooling and whose experience and commitment to conventional schools distort the information they present and make it inaccurate.

Therefore, you have what it takes to homeschool. This does not necessarily mean that you should homeschool. That's a separate question you need to answer for yourself. But it means you will be able to homeschool if that's what you decide to do. Remember this, especially during times of doubt that arise partly from living in a society that is so dominated by conventional schools and their approach to learning and living: You can homeschool.

Chapter 2

Getting Started: What Does It Take to Homeschool?

Starting homeschooling is exciting and challenging. Here are some suggestions.

• **First, take a deep breath.** Homeschooling has worked well for many families, and it can work for yours. There's no rush. You have time to decide how you want to homeschool, what curriculum to use, how to comply with the law, and all that. This handbook will help you enormously.
• **Learn what's required to homeschool in Wisconsin** and what's not required. See Chapter 3.
• **File form PI-1206 with the Department of Public Instruction (DPI).** It is illegal to homeschool in Wisconsin without filing this form. See Chapter 4.
• **Take a break from school work.** This will be a big help in starting homeschooling. Take the pressure off yourself and your kids. Don't worry about textbooks, worksheets, or curriculums for at least a week, ideally a month. Instead, help the kids find constructive things to do, or, better yet, do things together. Ask the kids what they'd like to do. Think of things you've wanted to do but haven't had time for-until now. Don't worry about how you'll get the 875 hours required by statute. You will be amazed at how much the kids learn during this break, and you'll have plenty of time later for more formal academics, if that's the type of curriculum you choose.

A break gives your family an opportunity to come together, get to know each other better, improve communication, reduce tension, and just plain have fun. Kids unwind, get their feet back on the ground, and relax. It's especially important for kids who have had difficulties in conventional school, whether because of academics, teachers, peer pressure, bullying, or whatever. Parents can focus on just parenting without worrying about teaching.

Good activities for the first days and weeks of homeschooling include:

- Reading what the kids choose, as long as you consider it acceptable.
- Watching appropriate movies, videos, DVDs.
- Sleeping. Many kids (and parents) do not get as much sleep as they need. Catching up on sleep often works wonders.
- Going for long walks or nature hikes.
- Playing at the park.
- Daydreaming.
- Going to the library and checking out fun stuff: videos, DVDs, music, magazines, colorful books from the children's section, cookbooks, anything that looks appealing.

- Taking a trip: a day trip to a nearby city or park, an overnight to a favorite spot or a new one you want to explore, or, if you can afford the time and money, a real vacation. If you give the kids as much responsibility as possible for planning, preparing, and managing the trip, they will learn without your having to do lesson plans or motivate them.
- For more ideas, see Chapter 6.

Many parents find they need to limit or prohibit activities they feel are unacceptable or unhelpful, perhaps computer games, television, etc.

However, if your family is really uneasy with this approach and would feel more comfortable doing something that seems like school each day, here are some suggestions.

1. Read each day, in whatever way works best for your family. Take turns reading aloud. Gather as a group and each read silently. Listen to books on tape. Stretch the definition of reading and watch a video or DVD based on a book. Read anything that appeals to you: magazines, picture books (no matter how old you are), novels, books about homeschooling (*Surviving the Applewhites* by Stephanie S. Tolan is a lively, short novel about a homeschooling family), you name it.
2. Get one or more of the books listed in Possibility #2 in Chapter 6 from the library. Each day, choose an activity that looks interesting, and do "school" for maybe an hour.

Activities like these will give your children plenty of learning opportunities while you take your time choosing a curriculum that will work for your family. You don't need to do at home what your children would have done if they had stayed in school. As you're doing activities from the books listed above, remember that anything we learn is helpful, so even if your kids learn something about math or science or whatever that isn't part of the standard curriculum for their grade, it won't be a waste and it will help them learn the material for their grade when (or if) you go back to it.

• **Take your time in choosing a curriculum.** Read Chapters 6 and 7. Explore what's available and try some of the suggestions in this book before you buy a curriculum. Trying to get kids to use a curriculum that you paid for but that's not working creates tension and makes learning more difficult. You'll have time for the 875 hours of instruction required by law, even if you spend a month or two choosing a curriculum. If your children attended a conventional school for part of the school year, those hours count toward the 875. While you are deciding, consider doing some of the activities in Chapter 6, make up your own, or ask your kids. Recognizing what they are learning now will help you choose a curriculum that works for your family.

If your kids aren't particularly interested in school work, especially if they've had a difficult time in a conventional school, see "Working with Teens Who Don't Like School" in Chapter 11.

• **Learn more about libraries in your area.** Most homeschoolers rely heavily on libraries. You can save hundreds of dollars on curriculum by using the library for most of your learning resources. See Chapter 8 for details.

• **Get in touch with other homeschoolers**. They will give you information and support, and your kids will be glad to know they aren't the only homeschoolers around. Contact your WPA Regional Coordinator (listed in the current WPA newsletter and on the WPA website) or call the WPA Voice Mail for information about support groups in your area. Visit as many as you reasonably can. Groups vary a lot, and it's worth spending some time to find one that works well for your family. If you can't find a group that meets your needs, consider starting one. (See Chapter 14.)

• **Expect some ups and downs.** Homeschooling is a big change; it takes time to adjust and feel confident. Expect to spend some time figuring out how you want to homeschool and gaining confidence. Then, just when you think you almost know what you're doing, things will change, and you'll need to adjust. Searching, trial-and-error, and mid-course corrections are all part of what makes homeschooling so exciting and why it works so well for so many different families. Just hang in there and you'll make it. See Chapter 16 for suggestions on how to solve problems that may arise.

- **Become a responsible homeschooler.** The present and future of homeschooling in Wisconsin depend on YOU and other homeschoolers. Actions of individuals like you are critical to maintaining our homeschooling freedoms. It's not difficult once you understand a few basic principles that you may not have thought of before. See Chapter 21.
- **Join Wisconsin Parents Association (WPA).** WPA provides the support and information families need to homeschool. In addition, Wisconsin has one of the most reasonable home-schooling laws in the country. Homeschoolers working together through WPA got the law passed in 1984 and have worked hard to maintain despite numerous challenges. (See Chapter 20.) WPA cannot do its work without members like you.

Chapter 3

Requirements for Homeschooling in Wisconsin

Understanding and Complying with Wisconsin's Homeschooling Law

In Wisconsin statutes, homeschools are referred to as "home-based private educational programs." They are required to provide "at least 875 hours of instruction each school year" and "a sequentially progressive curriculum of fundamental instruction in reading, language arts, mathematics, social studies, science and health." (See Appendix A for the complete text of this law.) Homeschoolers need to understand what the statute does and does not require, especially because many school officials are either misinformed or uninformed about it.

1. The statute requires 875 hours of instruction, which can be 175 days of five hours each or some other schedule. This does not mean parents and children have to spend 875 hours at the kitchen table with textbooks and workbooks. Among the activities that can be counted as instruction:

- reading books, listening to other people read aloud, listening to books on tape;
- completing workbooks and exercise sheets where they discover and use skills like math and penmanship;
- doing hands-on experiments and observing things that give them a chance to discover things for themselves;
- using computers (with parental supervision, if necessary);
- using educational audio-visual materials (films, DVDs, videos, audio tapes, etc.);
- participating in community activities, including field trips and volunteer service;
- learning practical skills such as cooking, cleaning, doing laundry, driving, gardening, home maintenance, etc.;
- working part-time in ways that are similar to work-study programs in conventional schools;
- playing educational games;
- playing individual sports and on community sports teams; and
- others.

2. The statute requires a "sequentially progressive curriculum." This is an educational plan in which new subject matter builds on what has previously been learned. Many different curriculums are acceptable. Some families choose a standardized curriculum similar to those used in conventional schools, either purchasing a published version or developing their own. Some families develop their own curriculum based on their children's needs, interests, and abilities, being sure to include the subject areas required by law. (See Chapter 7.)

The subject areas (reading, language arts, mathematics, social studies, science and health) are commonly understood and assure that the educational program is well-balanced. However, the 875 hours can include other subjects a family chooses, such as art, religion, music, auto mechanics, computers, household management, etc.

3. Parents or guardians are required to file form PI-1206 with the Department of Public Instruction each year they are homeschooling, beginning the year their child turns six on or before September 1. They need to continue to file a form each year they homeschool until their child is no longer covered by the compulsory school attendance law. (See Chapter 4.)

4. In addition, the definitions section of the private school law states that, "An instructional program provided to more than one family unit does not constitute a home-based private educational program." Disobeying this provision would jeopardize the homeschooling law. (See Chapter 28.)

The four additional requirements (#5-8 listed below) are seldom a problem. However, parents need to be familiar with them and comply.

5. "The primary purpose of the program is to provide private or religious-based education."

6. "The program is privately controlled."

7. "The program is not operated or instituted for the purpose of avoiding or circumventing the compulsory school attendance requirement under s. 118.15(1)(a)."

8. "The pupils in the institution's educational program, in the ordinary course of events, return annually to the homes of their parents or guardians for not less than two months of summer vacation, or the institution is licensed as a child caring institution under s. 48.60(1)." (This provision applies to boarding schools and other such institutions and not to homeschools.)

These requirements for home-based private educational programs are exactly the same as those for any other private schools. Home-based private educational programs are, in fact, private schools. This is clear from the statutes: "118.165 Private schools. (1) An institution is a private school if its educational program meets all of the following criteria: [those listed immediately above and listed on the form homeschoolers must sign]." Homeschools are called "programs" in the statutes only to prevent them from receiving federal or state funds paid directly to schools for things like school lunch programs and school bus service. (See Chapter 28.) However, private school students, including homeschoolers, are eligible for services provided by public schools, including courses in special education and other subjects. (See Chapter 32.)

For more detailed information about Wisconsin's homeschooling law, see Chapter 28.

Additional Considerations

Homeschooling is a serious responsibility. In addition to complying with the law, homeschooling parents consider questions such as:

• What are our goals for our children's education? In addition to instruction in required subjects, many parents include topics like: learning to take responsibility, appreciating beauty in nature and the arts, running a household, participating in a community and assuming social responsibility, developing religious and moral values, serving others, and using resources wisely.

• How will our children's progress toward these goals be evaluated? Many approaches to evaluation are available; flexibility is an asset. Observing children is one of the best approaches; homeschooling parents have many opportunities. A review of records that have been kept, along with samples of children's work, demonstrates progress. See Chapter 10 for more on evaluations and record keeping.
• How will the children be supervised? Usually at least one parent is at home full-time, but there are other options, depending on the age and abilities of the children, family circumstances, etc.
• How will we provide a social life for our children? Homeschooling makes it easier for children to have important contact with a variety of older and younger people. They get together with kids their own age through neighborhood activities, organized sports, homeschooling support groups, and youth organizations such as 4-H, church groups, and scouts.

Social life in conventional schools can be negative, including intense competition, bullying, and peer dependency. Many parents feel that the social aspects of a classroom setting need not be duplicated and in fact are best avoided. After all, school is the only place where people are required to interact with a group of people who are all the same age.
• What community resources are available and how will we use them? Much depends on opportunities available in the community; children's interests and abilities; and parents' imagination, time schedules, and willingness to chauffeur. Many parents seek opportunities for their children to serve as well as be served.

Some Things Not Required

Things not required by Wisconsin law and not necessary for homeschooling include:
• Review and approval of homeschooling families' curriculums and calendars by public school officials are not required. See Chapter 31 for information on handling contacts from public school officials.
• Testing or other assessment of homeschooled children is not required, although some parents choose to have their children take standardized tests while others keep records or monitor their progress in other ways.
• A certified teacher, a parent with a high school or college diploma, a hired tutor, or other "professional educator" is not required.
• Homeschooling does not need to be expensive. With planning and imagination, many resources can be borrowed from the library or other places, or obtained free or at minimal cost.
• Parents do not need to know everything children will need or want to learn. Parents and children can learn together, older children can work independently, tutors can be used, etc.
• A two-parent family is not required. There may be additional challenges for a single parent, such as scheduling and providing adequate supervision, but single parents can and do homeschool.

Chapter 4

Filing Form PI-1206

Step 1 Understand the Purpose and Importance of Filing Form PI-1206

To homeschool legally in Wisconsin, parents and guardians must send PI-1206 to the Department of Public Instruction (DPI) each year they are homeschooling. If your child is not currently enrolled in a public or conventional private school, you can officially begin homeschooling at the beginning of the school year and send your form to the DPI early in October, no later than October 15. (See Step 2, Part A below.) If your child is currently enrolled in a public or conventional private school, you cannot legally homeschool until the DPI has received your form, regardless of whether you are beginning before or after October 15. (See Step 2, Part B below.)

You should only send a form to the DPI during the years your children are covered by the compulsory school attendance law. This means children who turned six years old on or before September 1 of the current school year and those who have not yet turned 18 by the beginning of the current school year. (See the Appendix for the text of this law.) Children younger than six should not be included on the form.

Form PI-1206 serves two main purposes under the law. First, it provides a way for the state to determine the number of homeschoolers and their distribution by gender and grade. These data, together with data from public and other private schools, enable public school officials to plan for future space and teacher requirements.

Second, the form serves as a signed affidavit that you are complying with the homeschooling law and is important in documenting your compliance.

It is very important to realize that you are NOT applying to the DPI for permission to homeschool. As a parent, you have the right to educate your children at home. You also are NOT registering your children with the DPI, although the DPI uses that term. Homeschools are private schools and do not register with the DPI. You only need to report that you are homeschooling.

WPA urges you to comply with the reasonable law we have in Wisconsin, even if you do not fully agree with it. It is illegal to homeschool without filing the form. Many people worked long and hard to get this law passed in 1984. Homeschoolers have worked hard since 1984 to maintain it. If you don't comply with the law, you could jeopardize it and end up paying a fine and/or going to jail.

Step 2 Choose the Correct Time to File Your Form

Part A. If, like most homeschooling families, you have not enrolled your children in a public school or a private school that is not a homeschool for the current academic year, your form should be postmarked in early October, on or before October 15.

WPA encourages you not to file the form before October for two reasons. First, public and other private schools in Wisconsin base their reports on enrollment as of the third Friday in September and file their forms on October 15. Since homeschools are private schools, we follow this requirement. Doing so reminds school officials that we are sending the form to report enrollment. Second, complying with more than the minimum requirement of the law (in this case, sending in the form before public schools open in the fall or at some other time before it is due) encourages public officials to increase requirements and exceed their legal authority.

School officials sometimes pressure homeschoolers who have not enrolled their children in a public school for the current academic year to send the form before October 15. The date on which one files the form may seem like a small point, but waiting until early October sets a pattern of taking responsibility for complying with the law since the primary purpose of the form is to report school enrollment as of the third Friday in September.

Part B. If your children are currently enrolled in a public school or a private school that is not a homeschool, you cannot legally begin homeschooling until the DPI has received your form, regardless of whether you begin homeschooling before or after October 15. In other words, you can begin homeschooling at any time during the school year as long as the DPI has received your form. It is not necessary to begin homeschooling by October 15.

Step 3 Get a Copy of Form PI-1206

In August, the DPI sends the form for the current school year to families who sent them the preceding year. If you do not receive one, it is your responsibility to get it. It is not the DPI's responsibility to give you one.

The DPI requires the official three part form. You cannot print and send the form that is posted on the DPI website or fax your form.

If you need a copy of the form, call the DPI at 608-266-5761 or 888-245-2732 and leave a message or write to:

Wisconsin Department of Public Instruction
P. O. Box 7841
Madison, WI 53707-7841

The DPI mails forms on Fridays, so you may have to wait a week or more for your form. If you need a copy of the form more quickly, call the WPA Voice Mail for assistance.

With the form, the DPI send "Questions and DPI Responses Relating to Home-Based Private Educational Programs." Unfortunately, some information in it is inaccurate and misleading. WPA strongly suggests that you read this handbook instead. The DPI and the educational establishment have been opposing and misrepresenting the rights and responsibilities of homeschoolers since before the current homeschooling law was passed in 1984. Although they have grudgingly made certain corrections in their information, they are not a trustworthy source of information about homeschooling.

If you want or need to begin homeschooling as soon as possible, the quickest way to get a form is to go to the DPI offices at 125 South Webster Street, near the capitol in Madison. Complete the form (see suggestions and a sample form below). Go to a copier and make three copies of the completed original. Return the original and the yellow carbon to the DPI and request a letter acknowledging that they have received your form. Take home the three copies you made, the pink carbon from the form, and your letter of acknowledgement.

Step 4 Understand the Form

In 1984, in its first version of form PI-1206, the DPI claimed more authority over homeschoolers than it was given under Wisconsin law. Representatives of WPA met with legislators and DPI officials. As a result, the form was changed to be consistent with the law, and homeschooling freedoms were not unnecessarily lost. WPA has continued to watch the form carefully since 1984. For information on changes in the form, see the WPA newsletters.

The form quotes s. 115.30(3) of the Wisconsin statutes which states, "The administrator of each home-based private educational program shall indicate in his or her report whether the system or program meets all of the criteria under s. 118.165(1)." The "administrator" of a homeschool is the parent or guardian filing the form. This use of the term "administrator" recognizes that homeschools are private schools. "His or her report" means form PI-1206. The term "report" is used because PI-1206 is homeschoolers' version of the report that is filed by public schools and other private schools.

For an explanation of the language used in s. 118.165(1) as quoted on the form, see Chapter 3.

The form also states, "Recommendations: It is recommended that a copy of the school calendar verifying a minimum of 875 hours of instruction and course outlines verifying that there exists a sequentially progressive curriculum of fundamental instruction be maintained in your home." This is NOT a requirement. On the contrary, providing course outlines would exceed the requirements of the law, set unnecessary precedents, and undermine our homeschooling freedoms. For information on school calendars and attendance records, see Chapter 10.

Step 5 Complete the Form

A sample is included here. Note that the form does NOT require children's names, ages, or birth dates. In 1984, homeschoolers worked hard through WPA to ensure that the law did not require this information, to protect the privacy and independence of homeschoolers. Do not voluntarily give your school district this information. Doing so would undermine our homeschooling freedoms.

Step 6 Copy Your Form

Make three copies of the completed original (the white page). Do not rely on the pink carbon that you keep. You may need copies in the future, and it is difficult to make copies from the carbon.

Step 7 Request a Letter of Acknowledgment from the DPI

WPA strongly recommends that you get a letter of acknowledgment from the DPI each year as evidence that they have received your form. Keep these letters with your copies of your forms. Among the reasons:

Wisconsin Department of Public Instruction
HOME-BASED PRIVATE EDUCATIONAL PROGRAM
PI-1206 (Rev. 5-05)

INSTRUCTIONS: Complete and retain the pink copy for your records and return the original and the yellow copy to:

WISCONSIN DEPARTMENT OF PUBLIC INSTRUCTION
SCHOOL MANAGEMENT SERVICES / HOME-BASED
125 SOUTH WEBSTER STREET
P.O. BOX 7841
MADISON, WI 53707-7841

The sections listed are references to the Wisconsin statutes.
For additional information about the Home-Based Private Educational Program, call: (608) 266-5761 or toll free 1-888-245-2732, ext. 1.

School Year **2005-2006**

1. **Section 115.30(3)** On or before each October 15, each administrator of a home-based private educational program shall submit, on forms provided by the department, a statement of the enrollment on the third Friday of September in the elementary and secondary grades under his/her jurisdiction to the department.

HOME-BASED ENROLLMENT DATA
*Indicate the **Number of Children in Each Grade Level** and the **Name of the Public School District of Residence.***

	1st	2nd	3rd	4th	5th	6th	7th	8th	9th	10th	11th	12th	Ungraded 1-8	Ungraded 9-12	**Total No. of Children 1-12 and Ungraded** *In Program Only*
MALE				1											1
FEMALE		1													1

Name of Public School District of Residence
Name of your school district

2. **Section 115.001(3g)** "Home-based private educational program" means a program of educational instruction provided to a child by the child's parent or guardian or by a person designated by the parent or guardian. An instructional program provided to more than one family unit does not constitute a home-based private educational program.

Section 118.15(4) Instruction in a home-based private educational program that meets all of the criteria under s. 118.165(1) may be substituted for attendance at a public or private school.

Section 115.30(3) The administrator of each home-based private educational program shall indicate in his or her report whether the system or program meets all of the criteria under s. 118.165(1).

Section 118.165(1)

SAMPLE

(a) The primary purpose of the program is to provide private **or** religious-based education.
(b) The program is privately controlled.
(c) The program provides at least 875 hours of instruction each school year.
(d) The program provides a sequentially progressive curriculum of fundamental instruction in reading, language arts, mathematics, social studies, science and health. This subsection does not require the program to include in its curriculum any concept, topic, or practice in conflict with the program's religious doctrines or to exclude from its curriculum any concept, topic, or practice consistent with the program's religious doctrines.
(e) The program is not operated or instituted for the purpose of avoiding or circumventing the compulsory school attendance requirement under s. 118.15(1)(a).

The program meets all of the above-named criteria. *Check one*
☒ True ☐ False

RECOMMENDATIONS: *It is recommended that a copy of the school calendar verifying a minimum of 875 hours of instruction and course outlines verifying that there exists a sequentially progressive curriculum of fundamental instruction be maintained in your home.*

Name of Parent or Guardian *Print or Type*
Your name

Street Address *If mailing address is a P.O. Box, also list street address.*
Complete

City	State	Zip
Complete	Complete	Complete

Signature of Parent/Guardian	Date Signed *Mo./Day/Yr.*
➢ Your signature	Complete

• Technically, neither a copy of the original of your form nor the pink carbon proves that you actually sent the form and that the DPI received it. You could have filled it out but not sent it, or it could have been lost in the mail. Therefore, if anyone questions whether you filed the form, you can show them both a copy of your completed form and your letter from the DPI.
• Some families prepare their children for the possibility of a truancy sweep by giving them a copy of the form and the letter of acknowledgment. See Chapter 31.
• Sometimes colleges, the military, and others require proof that applicants have complied with their state's homeschooling requirements. Submitting copies of your forms and the letters of acknowledgment from the DPI is usually an acceptable way to meet this requirement.

To get a letter of acknowledgment, when you send your completed form to the DPI, include a self-addressed stamped envelope (SASE) and a note saying something like, "Please send me a letter acknowledging that you have received this form." The DPI will send you a short letter. (Note: The cover letter the DPI sends with the form says, "When the DPI receives the completed form, the registration process for the home-based program is complete. No other materials will be sent from the DPI." However, they will send a letter of acknowledgment despite this statement. Also, the term "registration" is incorrect. As homeschoolers we report to the DPI; we don't register with the DPI. Registering generally implies that a person intends to participate in something, such as registering for a class or to vote. We do not intend to participate in the DPI or its activities.)

Step 8 Send Your Form to the DPI

You can send it by regular, first class mail. If you are beginning homeschooling during the school year, it is wise to wait until you have received the letter of acknowledgment from the DPI before you begin homeschooling. (Be sure to request a letter of acknowledgment and include a self-addressed stamped envelope with your form or you will not receive anything from the DPI.) If you want to begin homeschooling as soon as possible, you may want to send your form in a way you can track so you know when it arrives at the DPI.

Step 9 If Necessary, Notify Your Local Public School District

Wisconsin law does not require that you inform your local public school district that you are homeschooling. The DPI sends them the yellow carbon from your form, but it may take several weeks or longer. In almost all situations, WPA strongly recommends that homeschoolers not exceed the requirements of the law, because doing so can set precedents that may increase the power and authority of public officials and undermine our homeschooling freedoms. Sometimes, however, courtesy and common sense indicate you should notify your district. If you do, you may also have to explain to officials what the law requires. Some officials don't know and some have been misinformed and have incorrect information.

Here are WPA's recommendations:
• If your children have never been enrolled in a public or conventional private school in Wisconsin, you do not need to notify any school or district since the DPI does this.
• If your children are currently enrolled in a public school or a private school that is not a homeschool, you are less likely to be charged with truancy if you notify the school. You can send a letter like the one below or call the school and give them this information.

Remember that you do not need school officials' permission or their approval of your curriculum, school calendar, learning resources, or anything else. If a school official asks what curriculum you are using, explain that under Wisconsin law, they do not have the authority to review your curriculum, so you are not going to discuss it with them.

If a school official claims that you cannot begin homeschooling until they receive a copy of your form from the DPI, explain that their information is incorrect. Wisconsin law requires that the form be received by the DPI, but not by the local school district, before a family begins homeschooling. The DPI will eventually send them the yellow carbon that you sent, but it may take several weeks or longer. If you think it would reduce tension, you can give a school official a copy of your completed form and a copy of your letter of acknowledgment from the DPI. You are not legally required to do this, but sometimes it helps avoid truancy charges and other difficulties. Giving your local school a copy of your form is one of the few times when it makes sense to do more than the law requires.

• If your children attended a public school or a conventional private school last year and you are starting homeschooling at the beginning of the school year, you are less likely to be charged with truancy if you notify the school they would have attended before school starts. You can use the letter below.

Sample Letter Notifying Your Local Public School District That You Are Homeschooling

Your street address
City, state, zip code
Date

Dr. or Mr. or Ms. (full name), Superintendent
__________ School District
Street address
City, state, zip

Dear Dr. or Mr. or Ms. (last name):

This letter is to inform you that I will be the administrator of a home-based private educational program beginning on [date]. I am the parent (or guardian) of ___________, who will be enrolled. [Note to parent writing this letter: On the ___________, put the names of your children if they have been enrolled in the local public school; if they have not been enrolled, give only the information on PI-1206, that is, the child's gender and grade, for example: a boy in tenth grade and a girl in fourth.]

I have read Wisconsin law concerning home-based private educational programs and am in full compliance with the law. I will be sending form PI-1206 to the DPI on or before October 15. OR I have already sent form PI-1206 to the DPI. Under Wisconsin law, I can begin homeschooling legally as soon as the DPI receives my completed form, even though you have not received your copy.

Sincerely,

Your signature

Your full name

Chapter 5

Beginning Under Special Circumstances

Beginning Homeschooling When a Child Turns Six

Wisconsin's compulsory school attendance law covers children from ages 6 to 18. Therefore, homeschoolers need to submit form PI-1206 to the Department of Public Instruction (DPI) by October 15 of the year in which their child turns six by September 1.

Wisconsin law requires that homeschoolers have a curriculum. However, this does not mean that you have to purchase a curriculum for your children when they turn six (or at any other time). See Chapter 7. Many parents feel there is nothing magic about age six. (In fact, some states do not require school attendance until children are seven or eight.) Children who have been learning at home since birth simply continue to do so after they turn six.

There is a wide range of normal behavior for six year olds. Boys are often a year or more behind girls in language development. Many homeschooling parents allow their children to develop various skills when they are ready, rather than pressuring them to learn specific things by certain ages. Many children learn well and easily and enjoy it when they can wait until they have the necessary physical, mental, and emotional maturity. Often, all it takes is time. Learning according to one's own timetable, instead of being limited by the pace of a classroom of kids, is a big advantage to homeschooling.

Beginning During the High School Years

Many families begin homeschooling during the high school years and find it a rewarding and satisfying experience. See Chapter 11.

Single Parents

Single parents can and do homeschool. There may be additional challenges such as working out scheduling and providing adequate supervision, but these can be managed. It often helps to develop a support system, perhaps including extended family, neighbors, and friends.

Beginning on Short Notice

Families sometimes need to begin homeschooling on short notice. They may have been considering homeschooling for a while and decide that now is the time to start. Their children's school situation may have become intolerable. Illness may be a factor. Or there may be other circumstances or concerns.

If a school official has told you that you have to homeschool, stop and think before you decide to begin. Officials cannot force you to homeschool. If you don't want to homeschool, or if, despite the information in this handbook, you can't figure out how to homeschool given your circumstances, then homeschooling may not be right for your family. You should find another approach to your children's education.

Fortunately, in Wisconsin you can begin homeschooling any time during the school year. You do not have to wait until the beginning of the next academic year or semester, as you would in some other states. However, you do have to file form PI-1206 with the Department of Public Instruction (DPI) before you can legally begin homeschooling.

The quickest way to get form PI-1206 is to go to the DPI offices at 125 South Webster Street, near the capitol in Madison. Complete the form. (See suggestions and the sample form in Chapter 4). Go to a copier and make three copies of the completed original. Return the original and the yellow carbon to the DPI and request a letter acknowledging that they have received your form. Take home the three copies you made, the pink carbon from the form, and your letter of acknowledgment.

If you cannot or do not want to go to the DPI offices, you can call the DPI at 608-266-5761 or 888-245-2732 and leave a message requesting a form. The DPI mails forms on Fridays. If you need a form more quickly than that, call the WPA Voice Mail for assistance. Complete the form and send it to the DPI following the suggestions in Chapter 4. It is wise to wait until you have received the letter of acknowledgment from the DPI before you begin homeschooling. (Be sure to request a letter of acknowledgment and include a self-addressed stamped envelope with your form or you will not receive anything from the DPI.) If you want to begin homeschooling as soon as possible, you may want to send your form in a way you can track so you know when it arrives at the DPI.

Then stop. Sit down. Take a deep breath. Relax. The more overwhelming your situation seems, the more important it is to take time to figure out what to do next. Homeschooling has worked for thousands of families, and it will work for yours, either as a short term solution or as a new adventure that changes your life. If appropriate, see "When Parents Are Reluctant to Begin Homeschooling" later in this chapter. See Chapter 6 for suggestions on what to do next.

Beginning During the School Year

You can begin homeschooling during the school year. You do not have to wait until the beginning of the next semester or school year. However, you do have to file form PI-1206 with the DPI before you begin. See Chapter 4.

Homeschooling Children With Special Needs

Children who have been labeled hyperactive, "learning disabled," ADD, ADHD, or with another term, or who have physical disability, or who are autistic or have other special needs often benefit greatly from homeschooling. See Chapter 9.

When Parents Are Reluctant to Begin Homeschooling

Some parents begin homeschooling because they feel their children need the support, opportunities, and flexibility that homeschooling offers. Others cannot find an acceptable alternative. Still others go along with their children's desire to homeschool, even though they themselves have little enthusiasm.

Parents who begin homeschooling reluctantly often find homeschooling is more manageable than they expected. Some even grow to like it. Here are some suggestions:

- Talk with other homeschooling parents. Contact your WPA Regional Coordinator (listed in the most recent WPA newsletter and on the WPA website) or call the WPA Voice Mail. Ask them what they like about homeschooling and what suggestions they have for making homeschooling more manageable.
- Attend the WPA conference. Workshops offer information, encouragement, and support.
- This handbook offers encouragement and information. Glance through the Contents. See the suggestions in Chapters 6 and 7 and "How Homeschooling Parents Can Find Time for Themselves" in Chapter 15. Look in the Index for topics of special concern.
- See Chapter 15 for reasons why it is easier to parent homeschooling children than people expect.
- Take a break from worrying about academics. Children have a lifetime to learn. They do not have to learn things in the order conventional schools teach them. They do not have to learn them at the same time as the rest of their classmates. They do not have to learn everything right now. A break is especially important if your children have just left a difficult school situation that has taken its toll on the whole family. Do things that you enjoy. See Chapter 2.
- Include in your homeschooling some activities that you enjoy yourself and some things that you personally would like to learn. If your children are not interested in them, do them yourself.
- Watch your children as they relax, learn, and grow. Let some of their energy encourage you.
- Realize that your commitment as a parent is important. With strong parental involvement, children do remarkably well. See Chapter 22 for research that supports the importance of parental involvement.

When a School Situation Has Become Intolerable

Families for whom a school situation has become intolerable often find that homeschooling provides a way to recover and get back to learning. Children who have had a difficult time in a conventional school, for whatever reason, usually benefit from a break from structured or formal academics. Many of the activities in Chapter 6 work well in this situation. Our society puts a lot of pressure on people to correct their weaknesses, but homeschooling parents often find it works better to set aside concerns about academics for a while and give children a chance to develop their strengths and interests. If appropriate, see "When Parents Are Reluctant to Begin Homeschooling" above.

When School Officials Recommend Homeschooling

School officials occasionally recommend that children who are having difficulty in school begin homeschooling. However, parents cannot be required to homeschool. In fact, Wisconsin law requires that school boards respond within 90 days to written requests from parents that the school provide their child with program or curriculum modifications. (See s. 118.15(1)(d) in Appendix A.) At the same time, if a school situation has gotten to the point that officials are recommending homeschooling, it might be worth considering. If appropriate, see "When Parents Are Reluctant to Begin Homeschooling" above.

When Children Have Had Truancy Problems

Take heart. Families whose children find school so intolerable that they become truants find that homeschooling works. Truancy is a complex problem that is not necessarily your child's fault. Young people sometimes deserve credit for standing up to a system that may be doing them more harm than good.

People who begin homeschooling are still liable for truancy charges stemming from evidence that they were truant before they started homeschooling. It is a good idea to take extra care in filing form PI-1206. See Chapter 4. Read about truancy laws in Chapter 31 and read the text of the truancy statutes in Appendix A. If you think you need an attorney, see Chapter 23.

Parents of children who have been accused of truancy may face three special challenges. First, the children may have been labeled "law breakers" or "criminals" and heard dire predictions made about their future. Such a picture of oneself is unsettling, to say the least, and may become a self-fulfilling prophecy unless someone is able to help the children change it. Some parents view truancy as an indication that there is something wrong with the school system, rather than something being wrong with their children, and are able to convey this to their children and help them make a realistic assessment of their strengths, abilities, and potential.

Second, parents of these children may believe they are being forced into something they don't want to undertake, aren't fully capable of doing, and don't have time to do. Parents who respond positively at this time to their children's genuine needs are often richly rewarded. They discover things they can do with their children that they both enjoy. They sometimes work with their children on learning projects. In addition to the rewards of seeing improvement in their children, these parents frequently end up liking homeschooling better than they expected to.

Third, school officials may scrutinize or harass a family whose children have had truancy problems. Some families deal with this by knowing what the law requires, complying carefully, and standing their ground firmly but politely in contacts with school officials. See Chapter 31 for more information on dealing with school officials. Some families also minimize the opportunities officials have to contact them by appearing as conventional as possible without compromising important principles. For example, they are careful that their children are clearly being supervised during conventional school hours. They explain their homeschooling to neighbors, relatives or others who might be concerned, which reduces the chance that these people will report the family to school officials or social services.

When Children Have Been Expelled

An increasing number of students are being expelled from public schools for a variety of reasons. The position of the DPI and some school officials is that these students still have to attend school, although this position does not seem to be enforced and has not been tested in court. However, on this basis, some people conclude that if these students cannot get into another public school or a conventional private school that they can afford, they have to homeschool. This does not make sense. Students do not have to homeschool simply because they have been expelled.

If your child has been expelled and you want to homeschool, many of the suggestions in "Homeschooling Children Who Have Had Truancy Problems" above may be helpful to you. Also, be sure to read Chapter 2 and, if appropriate, "When Parents Are Reluctant to Begin Homeschooling" above.

However, if your child has been expelled and you do not want to comply with Wisconsin's homeschooling law, do not submit form PI-1206 and claim you are homeschooling. Homeschooling is not the solution to the problems you are facing.

PART TWO

LEARNING THROUGH HOMESCHOOLING

Chapter 6

"Where Do I Get the Books?" Getting Going or Shifting Gears

Here are easy, low cost curriculums that have been life-savers for many homeschooling families. One or more of them may be just what you need if you're in a situation such as one of these.

• You've been considering homeschool for a while and have just decided you want to start NOW, so you want a curriculum right away.

• Something has happened (maybe a crisis at your children's school or an unexpected event in your family), and you've decided to begin homeschooling as soon as possible. o You've been homeschooling for a while. There are lots of things you like about it, but it still seems to be so much work, and you're tired of struggling, of being responsible for planning and directing your kids' learning, of hearing, "So why don't you just send them to school?"

• It's February in Wisconsin: cabin fever time. The kids keep squabbling. You're basically glad you're homeschooling, but you'd sure like to go on a cruise or at least do something different for a while.

• It's early May in Wisconsin. One day is sunny and warm, the next is in the 30's and drizzly. It seems like you've gotten what you're going to get from the curriculum you've been using all year, but it's not time to quit for the summer.

• You've heard other homeschoolers talk about relaxing their approach to homeschooling, and you'd like to try that. But you wonder what would happen. Would the kids learn anything? Would it be pure chaos? What would you do all day?

• You're facing a complicated situation that has nothing to do with homeschooling. You have a new baby, one of your parents is seriously ill, your husband's business has taken a downward turn and he's just asked you to take over the bookkeeping, which will take you four hours a day. (In situations like these, you may want to do some of the activities listed here. But more to the point, let reading this list help you realize that your children will learn invaluable lessons about real life by going through this with you, rather than being shuttled off to school each day and missing much of what is happening. Consider doing a unit study on newborns, or health and disease, or whatever. See the section on Unit Studies in Chapter 7.)

We are all only a slip of the foot away from disaster. Five years I stepped onto black ice, flipped up and landed on my head. Life changed in an instant. Driving, speech, vision, comprehension, and so on and so forth-traumatic brain damage seemed insurmountable. Friends whose children were in conventional schools said, "Aw, now you'll have to enroll your children in school." Homeschooling friends knew better and said, "Thank goodness you're homeschooling." For eight long months, while I slept 12 to 18 hours a day, our curriculum consisted of household management and brain physiology. We slowly resumed our routine. At no time did our yearly commitment to 875 hours of a sequentially progressive curriculum miss its target. Could that have happened in a state where we were tied to some governmental timetable?—From Opening Remarks, WPA Conference, 2000

Starting Homeschooling on Short Notice

Families who begin homeschooling on short notice often assume there is a standard set of textbooks and workbooks that homeschoolers use. This is understandable, since public schools cover certain subjects in each grade and use pretty much the same approach based on textbooks, worksheets, and homework.

However, homeschooling families are responsible for choosing their own materials and deciding how they will go about learning. This may seem overwhelming at first. But in the long run, once you get used to the idea, it has many advantages. You can choose or develop a curriculum specifically for your children that will work much better than anything a conventional school could offer them. Think of the possibilities! You are working with a small group of children you've known for a long time, not 25 to 30 kids you just met in September. You can focus on their individual strengths and interests and encourage them to learn in their own way and according to their own timetable. (Conventional teachers would have chaos if they tried to do that.) You are not limited to what you can bring into a classroom; you have the whole world to explore.

You can choose a curriculum similar to those used by conventional schools, but you don't have to. Many parents focus on what their children need to learn to lead effective adult lives, rather than on what they would be doing if they were attending a conventional school. They focus on helping their kids learn things like how to get a job and keep it, relate to other people, manage money, cook, run a household, etc.

Possibility #1 Follow a low cost or free curriculum similar to those conventional schools have. Get a copy of Rebecca Rupp's *Home Learning Year* by Year from your library or bookstore or an online bookseller. This book tells you what conventional schools cover each year from pre-kindergarten through 12th grade and suggests books and other resources you can use for each subject. You can get most of the books from the library, so you don't have to spend much money. Choose what you think will work best for your children, whether or not it's listed under the grade they're supposed to be in. It's fine to be doing math from the second grade, science from third grade, and history from sixth. Keep records of topics you study and resources you use so you can develop a transcript at some point if you want or need to.

Possibility #2 Do learning activities you find in library books. Check out one or more of the following books from the library. Choose activities that appeal to you and try them. Build on the ones that work. Ignore the ones that you don't like. Don't worry about grade levels; pick things your kids enjoy. They'll learn more if they're having fun, and you won't have to worry about getting them to do school work.

- *Family Learning: How to Help Your Children Succeed in School by Learning at Home* by William F. Russell
- *Family Math* by Jean Kerr Stenmark, Virginia H. Thompson, and Ruth Cossey

- *Family Math II* by Grace Davila Coates and Virginia Thompson
- *Family Math for Young Children* by Grace Davila Coates
- *Parents Are Teachers, Too: Enriching Your Child's Frist Six Years* by Claudia Jones and *More Parents Are Teachers, Too: Encouraging Your 6- to 12-Year-Old* by the same author
- *The Teenage Liberation Handbook: How to Quit School and Get a Real Life and Education* by Grace Llewellyn
- *Trust the Children: An Activity Guide for Homeschooling and Alternative Learning* by Anna Kealoha
- *The Unschooling Handbook: How to Use the Whole World As Your Child's Classroom* by Mary Griffith

Possibility #3 Buy a conventional curriculum and follow it. See "(1) Purchase a Curriculum" in Chapter 7. Some families are relieved to have an official-looking curriculum in the house and find that it works well for them. However, other families decide other approaches to learning work better. It's generally a good idea to try some of the free or inexpensive possibilities listed here while you spend some time learning about different curriculums you can buy. Look on the Internet, contact curriculum providers, ask other homeschoolers what they use and what they like and don't like about it, visit the Curriculum Fair at the WPA conference. Curriculums can be expensive, so you'll save time, money, and frustration if you do some checking before you buy one.

Possibility #4 Encourage your children to pursue their interests and turn that into your curriculum. You can start with any topic. It doesn't have to sound academic or be a subject that conventional schools teach. The more interested your kids are in it, the easier it will be for them to learn, and the less you have to do to get them to learn. Studying any topic will inevitably cover the basic subjects required by Wisconsin law (reading, language arts, mathematics, social studies, science and health). So let them choose music, football, chess, motorcycles, computers, cosmetology, hunting, fishing, etc. For more ideas about how to do this, see "Unit Studies" in Chapter 7 and "Homeschooling Teens Who Don't Like School Work" in Chapter 11 which includes an example of a curriculum based on motorcycles.

Possibility #5 Develop a curriculum based on CLEP tests. Young people homeschooling for high school can base their curriculum on CLEP tests. In addition to doing high school work, they also earn college credit, a huge advantage. See "The Many Uses of CLEP and AP Tests" in Chapter 8.

Possibility #6 Use the Internet. Many resources are available, lots of them free. You can find lesson plans, worksheets, sites especially for kids, and much more. Homeschooling websites like A to Z Home's Cool at www.homeschooling.gomilpitas.com are good places to start. Of course, you can use just plain information that's available at many websites; it doesn't have to be organized as lesson plans or labeled as school work. Another possibility is to enroll in online courses. For more information, see "Using the Internet" in Chapter 8.

Possibility #7 Learn from life experience. This is sometimes referred to as unschooling. Use the following ideas any way that works for your family as a spring board. Modify them so they fit the ages, needs, personalities, interests, and unique situation of your family. Many families find it helps to involve their kids in the planning and preparation, which means less work for parents, and kids (and adults) are more likely to participate willingly in activities that they have had a role in choosing. (Parents, of course, eliminate inappropriate or unsafe activities.)

These activities are worthwhile in and of themselves, whether or not you expect to learn something from them. But people do learn from them. Therefore, they can be counted as part of the "875 hours of instruction" and "sequentially progressive curriculum" required by Wisconsin law. To emphasize that point, each activity is followed by the names of some of the conventional academic subjects that could be learned. The claim is not being made that children will learn all the language arts, math, science, or any other subject that they need from these activities. But many parents find it helpful to realize that children learn basic subjects from activities such as these, just as they learn to walk and talk without formal lessons.

If you've been homeschooling for a while and are taking a break, you could set aside the curriculum you've been using and just do these activities. Or you could spend less time on your current curriculum. You could do these activities for a week and return to a more conventional curriculum or do things like this for the rest of your life, learning as you go. At some point, read Chapter 7 for more ideas about curriculum.

Try to find time to answer your kids' questions. If you don't know, say so and try to help them find the answers. But don't wear yourself and your kids out by constantly looking for opportunities to "teach" them something. Focus on their strengths, especially if they have been in a conventional school situation that emphasized their weaknesses.

If your kids complain that they are bored, congratulate yourself: You have managed to help them find some free time that they can decide what to do with. Ask them what they would like to do. List possibilities that they can choose from.

- Go to the library. Visit the children's section, no matter how old you are. Many nonfiction children's books provide basic, easy-to-understand explanations of complex topics, like how computers work. Check the adult section for books on other countries, history, and crafts; appropriate magazines; music; etc. Investigate other library resources: videos, DVDs, CDs, books on tape, etc. (Learning possibilities: Reading, how to use the library, music, just about any subject)
- Visit a near-by nature area, your own yard or neighborhood, or a park. Take a picnic. Enjoy being outside, looking, and listening. (Science, physical education, esthetics)
- Call the Wisconsin Department of Tourism at 800-432-8747 or visit their website at www.travelwisconsin.com. Plan a trip, deciding where you would go, what routes you would take, what you would do, and how much the trip would cost. If possible, take the trip. (Geography, science, math, reading)
- Make baker's clay by mixing together 4 cups of flour, 1 cup salt, and 1 1/2 cups of water (with food coloring, if desired). Knead until smooth. Shape. Bake in a 300 degree oven until dry, about an hour, depending on size and thickness. Paint or color with magic markers. (Art, math)
- Choose a craft you know little or nothing about. Ask someone with experience for help getting started, perhaps explaining that this is part of your homeschool. Many people are glad to be asked. Get some supplies and be creative. (Art, problem solving, math)
- Visit a pet store, looking even at animals that do not appeal to you at first. Try to find a clerk who is not too busy to answer questions. If possible, get a new pet. Observe it and keep records of what it does, how much it eats, etc. Draw pictures of it. Read library books about it. (Science, math, reading, writing, art, taking responsibility)
- Color Dover or other detailed coloring books on other countries, history, famous people, designs, animals, etc. (Art, whatever subjects the coloring books cover, such as social studies, history, science)
- Use library videos and DVDs to learn about science, other countries and history (both fiction and non-fiction), new skills (exercises, cooking, crafts, etc.), and more. (Whatever subjects the videos cover)
- Reorganize part of the house. Ask what materials people use most and want to have readily available, such as arts and crafts supplies, games, tools, musical instruments, and writing materials. Involve as many people as possible in deciding how to store these so they are easy to find and put away. Put what is used most often in the places that are easiest to reach. Get rid of things you don't use. Try to provide a large flat surface where people can work on projects for several days. (Home economics, planning and organizational skills)

• Paint or wallpaper a room. Choose the colors, learn how to prepare the walls, apply the paint or paper, etc. Study design, its history, cultural perspectives, etc. (Art, math, social studies)
• Choose a country. Think of as many ways as possible to learn about it. Read books and watch videos and DVDs, both fiction and non-fiction. Visit stores with imports from the country. Learn to cook foods or eat at a restaurant that offers foods from the country. Meet people from the country. Make a traditional costume. Have a party using the country as a theme. Draw a map. Make a book. Visit the country. (Social studies, reading, home economics)
• Plant a garden. Study seed catalogs and gardening websites. Find an experienced gardener to answer questions and perhaps sell you some plants for starters. Offer to help in their garden so you can learn from them. Visit a farmers' market for ideas. Learn to sprout alfalfa and other seeds. (Science, nutrition, math)
• Buy or build an inexpensive food dehydrator. See what you can dry and how they taste dried. (Science, nutrition, industrial arts if you build it yourself)
• Learn to do something new with the car, like checking fluids or changing the oil, the spark plugs, the filters, or a tire. (Auto mechanics)
• Fix something that is broken, or do something to improve your home. Put up a shelf or coat hooks, replace a cracked window, or build a bookcase. (Problem solving, reading if you consult books for information, industrial arts, wood working)
• Visit museums. Call the curator, schedule a tour in an area of special interest. Ask if you can use their library. (Science, social studies, language arts)
• Go to a music store and learn about the instruments available and how they sound. If possible, buy one and teach yourself to play, take lessons, or ask someone who plays the instrument to help you get started. (Music)
• Get tapes or CDs of singing lessons from the library or take voice lessons. Sing with your family, before or after meals, riding in the car, etc. Explore songs from other countries. (Music)
• Read aloud. Take turns choosing books. Good books appeal to a wide range of ages. Picture books with attractive art work appeal to all ages, and many young children enjoy listening to books that are supposedly written for older ones, especially if they can be part of a cozy family group. Don't insist that children sit still; some people listen better if they can move around. Encourage children interested in reading aloud to do some of the reading, but don't pressure them. It is more challenging to read aloud than to oneself, and it's more important that reading be a pleasant activity than that children learn to read aloud well at a young age. (Reading, plus whatever subjects are covered by the books you are reading)
• Interview a person with a job that interests you, an older person, or someone else you want to talk with. Plan questions ahead. Tape the interview, if it is easy and people are comfortable with it. Children can write about parts of the interview that interest them and possibly turn it into a book. (Social studies, writing)
• Put up maps and locate places that come up in reading or conversation. (Geography)
• Get a book of math activities. (A good one with activities for people of all ages is *Family Math* by Jean Kerr Stenmark, Virginia Thompson, and Ruth Cossey.) Do activities for fun, in relaxed way. (Math)
• Do "free writing" as a family. Everyone has a notebook and pen or pencil and spends 10 minutes writing without stopping. (People who are not yet writing conventional words can draw.) If you can't think of anything to write, just write "I can't think of anything to write" over and over until you think of something. For right now, don't worry about spelling or punctuation; it is more important to enjoy writing than to do it perfectly. (Writing)
• Make your own books. Sew some paper and cardboard down the middle by hand or machine and fold it in half, or find a book with more detailed instructions. Decorate the cover. Inside, draw, write, paste pictures, whatever. (Art, writing)
• Cook something you've never cooked before. (Home economics)

Chapter 7

Curriculums and Learning Resources

Academics sometimes weigh heavily on homeschoolers. Beginning homeschoolers ask, "Where do I get the books?" Experienced homeschoolers worry about whether their children are learning enough of the right stuff, are keeping up with their peers in conventional schools, and will be able to get a job or go to college. These are our children, after all, some of our greatest joys and biggest responsibilities. What if they don't learn something they need to know?

Actually, the academic parts of homeschooling are more manageable than they may seem when we're just starting, or when, after four years, seven months, and two days of homeschooling, we suddenly awaken at 3 AM, panicked, thinking, "We haven't diagrammed sentences!" To be sure, the number and variety of options may make choosing a curriculum seem complicated. But kids are learning all the time, and homeschooling works well (for a list of reasons, see Chapter 18). We're working with only a few children that we know well. It's okay (in fact, it's often an advantage) that most of us don't know a lot about curriculums used in conventional schools.

This chapter will describe options that are available and how to use them. But first let's consider some general ideas. The end of this chapter has suggestions for how to choose a curriculum for your family.

Why Choosing a Curriculum is Easier Than You May Think

• Your children will learn a lot no matter what you do or don't do. Have you spent time with a two year old lately? It's mind boggling what little kids learn without anybody teaching them. They learn to talk, walk, sing, and dance. They understand that some things are here and then disappear for good, like snow, but socks and puzzle pieces can be missing for a while and reappear. People leave and come back. Two year olds remember things from the past and know that water makes things wet and Mom doesn't want you to pour it on the floor. Life, time, movement, impermanence, constancy, two, more: these are complex ideas, and little kids master them. Kids are natural learners, and we are fortunate indeed to get to share the learning with them.

A father in our support group years ago said, "It's too bad children don't come with an indicator light, like the ones in your car. Just a little light on their forehead, with a sign saying 'Learning Now in Progress.' We could look at a child playing with blocks or running around the yard with her brother or reading a comic book, see that the light was on, and be reassured."-From Opening Remarks, WPA Conference, 2005

• You, a parent who has chosen to homeschool, are very good at helping your children learn. You love them, care about them, and want the best for them. You know how they learn: which ones love books, which learn better by having someone explain something to them, and which are determined to figure things out for themselves. You also know who likes numbers, who loves the sound of words, and who would rather fix something than work with either numbers or words. You only have a few kids to deal with. You don't have to keep a whole class on track and make sure they're prepared to do well on the fourth grade test they'll have to take soon and ready to do fifth grade work next fall. This means you can focus on what your kids are most interested in and go at their pace. You can choose the learning schedule that works best: spending a short time working on each of several different subjects or projects each day or spending the whole day reading a good book or building a castle and then working on math or learning about butterflies tomorrow. You can choose resources from the whole world, not just a classroom. You don't have to keep the principal, the school board, or the taxpayers happy. You don't need special teacher training because you don't have 20 or 30 kids you just met who you have to keep moving at the same pace and prepare for standardized tests, using only the materials that are in one room.

• There are many different ways to learn that work. So as homeschooling parents, it isn't our job to find the only right way or the best way. We are looking for a variety of ways that will work for our family. This may be different for different children, and for the same child at different times. That's fine.

• A curriculum is a plan of study. Many people think a curriculum is a stack of textbooks and workbooks. That's one type of curriculum, and certainly the one most widely used in conventional schools, but it's not the only one. Homeschoolers use different kinds of curriculums.

• You can take your time in choosing a curriculum. In the long run, you will save time, money, and frustration. Think about your long-range goals. Talk with your kids. Ask other homeschoolers what has worked for them and what hasn't. Start slowly. Don't spend a lot of money right away; take time to explore alternatives. Even if you spend a month or two, you will still have time to get in the hours of instruction that the law requires.

• You can use a variety of ways to learn about curriculums and learning resources. Read this chapter and other books about homeschooling. Look on the Internet. (The A to Z Home's Cool website is a good place to start.) Talk with other homeschoolers. Join a support group. Attend the WPA conference held each spring. Subscribe to one or more homeschooling magazines. Think about how you've learned the things that matter most to you. Most important, watch your kids, listen to your kids, think about how your kids learn and what they enjoy. (By the way, you might want to notice how you're learning about homeschooling. It's an example of how people learn, from a variety of sources, in a variety of ways. Understanding how people learn will increase your confidence in your homeschooling.)

• As you're learning about homeschooling, some approaches will appeal more to you than others. Sometimes you may think, "John would enjoy that" or "I bet Mary would like this book/video/game/experiment/whatever." Pay attention to what makes sense to you and appeals to you. You're looking for curriculum that will work for your family, not for what someone might claim is theoretically the best curriculum ever written.

• Accept the fact that, no matter which approach you choose, how much time you spend, or how hard you try, you will miss something, maybe something important. Kids attending conventional schools don't learn everything there is to know, or even everything they're supposedly taught. You don't have to include everything conventional schools supposedly cover. Neither you nor your kids nor any professional educator knows what your kids will need to know as adults, partly because some of it hasn't been discovered or developed yet. But that's okay, your kids will be able to learn what they need when they need it, as long as your kids know what to do when they don't know something. First, admit that you don't know. (How many adults have trouble doing that?!) Then try to figure it out yourself by thinking and trial and error, or ask someone, or look it up on the Internet, or research it at the library, or find a tutor, or take a class, or...

• Academics are not the most important thing in life or homeschooling. We call what we do homeSCHOOLING. We do it instead of sending our children to school. So it's tempting to focus on academics. To be sure, learning is important. But experienced homeschoolers know that academics are not the only part, or even the most important part, of homeschooling. It may be more important to be able to manage money wisely than to know how to calculate percentages. It may be more important to be a responsible and honest young person than to understand nuclear physics. It may be more important to be kind and gentle than to be able to spell. Of course, we want our children to learn both academics and the other things that are more important. But sometimes we have to choose. Sometimes too much emphasis on academics undermines our larger goals and takes time we need to work on them. That's why it's important to keep academics in perspective.

So don't let concerns about academics interfere with your enjoyment of your children or rob them of their childhood. Your kids will want to learn to read, use numbers, figure out how the world works or what happened in the past. They'll ask you and other people for help. Spend a reasonable amount of time on academics. But make sure your kids also have time to play, daydream, make a mess, be bored, exercise, be creative, get to know themselves and each other and you, learn about religion, sleep, do work that matters, decide between right and wrong. Take time to play in the snow, go bowling, watch a movie, talk about life, clean the garage, go for pizza, share religious and moral values, sing and read aloud and laugh and cry together. Your kids will learn invaluable lessons, and so will you.

We celebrate those moments that at the time seem so profound - when the light suddenly goes on in our son's mind and long division finally makes sense. We celebrate those moments that at the time seemed so small - when our daughter apologizes for saying something hurtful to a friend. And then suddenly we realize we have it backwards. Academic skills have value but having compassion is priceless.-From Opening Remarks, WPA Conference, 2004

• Homeschoolers do well working on different grade levels or even paying little attention to grade levels. Kids often enjoy and do well with material that is supposedly above their grade level. More challenging material that interests them is often easier than boring material supposedly at their level. Sometimes kids get a nice boost from material supposedly below their grade level that is inviting, fun, and less difficult. Pay attention to your kids, their interests, and their strengths instead of grade levels.

We know that our children are not pieces of clay that we mold or vessels that we fill. Knowledge is not gained in this fashion and development cannot be rushed.

We allow our children to be children, being ever watchful that everything has an appropriate time. And we give them that time to unearth the wonders of their world - to create without criticism - to ponder complex ideas and to draw their own conclusions. We know how difficult it is to trust that our children will learn when the time is right. In our fast-paced society where the trend is to push academics at younger and younger ages, we try to be patient while providing an environment where our children may learn at their own pace. Some years, this creates an inner struggle because we wonder if growth and learning are even happening. During these times, we may even see our children take one step backward before taking two or three forward. Today, we celebrate our ability to look beyond those feelings of doubt and uncertainty that we have from time to time.-From Opening Remarks, WPA Conference, 2004

- You don't have to know everything your kids want or need to learn. They can use the library, learning resources, tutors, mentors, the Internet, and other sources.
- Be flexible. If what you try first doesn't work as well as you or your children want it to, try something else. If one approach works for a while but then doesn't seem right anymore, change.
- There's no one right approach to education. Neither professional educators nor experienced teachers nor homeschooling parents can agree on the one approach, because people learn in different ways, have varying interests and talents, and need to know different things. Your family is in the best position to decide what approach to education will work best for each of you.
- People learn in different ways. Visual learners benefit from seeing things written down, while kinesthetic learners need to move around. In fact, Howard Gardner has identified eight different intelligences. (For more information, see Thomas Armstrong's *In Their Own Way: Discovering and Encouraging Your Child's Personal Learning Style.*) You don't have to figure out special ways to teach each child. Just encourage them to learn in ways that work best for them. Let kids move around while you read aloud rather than sitting still. Find projects for kids who learn more taking a broken motor apart than reading a book about motors. Find companions and mentors for kids who learn best with other people, and allow time and space for kids who like to be alone. If you stop and think about it, you are probably already doing a lot of these kinds of things. It's mostly a matter of recognizing how many ways people learn besides from books and conventional school activities.
- In the long run, the particular material you cover and learning resources you use are determined by what's available when you are looking, what you happen to find, what you can afford, what appeals to you and your children, and occasionally luck. Don't think you need to review everything that's available or make sure you choose the best.
- Try not to feel overwhelmed. A huge amount of material is marketed to homeschoolers, some of it very good. No family could begin to use it all.
- We all learn in many ways, every day, in everything we do. Unfortunately, this is something our society has lost track of. We are most aware of what we learn in school, because that's what we talk about and get tested and graded on. But actually most of what we know, we learned outside of school. We can learn more broadly and deeply if we don't limit our thinking to schooling. Anyone can do this, of course, but homeschoolers have more time and opportunities than children who put a lot of their time and energy into attending conventional schools. Also, some of what happens in school undermines learning. Bullying, humiliation, intense competition, fear, strict schedules, and continuous interruptions make it difficult for children to learn. Schools don't do this deliberately. It's partly an inevitable result of needing to try to educate 20 to 30 kids in one room at the same time, all of them roughly the same age.

This means schools are not a good model for homeschools because the situations are so different. Homeschoolers do what schools do when it makes sense and is consistent with their goals. But it's important to remember that as homeschoolers we don't have to do what conventional schools do.

Approaches to Curriculum

All that said, three approaches to homeschooling curriculum are discussed here so readers can get some sense of the possible choices. The three overlap; don't worry if they don't seem totally clear-cut. You can use any of them with whatever philosophical or religious approach you choose. You can also choose an approach to scheduling that works for your family. Some families do well following a set schedule each day while others are more flexible.

Three approaches to curriculum discussed below are:

1. Purchase a curriculum that tells you what children are expected to learn at each grade level. These curriculums are usually very similar to the approach to education used by either public schools, private schools, or alternative schools. There are three ways to purchase a curriculum. (A) Complete curriculum packages provide books, workbooks, lesson plans, and other materials plus specific instructions to follow. (B) You can buy a general outline of a curriculum without the supporting materials and then choose and locate materials from a list of possibilities. (C) Enrolling in a correspondence school means students complete the lessons that are sent to them, teachers at the school grade or evaluate them, and students earn credits and sometimes diplomas.

2. Develop your own curriculum. (A) You can start with basic academic subjects like reading, math, art, and religion, and either purchase or create your own courses. (B) You can start with a general topic like frogs or Peru and either purchase or create your own unit study. Easy steps are given below.

3. Make your curriculum or plan of study that your children will learn from life experience and from pursuing interests and projects at home and in your community, sometimes supplementing this with unit studies or learning resources or maybe a class. The claim is not being made that children will learn everything they need from life experience and pursuing their interests. But they do learn a great deal without formal lessons. If you need to convince employers, college admissions officers, relatives, your kids, or yourself that they really are learning, you can translate (or help your kids translate) what they have done into school language. See Chapters 10 and 12.

The classification used here is only one of the ways that curriculums could be organized. Another way would be to begin with approaches to education or philosophical or religious beliefs. For example, some families base their homeschools on the ideas of Charlotte Mason or the Montessori or Waldorf approach to education. Some want a classical education for their children. Others want a curriculum that emphasizes their religious beliefs. They choose one or more of the approaches to curriculum listed here (purchase a curriculum, develop your own, or learn from life experience) that meets their needs and is consistent with their approach or beliefs.

Still another approach is called eclectic homeschooling, in which homeschoolers choose what meets their needs from the range of approaches to homeschooling.

A Note About Resources

Homeschooling resources abound. This handbook can't list "The Best Resources," partly because each family needs to choose what works best for them. So it lists some books, periodicals, websites, and other sources of information about resources, rather than listing resources themselves. Try not to feel overwhelmed. Many families find they do very well learning together in their homes, communities, and public libraries, with perhaps just a few well-chosen learning resources in areas that especially interest them.

Only the titles and authors of books are listed in this chapter. For more information, see the Bibliography.

1. Purchase a Curriculum

Families purchase curriculums for different reasons.

• Some want their children to learn the things that are taught in conventional schools, so they will be like the majority of children. They think this is the best way for them to be as prepared for jobs, college, and adult life as children who attend conventional schools.

• Some families want or need to homeschool (perhaps because the situation in their local public school is unacceptable) but are not sure how to go about it. A purchased curriculum can give them the direction they need to get started homeschooling.

• Some want to have a curriculum based on religion.

• Some want their children to have the equivalent of a private school education, perhaps based on the principles of Waldorf or Montessori schools.

You can buy a curriculum as a complete package, an outline, or correspondence or online courses. Each is described below.

1A. Complete Curriculum Packages

Before purchasing a curriculum, especially an expensive one, it's a good idea to find out as much about it as you can.

- Read reviews of curriculums in homeschooling magazines, books, on websites, etc.
- Ask other homeschooling families which curriculums they have used and what they liked and didn't like about them.
- Visit the publisher's website or call or email and request information and samples.
- Attend workshops and look at curriculums at the WPA Conference and Curriculum Fair held each spring.

Some curriculum providers offer full-service curriculums, in which children's work is sent to the provider for grading. Some award high school diplomas to students who complete the requirements. Full-service curriculums are similar to correspondence schools discussed in (C) below.

Here are some of the largest and best known curriculum providers. WPA does not endorse or recommend any particular curriculum or approach to education; each family is in the best position to choose what will work. These curriculums vary widely in their orientation, content, philosophy of education, approach to learning, etc.

1B. Curriculum Outlines

You can buy a curriculum outline, without any books, workbooks, or other materials. Professional educators call such an outline a "Scope and Sequence," since it includes both the scope of the material to be covered and the order in which it is to be covered. Many outlines include suggested resources you can find yourself. Since an outline often covers more than one grade and learning materials are not included, it is much less expensive than a complete curriculum package. If you get most of the resources from the library, you can spend a lot less than a curriculum package costs.

An even bigger advantage to buying just an outline is that it is much easier to modify to meet your children's unique strengths, interests, needs, and learning styles. You can emphasize the subject areas, types of resources, and approaches to learning that work best for you. You can look at several different outlines, compare them, and pick what you want from each. You can also choose a grade level in each subject area that works for each child. Tom can use reading materials from the second grade level, math from third, and science from fourth, regardless of his age.

Curriculum Providers

Curriculum Providers—Religious

A Beka Academy
PO Box 18000
Pensacola, FL 32523-9160
800-874-3592
www.abeka.org

Accelerated Christian Education
PO Box 299000
Lewisville, TX 75029-9000
800-925-7777
www.aceministries.com

Alpha Omega Publications
804 North 2nd Avenue East
Rock Rapids, IA 51246
800-622-3070
www.aop.com

Bob Jones University Press
Customer Service
Greenville, SC 29614-0062
800-845-5731
www.bjupress.com

Christian Liberty Academy School System
502 West Euclid Avenue
Arlington Heights, IL 60004-5495
847-259-4444
www.homeschools.org

Christian Light Publications
PO Box 1212
Harrisonburg, VA 22803-1212
877-226-8010
www.clp.org

Clonlara School Home Based
Education Program
1289 Jewett
Ann Arbor, MI 48104
734-769-4511
www.clonlara.org

Covenant Home Curriculum
N63 W23421 Main Street
Sussex, WI 53089
800-578-2421
www.covenanthome.com

KONOS
PO Box 250
Anna, TX 75409
972-924-2712
www.konos.com

The Moore Foundation
PO BOX 98
North Bonneville, WA 98639
509-427-7779
www.moorefoundation.com

Seton Home Study School
1350 Progress Drive
Front Royal, VA 22630
540-636-9990
www.setonhome.org

Sonlight Curriculum
8042 South Grant Way
Littleton, CO 80122-2705
303-730-6292
www.sonlight.com

Curriculum Providers—Secular

AMSCO School Publications, Inc.
315 Hudson Street
New York, NY 10013-1085
800 969-8398
www.amscopub.com

Houghton Miflin
1900 South Batavia Avenue
Geneva, IL 60134
800-733-2828
www.schooldirect.com
www.eduplace.com

The McGraw-Hill Companies
PO Box 182604
Columbus, OH 43272
800-262-4729
www.mheducation.com

Oak Meadow
PO Box 1346
Brattleboro, VT 05302
802 251-7250
www.oakmeadow.com

Steck-Vaughn/Harcourt Achieve
Attn: Customer Service 5th Floor
6277 Sea Harbor Drive
Orlando, FL 32887
800-531-5015
www.steck-vaughn.com

One disadvantage to buying just the curriculum outline is that you have to track down the resources. It's also easy to assume you're supposed to do everything suggested and feel overwhelmed. You don't. Some families use an outline as a suggestion and choose what makes sense to them, covering some topics in greater depth than others.

Here are a few resources for people interested in curriculum outlines. These and others are available in libraries or through interlibrary loan.

Home Learning Year by Year: How to Design a Homeschool Curriculum from Preschool Through High School by Rebecca Rupp

Home School Manual: For Parents Who Teach Their Own Children by Theodore E. Wade, Jr.

The Three R's: Grades K-3 and *You Can Teach Your Child Successfully: Grades 4-8* by Ruth Beechick.

Typical Courses of Study, Kindergarten through Grade 12 by World Book. Available at www.worldbook.com/wc/browse?id=pa/tcs.

The Well-Trained Mind: A Guide to Classical Education at Home by Jessie Wise and Susan Wise Bauer.

What Your Kindergartener Needs to Know through *What Your Sixth Grader Needs to Know,* edited by E. D. Hirsch

1C. Correspondence Schools, Full-Service Curriculums, and Distance Learning

Another way to study what other people have selected is to take correspondence courses and perhaps earn a high school diploma. Conventional correspondence schools send students assignments to complete and require that exams be supervised by a librarian, pastor, or other such person. Full-service curriculum programs have teachers who grade assign-

Correspondence Schools and Distance Learning

American School
2200 East 170th Street
Lansing, IL 60438
708-418-2800
www.americanschoolofcorr.com

Clonlara School Home Based Education Program
1289 Jewett
Ann Arbor, MI 48104
734-769-4511
www.clonlara.org/homebased.htm

Indiana University School of Cont. Studies
Owen Hall 001
790 East Kirkwood Avenue
Bloomington, IN 47405
800-334-1011
www.scs.indiana.edu

Keystone National High School
420 West Fifth Street
Bloomsburg, PA 17815-1564
800-255-4937
www.keystonehighschool.com

Kolbe Academy Home School
2501 Oak Street
Napa, CA 94559
707-255-6499
www.kolbe.org

University of Missouri-Columbia High School
136 Clark Hall
Columbia, MO 65211-4200
800-609-3727
www.cdis.missouri.edu/MUHighSchool/HShome.htm

University of Nebraska Independent Study High School
PO Box 88400
Lincoln, NE 68588-8400
866-700-4747_
eeohawj.unl.edu/ishs

University of North Dakota Division of Independent Study
State University Station, PO Box 5036
1510 12th Avenue North
Fargo, ND 58105-5036
701-231-6000
www.dis.dpi.state.nd.us

University of Wisconsin Learning Innovations Center
505 South Rosa Road
Madison, WI 53719-1257
877-895-3276
www.learn.wisconsin.edu

ments and exams that children complete under their parent's supervision. (See [1A] above.) Virtual schools rely on distance learning, with teachers using computers and the Internet to communicate with students, sometimes using computers that allow teacher and students to interact in real time.

These programs tend to be relatively expensive, but some families feel it is worth the cost to have someone outside the family supervise and grade students' work and/or to receive a third-party diploma granted by an institution outside their homeschool. Some programs also offer consultation and support for homeschooling parents. For example, Clonlara School helps families plan individualized programs that meet Clonlara's graduation requirements. It has support teachers who consult with families. It is important to find a school or program whose philosophy and approach to education are acceptable to you.

For information about correspondence courses and schools and distance learning, see books like *Peterson's Independent Study Catalog*, and other resources listed in this chapter. On the preceding page are a few correspondence schools to help start your search.

2. Develop Your Own Curriculum

2A. Develop a Curriculum Based on Conventional School Subjects

Many homeschooling families begin developing their curriculum by choosing general goals. Here are some examples:

- Learning to read for enjoyment and information
- Learning to express oneself verbally and in writing and to communicate through letters, email, etc. (Conventional schools call this language arts.)
- Learning enough math to comfortably handle the numbers that are part of daily life and adding more math if kids enjoy it or need it for something they want to do
- Realizing that studying the past helps us understand the present and that different societies have different customs and ways of thinking (social studies)
- Understanding something about the workings of the natural world and the physical world around us (science)
- Knowing how to take responsibility for one's own health

Note: The points listed above are the subject areas that Wisconsin homeschoolers are required to cover. Many families add subjects such as art, music, religion, etc. The 875 hours of instruction required by Wisconsin law can be in any combination of required and added subject areas. See Chapter 3.

Many families also add goals such as:

- Developing moral and ethical beliefs and principles
- Developing an appreciation for beauty
- Learning to express oneself creatively through art, music, and other media
- Learning mechanical skills, driving, maintaining a car, taking care of a house, and doing simple repairs
- Whatever else you want to add

In other words, there's fairly general agreement in our society about the basic information that people should learn. You don't need to buy a curriculum package or even a curriculum outline. But at the same time, there are many, many different ways to study these broad categories. People who want to follow someone else's direction on this can purchase curriculums as described in 1 above. People who want to make their own decisions and choose and create their own pieces can develop their own curriculum.

If you want to compare your ideas with curriculums used in conventional schools, consult one or more of the books listed in "Curriculum Outlines" in (1B) above. But since these outlines cover so many possibilities, they can be overwhelming, and you may want to ignore them. Or you may want to use them as reference points; but if you do, don't feel your kids have to learn everything they include.

Once you have chosen your general goals, decide how you want to work toward them. Before you even start looking for learning resources, keep in mind what many parents, including homeschoolers, have found: that often the best learning resources are NOT the educational materials you buy, but just parts of the real world: Dad's tools, Mom's kitchen equipment, Grandma's sewing machine, Grandpa's fishing tackle. Kids are drawn to real things, especially what belongs to people they care about. So don't overlook the possibilities that are already in your home and community, and don't underestimate their importance just because you didn't buy them to be "learning resources."

An ENORMOUS number of learning resources are available to homeschoolers today. The problem is not finding them; it's not being overwhelmed. Here are some suggestions:

- Ask other homeschoolers what has and hasn't worked for them.
- Attend the WPA Conference and Curriculum Fair held each spring. Many workshops include suggestions for resources, and the Fair provides a great opportunity to examine resources and talk with exhibitors.
- Consult books about homeschooling and those that review educational materials and learning resources, such as
  - *Complete Home Learning Source Book* by Rebecca Rupp
  - *For the Children's Sake* by Susan Schaeffer Macaulay
  - *Home School Source Book* by Jean and Donn Reed
  - *The Homeschooling Book of Answers* by Linda Dobson
  - *The Successful Homeschool Family Handbook* by Raymond and Dorothy Moore
  - *Teenage Liberation Handbook* by Grace Llewellyn
- Visit homeschooling websites such as A to Z Home's Cool at www.homeschooling.gomilpitas.com and *Home Education Magazine* at www.home-ed-magazine.com

Here are a few of the many ways to study a subject. (These examples are not intended to be a year's worth of study in any of the subjects listed.)

Reading and language arts for a younger child: Listen to stories being read aloud. Learn to recognize and write your name. Tell someone about going sledding. Make a phonics notebook with pictures of things that start with a given letter on each page. Play games like "I'm going to Grandmother's house and I'm going to take an alligator, a banana, and a circus tent." (Each person in turn repeats what previous players have said and adds an object that starts with the next letter of the alphabet.)

Reading and language arts for a teen: Read novels from a country and century you choose. Research the authors' lives. Participate in a listserv on a topic of interest. Write a letter each week to a friend, relative, legislator, etc. Make a presentation in front of your 4-H group, church group, or other people.

Math for a younger child: Build with legos. Receive and spend an allowance. Work on the Miquon math series.

Math for a teen: Balance the family checkbook; write checks for your parent to sign. Open your own checking account. Buy the family groceries, staying within a budget. Work on geometry books from Key Curriculum.

Social studies for any age: Choose a country. Read fiction and non-fiction books and watch videos and DVDs. Cook food from the country. Visit import stores. Meet people from the country. Travel to the country.

Books such as those listed above under curriculum outlines can be helpful in developing your own curriculum based on basic subjects. If you want ideas for how to study history, for example, look in the history sections, choosing what appeals to your family, not being limited by grade levels or trying to cover everything.

2B. Unit Studies

Unit studies are a great way to organize the learning you want to do, stay motivated, have the flexibility to meet each individual's needs, keep records, and, if necessary, demonstrate to others that your kids are learning. To do unit studies, you start with a topic that interests you instead of a subject like math or social studies. You can start anywhere and learn what you need to know. The world is interconnected; it's not divided up into sections called reading, math, etc. Any topic you pick will provide opportunities to learn the basics such as reading, math, and social studies. Since no one can learn everything, it makes sense to learn what you are interested in.

What topics can be used for a unit study? Anything you want! You can use a topic that is generally considered academic, like the Civil War, sign language, or the solar system, or something that most people don't consider academic, like baseball, motorcycles, or cross stitch. They can be primarily thinking, such as trigonometry or the philosophy of John Locke, or primarily practical, such as baking cookies, driving a car, or refinishing furniture. Or they can be a combination of the two, such as gardening, where you can read books and seed catalogs and then grow vegetables.

A unit study can be any length and depth you want. After half an hour, you may decide you know enough about earthworms. Or what starts as a unit on rocks could lead to a career in geology. You may decide that identifying the Big Dipper and Orion is as much as you want to know about stars for now. Or you may end up spending several years learning about the history and culture of Chile and travel there. When you start a unit, you don't have to know how much time and energy you want to spend. You can decide as you go. People of any age can do unit studies, from the youngest (babies do units on crawling, walking, and human speech) to the oldest (elderly people learn to accept physical limitations and face death).

Sometimes a unit leads to a lifelong interest and even employment. It's easy to keep records you can use for transcripts, diplomas, college applications, or other credentials you need. (See Chapter 10.) Children and parents can plan them together. Parents can do units of their own, which is rewarding and sets a great example. Kids learn to take responsibility for their own learning, learn how to learn, and become lifelong learners.

You can make unit studies the foundation of your curriculum or include them with whatever else you are doing. If you think you might like unit studies, try one or two modest units.

You can buy individual unit studies, find websites on unit studies, or purchase curriculums based on them. For example, KONOS offers unit studies based on character traits. But many families find the best units are the ones they create for themselves, since these units cover exactly what they want to do in exactly the right depth. If you want to create your own, here are some general steps and a few rules.

Developing a Curriculum Based on Unit Studies

Step 1: Choose one or more things you want to learn more about. It works best, at least at first, to start with things that your children are interested in, so involve them in the planning. (Later, if you want, you can suggest units you think are important that your children might not be very excited about, at least at first, like spelling.) Let each pick their own unit(s). Encourage them to also work on some together; it's fun to share and easier for you if they work on the same topic part of the time. Choose a unit or two that you want to do yourself, and invite your kids to join you if they want. They're more likely to get involved if you're not pressuring them (even so, many parents love things that don't interest their kids in the least).

Step 2: Plan. Sit down with your kids when you are all well fed, well rested, and ready to concentrate for an hour or so. For each unit, have someone jot down responses to questions such as the following. (Planning may be easier if you organize the questions you want to use

into a one-page form, make copies, punch them, and keep them in a notebook. Later you can combine them with the notes you make at the end of the unit and have helpful records.)
• What do we already know about this topic? You just need a few notes here. A unit seems more manageable if you realize you already know something about it.
• How much of what we want to learn can we figure out for ourselves? Whenever possible, there are enormous advantages to getting raw materials and discovering things yourself. You feel the thrill of discovery, you're more likely to remember what you learn, and you increase your confidence. If you want to learn about how plants grow, why not put some dried beans from the kitchen against the side of a glass filled with moist soil or cotton and watch them sprout? Of course, it's not always safe or a good idea to try to reinvent the wheel, so it's good to maintain a balance between doing things yourself and learning from others, something that will be easier as you gain experience with unit studies.
• When can we go to the library? See below.
• Who do we know who would be willing to help us learn more about this topic? How could we work with this person? Think creatively. For a unit on World War II, invite a neighbor or relative who's a veteran to dinner. For gardening, volunteer to help someone in their garden in exchange for information and a few extra plants. Don't be shy. People love to be asked about their interests and experiences, and if you tell them it's part of your homeschooling curriculum, they may be even more willing. However, be reasonable, and do something for them in return.
• What field trips or other activities could we do? Books can be very helpful, but it is important to do as many things as possible that do NOT involve reading, writing, or computers. In other words, get involved in real life. Things you and the kids DO almost always make a stronger and more lasting impression than things you read about. These activities are also fun, and fun is an important part of any serious study because it keeps you going. For a unit on Mexico, go to a store that sells goods imported from Mexico to look at the patterns and colors, eat at a Mexican restaurant, get a Mexican cookbook and make dinner.
• What else can we think of about this topic? Jot down any other ideas you have.

Don't worry if you can't think of much to write. Even one idea gives you a place to start, which will lead to more information and new ideas.

Step 3: The library. See Chapter 8.

Step 4: Do what makes sense with the topic you have chosen. Experiment. Talk with other people. Read. Do stuff. Once you start investigating a topic, it's amazing how often you bump into it in unexpected places.

Step 5: Finish the unit. Try to end units at a good time. Some units become lifelong interests. Others are over in a flash. That's fine. Don't spoil people's enthusiasm by prolonging it. Some unit studies lead to something else, maybe the next unit. Some end quietly; you wake up one morning and realize your kids haven't tied any sailor's knots for several weeks. Sometimes you stop working on a unit and then come back to it months or even years later.

Whenever a unit ends, take five minutes (or more) to make at least a few notes or have your kids make them. Consider designing a form, making copies, and attaching it to your planning notes. Here are some suggestions:

- The name of the unit or the general topic
- Which children were involved
- Approximate dates (at least the year)
- Most helpful resources you used
- A few of the things you learned
- Academic subject areas covered (reading, language arts, math, etc.)
- Things you'd do differently next time
- Ideas for future units

Records help you and your children see how much you're doing and learning. They are invaluable when you have doubts about your homeschooling or when you need to convince someone else (a skeptical relative, a potential employer, a college admissions officer) that your children are qualified.

To explain unit studies more clearly, here are a few "rules."

Rule # 1: Ignore any of these rules that you don't like or that doesn't work for you. Make up your own rules.

Rule # 2: Have fun. People who know learning can be fun want to keep learning. If a unit stops being fun, either end it or shelve it by putting what you have into an appropriate container (a file folder, a box, or a newly purchased storage shed).

Rule # 3: Spend little or no money at first. Explore resources that are free or cost very little. Why? Unless you are independently wealthy, having spent money on something is likely to make you feel you should use it, which keeps you from ending a unit that isn't working. Once you know you want to pursue a topic, it may make sense to spend more money. See rule # 4.

Rule # 4: Make sure your kids have quality materials to work with. Suppose you want to do a unit on water color painting. Do you think your kids are more likely to have a positive experience if you buy several tubes of good water color paints (red, yellow, blue, and white are good choices) and good quality brushes or if you buy a $1.99 box of eight colored cubes and a wimpy brush that is losing its bristles? Of course, this rule seems to contradict rule # 3, and in some ways it does. Fortunately, your kids have you to think about these kinds of complexities and figure out how to maintain a balance between thrift and quality, excitement and satisfaction.

Rule # 5: Just plunge in. Don't try to find the beginning. Most subjects don't have a beginning-they're all interconnected. Of course, common sense will tell you to start someplace manageable, like starting with the thinner book with bigger print and more pictures or cooking a recipe that has five ingredients and seven steps rather than one that has 29 ingredients and takes two days. But don't worry if you don't understand very much of what you do or read at first, and don't wait to find a book titled *An Introduction to Field Mice.* Just start doing things and reading stuff, understand what you can, and let the rest wash over you. You'll be amazed at how soon you'll run into the same words and concepts, understand the terminology, and find things starting to make sense. The ability to just plunge into a new subject and start learning is one of the most important life skills you and your children can have. Don't underestimate it!

Rule # 6: Don't get overwhelmed. You don't have to learn everything there is to know about the unit you have chosen. Learn as much as you need or want right now, and let the rest go until later, or forever.

Rule # 7: Don't try to work all the basic subjects into each unit. If you just notice and start translating what your kids are doing into school language (see Chapter 10), you'll be surprised at how many units include reading, language arts, mathematics, social studies, science and health. If you feel you're not doing enough of an important subject (often it's math or spelling), you can either find learning resources or a course to fill the gap. Or you can decide to do a unit on multiplication or trigonometry or making words plural or whatever you feel is missing.

3. Learn By Living a Worthwhile Life and Pursuing What Interests You

A third approach is planning that your children will learn from life experience and from pursuing interests and projects at home and in your community, perhaps adding some unit studies or learning resources or maybe a correspondence course. (Whether you call what your kids are doing "following their interests" or "doing unit studies" may be determined by how organized you're feeling on any given day.) This is not to say that children will everything they need from life experience and pursuing their interests. But they do learn a great deal without formal lessons. If you need to prove to your mother-in-law, a prospective employer, a college admissions officer, your kids, or yourself that real learning is happening, you can review your records, photo albums, and memories and translate what your kids have done into conventional school subjects. For suggestions on how to do this, see Chapter 10.

So what do you do? What you and your kids want to do-assuming it's not life threatening, or morally threatening, or way too expensive. Can learning really be this easy and this much fun? Yes. Of course, reality helps. Getting hungry motivates you to learn to cook. Wanting to understand squiggles in books encourages kids to learn to read. The vast majority of people throughout history learned this way, devising solutions to problems of daily life and learning from people who had more experience which plants were poisonous or how to use the Internet. It's also how you have learned most of what you use in your work and daily life. How did you learn about parenting or computers? Even if you studied something in school, think about how much you've learned outside of school: how much more you know about driving than you learned in drivers' education, how much more you know about politics than you learned in civics class? Regardless of what approach to curriculum you choose, this is how your children have learned and will continue to learn a great deal, including how to walk, talk, get along with other people, etc.

Many homeschooling families who choose this approach like this quote from John Holt's *How Children Learn:*

All I am saying in this book can be summed up in two words-Trust Children. Nothing could be more simple-or more difficult. Difficult, because to trust children we must trust ourselves-and most of us were taught as children that we could not be trusted. And so we go on treating children as we ourselves were treated, calling this "reality" or saying bitterly, "If I could put up with it, they can too.

What we have to do is break this long downward cycle of fear and distrust, and trust children as we ourselves were not trusted. To do this will take a long leap of faith-but great rewards await any of us who will take that leap.

Want some suggestions? Here are a few:

- Spend time in nature, in your own back yard, a near-by nature preserve, or a national park.
- Volunteer: work at the library, visit a nursing home, deliver Meals On Wheels, clean up a park. The possibilities are endless, the experience valuable.
- Learn practical skills that will save you money: change the oil in the car, build shelves, make a pair of shorts, wallpaper your bedroom, reupholster a chair, grow tomatoes, make pickles, bake bread, knit a sweater.
- Get more exercise: walk, run, play tag, swim, organize neighborhood games.
- Browse through the children's section of the library (no matter how old you are) for attractive books on subjects you know little or nothing about.
- Do some of the activities in Chapter 6.

The best resource for this approach to curriculum is the world. Simply expose your children to as much of it as you sensibly can without exhausting yourself or them in the process. If you love to travel and do dramatic things, that's great, but don't neglect the opportunities of home, family, free time, and your back yard. The second best resource is your local library. Instead of looking for homeschooling books or educational resources, look for books, magazines, videos, classes, clubs, conferences, etc., on embroidery or China or diesel engines or whatever you're interested in. Kids often prefer "real" books written for adults to watered down versions for kids.

For more information about and support for this approach to learning, consider these:

Home School Reader: Collected Articles from Home Education Magazine 1984-1994 edited by Mark and Helen Hegener

The Homeschooling Book of Answers: The 88 Most Important Questions Answered by Homeschooling's Most Respected Voices by Linda Dobson

Homeschooling Our Children, Unschooling Ourselves by Alsion McKee

Learning All the Time by John Holt

Teach Your Own: The John Holt Book of Homeschooling by John Holt and Patrick Farenga

The Teenage Liberation Handbook: How to Quit School and Get a Real Life and Education by Grace Llewellyn.

Home Education Magazine and website at www.home-ed-magazine.com

A mother of adults who grew up homeschooling observed: *Looking back, I realize that the most important things our kids learned were from doing real things, many of them unplanned and unscheduled: cooking, hanging out, grieving for dead pets, coping when the pump broke, square dancing in the barn, camping, playing, managing on limited income. This is how they learned to think for themselves, analyze complex situations, earn a living, make responsible decisions, act with integrity, develop healthy relationships, be themselves.*

So How Do You Choose a Curriculum?

Given all these possibilities, how do you decide which curriculum is right for your family? There's no simple answer. There's no one best curriculum, or, put another way, each of these curriculums is best under the right circumstances. Most homeschoolers use more than one approach. A family using a complete curriculum package may get interested in ancient Egypt and develop their own unit study. Families focusing on unit studies may take a break and just do "stuff" for a month or so. A teen learning mostly from life experience may decide to purchase an algebra course from a curriculum provider or take a correspondence course on American history. Feel free to mix and match. Try not to label your family as "unschooling," "doing unit studies," or "doing school at home" and restrict yourself to what you think is allowed under that approach. Kids (and adults) learn all the time in many different ways.

Considering the following questions may help you choose a curriculum.

- What do you want your children to learn so they are prepared for adult life?
- How does each member of your family learn best?
- Is your family facing challenges that are more important than academics? Are you dealing with a serious physical illness, recovering from a bad school experience, coping with depression, going through a pregnancy, facing problems at work or the loss of a job, caring for an elderly parent? If so, choose a curriculum that supports the ways you are dealing with the challenges. For example, children recovering from difficult school experiences, depression, or anxiety choose activities that emphasize their strengths and give them the best possible chance to succeed. Many families in such situations choose a flexible schedule that allows lots of time for conversation, rest, and reflection. If you end up covering less material during this time and feel you are "behind," there will be plenty of time to catch up later. And remember that your children are learning some of life's most important lessons as you work together as a family. When your life has settled down and people are stronger, you can think about more challenging curriculums, more emphasis on academics, or whatever is important to you. See Chapter 9 for stories from mothers who have done amazing things while homeschooling children with special needs.
- How much money do you want to spend? You can homeschool well without spending much money, getting most learning materials from the real world, the library, and other free or inexpensive sources. In fact, some learning activities actually save money, like gardening and many do-it-yourself projects. Others, like starting your own business selling homemade

baked goods, end up making money. Interestingly enough, people who spend very little find that this approach has many advantages, even if it wasn't their first choice.

Purchasing a complete curriculum (1A) and distance learning (1C) are usually the most expensive. Other approaches can be quite inexpensive, depending on your choices. But if your family needs or would benefit from a purchased curriculum or distance learning, and curriculum outlines (1B) won't work, it may be worth the cost. Used learning materials are available from other homeschoolers, on the Internet, and at the used book sale at the WPA conference each spring.

• Are you or is one or more of your children a person who prefers to be told what to do? A complete curriculum package (1A) may be a good approach. If you are most comfortable using a purchased curriculum similar to those used in conventional schools, start there. You may want to add as much as you can that is of special interest to the kids. Many families find it works well not to spend a lot of money until they're pretty sure about what they're buying, so they don't end up either creating a lot of tension by trying to get kids to follow a curriculum that isn't right for them or having paid a lot of money for something they can't use.

• Do you want some general guidance on what conventional or alternative schools expect children to learn at various ages, along with the flexibility to choose how you will study them? Do you want your kids to be able to work at different grade levels for different subjects? A curriculum outline (1B) might be a good idea.

• Do you have a pretty good idea of what subjects you want your children to study? Consider developing your own curriculum starting with basic subjects (2A).

• Do your children have special interests they want to pursue in some depth? Do they do better if they can make some of the decisions rather than having to do what you tell them to do? Consider learning from life experience and pursuing your interests (3).

• Do you want to homeschool but also want to make sure that your children get an education that is as close as possible to what children are exposed to in conventional schools? Consider a curriculum package (1A) or purchasing a curriculum outline (1B).

• Do you feel you need to homeschool but are overwhelmed? EITHER a curriculum outline (1B) or learning by living and pursuing your interests (3). An outline will give clear directions, but you may have the challenge of helping them get motivated. In some families, this is not a problem; in others, it creates a lot of tension. On the other hand, if you choose (3) you may have to help your kids figure out what they're interested in and want to do and get started (depending on how old they are, how motivated they are, and whether they are recovering from negative school experiences). But being able to do what interests them may give them enough energy and motivation that this approach is more manageable in the long run.

• Do you feel overwhelmed with the work involved in homeschooling? Consider correspondence schools, full-service curriculums, and distance learning (1C), which will mean that someone outside of your family will figure out the curriculum, grade papers, etc. This is expensive but may be worth the cost

• Are you homeschooling several children of different ages? You can choose a curriculum package (1A) or a curriculum outline (1B) and have each child do their own work while you supervise everyone, with the older ones sometimes helping the younger ones, but that can be a lot of work for you. Developing your own curriculum (2A) offers more opportunities for kids to work together. Unit studies (2B) and learning from life and pursuing your interests (3) work very well because kids can work on the same topic or project, each working in their own way and at their own level. This may be easier for you, and the kids will learn a lot from each other.

• Do you want to make sure your children have time to play, express themselves, be creative, and explore their interests? Consider (2B) or (3).

• Do you want to make sure your children have the best chance of getting into college? Choose the approach that appeals most to you, keep records of what you do, and look for a college that will understand and appreciate the approach to learning that you have chosen.

Once you've chosen a curriculum, how well it works will be determined in part by how you use it. Any curriculum will work better if you are flexible: take breaks when the going gets tough, spend extra time on parts that really interest you, move quickly through sections that aren't particularly interesting or that the kids already know, and have fun whenever you can. If what you have chosen doesn't work well for one or more of your children, consider adding something from one of the other approaches or changing approaches altogether. Finding out what doesn't work is part of the learning process. Choosing and using curriculums will get easier as you gain experience homeschooling.

Have fun trying different approaches to learning and curriculum. Many experienced homeschoolers think the key is to watch your kids, listen to them, and help them find the ways of learning that work best for them from all the options that are available. Your family is in the best position to make these decisions for yourselves, and you can do it!

Perspectives From Two Homeschooling Mothers

We value the freedom to set our own schedules and determine priorities. This results in allowing our children to immerse themselves in a chosen interest whether it is snakes, skyscrapers, or scuba diving. They not only have time but we help them find resources and we rejoice as they strive to learn everything they can about a topic. However, this is not always easy. Some of us are squeamish when it comes to snakes and would find it hard to embrace one as a pet. For others this may mean supporting a daughter as she develops an interest in rabbits. Soon you are building cages for 100 rabbits, raising baby bunnies in the house and getting up at 4:00 on a cold Saturday morning, traveling to a show clear across the state. For other parents it may mean building a new garage for a son who has a passion for everything that has a motor - from weed trimmers to tractors. You soon get use to tripping over engine parts, housing broken 4-wheelers, and eventually seeing wrecked cars in your driveway, awaiting some body work.

As a homeschooling parent, you value that learning process. It's not the end result or the finished product that is most important. It doesn't matter that your daughter who raised rabbits for eight years no longer wants to become a veterinarian. We understand that was never the goal. We supported her interest so she could learn to be responsible while discovering something about herself. She learned to deal with competition and that life isn't always fair. She learned that success comes with a lot of hard work, a little luck, and some help from your friends. She experienced the thrill of winning and an ache in her heart when she mourned the loss of an animal she raised from birth. We serve our children well by standing by them, by speaking words of encouragement and by comforting them. And we honor each other for the energy it takes to do this for them, each and every day.-From Opening Remarks, WPA Conference, 2004

As our children experience learning as part of daily life, they come to know that work, family and community, the natural world, religious or spiritual life, play, and learning are all part of one whole. Life cannot be compartmentalized into separate realms of work, family, faith, society. They are all connected.

One word for this sense of the wholeness of our lives is integrity-and it is one of the greatest gifts we give our children. It is something many people in our culture are hungry for, and I think they recognize and appreciate it when they see it. So as we celebrate and honor these young people who are moving out into the world, we can know that this gift of integrity is one that they will pass on to the larger society, simply by the way they live their lives.-From Opening Remarks, WPA Conference, 2005

Chapter 8

Using Libraries, the Internet, Local Communities, and CLEP Tests

Looking for resources? Finding them is easy. The challenge is choosing among them. Questions you may want to ask when considering a resource include: Will family members be able to use it easily? Is it consistent with our family's beliefs? Can we afford it? Experienced homeschoolers know they will miss some great resources. Some are too general or too specialized or at the wrong level for their family. Some are too expensive. But mostly they don't have time for everything. It really is okay, though. We have the time to learn enough. So, do a reasonable amount of research, choose what your family is interested in and enjoys, and don't worry about the rest.

Using the Library

Ah! The key to affordable homeschooling. Libraries hold more resources than you could ever use, all of them free. Add in the advantage that the library wants everything back, so you don't have to add on to the house to make room. Let the library store them, let others use them, and when (or if) you need them again, you can check them out. Libraries carry trade books and rarely have textbooks in their collections. Many homeschoolers find that this means they can get into greater depth in the areas that interest them.

How do you make effective use of the library? Contact a nearby public library and explain that you are homeschooling. Call, email or walk in, but make an appointment for a personalized tour on how to use the library. Explain that you want to use the library yourself; you are not asking the librarian to do the work. Ask questions like:

- How do we find books on (choose a subject your family is interested in)?
- How do we use the library's catalog?
- Can we log onto it from our home computer?
- Can we renew books from home?
- Can we consult the catalogs of other libraries, request materials from them, and pick them up and return them here?

- How can we find materials in magazines, newspapers, and other periodicals?
- What other resources do you have that we might find helpful? Is there a parent/teacher area in the library or a library card for teachers to check out school materials?
- What can we do to make it easier for you to help us?
- Is there volunteer work we could do to help the library?

Don't limit yourself to what is on the shelves of your library. Consult lists of recommended reading in books you like, mail order book catalogs, websites, and other sources for titles of books and other materials. If your local library or library system doesn't have the item you want, ask how to borrow it through interlibrary loan. This service allows libraries to borrow from public and university libraries throughout Wisconsin and sometimes from other states. To determine if material is available in a Wisconsin library, go to WISCAT at www.wiscat.net. For materials outside Wisconsin, see WorldCat, which calls itself the world's largest bibliographic database, at www.oclc.org/worldcat. Be extra careful to return interlibrary loan materials on time, since your library has to get them back to the library that owns them.

Treat your library as the valuable community resource that it is and your librarian as a colleague. Express your appreciation. Teach your children to behave appropriately and respect other people using the library. Do not leave young children alone in the library. Return materials on time and in good condition. Cooperate with library rules and policies concerning computer use and other matters. If you want special privileges, pick a good time to talk calmly with a librarian. Allow plenty of time to check out all your materials before the library closes. Don't act as if it's the librarian's fault if specific material you want is unavailable; consider their suggestions for substitutions. Join the friends of the library group if one exists; if not, consider starting one. Participate in library book sales and other fundraisers. Donate books and/or money to the library. Take the library staff occasional treats that can be shared by the whole staff (they are not allowed to accept individual gifts): strawberries, tomatoes, or flowers in the summer; cookies or festive bread at holiday time.

Support your library in your community and in the Wisconsin legislature. Write letters to the editor of your local paper describing how important the library is to you and encouraging others to support it. Offer to testify at county, city, or town board meetings. Let your legislators know that you strongly support funding for libraries. Respond when WPA notifies its members about pending legislation concerning libraries.

Visit other libraries in your region for fun and variety. You may find a library that suits your needs better than the closest one and decide it is worth the drive. Some university libraries allow the general public to use their materials in the library; others permit them to be checked out.

Using the Internet

Many homeschoolers find the Internet a valuable addition to their homeschool. Among the possibilities:

- As a source of information about homeschooling. Websites abound. Good places to start include:

A to Z Home's Cool at www.homeschooling.gomilpitas.com is a very popular, comprehensive homeschooling website that offers support and encouragement, articles about different approaches to homeschooling, resources, links to other sites, calendars, homeschooling humor, and more. An excellent place to start if you're new to homeschooling and/or the Internet; a good place to browse if you're experienced.

Home Education Magazine's website at www.homeedmag.com is another excellent resource for new and experienced homeschoolers.

• Search engines: As a source of information when you need a straightforward fact like the population of Brazil. Typing a word or phrase into a search engine will almost always result in many (sometimes too many!) references. Often, it is more effective to type a statement with an asterisk in place of the missing information than to type a question. For example, try "There are * public libraries in Wisconsin" instead of "How many public libraries are there in Wisconsin?" Learning to search effectively (or encouraging one or more of your children to do this) will save you considerable time. Talking with a reference librarian or other experienced searcher and consulting books such as Sarah Milstein's *Google: The Missing Manual* can help you here. Ask reference librarians` for what you are really looking for, not what you think they have.

• Examples of reference sites:

Refdesk at www.refdesk.com is one attempt to make the Internet more manageable. It introduces itself: "On the Internet since 1995, refdesk indexes and reviews quality, credible, and timely reference resources that are free and family-friendly." It offers links to many sites organized by topic.

Wikipedia at www.wikipedia.org is a site that describes itself as a hyperlinked encyclopedia written collaboratively by its readers. The quality of articles varies. Many are excellent; some express strong opinions; a few contain errors. Wikipedia is not censored for the protection of minors, so parents need to exercise discretion.

• As a place to find information on topics your family wants to learn about. You can find a wealth of information on just about any topic you want to include in your curriculum. Some sites are developed specifically to help parents and teachers teach children. The A to Z Homeschool site mentioned above will help you find them. But remember that you can learn from sites that simply offer information on a topic. It doesn't need to be presented as a lesson plan. Many libraries have extensive links to sites that are safe for children and full of good information. Museums (for example, the Exploratorium Museum in San Francisco at www.exploratorium.org) and teachers' professional organizations (for example, the National Council of Teachers of Mathematics at www.nctm.org) are other good sources of kid-friendly sites, information, and lesson plans.

• As a way to get articles from many magazines, newspapers, and other periodicals without subscribing to them. BadgerLink allows Wisconsin residents to read, print, and email articles from a wide variety of magazines, newspapers, and other periodicals. Consult with your local reference librarian about using BadgerLink or go to www.badgerlink.org, click on Magazines and Journals on EBSCOhost, then click on MasterFILE Premier, then type a subject or the title of the article you are searching for.

Many of these publications normally charge for this service; BadgerLink is available at no cost as a part of Wisconsin's public library service. While you are at the BadgerLink site, check out some of the other offerings, including Searchasaurus, their search engine for kids. You can also access the WISCAT catalog discussed above through BadgerLink.

• As a way to earn high school or college credit through online courses.

• As a way to connect with other homeschoolers through online discussion groups or online chat rooms, if this kind of communication appeals to you. You can find them at the homeschooling websites listed above and many other places. Read the Frequently Asked Questions (FAQ) before you begin. It's easy to be overwhelmed by the number of messages posted. Remember you don't need to respond to them all; it is as if you were in a large room filled with conversations going on simultaneously.

Netiquette (Internet etiquette) and online safety are important skills in today's world. Many parents make sure their kids have them before they allow their kids to use the Internet by themselves. Here are some suggestions adapted from one site for children that is gated (you need permission to enter) and moderated (a responsible adult is monitoring all the postings).

- For your safety, do not give out personal information online such as your full name, email address, address, or telephone number.
- Tell your parents/guardians or teacher right away if you come across any information that makes you feel uncomfortable.
- Never agree to get together with someone you "meet" online.
- Do not respond to any message that is mean or that makes you feel uncomfortable. It is not your fault if you get a message like that. If you do, tell your parents right away.
- Do not give out your password to anyone (even your best friends) other than your parents.
- Respect the other members of the community.
- Make sure that the messages you post relate to the discussion topic and provide additional information or ideas. Don't bother to send messages that simply say "I agree" or "Me, too."
- Try to use correct spelling and grammar when posting messages. Don't use capital letters for entire messages (THIS IS CONSIDERED SHOUTING), and please don't use repetitive punctuation marks (!!!!!!!!!!).

Many homeschoolers keep their priorities in mind and limit the time they spend online.

Becoming Involved in Your Local Community

We celebrate that learning happens all day long, 365 days a year. It happens in the sandbox, at the theater, on vacation, in the barn, on the soccer field, in the car, at the neighbors, in the grocery store, and at the junk yard. Wherever life takes us, whoever we meet, what ever situation we encounter, there is a lesson. It doesn't matter if we homeschool using conventional methods or we consider ourselves unschoolers. Everyone here understands that our community is our "classroom" and our community is wherever we are. Rich environments surround us providing infinite learning opportunities.—From Opening Remarks, WPA Conference, 2004

Many homeschoolers are active in youth organizations such as 4-H, scouts, youth orchestras and choruses, theater programs, community sports teams, and church youth groups. These activities provide homeschoolers with social opportunities, and the learning that takes place allows them to be part of a homeschool curriculum.

Homeschoolers also participate in organizations and activities that are for people of all ages or primarily for adults. Young people can learn a lot and find mentors by joining groups that match their interests in gardening, knitting, flying model airplanes, cooking, etc. If the group is used to having only adult members, it helps to have a parent accompany the young person. Even adults who are prejudiced against children often change their minds when they have the opportunity to share their interests with respectful young people. It may take time for a group to warm up to young people, but it's often worth the effort.

If you can't find an appropriate group in your area, consider starting one. Find people who share your interest by posting a notice in the library or local stores. Starting small and growing by word of mouth often works well. Share the work; ask other people to take responsibility for specific jobs if they don't volunteer.

Many homeschoolers volunteer at nursing homes, libraries, community centers, churches, and other places in their local communities. Some join existing volunteer programs. In situations where programs do not exist, homeschooling families meet with people in places that interest them, determine what is needed that they could help with, and make adjustments as they learn from the experience.

Some homeschoolers volunteer in small businesses such as pet stores, repair shops, and bakeries while they are too young to hold jobs there. They learn about work in general and about the specifics of the place they have chosen. Such experience can be invaluable when they are deciding what kind of work they do (and don't) want to do and when they need references and experience in applying for jobs when they get older. Sometimes volunteer work leads to paid employment.

Consider exploring opportunities in your local community and learning something you hadn't even considered. Every community has its own unique groups and individuals who are surprisingly passionate about something. See if your library has a list of local groups. Check with the local paper for information about "famous citizens." Don't be afraid to call people you haven't met, explain that you are homeschooling, and ask if they would be willing to tell you and your children about their interest in model railroads, decorative painting, raising parakeets, or whatever. Some people may decline, but most people enjoy talking about their special interests and appreciate an audience.

The Many Uses of CLEP and AP Tests

College Level Examination Program (CLEP) tests provide a widely recognized way for people to document what they have learned outside conventional classrooms and to earn college credit for it. It's like taking a final exam for a course you have taught yourself. These tests can be invaluable to homeschoolers.

How you can use CLEP tests

• As a homeschooling teen, you can develop a high school curriculum based in part or almost entirely on CLEP tests. Choose the tests you are interested in, study, and take the tests. The time you spend can be counted toward the 875 hours of instruction required by Wisconsin's homeschooling law, and many of the tests will help you cover the required subject areas of reading, language arts, math, social studies, science and health. In addition, when you have completed high school, you will have an impressive and well-documented transcript and credits that will be accepted by many colleges.

• CLEP tests are by far the least expensive way to earn college credit. They cost $55 (plus an administrative fee of about $15) for three to six (and, for foreign languages, up to 12) college credits. Compare this to Internet and correspondence courses which usually cost $200 to $500 or more for three or four credits. Tuition at selective colleges can be $30,000 or more per year, during which students typically earn 30 credits, which averages out to be $3,000 for three credits and $6,000 for six.

• CLEP tests often save time. You get credit for what you already know (you may have learned enough already to pass a CLEP test without further study) and what you learn on your own, working at your own pace, without needing to spend time in a classroom or doing assignments for a correspondence or Internet course.

Important: Not all colleges and universities give students credit for CLEP tests. If you want credit from a college, be sure to find out directly from the college which exams they give credit for, what score you need to get credit, and how many credits you will get. Some colleges that do not give credit for CLEP tests will allow you to use them to meet basic requirements, so you can take more advanced (and often more interesting) courses and get more from the time and money you put into college.

For excellent information on alternative ways of earning college credit, including credit by examination, see John Bear's and Mariah Bear's books *Bears' Guide to Earning Degrees by Distance Learning,* which has helpful general information, and *Bears' Guide to College Degrees by Mail and Internet,* which profiles 100 top schools. The Bears' website is www.degree.net.

• College credits from CLEP tests are very useful even if you are not working toward a college degree. They can be used to convince a conventional school, a potential employer, and others that you have learned a significant amount about a specific subject. For example, if you are creating a high school transcript based on your homeschooling, you can include

CLEP credits and explain that since you have earned college credit in a subject such as American history, you have met and surpassed high school requirements in that subject.

- If you find it easier to study if you have a specific goal to work toward, CLEP tests can give you an outline of what to study and a sense of accomplishment when you pass.

Advantages to CLEP tests

- Because CLEP tests concentrate on general principles, you can focus on understanding the most important parts of a subject, things you're more likely to remember, and avoid getting bogged down in memorizing insignificant details that you may quickly forget.
- You can learn at your own pace and take the tests when you are ready, as long as you allow time for scheduling with the testing center.
- When you complete a test, you receive your score (unless you have done the essay portion that is an optional part of a few CLEP tests) and official documentation that you can copy and give to other people. You can also arrange to have your scores sent to one or more colleges, if you want. This means that no one knows your scores unless you tell them. You can retake a test after six months if you want to improve your score.
- Great test preparation materials are available. However, inaccurate, misleading materials are also published. You do need to be careful which materials you use.

Suggestions for Studying for CLEP Tests

Thirty-three CLEP tests are available from the College Board, the same corporation that produces the SAT. You can take CLEP tests at any age; you do not have to wait until you are 18. Each computerized test is 90 minutes long. Except for four tests that include optional essays, they are primarily multiple choice, although some tests do require the test taker to type a few words or a number for some questions. For more details, visit the CLEP website at www.collegeboard.com/clep.

To study for a CLEP test, get the *CLEP Official Study Guide* and guides for tests you want to take from the library or through the CLEP website. Review the introductory material. If you think you might know enough already, take the practice test. Determine your score. (Hint: If you don't look up the correct answers to the questions, you can use the practice test again later. If you do study the correct answers, you might remember the answers the next time you take the test, which means you won't get useful information about how well prepared you are for the test.)

Decide whether your score is high enough for you to meet your goals. If you get 55% to 60% of the questions right, you can probably get a 50 on the test (scores range from 20 to 80). If you just want to pass the test and move on with what you really want to do, or if the college you are planning to attend will give credit for a score around 50, you may want to take the test right away. But if you want a higher score than you got on the practice test, you may want to study before taking the test.

In preparing for a CLEP test, focus on basic principles and basic vocabulary. CLEP tests generally stick to the big picture and don't try to trip people up on picky details. Math questions cover basic operations and understanding of fundamentals and do not require complicated arithmetic to answer questions.

One very, very important point: The official CLEP materials say to study a college textbook on the subject. However, college textbooks have way too much detail and are more likely to be confusing than helpful for most people. Much better resources are:

- Guides to CLEP tests that are not published by the College Board. However, you have to be very careful here, too. Some guides include material that isn't even on the tests, meaning that you end up studying a lot of stuff you don't need that may be confusing. *Cracking the CLEP* by Tom Meltzer and Paul Foglino, published by the Princeton Review, is excellent and follows closely what is on the tests. Other preparation guides vary in how close they come. Before you choose a guide, compare it with the official CLEP list of topics covered by the test.

• Good books (not textbooks) written for middle schoolers and high schoolers. This material is often well-illustrated, fun to read, much easier to understand, and more in line with what you'll need to know. Check the children's section of the library. For example, if you want to take CLEP tests on American history I and II, consider reading Joy Hakim's series *History of US*, which is much more appealing than a college textbook and provides the needed information.

• If you decide to take tests in more advanced subjects like introductory business law, you will find few if any books for middle and high schoolers. However, you can check the adult section of the library for popular works written on the topic. Such books are often 200-300 pages, much shorter than college texts. Since they do not have the guaranteed market college texts have, they have to be clear and appealing or people won't buy them.

• Consider using resources available on the Internet. One website that offers Internet resources is www.clepbuster.com. However, as with printed study guides, be sure the material you are using actually corresponds to the tests you are planning to take.

• If all else fails and you have to use a college textbook, try to visit a college library or bookstore where you can compare several. Choose one that's attractively laid out and appeals to you. Ideally, it will have a one to two page summary for every chapter. Compare the table of contents to the list of topics on the CLEP test to make sure most, if not all, are covered.

Once you have selected a textbook, don't begin at the beginning and work your way through all 450-600 pages, one page at a time, unless that's what you really want to do. If your goal is to learn basic principles, pass the CLEP, and move on to what you really want to do, try just reading the summaries for the chapters covering topics that will be on the test. (Don't spend your time on the other chapters unless, of course, you want to learn more than is required because you're interested in the subject. But remember that there are many better ways to learn about a subject than through a textbook.) If you think you have a pretty good grasp of basic principles and vocabulary, take the CLEP practice test to decide if you need to study more and what kinds of things you need to know.

Strategies for Taking CLEP (and Other) Tests

• Don't cram. Study what you want to cover in the days, weeks, or months before the test. Then get a good night's sleep.

• Stay calm. Remind yourself that you have nothing to lose except about $70 if you don't score as well as you want. If you get so nervous taking a test that it interferes with your ability to answer the questions, find a book or two on test-taking strategies and choose the suggestions that appeal to you.

• Learn how the test is structured, and take at least one practice test before taking the actual test. The CLEP website at www.collegeboard.com/clep has helpful tips.

• Plan your time carefully. If you don't know enough about a question to make an educated guess, go on to the next one without wasting any time. You can come back to the more difficult questions if you have time after you answer the others.

• Answer every question. CLEP does not penalize for guessing.

• Don't worry about how well you are doing while you are taking the test. Focus on answering the questions. Remember that some of the questions on the test are being tried out for future tests and won't count in your score. If you encounter a confusing question, assume it's a poorly written trial question and go to the next question. Don't let it shake your confidence.

Advanced Placement (AP) Tests

Like CLEP, Advanced Placement (AP) tests are created and administered by the College Board and offer an opportunity to earn college credit or advanced standing. AP tests were developed for students who have taken AP courses in a conventional high school, but you can take tests without taking the courses. Thirty-five tests are available in 20 subject areas. Tests cost $82; an additional fee may be added by the school administering the test. You can take an AP test over to try to improve your score, but you have to wait a year, and your grade report will include all the AP tests you have taken.

Differences Between AP and CLEP Tests

• CLEP tests are offered year round; AP tests are given only in early May. To take an AP test, you must contact AP Services by March 1 by phone (609) 771-7300 or (888) 225-5427 or_email: apexams@info.collegeboard.org to get the names of local AP coordinators, and contact the coordinators by March 15.
• AP tests include multiple choice questions plus "free response" questions that require test takers to write an essay, solve a problem, etc. Each test is two to three hours long. CLEP tests are 90 minutes and most tests have only multiple choice questions.
• Some colleges will give credit or advanced standing for AP tests but not for CLEP tests.
• Both programs offer tests in subjects like US history and biology, but some subjects are available from only one.
• AP scores are available several months after you take the test. You get CLEP scores as soon as you complete a test (unless you have written an essay).

Much of the general information about CLEP tests above applies to AP tests. Resources to prepare for AP tests are available at www.collegeboard.com/student/testing/ap/about.html. Commercial guides also exist, including the Princeton Review's *Cracking the AP.* As with CLEP, make sure that guides you choose are appropriate to and match the tests. For more information, go to www.collegeboard.com/student/testing/ap/about.html.

In addition to CLEP and AP, you can get college credit for DANTES/DSST tests (www.getcollegecredit.com), tests offered by Excelsior College in Albany, New York (www.excelsior.edu), and other sources.

Chapter 9

Homeschooling Children With Special Needs

This chapter includes children who have been diagnosed and labeled as learning disabled (LD), attention deficit hyperactivity disorder (ADHD), on the autism spectrum, gifted, or who have other special needs or syndromes, or who are blind, deaf, or have other physical disabilities. It discusses advantages to homeschooling and general suggestions for dealing with any of these diagnoses and labels. But the most powerful part is the collection of stories at the end of the chapter from mothers who have homeschooled their special children.

Advantages to Homeschooling

• Children get individualized attention and care from someone who knows them well, loves them, and can focus on meeting their needs. Parents can choose or develop a unique program that meets the needs of their child.
• Homeschooling provides continuity and stability for children. They can focus their energy on developing their potential because they don't have to worry about where they are or who is taking care of them.
• Homeschooling gives parents much more control over what happens to their children. Parents know what happens each day, can avoid having their child treated in ways they don't want, and don't have to worry about inappropriate or harmful treatment from a teacher, staff member, or other children. Also, a homeschool can provide many, many things a conventional school cannot offer, such as fresh air, special diets, background music, pleasant surroundings, and more. The flexible schedule allows children to eat, rest, sleep, be active, etc., when it suits them best, instead of having to follow a rigid schedule imposed by the school.
• Parents can spend time and energy working with their child instead of having to meet with school officials and trying to convince them to treat their child the way the parents want.

Suggestions for Parents

• Trust what you know about your child, even when experts disagree. The stories below show how often parents are right and experts are wrong. This is not surprising, since parents have known their children well for most or all of their lives, have seen them in a variety of settings, and have a lot more information about them than experts who only see them once or occasionally. Experts often say that parents can't be trusted and aren't objective about their own children. However, many parents feel that their knowledge of and love for their children enables them to see realities and possibilities that experts who are objective often miss. To be sure, an expert probably has more details about the specific condition your child has, but you have much more information about your child. If you think an expert is wrong about your child, stick to what you know and tell the experts you don't agree with them (but don't be surprised if they overlook what you are trying to say).

• But at the same time, there may be times when you would benefit from information from professionals and others who have more experience with children who have the same diagnosis. Learn from other people's experiences and information, but choose your sources carefully, stick to what you know about your child, and don't be afraid to disagree with experts. Their experience may help you make decisions, although it may only help you decide what not to do. For example, experts have probably only seen children who attended conventional schools and may be unaware of the possibilities that homeschooling offers. Think carefully about what you hear and read before you accept it.

• One way to get experts to listen to you and take you more seriously is to learn some technical vocabulary associated with your child's condition. When you can use scientific names for parts of the body, diagnostic tests, test results, medications, etc., experts realize they are talking with a knowledgeable person. Information about various conditions is available at the library, on the Internet, from other parents, and from other sources. Ask people to spell the names of technical terms they use and to explain things to you. Write down, print off the Internet, or make copies of information that might be helpful. (Also keep records of your child's behavior, what experts tell you, test results, and related information.) You may feel overwhelmed at first, but gradually you'll begin running into finding more words you recognize, and the information will start making more sense.

• If appropriate, question the diagnosis. Some are clear-cut, such as obvious physical disabilities. But many children who have been labeled "learning disabled" have shown that they can learn well given a good learning environment, the support they need, and an opportunity to learn in their own way and according to their own timetable.

• Many parents choose to focus on their child as a person rather than on the label someone has given them.

• Be open to alternative approaches to your situation and seek information from a range of people. Some people have found that acupuncture, homeopathy, and other alternatives can help in a wide range of situations.

• Your decision to homeschool your child will probably be questioned and challenged by school officials, experts, and others. You will be told that you should not or cannot homeschool your child because you do not have special training. It takes extra strength to stand up against such challenges. However, there are many advantages to homeschooling children such as yours, and many parents have homeschooled children in similar circumstances and been very glad they did.

When talking with school officials who are trying to convince you not to homeschool, it may help to remember two things. First, they may want you to send your child to school partly because school districts receive extra money for each child with special needs. Also, without enough special students, special education teachers may lose their jobs. Second, despite the extra funds they receive, school districts often do not have the teachers, equipment, facilities, or time to deal well with children with special needs. Some teachers really want to help children but simply have too many students to give them what they need.

• If you choose to use services provided by public schools, be careful what you sign. If you give permission to have your child evaluated for learning disabilities, you may have to also agree to psychological testing, which you may or may not want. Parents of children in special education lost some ground late in 2005 when the US Supreme Court ruled that parents have to prove that an Individualized Education Plan (IEP) is not the right plan; school districts do not have to show that it is. Know your rights. For example, you can get out from under an IEP you are unhappy with by withdrawing your child from a public school. An IEP cannot follow your child into a private school, including a homeschool.

• All homeschooling parents need support; parents who are homeschooling special children need extra support. Think about what kind of support you need (someone to talk with, help with household tasks, a break from your daily routine, time with your spouse, etc.) and where you can find it. You may find some parents of children similar to your child are very supportive while others have very different approaches to the situation and may even challenge your decision to homeschool. You may find you have more in common with parents who understand and are committed to homeschooling even though their children are different from yours than you do with parents whose children are similar but who send them to a conventional school. If you need household help, teens (including homeschooling teens) sometimes work out well. Internet chat rooms offer support, but again, you will come into contact with people whose perspectives are different from yours. You are welcome to your own thoughts and opinions and do not need to agree with other people.

• You may want to work especially hard to protect your family's privacy in light of the records that exist on your child. See Chapter 33.

Children With Labels Like LD and ADHD

Children who have been labeled have often had such negative school experiences that beginning homeschooling is both a relief and a special challenge. However, many parents have found that homeschooling solves many problems and allows the children to grow and learn in amazing ways.

The first step in resolving such a situation is often the parents' realization that labels are frequently wrong. Sometimes children are misdiagnosed. The tests and techniques used to label children have been shown to be highly questionable. Although extensive research has been done, there is no clear evidence that children labeled "learning disabled" actually have neurological or other physiological problems. It seems much more likely that difficulties in learning are caused by a combination of factors, including the stress and tension of school, pressure on children to learn before they are ready, not allowing children to use the learning style or approach that suits them best, trying to teach children material they find boring or irrelevant, children's lack of experiences their teacher assumes they've had, lack of time with their parents, problems of poverty and lack of resources, and so forth.

We all have difficulties in learning at times. Some children have more difficulty than others in learning what is expected in a school setting. But having difficulty in learning does not mean people have a "learning disability."

Parents who wonder if a label is correct may want to read Lori and Bill Granger's *Magic Feather: The Truth About "Special Education."* The authors describe their experiences when their son was labeled, show how and why schools often mislabel and misdiagnose, stress the importance of parents' roles in protecting their children from labeling, and offer support and suggestions for what parents can do.

Many parents make it clear to their children and to other people they know that the school was wrong. They express confidence in their children and their abilities. They deal with their feelings but don't waste a lot of time on anger or guilt, moving on instead. Many find it works well to begin homeschooling with activities different from the conventional school assignments, workbooks, and tests that may have been part of the problem.

After homeschooling for a while, many children relax and regain their natural curiosity and desire to learn. It is encouraging to see how many problems resolve themselves, once a child is no longer under pressure to perform at a certain level. Parents are amazed at how much children learn easily and happily. Many parents also take advantage of this opportunity to help their children see how much ability they have and to boost their self-confidence.

Gifted Children

Many gifted children are either bored by the pace at which conventional schools move or frustrated because they cannot pursue what interests them most in their own way or both. Many parents feel special programs for gifted and talented students are not the answer and choose to homeschool to give their children the opportunities they need and want. Books could be written on the topic. Books have been. A very good one is *Creative Homeschooling for Gifted Children: A Resource Guide* by Lisa Rivero.

Mothers' Stories

The following stories have been shortened to fit in this book. Reading the complete stories on the WPA website is strongly recommended. To protect the children's privacy, their real names have not been used.

It was a difficult decision to take John out of the mainstream. We began to be worried in January when John began to cry daily before school, not wanting to go. Of course, I told him he had to go. I spoke with his teachers and principal, who offered no help but sympathy. He was labeled a low self-esteem child, and the school social worker worked with him with little improvement. By summer, I began reading anything I could on helping him with school. I also read some about homeschooling and talked with a homeschooler I knew.

In second grade, John's problem was worse. His teacher thought he was slow, he could not get his paperwork done, and he couldn't concentrate on the day's activities. He was a wreck at home. Asking him to eat his dinner or brush his teeth was too much-let alone any chores. It was a constant battle of nagging and punishment from after school until bed.

We still weren't confident to take John out, so we took him to a psychiatrist for more information. He felt John was hyperactive with an attention deficit. He offered a behavior modification program and advised us to prohibit TV action and violence. We were in favor of TV limitation. I was doubtful that the original program could do anything for John's depression and anger, and I knew the changes his teacher made in it would be more harmful than helpful.

We took John out in November, and by the following January, we were pleased to have a happy, cooperative child again. He soon realized he could read just about anything he wanted to read and is continually finding more to read, including some books from the adult section of the library. His judging of a book by the size of the print and number of pictures disappeared shortly after he was away from his reading program. It took nearly a year for John to be able to write papers such as math problems without great stress, but he is improving daily. The best improvement is that John has become interested in life's work and life's choices. He's become responsible for developing (with us) his curriculum and better at carrying it through.

Just looking at the improvement in John's behavior, attitude toward life, and ability to be cooperative and positive is enough to judge our program as successful. A great added plus is that he is also learning a great many things, some of which he might get in school but many not necessarily.

Before I begin, I want my readers to know that both of my daughters have given me permission to share parts of their stories. Because of space constraints, this article focuses on our older daughter, Esme. Both of our girls, ages 12 and 14, are on the autism spectrum. They have needs that can't be met in public schools.

We seriously considered homeschooling Esme when she was in kindergarten. But we decided to send Esme to half-day kindergarten. After a week, Esme came home with a stress rash on her face. Her teacher told us that she was "hysterical" much of the day. Our family doctor suggested a school team evaluation. I decided we would benefit from the results, but I intended to resume my plans to homeschool. However, the school psychologist suggested that Esme would benefit from daily exposure to other kids. The evaluation team recommended a compassionate teacher and gradual inclusion starting at 20 minutes a day so Esme could adjust to school. The schools did provide the therapy Esme needed in sensory integration, adaptation, help with motor planning, and physical education. Esme and her teacher formed a close bond and keep in touch.

Esme was schooled in the public school system until sixth grade. While Esme excelled academically, she struggled, as most children with autism spectrum disorder do, in multiple areas, including making friendships, working in small groups, distractibility, following multi-step directions, and organization. We found it was often hard to get school personnel, including many exceptional and highly respected teachers, to listen to our concerns or to respond. Teachers were stressed with too many kids, an increasing number of them with special needs.

There's a myth that children on the autism spectrum want to be alone because they're happier that way. But the fact is they choose to be alone because they don't know how to be with others.

School became increasingly challenging for Esme as the demands for self-organization and the complexity of instructions and social interactions increased. Her teachers handled this improperly, trying a behavioral approach that made the problem worse. I'll never forget the day I picked Esme up from school when she was crying and saying she did not want to return the next day, that she felt like killing herself.

When I approached the teachers, they were downright rude, insinuating that somehow I was causing Esme's stress. It took two weeks of letter writing to get the school principal, who initially sided with the teachers, to take the problem seriously and listen to our suggestions for helping Esme. I realized I was spending my time working with school people, not with my daughter, and it was negative time. I felt emotionally drained and sapped of all my energy. I decided to take responsibility for Esme, but I had to change my work schedule first. We decided to sell some property we used as a getaway to help us afford my reduced income, and I devoted myself to helping my daughter.

Since she was already academically strong, I decided we should focus on helping her participate in new experiences, tolerate frustration, compensate when she missed information, and communicate with her peers more effectively. Doing less academic work was hard for Esme at first. It was a bit of a culture shock when she began homeschooling. But she met all of the goals I set for her within a year, with individualized attention to her specific needs.

I have the freedom to support her as needed. For example, I can foreshadow with Esme what to expect during an upcoming activity, ensure that she does not miss any directions, or allow her to move to another area where there is less background noise and confusion. It makes a big difference that I know my daughter. I can review events with her afterward, which has helped her comprehend situations as a whole, rather than stressing about one detail or another.

Teaching what kids need to know in a way that revolves around their interests is key for any child, but especially for those on the autism spectrum. Without the burden of homework, Esme has been able to develop an array of gifts and talents, including poetry, photography, and public speaking. She is able to stay with a task despite frustrations for a longer period of time. Esme is generally more comfortable around homeschooled kids because they rarely tease and are more likely to share her interests.

Esme has days when she just needs to unwind with a book or indulge in a spontaneous writing project. We have the flexibility to allow this. With homeschooling, you have the power to prioritize. I cannot overemphasize the importance of this in our lives.

Based on our family's experiences, my reading, and my conversations with other parents, I have come to the following conclusions:

- It is very important for parents to be able to have the flexibility to make decisions that will work for their own unique children. This is especially true for kids who have special needs.
- It is a myth that children on the autism spectrum will learn how to socialize simply by being thrown into large groups of children without any support or guidance. Homeschooling allows parents the opportunity to teach social communication skills gradually, at whatever level the child is ready for.
- An advantage to homeschooling is more time for children to participate in activities in their communities and develop talents and areas of interest.
- I feel extremely fortunate that Wisconsin's homeschooling law allows parents the flexibility to do whatever it takes to meet the individual needs of their children.

An update: Recently Esme told me, "Mom, it used to be that I didn't like change and would do anything to avoid it. Now, I look forward to the unexpected...it's what makes life interesting." This was a monumental statement coming from a person with autism, since a hallmark of the condition is to have great difficulty with change. Since life is full of changes, you can imagine how learning to cope, and even enjoy, change would be "life changing" for the whole family. I would not have been able to help Esme develop this ability if I had not had the opportunity to gradually expose her to small changes in a safe environment, without the additional social and homework pressures of public school.

A few weeks ago, my 10-year-old daughter read a short chapter book.

That may not be too impressive to you. But for me, it was an exciting breakthrough that brought tears to my eyes. It was another proof that homeschooling works, as well as proof that our current Wisconsin law gives us the freedom necessary to achieve great things.

You see, we'd already been homeschooling for many years when my youngest child came along. Her first years were full of doctor visits and surgeries. Her next hurdle was learning to talk. When Liesl was five, a specialist diagnosed a particular genetic abnormality that manifests itself in physical defects, speech difficulties, and learning disabilities. We were told that Liesl would need special education classes and would probably never live independently. Although many doctors and nurses were supportive of our intentions to homeschool Liesl, some "experts" were vehement in their opposition. Some said we just didn't have the expertise needed to provide specialized education.

One of the many sad prognoses was that Liesl would not be able to read. Yes, they said, she could learn phonics and be able to decipher a job application at McDonald's. But her comprehension would be minimal, and she would never enjoy the pleasures of curling up with a story book. Even worse, this wasn't just a doctor's worst-case-scenario prediction; it was commonly acknowledged by other parents of kids with this syndrome.

Because we were "lacking in expertise," we proceeded to educate her in a way that was NOT in accord with standard operating procedure. Had we lived in a state that required standardized testing or portfolio review or curriculum oversight by the local superintendent, it's very unlikely that we would've been allowed to continue homeschooling the way we did in Wisconsin.

A year or so ago, we rejoiced when Liesl began to read easy chapter books. She was not capable of reading a book unless she had previously heard it read aloud more than once. Still, it was progress. And most importantly, she was enjoying these books. I wished she would be able to read new material, too, but it seemed that was not to be. She would try and then give up because the words were senseless. Maybe the experts were right. Maybe her reading comprehension would always be seriously limited.

Then a couple of weeks ago, I read aloud a "Russell" book. It wasn't long, only 1.5 hours for the whole story. She wanted more. But I had work to do, and my voice box was wearing out. An hour later, I discovered that Liesl was two-thirds of the way through a different "Russell" book. She read it. With no bribes from me. She read it. And understood it. She read it. And enjoyed the funny parts. Not only that, but on our next library trip she also wanted to find the series so that she could continue reading these chapter books. Books that the experts said she could never read. What joy that brings to a mommy's heart!

As homeschooling has become more mainstream, many people have become aware of its positive results with regard to academics. Many of us are proud to tout the academic record of homeschoolers. And that's okay. But we must never become so confident in our academic success that we're willing to request favors from the government (be it tax credits or sports in the public schools or something else) based on homeschoolers' ability to measure up academically. "Oh, we don't have to worry if the state checks up on homeschoolers because, after all, we're doing so well anyway!" Please remember that there are homeschoolers who cannot compete in the academic contests. Those children are very likely doing better academically in homeschool than they would in conventional school, but they still wouldn't measure up if the government increased its regulation of homeschoolers. All of us, because we are their parents, have the right and the authority to homeschool our children. It is not a privilege parceled out by the state only to those who measure up. It is critical for homeschoolers to recognize this and never to ask for "help" from the government which will come with strings attached. Those strings may be something you're willing to live with, but those just might be strings which strangle another family out of the homeschooling lifestyle, a family which may be desperate for an alternative to conventional schools.

I wish to share the story of our son, Tom. My husband and I have three children. Mark is presently 13, Tom, 9, and Mary, age 6. We have always homeschooled our children.

From the time Tom was two years old, I could see that he was a more challenging child. He was frequently in trouble, and experience didn't always prevent him from getting into the same trouble again and again. We have had to be very consistent disciplinarians with him. We were also very loving, and he is a sweet, loving child in return. By the time he was in first grade, I had learned some about Attention Deficit Disorder and elected to have him tested by our family pediatrician. He was a difficult child to teach as he couldn't sit still and was not really learning to read. The pediatrician diagnosed him as ADD. I know that, had he been in school, he would have also been diagnosed.

We were given a prescription for Ritalin, and I discussed with the pediatrician how I planned to use it. Dr. Smith completely supported me. I never gave Ritalin to Tom when we were at home, only when we were on field trips. Tom is a tactile learner but is so highly distractible that it was hard for him to learn in his best learning environment! Thus, the Ritalin really helped him when we were on field trips. Also, he used it for soccer games, as otherwise he was unable to concentrate on where the ball was!

At home, I was able to be patient with him and didn't mind if he was standing on his head when we were doing a reading lesson. I understood that was how he operated. Had he been in a classroom situation, I know he would have been on Ritalin daily, as a teacher could not tolerate his behavior with an entire classroom as I could at home—he would distract everyone.

Although he did well in math, his reading progress was very slow. I tried a number of different approaches to teach him and ended up with a combination of A Beka phonics and library books as ideal for him—a different approach than I used with his older brother. He made very slow progress until the third week of January in his second grade year. That week, a "light" went on for him, and he has been reading well ever since!

I've been so thankful that I was teaching him at home because he was never really frustrated. He had no idea that everyone else his age was reading and he wasn't. His self-esteem stayed intact because I always let him know he was doing well. Most ADD children really struggle with self-esteem; Tom doesn't very much.

Now in fourth grade, Tom is doing well with reading. He is a little slower now in math. His fine motor skills are terrible, as his hand writing quickly illustrates. But he is much more independent now and enjoys reading and learning. We have worked very hard with him and been very patient, and our efforts are paying off well. He still doesn't "think before he acts" and will probably always have some struggles in life his brother and sister won't have. But I feel that he is working at his potential and is a happy, loving child. Further, he has not had Ritalin in over half a year now. We travel a lot, and I still take it with me, but he has been successful without it.

I especially wanted to tell Tom's story because I am a special education teacher. I am certified in elementary education K to 6 and special education Learning Disabled, Mentally Retarded and Physically Handicapped K to 12. I taught special education for seven years. I am presently a substitute teacher at a small Christian school. To me, the important part of my story with Tom is that my teaching background really did not help me a lot with Tom. I didn't do anything any differently than any other conscientious mom would have. Perhaps I am a little more confident in my abilities or have an easier time locating materials, but I am not a better teacher to my children than any other mom.

The entire key to working with Tom was patience. I worked at his pace. I kept trying different materials until I found what worked for him. I prayed for him. I loved him as only a mom loves her child—which kept me motivated to work with him even when it seemed difficult. Any caring mom could do this.

This was the same approach I used when I was teaching brain-injured children who were six to nine years old. I worked at their pace and kept trying materials until I found what worked for them. I also worked hard on social skills and teaching general information. I wanted my students to learn to be polite and respect people, to be socially acceptable in public, and to be able to hold a friendly conversation—to be interesting to talk to. I knew they would never succeed academically, but I wanted them to be the best people they could be.

When we get down to it, that is a lot of what I want for my own children. If they go far academically, that's great. But it is more important that they love God, are happily married, are conscientious parents, and contribute back to their communities. I want them to enjoy learning all their lives. I want them to be responsible for their actions. I want the world to be a little better place because they were here. By homeschooling, I'm not teaching to a test, or teaching to someone else's values. We are teaching what we believe. We are teaching because we completely accept the responsibility for the children we brought into this world. Some day, when they are grown, I believe we will look back and say, "We did the best job we could." I believe we will be pleased.

Our second son, Todd, was born with Down Syndrome. We were a bit overwhelmed and figured we needed all the help we could get. Our doctor referred us to the Early Education program in our school district. To be honest, we appreciated the information we received about Down Syndrome from the early education teacher. What we could not stand was someone telling us how to raise our children and what was best for their growth.

Our first of many battles came when Todd turned two. It was strongly recommended that we send him to school to learn daily living skills with other children with disabilities. The idea of sending our child to school to learn how to function with and from other children who were dysfunctional seemed a little ridiculous to us. We chose to keep Todd home to learn from his big brother, who was more then happy to play, interact, and teach his little brother how to be a normal kid. It never occurred to our then four-year-old normal child that there was anything different or slow about his little brother. The boys developed a loving respect for each other and a solid friendship that still exists today. This experience was something school could not provide. We knew we were doing the right thing, but our decision did not endear us with the school system. They felt we were depriving Todd of a greatly needed education that by law he had a right to. Talk about a guilt trip! It was a good thing we decided early on to stand up for what we believed was right for our kids, because intimidation was the name of the game!

At six Todd started school. He had a mind of his own and was very determined. We had taught him the alphabet by phonetic sound only. We were hopeful that in school with a real teacher, he could make great strides. So we sent the little boy we were so proud of off to school.

After one week, we realized school was going to be a struggle. The teacher explained, "Todd is not listening to directions. He sits where he wants to sit, not in a circle like all the other children who have been in school for four years. Let's be reasonable, Mom. You only think he knows his alphabet; don't be surprised if reading is a skill he won't be able to learn because he can't talk after all. Besides children with Down usually aren't capable of learning to read." Imagine the teacher's surprise when a month later she noticed that instead of sitting in the circle, Todd was actually sitting on the carpet square with the letter of the day. She finally agreed he did know his letters. This little episode made us realize the necessity of staying involved in Todd's learning.

Armed with knowledge of our son, a firm belief in our child's ability, and an unbeatable determination, we stood our ground and said, "Let the battle begin." After all, Todd had a right (by law) to a good education, and we were willing to fight for that right. Year after year we attended every Individualized Educational Program (IEP) meeting as a couple and submitted our own list of expectations to be covered with Todd for the following year. When the school didn't have the necessary materials, we found them and took them in.

We started to realize we were winning some short-term battles, but basically we were losing the war. Todd was becoming more and more frustrated and unruly. All our time and energy were being spent on fighting for education. We finally decided to use that time and energy to teach him ourselves.

At age twelve, we pulled our frustrated, angry son out of school and started homeschooling. We gave him time to learn what he wanted to learn. He spelled words and read everything from cereal boxes to children's dictionaries. He became very handy with a calculator and loved playing educational games on the computer. And much to our surprise, Todd started to play the piano. He taught himself, with a little help from Dad, to read music. Todd started to enjoy learning, and rather than just doing what was expected of him, he was always doing more. Our angry, withdrawn son again became a happy, relaxed child with a great sense of humor. Todd started reaching out to others outside of the family. We were so excited with the changes in Todd because of homeschooling, we also pulled his two younger brothers out of school.

In June, we had a graduation celebration for Todd. He has become a confident, loving, happy, and independent young adult. In the last year, Todd and his dad sang a duet at the Very Special Arts Choir concert. He also played the piano for the audience while his dad sang a solo. Todd reads at a third to fourth grade level, has started writing simple sentences, and if he says a word we can't understand, he just spells it out for us. And much to our surprise, he has turned out to be a good photographer. We gave him a Polaroid camera as a graduation gift, and he took nicely posed, perfectly centered pictures of everyone at his party. Must be time to enjoy another talent!

It's true; every child has the right to a good education. It's their God-given right, which has nothing to do with the "law." Homeschooling has been an answer to our prayers. Through this wonderful experience, we have come to realize that, not only do we love our four boys, we also recognize and appreciate who they are and the responsible men they are becoming. We certainly have been blessed. Life is good!

Chapter 10

Recognizing and Evaluating Learning and Keeping Records

Translating Learning Into Conventional School Language

Many homeschooling parents are very aware, just from watching their children and interacting with them, that their children are learning a lot of important things. However, there are times when children's activities and experiences that are less obviously "educational" need to be translated into conventional school language. For example:

• Homeschoolers who are applying for employment, college, or other opportunities need to show that they are qualified. Often homeschoolers' experiences differ from those of people who have attended conventional schools, and the latter is what potential employers and others are expecting. Homeschoolers can increase their chances of being accepted if they can do the work of helping other people understand their qualifications instead of expecting non-homeschoolers to be able to figure it out. See Chapter 12.

• Translating can help prepare homeschooled children to respond to questions from other children and from adults. Our society is strongly dominated by conventional schools. Even children who have not attended a conventional school often try to compare what they know with what they think other children their age have learned in conventional schools. Because our society has such a strong bias toward conventional schools, many homeschooled children feel they are behind their contemporaries and know less. Many homeschooling parents try to help their children realize the wide range of things they are learning, some of which are not even included in conventional schools. But translating can be a way of helping homeschooled children realize how much they are doing and learning that is like what children learn in conventional schools, so they feel more confident and comfortable with themselves and so they can respond to challenges from other children. "Can you read?" "What's 9 times 12?" "What's the capital of Brazil?" Some homeschoolers respond to such challenges by saying, "I don't really like those kinds of school games. Do you? Let's do something that's more fun instead."

• It often helps non-homeschoolers relax and maybe even become supportive of homeschooling if they can see that conventional school subjects can be learned through hands-on activities and what may first appear to be "play." For example, when children set up a pretend store, weigh food, and wait on customers, they are learning math and social skills.

• Translating helps parents who usually have confidence in homeschooling but who occasionally have doubts. They realize how much their children are doing that even non-homeschoolers would recognize and give them credit for.

• If homeschoolers are questioned about truancy, they might find it helpful to include some examples in which they translate what they have been doing in their homeschools into conventional school language.

At the same time, however, many homeschoolers work very hard to remember that they are only doing this translating to help other people understand homeschooling, to bridge a gap that exists because our society is so dominated by conventional schools. When homeschoolers translate, they are not saying that conventional schools are the standard for education and learning that homeschools have to measure up to. Homeschoolers are not saying that the only learning that really matters is what can be shown to be like the learning that goes on in conventional schools, that the only subjects worth studying are those that are included in conventional schools, or that the only way that homeschools can be legitimate is by showing that they are really a lot like conventional schools after all. Homeschoolers know that homeschooling has a legitimacy and value all its own, just by virtue of being what it is, learning together as families. Homeschooling does not need to earn legitimacy by showing that it is like conventional schooling.

Here are some specific examples of translating experiences and activities into the language used in conventional schools. This is a responsibility that homeschoolers have to take themselves, because no one else will do it for them.

• Children playing with blocks or legos are learning arithmetic and geometry as they discover from direct experience important concepts such as how various shapes fit together, how smaller units can be added together to form larger ones, and how numbers as represented by blocks relate to each other.

• Children talking with older relatives and friends about times past or with people from other countries about their cultures are learning history and social studies as they learn about the past, changes that have brought us to the present, and how other people live.

• Children who know something about Wisconsin's homeschooling law and the way in which homeschoolers have worked to protect their rights know a lot about government, civics, law, and reclaiming and maintaining rights.

• Children listening to someone reading aloud and recognizing stop signs are learning to read as they understand how words fit together to make a story and how symbols are used to represent words and ideas.

The list goes on. (See Chapter 6 for more examples.) The possibilities are endless. Experienced homeschoolers have many examples of their own to add.

This translation process makes it possible for us as parents, for our children, and for others who are concerned about our homeschooling to see that real and important learning is taking place even when our children are not necessarily doing the same things that children do in conventional schools. When we recognize some of the basic differences between a homeschool and a conventional school, we can provide our children with many more learning opportunities than a conventional school can. We can encourage them to learn in many more ways than children in conventional schools do.

Evaluating the Learning of Homeschooled Children

Parents need to evaluate the progress their children are making toward their goals. Fortunately homeschooling provides many opportunities for parents to observe what their children are capable of doing and what they have learned. For example:

• Parents observe and evaluate their children without needing to plan or think about it. They do this naturally and automatically because they like their children, are interested in what they say and do, and want them to have opportunities to learn about the world. Parents then make adjustments as a result of these observations. They may do extra reading with children who are having trouble recognizing words, write notes to children who need encouragement to write, or talk about the price of groceries with children who say they don't like math.

• Many parents also make deliberate and self-conscious observations of their children. These observations are guided by the family's goals and curriculum. Parents ask themselves questions like: What interests my children? What skills have they mastered or made progress on? What do they do with their free time? What kinds of questions do they ask? (Someone once said that the real measure of intelligence is not the ability to answer questions but the ability to ask them.)

• Evaluating children's learning environment can also be helpful. Many parents ask themselves what more they could do to encourage learning. Do the children have a variety of things to look at, listen to, and work on? Are there enough of the right kind of reference books? Maps on the wall? Are there other learning aids that would be intriguing to the children? Many parents find that some of the best learning aids are the tools and materials that adults use. Children learn a great deal from using their parents' sewing machines, wood working equipment, computers, garden tools, and other such equipment.

• Many parents find it helpful to review their homeschool records (see below), comparing what children were able to do in the past with their present abilities.

• **Some parents use standardized tests and other assessments** as part of their evaluation of their children's learning. If you want to use them, it is a good idea to have testing privately done and make sure the results are reported only to you and not made part of any government agencies' records on your children. For up-to-date information on having your children tested, go to the A to Z website and search for "testing services." However, many homeschoolers avoid standardized tests and assessments, since they know their children well from working with them. They are also concerned because standardized tests and assessments have been shown to be biased, unfair, and inaccurate. They undermine children's confidence and interfere with the learning process. Their results can have far-reaching negative effects on children. See Chapter 24 for information on problems with preschool screening. Many of these concerns apply to any standardized testing and assessment, for people of any age.

For me, the questions that Dan and Ben ask say a lot about what they understand. When one asks, "How many words are there in English?" or the other asks, "Why are all the Noble elements gases?" I get a pretty good idea of how they are relating that knowledge to their understanding of the rest of the world.

The questions I want my children to be able to answer are the questions they raise themselves. Can they determine that they know enough for their own needs? Can they trust their own assessments without having to call in some outside expert? Do they know how and where to find more information if they need it? And can they learn that ignorance is not the same as stupidity?

Maybe, somewhere along the way, they'll learn wisdom.—From Opening Remarks, WPA Conference, 2000

Record Keeping

To decide what records to keep, many families ask two separate questions. First, "What records should we keep to be in compliance with Wisconsin's homeschooling law?" Second, "What additional records do we want to keep for ourselves?"

Although there may be some overlap, generally different records are needed for these two purposes. Each family needs to decide what kinds of personal records will best serve their approach to education and their unique situation. Personal records may have a strong impact on a individual family, but they generally have little effect on other homeschooling families. However, the records we submit in response to a legal challenge can affect other homeschoolers and our homeschooling freedoms. When we are careful to give to the state only the minimum records and reports needed, we are making an important contribution to maintaining homeschooling freedoms for our families and others. Conversely, when we submit more records and reports than are necessary to deal with a legal challenge, we threaten the homeschooling freedoms of our family and others.

Records Required by Wisconsin Law

According to Wisconsin law, homeschools should keep attendance records as other private schools do.

WPA recommends keeping a daily attendance record that shows that children attend their homeschool each day. Such records document that children are complying with the compulsory school attendance law. Homeschooled children can be marked "present" when they are learning away from home, such as on field trips or more extended excursions. Some parents indicate as "sick" days when children are not feeling well, although many children who are not seriously ill learn a great deal on these days. Therefore, one could ask how homeschooled children could ever be absent other than in a few extreme situations, such as runaways. Nevertheless, it makes sense to comply with a clear-cut requirement of what is basically a reasonable homeschooling law.

If a truant officer comes to the door, show the official your attendance record and/or offer to send in a copy of it; keep the original. Often officials simply need a piece of paper to put in their files, and your attendance record will suffice, especially if you remind them that the law requires compulsory attendance but not compulsory education. See Chapter 22. Your attendance records document attendance. Unless you are called into court because a prosecutor has convinced a district attorney that there is substantial evidence that you are not obeying the homeschooling law, you are not required to show your curriculum or evidence that your children are learning.

Having shown the official your attendance record, you can then explain that you are busy working with your kids. If the official has additional questions, ask that they be sent to you in writing or that an appointment be made for a convenient time. See Chapter 31.

Attendance records are simple and easy to keep. When families begin homeschooling, they establish a calendar that will provide at least 875 hours of instruction. Some families adopt their local school district calendar so they are on the same schedule as the rest of the neighborhood. Others feel that children learn every day, so they mark attendance every day. For a sample chart, see the next page.

In addition to keeping attendance records, many families save samples of their children's learning so that in the unlikely event they were called into court on a truancy charge, this material would support their claim that they have complied with the requirements of Wisconsin's homeschooling law. The materials might also be used to document a transcript or an application for a job or college admission. Use common sense; don't go to extremes. Even without such samples, homeschoolers are very good at figuring out ways to show officials that they have been complying with the law and to convince potential employers that

	August					September							
	26	27	28	29	30	2	3	4	5	6			
Mary	P	P	P	P	P	H	P	P	P	P			
Johnny	P	P	P	P	P	H	P	P	P	S			
Sally	P	P	P	P	P	H	P	P	P	P			

P = present A = absent S = sick H = holiday

they are capable and have learned important things. Most homeschoolers' records are not in the form or detail that is sometimes required in a conventional school. But if necessary, homeschoolers can use notes, examples, and memories to make their case.

Occasionally a family finds its homeschooling challenged by a public official. These challenges may arise because we are unlucky enough to live in a school district where officials are suspicious of homeschoolers and are threatening and intimidating them. Or perhaps someone we know has told school authorities or social service workers that they are worried about our children and think our homeschool should be investigated. Or we may be involved in a custody dispute. A reasonable goal in responding to such challenges is to provide enough information to minimize or resolve the challenge without providing so much that we set precedents that will be difficult for other families or us to meet in the future.

Personal Records Not Required by Law

Homeschoolers who keep attendance records are in compliance with the record keeping portions of Wisconsin's homeschooling law. The law does not require that homeschoolers keep records of their educational activities or accomplishments. The law is written to be consistent with the principle of "innocent until proven guilty" by requiring that the state show that a family is not complying with the law.

Each homeschooling family decides what kind of personal records will work best for them. Some have extensive records; others have few. It is obviously more important to enjoy spending time together as a family and to have a wide variety of experiences than it is to worry about trying to record them all, especially if the record keeping interrupts the activity or becomes a chore that takes the fun out of it.

Reasons to Keep Personal Records

• Records highlight and celebrate what we have done and help us remember. Putting together some kind of presentation can be a way of making part of learning visible, tangible, and appreciable. The presentation may be a recital or show, a collection of pieces of work assembled on the dining room table, a scrapbook, a video, a written report, or whatever else we decide is appropriate. We may want to record the presentation itself by taking photos.

• Personal records boost confidence. As homeschooling parents, we are alert for ways to increase our confidence and that of our children. Assuming so much responsibility for our children's learning is a serious undertaking. It can be difficult to feel sure about what we are doing, especially when most non-homeschoolers assume that children should attend conventional schools. Keeping records that we want to have, records of activities and ideas that we feel are important, can boost our confidence.

Records can also help our children realize how much they are learning and prepare them to respond to challenges from others. Many children have more confidence and a better idea of how much they are learning if they can look at records their parents are keeping or they are helping to keep.

• Personal records also help us develop and keep long-range perspective. They provide an overview and show us patterns in learning and development that we might otherwise miss. They demonstrate that more learning is taking place than we might recognize without records. They are a wonderful support at times when we doubt ourselves, our children, or the very idea of homeschooling. They help us learn to trust our children and ourselves.

Many families include in their records areas of special concern. For example, if a parent, a young person, or someone outside the family is concerned about socialization, the family can simply note each time they interact with other people, including visits with others, outings, phone conversations, and letters and email. Similarly, if there are concerns about math, the family can record each time they work with numbers, spatial relationships, and other aspects of math. In most cases, the records are very reassuring; if not, they provide additional information on problems to be addressed.

• Personal records help families set their own goals and move toward them. Deciding what to record is an exercise in goal setting. Knowing an activity will be recorded gives extra incentive to do it and makes us more likely to notice and remember it when it happens.

• Personal records can be useful for explaining homeschooling to others (except for school officials and truant officers). They provide valuable raw material for applications and credentials. As homeschoolers we often have the opportunity and the responsibility to develop our own diplomas, transcripts, and other credentials and to convince employers that they should hire us and volunteer programs and colleges that they should accept us. Records are invaluable in stimulating our thinking, creativity, and confidence at such times.

• Some families feel more comfortable and secure knowing that they have records available if they ever need to show them.

• The process of keeping records can be a good learning experience, especially if older children help keep their own records.

Choosing a Focus That Supports Learning

Record keeping works best if the personal records we keep are consistent with and support the approach to learning we are following.

Families who choose an approach to learning similar to that used in conventional schools often organize their personal records according to conventional school subjects such as reading, writing, math, and social studies. This shows parents, children, and others that homeschooling includes the kind of academic work that people assume children do in conventional schools.

However, organizing records by academic subjects also keeps families tied to the school model, and many families are homeschooling because they want an approach to life and learning that is different from that of conventional schools. Such families often simply record children's activities without labeling them as conventional school subjects.

	Sun.	Mon.	Tue.	Wed.	Thur.	Fri.	Sat.
Reading							
Language Arts							
Mathematics							
Etc.							

Actually most families use a combination of these two approaches. Families using conventional academic curriculums include ways in which children learn in addition to the planned academic studies, such as things they learn from hobbies, travel, involvement in church and volunteer organizations, and other activities. Families that emphasize alternative approaches to learning find that some of their activities inevitably include conventional academic subjects such as reading and writing about all sorts of topics, using math to figure out how to build something, or using science resources to help understand phenomena they have observed. The kind of translating discussed at the beginning of this chapter is an important part of record keeping because it sometimes helps us to record as much of the learning that our children are doing as possible.

Feeling overwhelmed with record keeping is not a good reason to give up homeschooling.

Ways to Keep Personal Records

Possibilities for personal homeschooling records are limited only by homeschoolers' creativity and imagination. Personal homeschooling records do not need to be modeled on conventional school records. Conventional schools keep records so they can keep track of students who encounter new teachers each year, so they have information available on students that few if any people in the school may know well, so they can convince legislators and voters that the schools are doing a good job and that problems arise from students and their families, so they are covered in case someone takes legal action against them, so they can determine who is the valedictorian and who is eligible to play on the school's sports teams, etc. Homeschoolers by and large don't need records for reasons such as these. It's certainly to be expected that homeschooling records can be very different from conventional school records.

Flexibility is a key to keeping homeschooling records. Many families try different approaches, building on what works and discarding what doesn't. If record keeping is interfering with a family's enjoyment or bogging them down, they can try a different approach or simply stop keeping the records that are causing them problems.

Some examples of the kinds of records that homeschoolers find helpful:

- A daily or weekly journal can record children's activities. It can be a narrative, a brief list of activities, or some other format. Some families make a "to do" list each morning, check off what they do, add unplanned events that occurred, and use this as a record.
- A monthly or quarterly summary that reviews what has been done and summarizes important developments. "John is now paying more attention to words on cereal boxes and pointing to the ones he recognizes." "Mary has made two blouses and a dress in the past three months and obviously feels more confident in her sewing abilities."
- Some families who want records by subject area use a chart such as the one shown here. Any subject can be listed. In the boxes notes are made about activities and perhaps the amount of time spent on each. For example, the rectangle for reading on Tuesday might say, "Little House in the Big Woods, 1 1/2 hours." Language arts on Thursday might say "Wrote to Grandma, 3/4 hour." Not every subject needs to be covered every day. Families select the subjects they want to include and need not limit themselves to subjects their children would be studying in a conventional school. This chart is quick and easy to fill in, and it shows whether any subjects are being overlooked.
- Some families using purchased curriculums record when they do the parts of the curriculum they choose to do and add other learning activities that supplement the curriculum, such as reading aloud for pleasure, cooking, and going on nature walks and other field trips.
- A quick and easy approach is to simply collect, in a file folder or box for each child, some samples of their written work and art, lists of books read, snapshots of projects in progress or completed, brochures from places visited, and similar materials with dates on them. They can be kept as is or used to make a scrapbook or portfolio.

• A scrapbook or portfolio can be made with samples of children's work. Many families include more than paperwork. They write a description, include drawings, or take a photograph of accomplishments like cooking dinner, raising an animal, producing a play, or building an elaborate block structure.
• Photo albums provide rich and easy records. Just remember to take pictures of typical activities, special projects, children working with adults, places you visit, people who visit you, etc.
• Parents' and children's memories are an important part of record keeping, even though they are informal and require little conscious effort. Memories can be the mainstay of personal homeschooling records; some families have few if any personal records beyond their memories. Memories are richer and more detailed than tangible records can be. In fact, sometimes photographs and written records may interfere with our memories, as we either subconsciously decide we no longer need to remember an event or a scene because a photograph has been taken, or we remember the photograph but have trouble calling to mind the actual event or scene itself.

For information on developing transcripts, portfolios, and credentials to demonstrate homeschoolers' qualifications, see Chapter 12. For making records of unit studies, see Chapter 7. For additional information, see Loretta Heuer's *Homeschooler's Guide to Portfolios and Transcripts.*

Responding to Officials' Requests for Our Records

A frustrating irony of record keeping is that, in a sense, the more complete and extensive our records are, the more careful we need to be about when and to whom we show them. WPA strongly urges homeschoolers to give careful and serious consideration to any request for our records and to show them to officials only after we have clearly established that it is essential that we show them and in the best interests of our own family and other homeschoolers in Wisconsin.

If you are contacted by letter, phone, or in person by a school official who asks to see your records, see Chapter 31.

Chapter 11

Homeschooling for High School

Can you really homeschool for high school? Questions abound. Some teens wonder about missing the social life at school, getting into college, being prepared for the "real world," being bored, getting tired of younger siblings, and so on. Some parents worry about helping kids learn things they don't know themselves, getting enough equipment for chemistry without blowing up the house, having to spend so much time with a volatile teen, getting teens to learn math and spelling, and helping them get into college.

Questions and doubts are to be expected, especially given the unfairly and undeservedly negative attitude our society has toward teens. But families who have homeschooled for high school can tell you that it's possible to answer these questions positively. In fact, homeschooling for high school is better than attending a conventional school. You can have friends your own age and older and younger. You can learn at your own pace and explore what interests you. Spending more time together as a family reduces tensions, strengthens bonds, and paves the way for interacting as adults. Your flexible schedule makes it easier to find part-time jobs. There's time for music, art, sports, and community service. Colleges increasingly are seeking homeschoolers. You have more control over your life. And, yes, you can either go to the prom or decide other things are more important. Just expect that the question you'll be asked most is, "What about the prom?"

Here are ideas for new and continuing homeschoolers. The information is for both teens and parents. But since it had to be addressed to one or the other, it's mostly directed to teens, assuming that parents are reading, too. Many families also find that workshops for teens and parents at the WPA conference provide important information, support, and encouragement that are difficult to find elsewhere.

A few years ago, I was asked to speak to a workshop on "simple living" about some of the choices our family has made over the years. When I mentioned how much I'd been enjoying my sons' teenage years, one of the participants commented "You're the first person I've ever heard say they enjoyed their teenagers!" He was completely amazed. That brought home to me just how unusual good connections between parents and young people are in our society today-and it made me feel sad for the people who are missing them. I'm guessing there are a lot of parents in this room who are enjoying your teenagers. Don't take that connection for granted-it is something valuable.—From Opening Remarks, WPA Conference, 2005

Choosing an Approach to Curriculum and Learning

Having so many choices for curriculum and learning can be both exciting and overwhelming. Some homeschooling teens and their parents begin by listing:

- Current interests, including topics you know a lot about; things you want to learn more about; hobbies, sports, and other activities you enjoy; skills you want to acquire or improve; and anything else that's important to you.
- Short-term goals and plans, including things you'd like to do this week and this month.
- Long-range goals, including things you'd like to do, trips to take, work and careers to explore, and what you're thinking at this point about going to college.
- Strengths, including what you're good at, talents and abilities you have.
- How you learn best.
- Resources, including people you know and opportunities available near home.

A good website for learning more about yourself and career possibilities is the University of Waterloo's "Career Development eManual" www.cdm.uwaterloo.ca/steps.asp. Helpful books on setting goals and reaching them are Richard Bolles' *What Color Is Your Parachute? A Practical Manual for Job-Hunters and Career Changers* and Barbara Sher's *Wishcraft: How to Get What You Really Want.*

For information about approaches to curriculum, see Chapter 7, which applies to kids of all ages. Here are ideas particularly for teens.

- You can base your curriculum on what teens usually learn in conventional high schools, but you don't have to. Many homeschooling teens pursue their interests and passions in greater depth than conventional schools allow time for, whether playing violin or drums, visiting American Civil War battlefields, swimming, hosting websites, serving others, learning another language, or something else.
- Teens are usually more interested in and motivated to use a curriculum they have helped select or develop. Many parents involve their teens and give them as much responsibility as possible for their own learning. Teens who know how to learn and enjoy it are likely to keep learning long after their parents and Wisconsin law require that they do.
- An outstanding resource for teens who want to plan their own curriculum is Grace Llewellyn's *Teenage Liberation Handbook: How to Quit School and Get a Real Life and Education.* It explores many conventional and unconventional ways to learn just about anything, and the author's enthusiasm is contagious.
- Some families use the CLEP and other tests for part of their curriculum. It can be satisfying and rewarding to choose a subject area, study for the test, take it, receive college credit, and save a great deal of time and money in the process. See Chapter 8.
- Most of the curriculum packages, outlines, and correspondence schools listed in Chapter 7 offer materials for high school.

• Some homeschooling teens take classes in a community college or technical school before they are 18. They gain college experience and earn college credits. Transcripts from these courses strengthen applications to other colleges.
• Homeschooling for high school takes balance. There is a lot of pressure to prepare for adult life, but getting too caught up in the future can mean you miss some of the fun, excitement, and wonder of each day.

Starting Homeschooling During the High School Years

Many families begin homeschooling during high school and find it rewarding and satisfying. If you are beginning during high school, you have good reason to feel encouraged about the prospect, even if it's because of health concerns, a difficult conventional school experience, truancy, failing grades, or other less than ideal circumstances.

Experienced homeschoolers recommend taking a break from academics, especially if you've had a difficult experience in school. This is especially important for teens. Plan a week, a month, or more to rest, recover, and reconnect with your parents, your siblings, and others. Don't be surprised if you sleep a lot. Most students in conventional high schools don't get enough sleep, and fatigue contributes to whatever problems they face. Many parents find they need a balance: giving teens some space and letting them make some choices while at the same time offering support, making suggestions, guiding their decisions when necessary, and listening when they want to talk.

Activities that work well for this time include: physical exercise, spending time in nature (sitting in the back yard, hiking in a nearby park, camping at the Grand Canyon), creative work (taking snapshots, doodling, doing counted cross stitch, building a doghouse). Discovering that you're capable, needed, and appreciated does wonders, whether it's driving an elderly neighbor to the doctor, painting the garage, walking the dog, or organizing a game of tag for neighborhood kids. Taking a trip is a great way to make the transition from school to homeschooling. Could the whole family manage a weekend away, or even just a day trip to a nearby park or activity? Do you know someone who supports homeschooling who you could visit? Getting away is a relief, offers new perspectives, and opens the door for a fresh start.

Don't feel pressured or hurry to get into academics, and don't buy a curriculum, especially an expensive one, until you've considered the options. You'll quickly realize that you are learning by doing the activities listed above, and you may want to add some from Chapter 6. To meet Wisconsin's requirement for 875 hours of instruction each school year, you can start counting what you are learning now. For ideas on how to do this, see the section on translating what kids do into school language in Chapter 10. If you attended a conventional school for part of the year, you can count those hours toward the 875.

When the time is right, read Chapter 7 and decide which approach to a curriculum you want to start with. If you're not interested in "school work," see "Homeschooling Teens Who Don't Like School Work" below.

For information on diplomas and other credentials, see Chapter 12.

Homeschooling Teens Who Don't Like School Work

Lots of teens don't like school work. Some had negative school experiences and are convinced they don't like studying or are no good at it. Others think school work is dull and boring. Fortunately, there are many ways to learn, and the approach used by conventional schools is only one. For many people, it's not the best. As a homeschooling teen, you can learn very important things in ways that work well for you. Some people learn well by working with their hands and have amazing abilities to build, fix things, and keep things running. Some learn and work best on projects that involve people working together for a good cause. Some rise to the occasion when given the opportunity to serve those in need, including children, the sick, and the elderly. Artists and other creative types learn by creating and make important contributions through their work. Teens benefit from having the opportunity to do real work that matters.

So don't despair if you didn't do well in school or don't like to do school work at home. It's good that you know that this isn't the best way for you to learn and that you have the courage to say so. (Think how many people know school doesn't work for them but are afraid to say anything, so they just put in their time.) You can discover and develop the important gifts and talents you have and use them to do important work that will make a contribution, whatever it may be.

Consider developing your own curriculum. Developing a curriculum is much easier than it sounds. A curriculum is a plan for learning what you want to learn the way you want to learn it. Suggestions for homeschoolers who don't like school work include:

- Concentrate on your strengths. People have abilities in different areas. Unfortunately, our society tends to overemphasize reading, writing, math, and doing well in school. Much less credit is given to people who have mechanical, musical, physical, or artistic abilities; social skills; problem solving skills; common sense; or other abilities, even though these are at least as important and valuable as doing well in school. (Thomas Armstrong's book *In Their Own Way: Discovering and Encouraging Your Child's Personal Learning Style* discusses the different types of intelligence that people have and the variety of ways in which they learn.) Find the non-school things you're good at (if you don't already know what they are), emphasize them, and worry a lot less about the school stuff. On the other hand, if you really like school stuff but don't like being treated the way schools treat people, now that you're homeschooling you have a chance to learn the way you want to learn, concentrating on the areas that excite you and worrying less about things that don't. If you work on what is important to you, you'll learn the math, spelling, or whatever you need along the way, or you'll discover that you really need them and be motivated to study them.
- Many families start with what interests their teens. Homeschooling lets you build on what you are doing now that works well, on activities that you enjoy and want to do. Don't worry if your interest is motorcycles or photography or baking or something else that isn't usually covered in conventional schools and that doesn't sound like school work. Teens who pursue their interests usually cover the subject areas required by Wisconsin law (reading, language arts, mathematics, social studies, science and health).
- Instead of thinking about what you would be doing if you were going to a conventional school, think about what you need to learn to be an effective adult. Some families build a curriculum based on life skills: learn to get a job and keep it; learn new skills; deal confidently with change; run a household; manage money; buy a car or truck and keep it running; etc. They find that this prepares their kids for life more effectively than a conventional high school curriculum would.
- Every subject offers learning opportunities. Don't limit your homeschooling to things that sound like school subjects. You can learn an amazing amount from baseball, motorcycles, chess, cooking, gardening, caring for animals, repairing equipment, etc.
- Think in terms of learning by doing. We all learn this way. Ask your parents how they learned to do a lot of what they do each day: driving, cooking, things they do at work, parenting, etc. Most people spend most of their lives doing things, not studying.
- Find someone who knows what you want to learn and ask if you can work with them. It could be one of your parents, a sibling, a relative, a neighbor, a friend, or someone you don't know yet. Tell them what you want to learn. Ask them if they will answer questions, share tools and equipment, and things like that. Ask how you can help them, too, maybe by doing easy tasks, cleaning up, or answering the phone for them.

• Include learning to make money in your curriculum. (Conventional schools call this work-study or vocational education.) Call some places that sound interesting and ask if you can visit and find out what people actually do there. Look for part-time jobs that you'll learn from. If a paying job is not available at a place you'd like to work, see if you can be an apprentice or an intern and not get paid. You'll still learn a lot, and it will help you get your next job, since employers want to know what experience you've had. Another possibility is starting your own businesses. Lots of teens baby-sit, mow lawns, and shovel snow. Think about other possibilities: selling homemade specialty breads, making cloth dolls, walking dogs, reading to nursing home patients, setting up and troubleshooting computers, and repairing bicycles. Look for things that need to be done and figure out ways to do them.

• Life skills can be included in any curriculum, offering learning opportunities and practical benefits. Consider cooking, cleaning, laundry, keeping a car running, balancing the family check book, gardening, sewing, home repair, interior decorating, and learning how to work cooperatively with other people (in this case, your family) to get work done so everyone benefits. Conventional schools call this learning "home economics," "industrial arts," and/or "financial management." But these activities also include the basic subjects of reading, language arts, mathematics, social studies, science and health, and learning how to work cooperatively with other people (in this case, the family) to get work done so everyone benefits.

• Many teens find it helps to spend time on their health. If you already like playing sports and doing other physical activity, count that as part of your curriculum. If not, now is a good time to get more exercise. Consider learning or improving your skills in sports and activities that you can do for years to come: swimming, volleyball, yoga, walking, jogging, whatever appeals to you. Learn about nutrition and improve your diet. Grow a garden. Learn about alternative approaches to health and healing, like acupuncture or herbs.

As an example of how you could develop a curriculum, suppose you're interested in motorcycles. Your curriculum could include some or all of the following, plus other things you think of.

- Visit motorcycle shops. Learn about different cycles. Ask questions. Look at brochures, manuals, etc.
- Buy an old motorcycle or get one from a junk yard. Take it apart and put it back together. If it doesn't run, try to fix it or at least figure out what's wrong with it.
- Start with some money and figure out how you want to spend it: buy a motorcycle, buy gas for the cycle you already have, buy tools, whatever. Keep track of what you spend.
- Visit a motorcycle repair shop. Ask if you can watch the mechanics work. Consider asking if you can work there part-time or help out without getting paid.
- Subscribe to one or more motorcycle magazines. Get catalogs of motorcycles and gear.
- Read the history of how motorcycles have been manufactured and used throughout the world.
- Learn how and why Japanese companies have become the major manufacturers, leaving the US with only one significant manufacturer, Harley-Davidson, in Milwaukee.
- If you have a computer or can use one at the library, find websites about motorcycles. Consider joining a chat room for people who are interested in motorcycling.
- Design a motorcycle, making the drawings as detailed as you want.
- If you have your own motorcycle, keep track of how much you spend on gas, repairs, etc.

With a curriculum like this, you learn by doing. You cover the basic subjects required by law. Activities such as reading instruction manuals and magazines, using the Internet, and talking with others about motorcycles are reading and language arts. Figuring the cost of motorcycles and parts and miles per gallon of gas and using metric measurements are math. Talking with older cyclists about how motorcycles have changed, studying the history of the manufacturing and use of motorcycles, and understanding laws governing motorcycle riding are social studies. Science and health are studied by learning how motorcycles run, safety measures, first aid in case of a mishap, etc.

Finally, try not to get stuck thinking of yourself as someone who doesn't like school work or isn't any good at it. Some teens find that once they are working on a topic that interests them or makes sense to them, they are better at reading, writing, and math than they ever thought they would be. Leave the door open to discover this about yourself.

Note to parents: It may be hard to give up the idea that your teens really should be learning school stuff in conventional school ways and to trust that they will be all right if they learn and do what interests them in ways that work for them. However, many families have found that this approach works. Some very famous people, like Thomas Edison and Albert Einstein, did not do well in school. And if school stuff clearly isn't working for your teen, isn't it time to try a different approach?

Enriching Experiences

Whatever approach to learning you have chosen, it is often helpful to think seriously about including practical experience. Here are some possibilities:

• **Apprenticeships and internships**. Some homeschooling teens participate in formal, conventional apprenticeships that are widely recognized, such as those in the building trades, although most require at least a high school diploma. Others design their own informal apprenticeships that involve working, perhaps as a volunteer, with a person or an organization in an area that interests them. Many organizations offer internships in which they hire young people to work with them in exchange for practical experience. (There is considerable overlap between internships and apprenticeships.)

Internships: The Guide To On The Job Training For College Students published by Peterson's Guides is an excellent resource that lists thousands of internships. You can read the sections that interest you and contact organizations that sound promising. Figure out creative ways to meet the requirements for schooling. For example, if an internship requires "one or two years of college," you can explain that as a homeschooler, you study and learn independently. Describe some of the things you have done that are related to the internship. If you have college credit from CLEP tests, technical school, Internet courses, or other sources, mention that. (See Chapter 12 on diplomas and other credentials.)

If you want to do an internship with an organization that does not offer internships, you may be able to set one up yourself, perhaps modeling it on internships you have heard or read about. You will have a better chance of working something out if you are as flexible as possible about what hours you are available, how many weeks or months you are willing to work, what you are willing to do, etc. However, be clear about your goals and expectations. You will probably be asked to do some routine tasks, like data entry or photocopying, but indicate while you are making arrangements that you only want to spend a quarter of your time (or whatever amount you choose) doing this type of work. Then if you are asked to spend most of your time this way, you can refer to the agreement that was made.

An internship in an area of interest can give you good experience, impressive credentials, and a clearer idea of whether you want to explore the area further. Some organizations frequently offer interns full-time jobs at the end of the internship. But if you decide you do not want to pursue this area, realize you saved yourself time and possibly money by finding that out now instead of after you'd invested in a degree or training in the area. On the other hand, an internship in an area you have no intention of pursuing can be an interesting learning experience and a chance to do something different before you settle down.

You can do an internship in your home town or in another place, giving you a good opportunity to learn about another part of the country or the world. Organizations are often willing to help interns from out of town find housing.

In short, internships are a good way to learn and gain practical experience at much lower cost and sometimes in more interesting ways than enrolling in a technical school, college, or university. Some interns actually earn money; some get a large enough stipend from the sponsoring organization to break even.

• **Employment.** Many approaches are possible. A good source of books and videos, including many unconventional ones, is *The Whole Work Catalog,* Box 339, Boulder, CO 80306. (303-447-1087) Website: members.tripod.com/~ncc1/index.html

Usually, people under 18 need a work permit. For specific information about who needs one and what hours people under 18 are allowed to work, see the brochure titled *Wisconsin Employment of Minors Guide,* available from the Wisconsin Department of Workforce Development, Equal Rights Division, 201 E. Washington Ave., P O Box 8928, Madison WI 53708, 608-266-6860 or online at www.dwd.state.wi.us/er/labor¬_standards_bureau/publications_erd_4758_pweb.htm.

To get a work permit:

1. Get a job.
2. Get the following:
   –A note or form from your employer stating your duties and the hours you will be working.
   –A note (or sometimes a portion of the employer's form) signed by your parent stating that they understand and agree to your duties and hours of work.
   –A copy of either your birth certificate or your baptismal certificate with your birth date on it.
   –Your social security card.
   –Money to cover the small fee. (This will be repaid to you by your employer, often in your first paycheck.)
3. Submit these items. Most public high schools have someone who gives work permits to students in public and private schools, including homeschools. In some places you need to go to a county office instead.

• **Volunteer work.** Volunteering often gives teens the opportunity to serve and to gain valuable experience in areas where jobs are not available or teens are not yet qualified. Teens have volunteered in places that do not usually have conventional volunteers, such as veterinarians' offices, bakeries, pet stores, and other small businesses. Often such work eventually leads to paid employment.

• **Travel.** Again, possibilities and sources of information abound.

Teens and Their Families

Many families who homeschool for high school discover that homeschooling makes the teen years even better. Teens who do not have to cope with the problems and tensions of conventional schools are more confident and easier to get along with. Families who spend significant time together get stronger.

Many parents find ideas like these helpful. Use what works for your family and ignore the rest.

• Many parents try to concentrate on the positive characteristics of teens, like their energy, enthusiasm, courage, and sense of humor. At the same time, they try to minimize the strong messages our culture gives us that teens are difficult and that the teen years are a time of trouble, conflict, and heartache. This doesn't have to be true. Worse, this message tends to become a self-fulfilling prophecy because people (including teens) tend to act in ways they think others expect them to act and because people (including parents) tend to interpret what others say and do on the basis of what they are expecting. Positive expectations really help.

• Work to develop and maintain a strong relationship with your teens. Make time for activities that you enjoy doing together. Go for walks, go shopping, watch movies, read aloud, listen to music, cook favorite foods, and share household tasks. Make communication a priority. It takes a lot of time and energy, but try to be available to listen when teens want to talk and try to see their perspective, remembering that sometimes teens make statements to test out an idea or start a discussion and not because they firmly believe what they are saying. It helps to make eye contact, hug them, and make sure they know you're on their side and you love them.

• Encourage sibling interactions. The strong relationships that can develop among siblings are one of the biggest advantages of homeschooling.

• Ups and downs are an inevitable part of the teen years. One minute a teen may be so mature, thoughtful, and cooperative that their parents are congratulating themselves on what a good job they have done in raising them. A few minutes later, the very same teen may have lost it and have, from the parents' perspective, blown some minor detail totally out of proportion and turned it into a crisis. Understanding that these ups and downs happen to teens, and remembering that they will happen less as teens get older can help parents stay calm and offer their teens support and love.

• Respect teens' privacy. Don't read notes, journals, or mail unless they ask you to. Treat what they tell you as confidential, even if they haven't said, "Promise you won't tell," with the understanding that you may have to share information they give you with their other parent. Many parents feel that teens' triumphs, worries, experiences, and ideas are the teens' to share, not the parents'.

• Ask your teens before you make commitments for them, even if you're sure they'd like to go to the movies with the Browns or you really want them to shovel Mrs. White's sidewalk. Simply say, "I've learned not to make commitments for other people without checking with them. I'll ask John and call you back." Or better: "I'll ask John to call you."

• Many parents learn to care but not to worry. Obviously, they want their teens to be safe, so they discuss concerns they have with their teens, perhaps asking, "What are you doing to make this safe?" They point out that knowing where someone is going and when they expect to be back is a safety issue, not an attempt by parents to control or ruin their teens' lives. (After all, parents don't just disappear without telling anyone where they are going and when they expect to be back.) Once an agreement has been reached, try to relax and trust that all will be well. Worrying takes a lot of energy and is hard on the person who's worrying. It can also undermine the confidence of the person who's being worried about. Keeping their worries under control is one of the most important things parents can do to strengthen their relationship with their teens. Parents can do things like setting an alarm clock for the time teens are supposed to be home at night and then going to sleep. If the teens get home on time, they turn the alarm off. If not, the alarm wakes the parents, and they can decide what to do next. An arrangement like this gives teens a vote of confidence, a reasonable amount of responsibility, and a safety net while parents get more sleep and avoid pacing the floor and then getting upset with returning teens because the parents are so tired and so relieved.

Teens play a very important role in how well parent-teen relationships work out. Here are some ideas. Again, use what works for you and ignore the rest.

• Sometimes teens have to remind their parents just how mature and capable they are. For years, parents were responsible for keeping their young kids safe, warm, fed, clothed, and all. It's understandable that they occasionally benefit from a gentle reminder that teens can handle parts of their lives now. If your parents aren't giving you as much independence and responsibility as you want, ask yourself and them what you could do to change this.

• Try to see things from your parents' perspective as well as your own. They may be worried about their job, money, their parents, grey hair, new tires for the car, you name it. They could probably use some support and encouragement from you.
• Let your parents know what you appreciate about them.

Teens and parents who spend time together working, playing, learning, and living daily life, who respect each other, and who take time to listen to each other, develop strong, mature relationships that are an enormous help to everyone involved throughout their adult lives.

Social Life

"What about the prom?" Homeschooling teens are often asked about social life, the assumption being that theirs is lacking. Many homeschooling teens enjoy their social lives, and some do attend proms-either those held by conventional schools or events planned especially for homeschoolers. Here are some ideas:
• Homeschooling offers people, including teens, great opportunities for wholesome interactions with people of all ages. Therefore, many families consider the social life of homeschooling teens better than that available in conventional schools.
• Homeschooling teens usually develop strong relationships with their parents, siblings, and extended family. It's a big advantage to have a flexible schedule and time to spend with these important people. Many teens feel these relationships more than compensate for any positive social opportunities they might miss by not attending a conventional school.
• Many families help their teens find groups that focus on things they enjoy, like playing sports, producing a play, making music, gardening, learning to spin, or playing chess. If groups do not already exist, consider starting one, which is easier than most people think. Some teens and their families find it works well to plan events that can include the whole family in different ways. For example, everyone could share in a potluck. Then the teens could play active sports, board games, music, or other such activities. Parents could organize informal discussions or just chat. Younger children could do crafts, active play, or other things.
• When teens want to attend a conventional school for the social life but homeschooling really may be a better alternative, some parents conclude that this decision is too important to be left to teens who do not have the life experience necessary to realize the many ways in which public schools impact people. Some parents ask their teens questions such as: Looking realistically at what conventional high school is like, would your social life really be better? What are you missing that's positive? What are you glad you don't have to deal with? If you went to school, how would you handle the negative? What are the positive and negative aspects of homeschooling that you would lose by going to school? How could you improve your social life other than by going to school, and how could we help you?

Obtaining Good Student Discounts on Auto Insurance

Most automobile insurance companies offer discounts for teen drivers who qualify as a "good student" according to the company's criteria for good students. (Some companies require a B average, others a certain class rank, etc.) Homeschoolers have succeeded in getting discounts, setting a helpful precedent.

To get a discount, ask your insurance agent what your company requires and how most people demonstrate that they qualify. Usually, a copy of a report card or a semester or full year summary of report cards or a transcript is required. Sometimes a letter from the school principal stating that the student has, for example, a B average meets the requirement.

Parents can then submit a homeschooling equivalent of what is required, formatting it so it looks as much like it came from a conventional school as possible. You can purchase official forms from a school supply company. Or you can make your own, perhaps using an example from your local public school that a friend has shared with you. Under Wisconsin law, parents or guardians are the official administrators of homeschools, so you have the right and authority to create a report card, assign letter grades, etc. You do not have to purchase a curriculum to do this. You can develop your own curriculum (see Chapter 7) and assign grades. Insurance companies are more likely to understand that you qualify for a discount if most courses are similar to conventional high school courses. As a parent or guardian, you are authorized to sign the transcript as the administrator of your homeschool, just as you sign form PI-1206 to submit to the DPI.

If your agent seems quite open to the idea of giving good student discounts to homeschoolers, submitting the required forms may be enough. However, if they seem skeptical, it is probably a good idea to include a cover letter with information to convince the agent that your son or daughter meets the requirements. If necessary, your agent can use this information to help convince the company to grant the discount. It may be helpful to name your homeschool and create official stationery. Among the points you may want to include in the letter:

- Many insurance companies grant good student discounts to homeschoolers.
- Under s. 115.30 (3) of Wisconsin statutes, you as the parent or guardian are the administrator of your homeschool (called a home-based private educational program in the statutes). Therefore, you are qualified to sign the enclosed transcript.
- Many other organizations accept transcripts from homeschoolers. For example, the federal government accepts them as qualifications for student loans. Colleges and universities accept them as part of applications for admissions.

If your initial request is denied, you will probably need to write to the management of the insurance company, since agents cannot change company policy. Write to the person who made the policy that is denying you equal and fair treatment. Include a copy of your original letter and your transcript or report card. Send a copy to your insurance agent. You can include the points listed above in your letter and also add:

- Homeschools are private schools. There is no basis for thinking that the grades reported by homeschoolers are less reliable than grades issued by other schools.
- It is discriminatory for insurance companies to refuse to grant homeschoolers the same discounts they offer students in public and other private schools, unless they have compelling evidence that homeschoolers who receive discounts result in more claims at greater expense to insurance companies than non-homeschooling students who receive such discounts. Therefore, companies should adopt a policy consistent with the principles and procedures of Anglo-American jurisprudence, including innocent until proven guilty, equal treatment under law, and non-discrimination.
- It is discriminatory for an insurance company to deny good student discounts to homeschoolers because it does not understand homeschooling.
- Studies have shown that the single most important factor in influencing students' grades is the involvement of parents in their education. Since homeschooling requires strong involvement of parents, it is not surprising that homeschooled students generally receive high grades.

You may want to include a statement indicating you are considering switching to an insurance company that gives good student discounts to homeschoolers who qualify.

Finally, while you're working to get a good student discount, it may help to realize that this is good practice for the times in the future when you will need to submit official homeschooling transcripts and other records to potential employers, colleges, organizations that offer internships, etc. See Chapter 12.

Chapter 12

Diplomas, Other Credentials, and Opportunities After High School

Because homeschooling offers opportunities to learn in more ways than conventional schools offer and to gain practical experience in the real world, credentials that homeschoolers develop are different from (and, dare we say, often superior to) conventional transcripts, diplomas, and resumes. Homeschoolers' credentials help make possible a range of exciting opportunities after high school. As a homeschooler, you can feel good about the opportunities that credentials give you to present your experiences and qualifications. You don't need to apologize or worry about not having conventional credentials. Of course, it takes some effort to develop your own credentials. But learning to present yourself well is a very valuable skill that will help you gain access to the opportunities discussed later in this chapter.

Although homeschooling parents may find this chapter very helpful and wish to work with their teens in the ways suggested, this chapter is directly addressed to homeschooling young people who would like to take an active role in presenting themselves.

General Perspectives on Credentials

• Start with a realistic and positive attitude. Homeschoolers are a minority, different from the dominant culture. Therefore, you need to take responsibility for demonstrating that you are qualified. You won't be handed a widely recognized high school diploma and transcript. You have to translate what you have done into terms that people with conventional backgrounds and experience will understand. See Chapter 10. You need to show them that your experiences and knowledge fit their categories and requirements. When you realize that this is inevitably your responsibility simply because you are a member of a minority, when you expect to have to do these things, and when you realize you can in fact do them and do them well, you may see this process as an interesting challenge and an opportunity to exercise your creativity.

• Realize that YOU are your most important credential. You as a capable, experienced, energetic person are far more important and impressive than any diploma, transcript, or test score. You can get the credit you deserve by submitting documents that are clear, neat, and direct. When you are meeting someone in person, dress appropriately, make eye contact, shake hands firmly, and speak clearly and directly. If you'd like more information about how to present yourself, ask a parent, family friend, someone you know in business, or another supportive and experienced person, or check the library for books on resumes and job interviews. Also see the *Career Development Manual* from the University of Waterloo in Canada, which offers excellent steps for career/life planning success. (www.adm.uwaterloo.ca/infocecs/CRC/manual-home.html)

• Whenever possible, tell the person you are contacting what you can do for them rather than asking them to do something for you. Saying, "Think how your business would benefit from having a responsible, energetic teen to serve your customers" is more likely to get the attention of a potential employer than "I'd like to work in your hardware store because I've always liked tools."

• Emphasize your strengths. For example, if you feel your age is an asset, put it near the top of your resume. On the other hand, if it's likely to be a handicap, place it at the bottom or omit it altogether unless you're specifically asked.

• Think outside the box. Don't limit yourself to the style, format, or content of conventional credentials. Submit samples of work you have done, letters of recommendation, and anything else that shows how qualified you are. Show how past activities have prepared you for what you want to do now. For example, point out that you have taken responsibility for a daily paper route, done child care, and organized a neighborhood softball tournament as evidence that you have the skills, responsibility, and experience to work in a city recreation program. Include ways homeschooling has prepared you for whatever you are applying for. (Since many people are not very familiar with homeschooling, they will not realize this unless you tell them.) For example, "As a homeschooler, I am used to taking some responsibility for my own learning. I have been able to spend extra time studying science, which strongly interests me."

• If there's time between now and when you need to develop your credentials, and you're not already keeping records, start now. If you need to develop credentials now and you don't have very organized records, make lists of as much as you can remember. It is easy to forget or overlook activities and accomplishments. Include as many activities as possible that show yourself acting responsibly, taking initiative, exercising good judgment: hobbies, employment, volunteer work, internships, special projects, presentations, and performances. It is impossible to predict now what might be helpful in establishing qualifications in the future.

• Request letters of recommendation, addressed "To Whom It May Concern," from people who know from experience what you can do. This can include youth group leaders, employers, neighbors, pastors, and others. Request the letters when the activity or connection ends, before you lose track of them or their memory fades.

• Develop ways to meet requests and requirements. Try to show how your experiences fit conventional categories, rather than claiming you're so different that you just don't fit. For example, if a college application requires a recommendation from a high school guidance counselor, rather than writing, "Homeschooler—no guidance counselor," your mother could write something like, "As John's mother, I have also functioned as his guidance counselor. I have observed that he is generally..." Or, better yet, ask someone who has seen you in a learning situation, such as a 4-H or scout leader or a mentor you have worked with, to write a letter to fill the requirement for information from a guidance counselor. This is legitimate to do. Remember that administrators who are responsible for getting credentials from applicants, especially in large organizations or institutions, are often more concerned about filling in blanks than they are about what is actually written on the blank. Once you have filled in the blanks, you can be considered for the next step in the process.

• Consider arranging a personal interview, even if it is not part of the normal selection process. Many people are somewhat surprised to discover how "normal" and qualified homeschoolers are in person.

Helpful resources for convincing others you are qualified: Charles D. Hayes' *Proving You're Qualified: Strategies for Competent People without College Degrees* and Richard Bolles' *What Color Is Your Parachute? A Practical Manual for Job-Hunters and Career Changers.*

High School Diplomas

Homeschoolers can earn high school diplomas in a number of ways. But first, a few general points:

• High school diplomas have become an issue among non-homeschoolers these days. Conventional wisdom says you need a diploma to get a good job and be prepared for adult life. But despite the hype, nationwide roughly one quarter of high school students do not graduate. According to the Department of Public Instruction (DPI), about 40 percent of Wisconsin residents over 25 have not earned a high school diploma. In addition, many employers, legislators, and members of the general public are increasingly losing confidence in a diploma as an indication that a person is well educated. Some states have tried to address this problem by instituting 12th grade tests and sometimes requiring them for graduation. Given this climate of opinion among the general population, people may overreact to questions about diplomas for homeschoolers for reasons that have nothing to do with homeschooling.

• Don't assume that you can homeschool for part of high school and then enter or re-enter a public high school and graduate with your class. While a few high schools and school districts are reasonable about giving homeschoolers high school credits, many others are unfriendly and unreasonable. For example, some districts will not give homeschoolers credits unless they can pass the final exam from a class they would have had to take to earn these credits by attending high school. Therefore, if you want to homeschool for part of high school and then get a public high school diploma, discuss this with your local high school first. If you didn't make such arrangements but now find that you want credit for work you did while homeschooling, the suggestions for working with public school officials in Chapter 32 may help you negotiate with them.

• Many people begin planning for diplomas by asking when or why a diploma will be required. Answers to these questions determine the type of diploma needed. Many employers, especially in small businesses, do not require an official diploma. Very few colleges require a "third-party diploma" from homeschoolers for admission, and the federal government no longer requires them for student loans or federal scholarships. (When two parties enter into a contract that is witnessed by a third party, it is called a "third-party contract." So diplomas awarded by an institution outside of a homeschool are called "third-party diplomas.") Even in situations where diplomas are ostensibly required, many homeschoolers find other ways of demonstrating that they are qualified. Therefore, some homeschoolers find that they do not need a diploma.

If you need or want a diploma, here are some possibilities:

• Conventional schools that are accredited will award official third-party diplomas to homeschoolers who have met their graduation requirements. Some of the organizations listed

under curriculum providers and correspondence schools in Chapter 7 do so. These diplomas are widely recognized, but meeting the requirements set by these institutions costs time and money and may mean that you have to do things you wouldn't otherwise choose to do.
• Homeschooling families can grant their own diplomas as long as they have homeschooled in accordance with Wisconsin's private school/homeschool law, and the person receiving the diploma has completed the graduation requirements established by their homeschool.

These diplomas are as valid as diplomas from other schools. It's common knowledge that graduates have a wide range of abilities whether the school from which they graduated is accredited or not. For more information on the questionable value of accrediting institutions, see *Bears' Guide to Earning Degrees by Distance Learning* by John Bear and Mariah P. Bear.

It's a good idea to support any diploma with documents such as a transcript (see below); a list of books you have read; descriptions of projects you have done; examples or photographs of work you have completed; standardized test scores (see below); and/or transcripts from correspondence courses, classes taken at a community college, or other formal course work. These are suggestions, not requirements. The purpose of a diploma is to demonstrate that you have a high school education. Therefore, think about what would be likely to convince your intended audience.

Forms for diplomas and transcripts can be found in some school supply stores or on the Internet or prepared by you or a calligrapher.
• You can use passing scores on CLEP tests (see Chapter 8) in a number of subjects as the basis for a diploma, pointing out that if you have earned college credit, you clearly have more than the equivalent of a high school education.
• Some homeschoolers get either a General Educational Development (GED) certificate or a High School Equivalency Diploma (HSED). To get a GED you must pass five tests, one each in math, English (including writing skills), science, literature, and social studies. You can get an HSED by passing the five GED tests and meeting additional requirements in health, citizenship, employability, and career-awareness. If you already know the material covered by these tests or can learn it fairly easily, perhaps using one of the preparatory books available, the GED or HSED is a much quicker and less expensive way to obtain an "official" certificate or diploma than attending classes or taking correspondence courses.

However, the GED and HSED have drawbacks:
—Some people and institutions will not accept or honor a diploma based on a GED or HSED, arguing that they are too easily obtained, are not the equivalent of a high school education, and are no substitute for spending three or four years in high school.
—Some people distrust or look down on the GED and HSED, thinking that they are only for people who have failed or dropped out of a conventional high school. Therefore, homeschoolers with a GED or HSED may be viewed as high school dropouts and not as people making creative use of the GED or HSED to meet a formal requirement for a diploma.
—You cannot take the GED or HSED tests until you are 18 1/2 years old or until the class with which you entered ninth grade has graduated from high school unless you are incarcerated or participating in a federal job core center program. (This rule stems in part from the fear that, if it were an option at an earlier age, many students would quit high school, take the GED or HSED, and do something more interesting and worthwhile than attending high school.)
—Some homeschoolers object to the principle of turning to the state to judge and certify learning.

For Wisconsin's Administrative Code governing the GED/HSED, request information from the Department of Public Instruction's GED/HSED Consultant/Coordinator, 125 South Webster Street, P. O. Box 7841, Madison, WI 53707-7841 or visit their web site at www.state.wi.us/agencies/DPI/.

If you are told that a diploma is required for something you want to do, and you have a third-party diploma, it should be no problem to simply submit what's required. Homeschooling is now well enough known and respected that people realize the significance of your diploma. The obvious disadvantage to this approach is that you have to go through the work and expense of earning the diploma.

If you don't have a third-party diploma, you will have to figure out a way to respond to the request, which is often not difficult. Many homeschoolers prefer this to the time, effort, and expense involved in earning a third-party diploma, especially since many people do not need one. Among the possibilities:

- Make sure that a diploma is actually required. Officials are sometimes misinformed and give you inaccurate information. If you are told that a diploma is required by law, ask them to show you the statute, read it yourself, and make sure that it does in fact require a diploma and does not offer alternatives. If you are told that an organization's or institution's rules require a diploma, request a copy of the rules and see if they offer an alternative.
- Explain that the federal government no longer requires that homeschoolers have third-party diplomas for student loans and scholarships, and that many other institutions and organizations also have adopted this approach.
- Explain that you do have a diploma. (See above for ways homeschools grant diplomas.) This is acceptable to many colleges and universities, employers, and others.
- Take CLEP tests if you have not already done so and submit your scores. See Chapter 8.
- In some circumstances, it may be worth the effort to earn a third-party diploma, a General Educational Development (GED) certificate or a High School Equivalency Diploma (HSED). See above. However, remember that these have drawbacks which are also discussed above.

Developing a Transcript

A transcript is a one-page summary of subjects studied, grades received, and credits earned. Developing your own transcript can be a challenge, especially if you have based your curriculum on unit studies or pursuing special interests and learning from life experience. Suddenly you are asked to condense years of learning onto a one-page form that was developed to summarize what kids in conventional schools do. How can you give yourself credit without appearing to claim to have done something you haven't done, especially when the brevity of the form doesn't give you a chance to explain?

Let's put transcripts into perspective. A transcript is a quick summary that assures an employer, college admissions officer, or some such person that you have worked on a number of general subjects. It is not an ideal way for you as a homeschooler to show what you have done. But when a transcript is required or requested, you are likely to handicap yourself if you don't provide one, so it's a good idea to translate what you have done into the categories presented on the form. Anyone who really wants to know about you will ask for more than a transcript; they'll want samples of your work, a portfolio, a personal interview, standardized test scores, etc. A transcript is a quick overview to meet a formal requirement; don't worry about trying to make it more than that.

You can develop a transcript based on either (1) the number of hours you spent studying a subject (also called "time on task") or (2) what you have learned.

(1) Many conventional schools give one semester credit for 90 hours of class work plus homework. Some homeschoolers use this guideline to develop a conventional transcript with something like 8 semesters of English; 4 to 8 semesters of science; 4 to 8 semesters of math; 2 semesters of American history; 2 semesters of world history; 1 semester of American government; and electives such as art, music, religion, foreign language, industrial arts, home economics, sociology, psychology. This is usually easier to do if you keep

track while you are doing the work, jotting down two hours of English literature right after you spend two hours reading *A Tale of Two Cities,* etc. But you can also look back and estimate the time you spent; creating transcripts is not an exact science.
(2) You can develop a transcript that lists general subject areas you have learned about. Since conventional transcripts are organized by year, it's a good idea to do yours that way. If, during the year you would have been a freshman in a conventional school, you learned more about reading, writing, and expressing yourself orally, you can list English. If you read a reasonable number of novels, short stories, and/or poetry, you can list American, British, or world literature. If you learned about political developments in the U.S. and abroad by reading newspapers or other periodicals and perhaps working on a political campaign or opposing legislation that undermined homeschooling freedoms, you can put down political science. And so on. You can use terms like "General Math" or "General Science" if you didn't focus on specific areas such as geometry or chemistry. If the place you are applying requires trigonometry or physics, you can study those subjects to fill in gaps you may have.

Obviously, developing a transcript is easier for people who followed a conventional school curriculum or developed their own curriculum based on conventional school subjects like reading, math, and science. But if you did unit studies, you can group the units under their major subject areas. (For example, frogs and dogs would go under biology, Ancient Egypt and the Civil War would go under history.) Then, since some of your units undoubtedly included reading, writing, and math, you can add English and math for each year. Or you can explain that you used an interdisciplinary approach that covered basic subjects by focusing on . . . (the major units you studied). If your curriculum was based on learning from living a worthwhile life and pursuing your interests, either translate what you did into conventional school language or explain that you used an interdisciplinary approach and list your major projects.

If you will be having a personal interview based on your transcript, it would be wise to think ahead of time about how you would answer questions like, "How did you study science?"

Conventional transcripts include letter grades for each subject, and families can give grades. Don't be modest. A family that has taken responsibility for education, worked hard, and learned a lot deserves credit.

For more information on transcripts, see Loretta Heuer's *Homeschooler's Guide to Portfolios and Transcripts.* However, don't be intimidated by the examples. You can create satisfactory transcripts that are much shorter and simpler than the ones in this book.

Developing Portfolios

Although portfolios are longer than transcripts, they are usually easier to develop because you have flexibility to include what you want and to explain what you have done. Feel free to be creative and present whatever you think will best communicate your strengths and experiences to your audience. For encouragement, ideas, and examples, see Loretta Heuer's *Homeschooler's Guide to Portfolios and Transcripts.*

Using CLEP and Other Standardized Test Scores as Credentials

Scores from CLEP and other tests are helpful credentials. See Chapter 8.

Graduation Ceremonies

Some families participate in the recognition of graduates that is a very moving part of the Opening Session at the WPA conference each spring. Some celebrate the completion of high school with their own graduation ceremony. This can be done for one student and can include a rented cap and gown, guest speakers, musical performances, special awards for younger children in the family, photographs, a reception for friends and relatives, and newspaper coverage. Some choose alternative celebrations and have a family outing, a trip, or whatever they prefer. And some pay little attention to graduation, emphasizing instead the continuity that comes from viewing learning as a life-long process.

Choices Available After High School

Although many people expect teens to either go to college, get a full-time job, or join the military after they turn 18, a small but increasing number of young people are choosing to continue homeschooling during the "college" years. Some homeschoolers who could easily go to college decide to continue learning in other ways. Some of them are so good at learning in their own way at their own pace that the idea of college does not appeal to them. Some decide they would rather spend the time and money that college requires to learn in other ways. Since they are saving so much money by not going to college, they feel they can afford to do volunteer work, travel, or continue learning at home rather than needing to find a job immediately. If they need credentials, they consider using CLEP tests (see Chapter 8) or other non-traditional approaches to college discussed in *Bears' Guide to Earning Degrees by Distance Learning* by John Bear and Mariah P. Bear or find other ways to meet requirements.

If you decide to postpone college or skip it altogether, there are many possibilities: independent study, internships, apprenticeships, volunteer service, travel, etc. You can take advantage of opportunities you may not have again to explore the world and pursue your special interests before you're tied down by serious responsibilities. You can learn more about what interests you without incurring college debt.

One of the biggest challenges of continuing homeschooling is dealing with the seemingly ceaseless questions people ask you. Say you're going to college, and warm smiles and nods appear. Say you're not, and brows furrow. Such responses can be very discouraging, especially if you're not a hundred percent sure of what you're doing yourself. It helps to have a few pat answers ready to hand. Try to use language that sounds familiar to questioners. Say you're studying independently. If you've taken CLEP tests, you can say you're earning college credits independently. If you're mowing lawns or selling handmade dolls or specialty breads, you can say you're running your own business. You can be disarmingly honest: "I haven't figured that out yet," or "I don't know." Or try humor: "I'm getting my mid-life crisis over with now." Really, it's not fair that our society accepts people in their 30's and 40's and 50's deciding to change jobs and careers but expects 18 year olds to know exactly what they plan to do with the rest of their lives. But that injustice will not prevent people from asking you what you're doing. Some mean well and want to be supportive; some are just plain nosy. You can guess what's motivating them and respond accordingly.

Sometimes young adults continue to live at home, or to use home as a base between trips and other explorations, or while they attend college. In such cases, everyone needs to make adjustments as a family of parents and children turns into a community of adults. But family members can continue to learn from and support each other; parents and adult children can develop mature relationships; and siblings can stay in close touch. It often takes continuing effort to devise good ways to share household chores. There's no one right way to handle finances, but families make arrangements based on the needs and incomes of each person. Some have a family fund that people contribute to in various ways and that covers shared expenses such as food, rent or house payments, and car expenses. The rewards of continuing to learn, work, and play as a family are great.

Resources for opportunities after high school include:

Career Development Manual of the University of Waterloo in Canada. www.adm.uwaterloo.ca/infocecs/CRC/manual-home.html

Internships: The Guide To On The Job Training For College Students from Peterson's Guides (updated annually)
Bears' Guide to Earning Degrees by Distance Learning by John Bear and Mariah P. Bear
What Color Is Your Parachute? by Richard Bolles
The Whole Work Catalog, PO Box 339-AB, Boulder, CO 80306. 800-634-9024
You're Certifiable: The Alternative Career Guide to More Than 700 Certificate Programs, Trade Schools, and Job Opportunities by Lee Naftali and Joel Naftali

Considering College and Applying for Admission

Homeschoolers don't have difficulty getting admitted to most colleges. Although some colleges are highly selective, over 75% of colleges and universities admit between 75 and 99% of those who apply, according to *Barron's Profiles of American Colleges.* In addition, colleges sometimes see homeschooling as an advantage. Some actively seek homeschoolers since they have found them to be serious, responsible, capable students who take initiative. Few if any colleges refuse to admit homeschoolers; a college so narrow-minded that it will not even consider homeschoolers is probably too rigid for most homeschoolers anyway. One unfortunate reality is that private colleges are often easier to get into, but more expensive to attend, than state colleges and universities.

Find out as early as possible what is required by colleges of the type (or types) you may want to attend. Public libraries sometimes have collections of college catalogues. Grace Llewellyn's *Teenage Liberation Handbook* has information on what colleges are looking for in students and how homeschoolers can meet these requirements.

During the application process, use the suggestions above for convincing others that you are qualified. Be reasonable and use common sense. If a college requires something that seems unreasonable, try to negotiate a more realistic requirement. Remember that you are setting precedents that other homeschoolers, including perhaps members of your family, may have to meet.

Standardized tests such as SAT and ACT are required by some colleges and can be a real asset for those who happen to be good at taking tests. You can prepare for tests and increase your chances of scoring well by using books like *Ten SATs* (published by the College Board), Neil Fiore and Susan C. Pescar's *Conquering Test Anxiety: or How To Psyche Up for the SAT, GRE, GMAT, LSAT, MCAT, or Any Other Standardized Test,* and Adam Robinson and John Katzman's *Cracking the System: The SAT.* Or find a college that does not require such tests.

Instead of attending a conventional college or university, college credit and a college degree can be earned from "real," recognized, and accredited colleges on the basis of correspondence courses; tests such as CLEP and DANTES; and learning from life experience that is documented in a variety of ways. Although these programs were originally developed for adults, they are adaptable to homeschoolers and are an excellent alternative for teens who prefer independent study and/or learning from experience. The tremendous savings of time and money alone makes them worth serious consideration. *Bears' Guide to Earning Degrees by Distance Learning* by John Bear and Mariah P. Bear and *Earn College Credit For What You Know* by Susan Simosko are excellent resources.

Resources for homeschoolers considering college include

The Homeschooler's Guide to Portfolios and Transcripts by Loretta Heuer
Homeschoolers' College Admissions Handbook by Cafi Cohen
The Question is College: Guiding Your Child to the Right Choices After High School by Herbert Kohl

Writing Successful Scholarship Applications

Almost all financial aid for college students is handled by the institution you attend. Colleges and technical schools usually require that parents submit the Free Application for Federal Student Aid (FAFSA) which can be found at www.fafsa.ed.gov. It requires private information about your family and its finances, based on information submitted to the IRS. It is used to determine how much your family is expected to contribute to the cost of your education. This amount is nearly constant no matter where you go to college. For example, if the FAFSA determines that your family should pay $6,000 a year, a state college and an Ivy League university will both expect your family to pay that much of the total cost per year, whether it's $7,500 or $43,000. Schools usually offer financial aid to cover the rest. However, the proportions of loans to grants (scholarships) may vary. Obviously, the larger the loans and the smaller the grants, the more debt you'll end up with.

Private scholarships and grants are offered by organizations and individuals that are not connected to a specific school. These awards are not based on how much money your family has. Many fewer students apply for them than request financial aid from a given college, so they are a very good option to consider. However, they are subtracted from the financial aid the school is giving you, not from the amount your family is expected to contribute, until the private scholarships and grants you have gotten total more than the school's financial aid.

Here are suggestions for applying for these private scholarships and grants.

• Start early. Two years before you plan to go to college is a good time to begin. Writing essays and collecting information always take more time than we expect. To be eligible for some scholarships, you have to take the Preliminary SAT (PSAT) or the National Merit Student Qualifying Test (NMSQT) in the fall of your junior year. Students who score well on the NMSQT are awarded grants based on their scores, but the test results are also used by others.

• Look widely. No one place lists all the scholarship opportunities. Scholarship offers may be posted on the bulletin board at the bank or your grandmother's place of work. The public library has books at 378.3. Free Internet screeners abound. (Places that charge a fee are likely to be a scam or to do the same service offered for free elsewhere.) The free Internet sites do require you to reveal personal information, especially about your abilities, background, and interests, to identify possible matches. Each year scholarships go unused because the left-handed piccolo-playing descendant of an Italian firefighter can't be found.

Places to look include:
Cafi Cohen's *Homeschoolers' College Admissions Handbook*
Fastweb www.fastweb.com-the most widely known scholarship website
The SmartStudent ™ Guide to Financial Aid at www.finaid.org/scholarships/other.phtml
Kohl Excellence Scholarship Program at www.kohleducation.org/students
Scholarship Resource Network Express at www.srnexpress.com
Scholarships.com at www.scholarships.com
College Board Pay for College at www.collegeboard.com/pay

• Check out the sponsors. Does the scholarship or its sponsor have a website? How much money do they give out? Are there multiple scholarships or just one? How many people applied last year? Being one of twenty applicants gives you a better chance than one of twelve hundred. You may even see essays from last year's winners and get a better idea of what the sponsor is looking for.

• Apply for scholarships that match your strengths. You have unique qualities, talents, and heritage. The largest scholarships ($10,000 to $100,000) are awarded to those who have completed some special project. The grand prize of them all, the Siemens-Westinghouse Science Competition at www.siemens-foundation.org may not be your cup of tea, but perhaps the citizenship-oriented Ronald Reagan Future Leaders Scholarship at www.thephillipsfoundation.org/futureleaders.htm is.

• Be neat. On applications, neatness counts. Do not have Mom fill it in even though her handwriting is better. The gender and generation of the writer are fairly easy to figure out. Typed applications are even easier to read and make it look as if the applicant is taking time and care.

• Be complete. Think of applications as a way for the people giving scholarships to get to know you. Of course, most applications are oriented to conventional schools and ask about after-school clubs, student government, and team sports. Think creatively about how you can introduce yourself, fit your experiences into their categories, and show them why you are so wonderfully deserving of their scholarship. Put something in every section; incomplete applications get eliminated early in the process.

Well-rounded students always look good. Even if you love nothing but baseball, you can demonstrate how much you've covered. Statistics are math as a hobby, running the fundraiser for your team demonstrates leadership, making announcements at the game is public speaking, photographing the team qualifies as art, and sports-easy deal, say baseball. Suddenly a narrowly focused individual has a finger in every pie.

Letters of recommendation are opportunities to present additional perspectives on who you are to people reviewing scholarship applications. No matter how disinterested they try to be, parents' letters are easily discounted. Students who attend conventional schools may use no one but teachers for letters of recommendations, but homeschoolers need more variety. Your pastor, choir director, and Sunday school teacher look like one recommendation to the scholarship reader since they come from the same place. Try to have a set of recommendations from people who know you from different viewpoints, perhaps one from someone from church, one from an employer or volunteer supervisor, and one from someone who has experience with you as a learner (a 4-H or scout leader or a teacher from a class you took). Ask them for reflections on you as a motivated and mature person.

Essays can make up for great weaknesses in the rest of an application, but only if they are great essays. Write, wait a day, and then reread and rewrite. Get comments from others. Rewrite again. Check out examples of good essays in the public library in the section on essays and applications, 378.1. One good collection is *Essays That Worked for College Applications: 50 Essays That Helped Students Get Into the Nation's Top Colleges* edited by Boykin Curry, Brian Kasbar, and Emily Angel Baer. Reread those winning essays from years past at the scholarship sponsor's website. And rewrite again.

Remember you are trying to earn money here. If you regularly earn $10 an hour, a $5,000 scholarship is equivalent to 500 hours of work. Doing a thorough job, putting in 25 hours on an application, means you could be reaping $200 an hour, and you can use the information you have gathered again and again. You may be able to use the same letters of recommendation, different versions of the same information, perhaps even variations of the same essays on other scholarship applications and even college or apprenticeship applications. Opportunities are there if you look hard enough.

Attending Technical College

The Wisconsin Technical Colleges System consists of 16 colleges with 47 campuses throughout the state. Here are general admissions policies. Because each college has some control over its own policies, you may find that the campus you contact has different policies that work in your favor or against you.

You can take individual courses as a special student when you are 16 years old (or younger if the dean of the college determines that you can handle the course). These can be counted as part of the 875 hours of instruction required for homeschooling. To enroll in a certificate or degree program, private school students, including homeschoolers, must have a high school diploma. (Public school students can enroll in a certificate or degree program and take courses before they have graduated from high school through the Youth Options program, but that opportunity is not available to private school students.) A homeschool diploma awarded by a parent or guardian is acceptable if it is accompanied by a transcript that identifies the subject areas and explains the grading system and by a statement that the high school course of study was completed and a diploma awarded. For some programs, a diploma awarded by a homeschooling parent or guardian can be used, but some programs, such as nursing, require a GED, an HSED, or a third party diploma issued by an outside institution such as a correspondence school. Also, some high school courses that are prerequisites must be taught in specific ways. For example, some science courses must include lab work. An additional, unusual, and unnecessary rule states that homeschoolers who are still in high school cannot take courses during hours that public schools are in session.

Since some technical colleges may not have much experience with homeschoolers, they may not have firm policies or may initially say no to your requests simply because they are uncomfortable dealing with uncertainty and change. If so, it often works well to keep things somewhat open and fluid, ask who else you could talk with, and keep going until you reach someone with the authority and flexibility to give you a better answer. Feel free to suggest alternatives and solutions to problems. You are, after all, a creative and experienced homeschooler who will get farther if you take responsibility for yourself rather than just accepting what other people tell you.

If you are considering attending a technical college, contact them and ask questions like those suggested below. Make detailed notes that include the name of the person you spoke with, their title, the date, and their responses. If their answers are definite enough and what you were hoping to hear, you may also want to write them a letter in which you state your understanding of what they told you and ask them to respond within 10 days if anything you have stated is incorrect.

1. What are the admissions requirements for the following courses or degree or certificate programs? (List the ones you are interested in.)
2. May I take individual courses as a special student before I graduate from high school and count them toward a degree or certification program once I have graduated?
3. If there are high school courses I must take before I enroll in courses I want to take, are there special requirements for how they are taught?
4. What type of high school diploma is required for the degree or certificate program I am interested in?
5. Can credits from CLEP, AP, or DANTES tests be used to meet the degree or certification program I am interested it? (See "The Many Uses of CLEP and AP Tests" in Chapter 8.)
6. Is there anything else I should know?

For more information, contact the Wisconsin Technical College System Office, P.O. Box 7874, Madison, WI 53707-7874. For general information, call 608-266-1207. Or go to www.witechcolleges.com.

Military Service

Some homeschoolers enlisting in the military have been able to get Tier I status (reserved for high school graduates) rather than Tier II (recruits with non-traditional diplomas or GED certificates) or Tier III (dropouts). Here are suggestions for those who are interested:

- Keep copies of your PI-1206 forms and be sure to get letters of acknowledgement from the DPI, especially during your high school years. (See Chapter 4.) They will give you something official to give to a recruiter.
- Provide a transcript of your homeschooling years and a diploma. You can submit a transcript and "third party diploma" from a correspondence school or homeschool program from which you graduated. Or you and your parents can create your own, following suggestions earlier in this chapter. Include any "third party" certification you have, such as transcripts from courses you have taken in college, technical school, or through distance learning; or scores from ACT, SAT, CLEP, or DANTES tests (see Chapter 8). Explain to the recruiter that many employers and colleges, universities, and technical schools accept homeschoolers' transcripts and diplomas. The federal government considers them valid for student loan applications.
- One semester (fifteen hours) of college credit can be used by recruits, including homeschoolers, to gain Tier I status.
- If the first recruiter with whom you talk will not grant what you want, find another recruiter.
- Check recent WPA newsletters to see if there have been further developments on this topic.

Chapter 13
Socialization

"What about socialization?" Homeschoolers are frequently asked this question. Many non-homeschoolers can understand that children could learn basic subjects at home, perhaps even better than in conventional schools. But what about socialization? Aren't homeschoolers too isolated? How do homeschooled children learn to get along with other people, especially those with backgrounds different from theirs? How do they learn to hold a job?

In response to such questions, homeschooling parents explain that actually homeschooling is a big advantage when it comes to socialization, for reasons such as the following.

• Homeschooled children have many opportunities to interact with their peers. Homeschoolers are often active in youth organizations such as 4-H and scouts, church groups, sports teams, and others. They interact with children in their neighborhoods and in homeschool support groups.

• Homeschooled children interact with people of all different ages, benefiting from the rich experience and perspective that this gives them. They play with and baby-sit for younger children and participate in activities that include children of a range of ages. They get to know adults through jobs, apprenticeships, community organizations, neighborhoods, volunteer work, shared interests, and in other ways. They may volunteer in nursing homes, visit senior citizen centers, and get to know older relatives.

Many homeschooling parents feel that it is better for their children to grow up surrounded by people of different ages than to be limited to children their own age. School and army boot camp are about the only times people spend limited to people their own age. It helps a lot to have older, more mature people around as role models. It is usually difficult to find strong role models in a classroom of children who are close to the same age.

• Homeschooled children learn a great deal from the interactions they have with members of their immediate family and often their extended family as well. They have more opportunities to spend time with their families, to get to know them well, and to develop strong bonds. They learn how to maintain relationships over time and to work out long-term solutions to problems rather than moving on to a new set of friends.

• Homeschooled children have good opportunities to develop a strong sense of identity and a commitment to their values and beliefs. People with this kind of inner strength are often better able to get along with others, including people who have ideas and beliefs very different from theirs, than are people who are less sure of themselves and therefore more easily confused and threatened.

• Homeschooled children have more opportunities to see and participate in real life on a daily basis. They are home while the plumber repairs the pipes and the neighbors' house is built. They have a clearer and more realistic sense of what grown ups do in their jobs and in other interactions. They observe their parents solving problems, managing the household, and pursuing their own interests. They have opportunities to participate in things that happen in the real world, to balance the family check book, to change a flat tire, to help redecorate the family room. They watch younger siblings and friends' babies grow, and they have a clearer sense of the responsibilities of parenthood.

• Many homeschooling parents feel that the social interactions that take place in conventional schools are negative often enough that they are glad their children do not have to have these experiences at such a young age. As John Holt put it, "If there were no other reason for wanting to keep kids out of school, the social life would be reason enough." Homeschooled children learn to resolve conflicts, deal with difficult people and challenging situations, speak up for themselves, and work well in groups, even though they are not forced to deal with challenging situations in classrooms, on the playground, and on the school bus. Many homeschooling parents feel that because their children have the opportunity to grow up in a secure family environment, with many positive role models to follow within their family and outside it, they become strong individuals who are very capable of dealing with problems and challenges as adults. They are not limited because they did not grow up facing difficult situations in conventional schools. Rather they are stronger because they had a chance to grow up in a more supportive environment.

• Colleges and employers are discovering that grown homeschoolers are strong people who can take responsibility, exercise initiative, cooperate with others, participate in a team effort, and function very well as young adults.

• The idea of doing research on homeschoolers raises serious concerns. (See Chapter 24.) However, some homeschoolers may face serious situations (such as custody disputes) in which they need as much evidence as possible that socialization is not a problem for homeschoolers. Studies, including one by Larry Shyers at the University of Florida, may be helpful. See Barbara Hall Palar's article, "When School is at Home," *Better Homes and Gardens*, March, 1995, pages 40-44. Also consider articles such as "Homeschooled Students Make the Grade at BU" by Cynthia K. Buccini in Boston University's Winter 2003 issue of their *Bostonia* magazine (www.bu.edu/alumni/bostonia/2003/winter/homeschoolers), "Homeschooling Comes of Age" by Jennifer Sutton in the Jan/Feb 2002 issue of the Brown University alumni magazine (www.brownalumnimagazine.com/storyDetail.cfm?ID=672), and "In a Class by Themselves" by Christine Foster in the *Stanford Magazine* Nov/Dec 2000 (www.stanfordalumni.org/news/magazine/2000/novdec/articles/homeschooling.html

How many of you have ever had someone comment on how unusual your child is because he or she can carry on a conversation with an adult, or play with children of a different age?

As our children grow up, at some point we see that they are ready for experiences beyond the home. For homeschoolers, this will probably be in a family-to-family context-a church or community group, homeschool support group, 4-H club -where we interact with people of all ages and generations. This is very different from the kinds of interactions that happen in institutional settings where people are segregated by age or ability or interest. I believe these family-based relationships are healthier for children-and for adults. . . .

In addition, every child is learning about his or her place in the family and community, about responsibility, respect for others, communication, interdependence. This kind of "socialization" is far more valuable than the hierarchical, age-segregated institutional social life kids get in school.—From Opening Remarks, WPA Conference, 2005

Chapter 14
Support Groups

Participating in Support Groups

Homeschooling support groups serve several important functions.

• Many homeschoolers value the opportunity to share experiences, concerns, and resources. It can be affirming and strengthening to talk with others about common values and concerns. Hearing about other families' homeschooling experiences can help new homeschoolers get off to a good start. It can also be reassuring to experienced homeschoolers and give them fresh perspectives, new ideas, and strong support. It's a nice change to be with a group of people who celebrate a family's decision to homeschool instead of questioning it.

• Children often benefit from a chance to meet and interact with other children. They enjoy finding other children who are also homeschooling, which helps them deal with being different from conventionally schooled children.

• Support groups also provide a means by which homeschoolers can coordinate their efforts and work together to promote a favorable climate for homeschooling and solve problems on the local and state level. Groups can plan ways in which they will deal with local schools and school boards, share experiences they have had, meet their state legislators, decide who is in the best position to meet with a reporter requesting information about homeschooling, and work together in other ways so that their actions are more effective. Sometimes people who feel they are being forced into homeschooling by threats of prosecution for truancy, or who are headed for legal difficulties for some reason, are able to avoid problems because of what they learn from support group members and meetings.

Support groups come in all sizes, have a variety of purposes, and choose their activities from a wide range of possibilities.

• Some groups have primarily activities for children and the whole family. Field trips are popular. If parents take turns making arrangements, the planning and organizing take much less time than if each family planned its own outings. Parents, older children, or outside resource people can lead craft activities, science experiments, folk dancing, singing, and sports activities. Guest speakers can cover a wide variety of topics. Activities in which many people participate also work well, such as talent shows or evenings in which each family dresses in the clothes of another culture and brings food from that culture.

• Some groups emphasize meetings for parents. These may cover legal and political issues or approaches to learning, or provide opportunities to share experiences and concerns.
• Some groups publish a newsletter.
• An email loop makes communication rapid and effective.

Many homeschoolers belong to both WPA and a local support group, since each of these organizations provides different kinds of assistance to homeschoolers. WPA works with support groups in a number of ways. Homeschoolers can support their local group and WPA at the same time by joining WPA through their support group. The group keeps part of the membership fee and sends the rest to WPA. The homeschoolers have the benefits of full membership in WPA. It works best if as many people as possible from a support group are also members of WPA. Then each family receives its own copy of the newsletter and special bulletins, and WPA is better able to continue its work. When a support group counts on receiving important information from just a few people who are members of WPA, communication and effectiveness are much more limited.

For information about support groups in your area, contact your WPA Regional Coordinator. Since groups differ, consider visiting more than one, if possiblel.

Starting a Support Group

If there is not a support group in your area, consider starting one, even if you have not done this kind of thing before. Here are some suggestions that may be helpful:
• Talk with other support group leaders. Your WPA Regional Coordinator can give you the names of leaders in the areas surrounding you.
• Support groups often work best if they meet the needs and desires of the families involved, so feel free to plan your support group so it suits the people participating. You may want to have the first meeting be a potluck of either snacks, brunch, lunch, or supper, since food brings people together and breaks the ice. Then there could be a general discussion of what kinds of activities the people in the group would like. Many groups find it pays to be flexible and willing to make changes as the group grows and develops. Remember that getting started is often the hardest part. Once the group has some experience, it can build on events and activities that have worked well in the past.
• Decide how the group will be oriented. Some groups focus on homeschooling in general and welcome anyone interested in homeschooling, regardless of their approach to education, life style, religion, etc. Other groups prefer the support that comes from being with a group that has more in common, so they limit the group to people with a particular perspective on homeschooling or religion. Each of these approaches has advantages and disadvantages.
• Keep the organization of the group as simple as possible, but share the work as much as possible so one person or a few people do not have all the responsibility. It often works well to start by having the person who is most interested in a given activity (like field trips) be its coordinator.
• Feel free to start small. Two or three families is enough to start a group. Small groups are often easier to manage than larger ones. If a group starts small and grows, members have a chance to learn a lot while the group is still small and be prepared for the challenges of a larger size.
• Tell your WPA Regional Coordinator about your group. If you are looking for new members, ask them to mention the group to people who call for information about homeschooling.
• Many groups grow by word of mouth. Most homeschoolers know at least a few other homeschooling families. Other approaches to publicity include an article or ad in a local newspaper and posters in your library, place of worship, natural foods store or coop, and children's book store or resale shop.

Perspectives from an Experienced Homeschooler

An experienced homeschooling mother wrote:

Years ago, homeschoolers belonged to support groups because the law was difficult, materials were difficult to find, homeschoolers were scarce. We joined in mutual support no matter why or how each family chose to learn.

We belong to Wisconsin Parents Association because we still need to keep abreast of those legal concerns. But why are we in a local support group after more than a decade of homeschooling?

There are the easily seen advantages of activities and field trips. Those new to homeschooling find somewhere to start to find information. There are opinions on books and materials, some even available for your use. And if you are moving to another state, someone in the group is sure to have some sort of contact there to find out about the legal situation. But what besides potlucks does a group offer to those who've been around for a while?

Support. Perspective. It is really quite simple. Thank goodness that on the day when it seems that little Elroy will never learn to read (and the kids squabble, dinner burns, the dog runs away, and you have the flu), someone else can listen and remind you of the day when Elroy figured out the tax on the Christmas tree. And you can help the someone else on his or her bad day.

Further, we can see examples of the variation in styles and aptitudes of our family members. My child may sink his teeth into specialized subjects and never come up for air and I fear that he'll never master basics like spelling. Your child may have a thorough grasp on all those essentials but hasn't ever been passionately interested in something, anything. Or it may be that Elroy's brother Eddie learns only through music, a fact unimagined by mother Edwina until she saw Beauford's daughter Beatrix memorize, in one afternoon, four pages of her role in a play by singing it to herself. Or it may be that your way of explaining how to divide numbers with decimals is easier to understand than mine.

Group members whose children are older can give us some idea of what to expect in days to come. I remember being so envious of Martha when she described the many things George was doing at twelve. He was so capable, mature, so independent! It sounded so far away from what our son, then ten, would or could do. Now I have a twelve year old and he is so capable, so mature (usually), so independent. And so am I.

And younger children remind those with older children that some skills have been learned that were previous challenges. Tying those shoelaces may have seemed like climbing Everest until figured out. Then it was as forgotten as was the process of learning to walk.

From those ahead, I see that there will always be something to worry about. Reading and arithmetic, then spelling, then to: Are they getting enough challenge in science? Do they need more foreign language? And I realize I will always have something to be concerned about in a conventional school or at home. A speaker said at a WPA Conference a few years ago that after 17 years of homeschooling, she felt she was finally getting the hang of it. Her message reminded me that although I often tell my children that mistakes are part of life and learning, I still expect my parenting and my homeschooling to be perfect.

When your friend with children in conventional school complains, you are the safe listener—uninvolved, unlikely to cause a problem with the status quo. Yet were you to have a conversation where you mentioned some problem with homeschooling, your schooling friend immediately suggests that putting your child into a conventional setting is the answer. You won't have to hear that in a support group!

Support and perspective. And friends whose values of family are similar to our own. Our family still belongs in our local support group.

Chapter 15

Parenting Homeschooled Children

We understand that homeschooling is not just a form of education, it is a lifestyle. As families we immerse ourselves in the rhythm of life and relish each and every moment.
~We share our child's joy as they discover the quiet magic of a butterfly.
~We witness our child's pride when they master a new skill such as tying their shoes.
~We dry their tears when the family dog dies and are surprised when they comfort us in return.
~We worry when our newly-licensed teenager drives off alone for the very first time.
~We experience those bittersweet feelings when a child moves away from home and we wish them all the luck in the world as they take the next step on their journey.
~We hope our adult children will find a soul mate with which they can share life's adventure.
~And, we stand by as they struggle to overcome defeat for that is what life hands all of us at times

Some may say these experiences are not unique to homeschooling families and indeed they are not. What makes us different is that we simply experience more of these events. We not only spend a lot of time with our children, we embrace the opportunity. And as a result, our lives are enriched and we are forever changed.—From Opening Remarks, WPA Conference, 2004

From an at-home father trained as a corporate lawyer: When I think back on this half-finished journey, and ponder alternative paths I could have taken, I am convinced that nothing I could have done in this wide world would have been more important or fulfilling than what I have done and am doing. I feel incredibly fortunate to be so fully involved in the lives of my two children and to enjoy a closeness to them that sadly seems all too rare.—From Opening Remarks, WPA Conference, 2002

Many homeschooling parents find it's helpful to think about how they will parent as homeschoolers. The more confident and comfortable they are with the approach to parenting they have chosen, the more smoothly their homeschooling goes. In fact, some homeschooling parents feel that parenting is the most important part of homeschooling. When parenting is going well, whatever approach to learning they have chosen seems to go well, too.

Of course, parenting homeschooled children does not always go smoothly. But it is much more manageable than it may seem at first. People who are not homeschooling sometimes think about the time that families whose children attend conventional schools spend together morning and evening, on weekends, and during school vacations. They imagine that homeschooling is like that 24 hours a day. But homeschoolers find that the time they have together as families is very different from the time that is leftover after children attend a conventional school. It is more even, more manageable, more enjoyable (most of the time), and more satisfying.

Homeschooling parents often find it is easier to parent children when they are homeschooled than when they attend conventional schools. Among the reasons:

• Homeschooled children are often more relaxed and easier to get along with than children who need to deal with the inevitable tensions and stresses that result from being with a large group of people for long periods of time in a big and impersonal institution.

• Homeschooled children and their parents spend more time together and share more experiences than they would if the children attended conventional schools. Therefore, they generally know and understand each other and get along better. Homeschooled children also have more opportunities to develop strong relationships with their siblings.

• Homeschoolers have more flexible schedules than conventional schools. Homeschoolers can reduce tension by doing things at a more reasonable pace. They can take time to deal with problems and conflicts when they arise. They can get enough rest.

• Homeschooling parents can support and encourage their children more through homeschooling than can parents of children attending conventional schools. Homeschoolers can choose the curriculum and schedule they want to follow, the food they will eat, the physical setting in which they will work, and other important things. Many parents find that even with the work and responsibility that homeschooling involves, it is easier than trying to work with conventional schools to provide learning environments, curriculums, social interactions, safety, and other things they want for their children.

Homeschooling also nurtures connections between siblings. When we first started homeschooling, a neighbor told me that during the school year, her children, though only a year or so apart in age, would have nothing to do with one another. It was not "cool" to like one's brother or to spend time with someone in a different class or age. During the summer, the siblings would gradually come to enjoy one another's company. "They're just getting to be friends with each other about the end of August," she said, ". . . and then school starts again and that is all lost." I really value the deep connections my children have with one another-and I often forget to appreciate how out-of-the-ordinary that is in our culture.—From Opening Remarks, WPA Conference, 2005

Learning More About Parenting

Learning to parent can be challenging. Many people do not want to simply follow in their parents' footsteps. Our society has multiple approaches to parenting, not one "right" way. However, the choices that are available do give parents the opportunity to parent in ways that they feel are right, and that work for them and their children. WPA is committed to working to reclaim and maintain parents' and families' rights and responsibilities. WPA does not recommend any particular approach to parenting, feeling strongly that each family needs to make its own decisions.

Here are some suggestions for ways many parents have used to learn more about parenting:

• Parents talk with other parents. They find it helps to spend time with parents who are parenting the way they want to parent, to learn from the examples and experiences of other parents. Some form support groups in which parents meet regularly to share their concerns. (See Chapter 14 for ideas about starting a group like this.)

• Some parents find it helpful to read about parenting. Given the wide range of books available, they choose carefully, concentrating on books that make sense to them and support

their ideas and beliefs and ignoring books that they disagree with. They may rely on a source they trust for suggestions, such as friends, an author whose writing they like, or an organization or catalog that recommends and sells carefully selected books on parenting.
• Many parents gain knowledge and direction about parenting from their religious and moral beliefs and practices.
• Many parents learn about parenting from their own experience and from watching their children and interacting with them. They build on what is going well for their families and work to solve problems that arise.

Some Ideas for Parenting Homeschooled Children

Many parents find that ideas like these make parenting homeschooled children more manageable and enjoyable.
• Many families work hard to develop and maintain respect for each other as unique and important individuals who have important things to contribute to the family, depending on their age and talents. They develop and maintain patterns of communication that demonstrate this respect by trying to emphasize the positive.
• Many families make communication a high priority, reasoning that if they can communicate effectively, they can solve problems. Good communication takes a lot of time and effort.
• Many families are careful about labels. Negative labels limit people's ideas about themselves. They tend to become self-fulfilling prophecies, because people often do what's expected of them and observers generally interpret what they see so that it fits what they're expecting, thus confirming the negative label. People often get stuck living up to a negative label. Even positive labels cause confusion and problems. How can someone who is "the musical one" have trouble understanding sharps and flats? What are people who have been labeled "always cheerful" supposed to do when feeling down?
• Many families make it a priority to discover and develop ways of doing things together. Working and relaxing together strengthen family bonds and give children good opportunities to grow. With the rapid pace at which many people today live, it often takes extra effort to ensure that family members have time together, but doing so pays rich rewards. Families share household tasks, attend religious services together, play active and quiet games, read aloud, cook special meals, go on short and long trips, play music, and do other activities. These shared experiences make it easier to get along together and maintain a strong family.
• Some families find it helps to give children opportunities to make some of their own decisions, in ways that work within the family structure. Young children can be asked whether they want to wear the red shirt or the blue one. Older children may participate in the family decision making process in a variety of ways, depending on how the family functions. Children who have the opportunity to make decisions are often more cooperative, feel they have a part in what is happening, gain valuable experience, and are more prepared for adult life.

How Homeschooling Parents Find Time For Themselves

Finding time for everything that needs to be done is a challenge for most parents, including homeschoolers. Sometimes it seems like parents' time for themselves gets sacrificed first. Here are ways some parents deal with this.
• Start with realistic expectations. Homeschooling takes a lot of time and energy. Some parents find that if they expect to be interrupted frequently, they are less likely to be surprised or annoyed by interruptions and more able to deal with them calmly and return to what they were doing.
• Many parents make it a priority to meet the needs of everyone in the family, including themselves. They try to ensure that everyone gets enough rest, eats nourishing food, has a chance to relax, and has attention paid to whatever special needs they have as individuals.

• Some parents include plans for their own learning when they are planning their family's curriculum. They may study some of the same topics their children are studying but on a more advanced level, like reviewing American history or learning Japanese. Or they may pick a topic that interests them that is separate from their children's curriculum. Then, while the children are studying independently, the parents can do their own work. Parents who are actively learning and enjoying it set outstanding examples for their children. Some parents keep a project of their own going, such as writing or needlework. (It is less frustrating to do projects that can easily be interrupted and do not require lots of equipment or big blocks of time.) Some families have times when each person reads their own book or writes in a notebook. Some parents also find that they enjoy so much working with their children, exploring and learning new things themselves, that they count this as time for themselves as well.

• Sometimes parents need a change of pace, a break from daily routine. It may help to spend several hours reading aloud, go on a field trip, or get together with another homeschooling family. Sometimes just getting out of the house helps. It is important to take time for fun with children. These are times from which memories are made and family bonds forged.

• Sometimes it helps to see if there is anything else, not related to homeschooling, that could be eliminated. Some people reduce the amount of time they watch TV, others begin saying "No" to requests from people outside the immediate family, and others figure out ways to spend less time cleaning house while still meeting the necessary standards of order and cleanliness.

• Think about the alternative, not homeschooling. Having children in school takes a lot of time and energy, too, and parents have much less control over the whole situation, the results of which may be far less satisfactory than homeschooling. The peace of mind that comes from knowing one is giving one's children a very important opportunity to learn at home keeps a lot of parents going even when they have little time for themselves. Many parents feel that, demanding as homeschooling is, they end up getting more than they give. By giving serious thought to their parenting, they find that they learn a lot about parenting as an important part of their homeschooling.

Chapter 16

Solving Problems

Homeschooling works and is exciting. But sometimes homeschools don't run smoothly. Conscientious parents may worry, question what they are doing, and get discouraged. Here are observations that may help. In addition, the WPA conference held each spring offers many workshops on preventing and solving problems.

Many parents put homeschooling "problems" in perspective by looking carefully at their size and cause. Was it really a bad day, a whole day? Wasn't it actually a difficult 15 minutes, or maybe two challenging half hours? Should a whole day be labeled and sacrificed because one or two things went wrong? How much difference will these "catastrophes" make an hour from now? In a week? A month? By any chance do they have a funny side that could be laughed about now?

Is this a homeschooling problem? Or is the real problem perhaps worries about money, a serious illness, difficulties with a parent's job, or rude comments a neighbor keeps making? Pressure and stress that have nothing to do with homeschooling can create tensions that interfere with learning, but these are not homeschooling problems. Some that could be called homeschooling problems are:

It seems like no one's learning.

To whom have you been listening? Comparisons can be dangerous. Of course, they are tempting and may even seem necessary. After all, we've undertaken a big responsibility by deciding to homeschool. Don't we need comparisons so we know we're on the right track and our children are doing all right?

To be sure, some kind of reassurance is helpful. Unfortunately we can't get it from comparisons. All of us, parents and children, are unique. There has never been another person just like us. We can't compare ourselves to other homeschoolers and try to become like them. There are some basic similarities. We can learn from and be inspired by others. But homeschooling on the basis of comparisons just doesn't work.

Another problem with comparisons among homeschoolers is that we tend to combine things inappropriately. We listen to several other parents and conclude we should be learning fractions the way the Smiths are, and studying astronomy like the Joneses, and working on Spanish like the Browns, and playing music like the Greens. We forget that even if it made sense for us to try to follow the one example, it would be way too much for us to try to do them all. Not one of these families is doing all of the things the other families are doing. We should concentrate on deciding what would be best for us.

Okay, but what can we do on those dark days when it still seems like no one is learning anything? Maybe this would be a good time to think back to what we were doing a month ago, six months ago, a year ago, or even farther back. We can look over records we are keeping. We can remember what it was like before we started homeschooling. It becomes clear that everybody (parents included) has learned a lot recently–maybe not this morning or last week, but over the last six months or year.

In a review like this, many homeschoolers find it helpful to remember that children learn all kinds of things in all kinds of ways. It isn't just a question of whether John has memorized the multiplication tables. Is he developing a sense of the way numbers work together and how he can use them to help him with other projects? Many parents also find it helpful to review their non-academic goals and the progress their children are making in these areas. These goals may be more important, anyway. People can learn basic math with a fairly short period of concentrated work (if they are ready and motivated). But spiritual and moral values, ways of getting along with other people, and social responsibility cannot be learned this way. They are the result of years of thinking and doing. Parents also find it helpful to understand that they can't always see what their children are learning, but learning is taking place nonetheless.

Our children are having trouble with reading (or math or whatever).

Learning is exciting and satisfying, but it can also be hard work. Everyone is challenged in some way when they try to learn. But having difficulty does not mean they have a disability. It helps to be calm, patient, and positive. Many parents find it also helps to ask the children what they think the problems are and what they would like to do about them. The reason for these questions is not to let children just do anything they please, but rather to get their perspectives and insights on the problem and possible solutions. Sometimes what seems like a difficult problem has a surprisingly simple solution, one that perhaps the parents hadn't thought of.

There are various ways to handle difficulties while learning, including the following.

- Try a different approach. Written material that is incomprehensible when you are trying to read it silently to yourself can become much clearer if someone else reads it to you, even if you are an experienced reader. Or if you are having trouble with cursive, maybe learning to type or write on a word processor would be a better alternative.
- Change books. The new perspective from a different approach or a different way of explaining things may clarify material. Some families select books from different sources to get the benefits of a variety of approaches.
- Hands-on experience provides learning opportunities not available through books. Math manipulatives make concepts concrete and real in a way that work sheets don't. A meal in an ethnic restaurant can help another culture come alive. Museums and nature centers are well recognized for their educational value, but a great deal can be learned from close observations in the back yard or a nearby park. Balancing the family checkbook demonstrates the importance of math while one is learning a valuable skill.

• Sometimes it helps to set aside material causing difficulty for a while. Things may go more smoothly with a fresh start after a break. The material may be more manageable when children are older. Children having trouble with fractions could work on percents or graphs instead. Sometimes homeschoolers set aside a whole subject area, like math, for a while. Some problems even seem to resolve themselves. Many children have found that their spelling improved greatly when they stopped trying to memorize word lists and instead concentrated on reading widely and writing for fun.

Our children won't settle down and study.

Some parents talk with their children. Would studying be easier if they worked in a different place? At a different time? The reason for asking these questions is to discover more about the problem and possible solutions.

Some families try a different approach to one or more subjects, such as those described above.

Some parents' main goal is to help their children learn how to learn and start on a path of lifelong learning. These parents reason that it is more important that their children generally enjoy learning than that they learn today or this week to read or add or locate Spain. Many learning opportunities appear when children discover and pursue activities they enjoy, whether these be arts and crafts, wood working, gardening, visiting an elderly neighbor, or raising an animal. Desire to find out more about a special interest has led many reluctant children into academics.

Taking a break often allows children to discover new interests that lead them back to studying in a new way or at least with less resistance.

The children seem to squabble so much.

Having one or more siblings provides learning opportunities along with conflict. Many parents feel that, on balance, siblings learn much that is positive by interacting with each other and try to take a reasonable amount of squabbling in stride.

It often helps to give everyone their own place. A whole room for each person is great, but many children manage well with a clearly marked part of a shared bedroom, or even a corner or desk. What is important is respecting each person's privacy and possessions.

Comparing siblings can contribute to an antagonistic atmosphere. When parents value children's uniqueness, it encourages siblings to accept each other and get along. It may also help to point out that learning is available to everyone. Mary's learning to multiply does not reduce John's chance to learn it, too.

Sometimes siblings squabble because they are bored. Parents try to find opportunities for them to do things of interest.

Some families develop a list of relaxing activities for times when tensions start building. Reading aloud, listening to music, or going for a family walk are ways of encouraging siblings to do something constructive together.

Friends, relatives, and neighbors sometimes criticize our homeschooling.

See Chapter 26 for ideas on dealing with critics.

As homeschooling parents, we don't have enough time for ourselves.

See Chapter 15 for ideas on how parents find time for themselves.

Solving Family Problems

We are in the best position to solve our family's problems. We understand the underlying issues and know what resources we have. Solutions to whatever problems we face often grow out of the fabric of our own families, the unique strengths and abilities and talents of each member and the group as a whole. Some families seem to solve problems without actually concentrating on them. Others use a model and step-by-step suggestions. Here's one possibility. Parents can use it themselves, but it's even better to include others in the process.

1. Identify the problem. Write it down. Sometimes we assume the problem is one thing only to discover, when we focus on it, that it's really something else. Sometimes we have a vague sense something is wrong for a while before we figure out the problem. Ask what you can learn from the problem, what it has to teach you.
2. Ask what you're doing now in this area or a related area that is working. It may take a little while to think of something, but there's almost always at least a little bit that's going right.
3. Write down as many solutions as you can. See how many ideas you can come up with. Don't try to decide whether something will work. Don't say, "But we can't..." or "But we don't have any..." If more than one person is working on this, listen to everyone.
4. Review the alternatives and cross out the unacceptable or impossible ones. Again, make sure everyone is heard.
5. Choose a solution and figure out specifically how it will work. If more than one person is involved, this step isn't done until you've figured out something everyone agrees to. Consider writing down the solution.
6. After an appropriate length of time, review the situation. Was the problem correctly identified? Is the solution working? If not, what changes or alternatives should be tried?

Problems provide opportunities to learn and grow. They give us strong incentive and get us going on things we might not get around to otherwise, some of which are too important to miss. If this sounds too unrealistically positive, think about the most important things you've learned in your life. How many of them were learned in response to a problem? There is much to be gained through solving problems.

Dealing With Discouragement

Here are suggestions for parents who want to continue homeschooling but are feeling overwhelmed, tired, or confused.

- Try not to make comparisons. Enjoy your children as they are without comparing them to others. Expect your house to look more lived in than those of families who are away from home all day. Remember that homeschools are different from conventional schools and do not need to duplicate them.
- Consider trying a different approach to curriculum. See Chapters 6 and 7 for possibilities.
- Think about taking a break from academics, or at least the part that is frustrating you or your children. Take off a day, a week, a month, or more. After all, you may be homeschooling for years, and your children can continue learning throughout their lives, so you can certainly afford to take a little time off. Or, if taking a break for a week or longer sounds too risky, try taking every Friday off. Start by doing the day's household tasks, then decide what you most want to do for the rest of the day. Try some of the activities in Chapter 6 or think up your own.

At the end of the break, look around. What have the kids learned? What have you learned? Most families who try this are amazed at how much they learn during times like this.

- For ideas about parenting homeschooling children, including finding time for yourself, see Chapter 15.
- Start a small parents' group. One possibility is to invite a few families for a brown bag lunch or a potluck lunch or supper. Parents can talk informally or discuss a specific topic

while the children play. (This may not be a good time for children's activities designed to promote learning.) If the children need some help, give them paper and magic markers, board games, play dough, ingredients to make cookies, or a place to play games like tag. (If neighbors are likely to be concerned, explain that it's physical education.) It helps if the kids can interrupt when they need you. If the gathering works well, pick a date to meet again, and ask someone to plan and host that gathering. If not, try again with a different group of people.

- Remember that many problems are "life problems" or "kid problems" and not "homeschooling problems." Some would be even more difficult to deal with if the children were attending conventional schools.
- Think about the alternatives to homeschooling. Many homeschoolers feel that even at difficult times, they are still better off than they would be if the children were attending conventional schools.
- Include topics and activities that you enjoy in your family's curriculum. Homeschooling provides many opportunities for us as parents to grow, to explore new areas, to learn things that we were told in school we did not have the ability to learn, and to express ourselves creatively. These are opportunities not to be missed. By setting an example, we are doing important things for our children and our communities, as well as ourselves.
- Attend the WPA conference each spring. Many homeschooling parents find the conference provides information, encouragement, and support that help prevent and overcome discouragement.

Custody Cases

Homeschooling sometimes becomes an issue for divorced homeschooling parents whose ex-spouses oppose it. Many of them recognize the advantages to resolving conflicts without going to court. Most attorneys and judges know little about homeschooling; many are biased against it. Judges often rule that parents can only homeschool if they agree to do more than the law requires. Parents have more flexibility, freedom, and choice if they make their own agreements instead of being restricted by court rulings they have to obey, even if both parents later decide the rulings are a mistake. Staying out of court also saves a lot of time and money and avoids the tensions surrounding court appearances that affect children as well as parents.

Testing is a complicated question in custody cases. Wisconsin law does not require that homeschoolers take tests, and the vast majority of homeschoolers oppose state-mandated tests. Moreover, test results do not automatically resolve conflicts and can lead to more testing, including psychological testing. But sometimes parents feel having their children tested is worth the risks if it's enough to convince their ex-spouse to drop their opposition to homeschooling or to avoid having the guardian ad litem argue that the homeschooling parent should no longer have primary or joint custody of the child. Also, judges often want testing done. Parents who agree to testing work to get the minimum number of the least objectionable academic tests and do not allow psychological testing.

If court is unavoidable, you are much more likely to get a favorable outcome if you work closely with your attorney rather than turning your case over to them. Tell them to prepare your case based on laws, educating judges about them if necessary and preventing judges from making decisions based on their opinion of what would be in the best interests of the child. As a parent, you have the right, recognized by Wisconsin statutes, to homeschool your children, regardless of whether the judge or guardian ad litem thinks homeschooling is a good idea. Make sure you and your attorney are very familiar with what Wisconsin's homeschooling law requires. See Chapters 3 and 28 and the texts of statutes in Appendix A. In addition, your attorney can point out that the compulsory school attendance law requires attendance; it does not require compulsory education. This should limit judges' ability to insist that homeschoolers prove that their children are learning by submitting test scores, evaluations by public school teachers, etc.

Guardian ad litems appointed by the court have enormous power and can turn a case you and your attorney have carefully prepared against you. They are very much a part of the conventional educational, judicial, and social service systems. Their job is to uphold these systems. It's not surprising that most of them are at least skeptical of homeschooling, and many are opposed. Their reports can displace statutes concerning education, the strong wishes and desires of children and their parents, and other things. Despite this, however, there are some guardian ad litems who can be convinced to support homeschooling. Therefore, begin by presenting homeschooling in the most reassuring and conventional terms you can. If the guardian ad litem objects to homeschooling, see if you can reach a better understanding about it.

If your guardian ad litem continues to oppose homeschooling, find out as much as you can about what they are likely to report. Any time after 120 days following the appointment of a guardian ad litem, you may request that the court schedule a status hearing related to the guardian ad litem's actions and work. This can be repeated 120 days after each status hearing. WPA strongly suggests that you request such status hearings unless you are very certain that the guardian ad litem supports your position concerning custody and homeschooling.

Often the only way to counter a biased or unfavorable custody evaluation presented by a guardian ad litem is to have a private evaluation performed by an independent professional. Unfortunately, this can cost between $2,000 and $8,000, but in some cases, it may be necessary

Chapter 17

Secrets of Experienced Homeschooling Families

To help new homeschoolers get started and experienced homeschoolers keep going, some long-term homeschoolers were asked what helps them homeschool. Here are their responses. As with the rest of this book, take what you can use and ignore what doesn't work for your family.

• **Take time to enjoy your children.** Homeschooling is all about relationships. Each child is a miracle. Homeschooling gives us extra opportunities to appreciate them. One of the most important things we can do for our children is let them know how much we love them and enjoy being with them. Our enjoyment of them as people helps them develop the confidence they need. The heart of homeschooling is families spending time together and learning together. Don't miss it!

• **Create your own version of homeschooling.** There's no one right way to homeschool. There's room for every approach to education, every learning style, every special interest, every individual's unique timetable. You can learn from the experiences of other homeschoolers, but don't try to duplicate what they have done. Instead, do what's right for your family, based on your principles and beliefs.

• **Slow down and take your time.** Learning is a life-long process. Your relationships with your children and their self-confidence are much more important than whether they learn to add fractions today. Also, many things are easier to learn at a later age, when you have more context for them and more experience living and learning.

• **Encourage your children to pursue their passions.** Learning is easier when we're pursuing something we love. We have more energy and motivation. We don't need someone else to set goals for us or keep us going. Sometimes this leads us to discover our life's work.

• **Focus on learning rather than teaching.** Trust that your kids will learn. Some parents say, "I don't teach; we learn together." Or "I'm just one more resource for our kids." Don't draw lines between living and learning. People learn all the time.

• **Help your kids learn how to learn.** One approach: First, admit that you don't know something. (How many adults can't do that?!) Then try to figure it out yourself, ask someone, look it up on the Internet, research it at the library, find a tutor, or take a class. As long as your kids know how to learn, they'll be able to learn anything you missed while they were growing up, so you don't have to worry.

• **Take a break from topics that the kids can't seem to understand right now.** If parts of speech aren't making sense today, set them aside for a day, a week, a month, or longer. "First, do no harm." It's better for kids to know very little about a subject than to become convinced that they hate it or are no good at it. If you let go of things that they're not ready for today, there's a greater chance they'll be interested, want to learn them, and be able to learn them later.

• **Often the way you use a curriculum is as important as which one you choose**. Many homeschoolers make their curriculum fit their kids, instead of trying to get their kids to fit the curriculum.

• **Homeschooling isn't "hard," like school is.** Sometimes homeschooled kids think they're not learning because they haven't gotten to "the hard part" yet.

• **Don't try to find the beginning of what you're learning.** Wherever you start IS the beginning.

• **Learn, yourself.** Learn things your kids are interested in, even if you've never cared how a car runs or always thought bugs were disgusting. Learn things that you want to know, even if your kids aren't enthusiastic when you announce that you're going to learn Spanish or grow zinnias or bake whole wheat bread.

• **Find things to do with your children that nurture you as well as them,** and learn to be nurtured by things they love to do. If you love to be outside, spend hours outdoors with them and marvel at what they learn without lesson plans or textbooks. If you love crafts, share your enthusiasm, give them their own supplies, and accept the fact that you'll get a lot less accomplished while you are working with them, but you may end up with children who share your passion or at least understands how important it is to you. Choose books to read aloud that you love, from picture books on up. Play in the snow, build sand castles, rake a pile of leaves and jump in it. Do what you loved to do as a child and what you always wanted to do but never did. Sing (even if you think you can't carry a tune). Dance (even if you never learned how). Write your own stories. Paint with water colors.

• **Consider limiting (or even eliminating) the use of TV and computers.** Families who limit TV are freer from advertising, violence, and values they object to. They have more time and incentive to do real things together. Other families prefer to own one small TV and carefully limit its use. Information and support are available from books like Jerry Mander's *Four Arguments for the Elimination of Television* and Marie Winn's *Plug-in Drug.*

Some families use computers in public libraries. Others limit their use. One can get an outstanding education without any educational software, some of which is misleading and inaccurate. Concerns about negative effects of computers on children, especially young children, are raised in books like Jane Healy's *Endangered Minds* and *Failure to Connect.*

• **Understand the value of our homeschooling freedoms.** Wisconsin has one of the best homeschooling laws in the nation only because many homeschoolers worked hard through WPA to get and maintain it. If we don't continue to work to maintain our freedoms, we will lose them. Chapter 21 tells why our freedoms are being challenged and what we can do. What we do or don't do will affect the future of homeschooling for us and others. The wonderful possibilities homeschooling offers will be lost if homeschools are unnecessarily regulated by the state, and many ideas in this chapter will no longer be possibilities.

• **Develop a support system that works for you.** Possibilities include joining an existing local support group or starting your own, getting together with one or a few other homeschooling families, keeping a few favorite homeschooling books nearby to reread when you need reassurance, having a few people who you can call when you need to.

• **Attend the WPA conference.** Besides the stimulating, helpful workshops, the conference offers the chance to be with lots of other homeschoolers, an experience you and your family may find energizing and encouraging.

• **Expect to be discouraged sometimes.** Homeschooling is great, but it's also intense and tends to change your life. Then there are the times you wake up in a panic, thinking, "Our kids haven't learned how to add fractions." Talking to someone about your discouragement can be a big help, but don't complain to people who are critical of homeschooling. Their response is likely to be, "Why don't you just put the kids in school?" Instead, call another homeschooler who can say, "Yes, I know. I've felt that way, too. You'll feel better soon." Then be prepared to say this to her when she gets discouraged and calls you.

• **Take a break when you need one.** Set aside "school work" for an hour, a day, a week, or more. Do things you really want to do. Then look back, see how much you've learned when you weren't even trying to, and perhaps ask if you could spend less time on "school work."

• **Accept the fact that your kids will miss some things,** quite possibly some big important things that they will need later in life. (Kids who attend conventional schools certainly do.) Learning doesn't end at age 18. If your kids need to know something, they'll learn it, no matter how old they are. Think how much of the knowledge you use today you have learned SINCE you finished school.

• **Remember that you can homeschool.** You can give your children much better learning opportunities than any conventional school can, simply because you are not confined to a school building or to conventional "school work," because you have only a few young people to work with so you can be more flexible and offer them more opportunities than you would be able to if you had 20 or 30, because you know them better than classroom teachers can possibly get to know their students, and because you love them.

• **Don't be overwhelmed by the number of homeschooling resources.** There are far more good, even excellent, resources than anyone could possibly use. The problem is not finding resources but keeping yourself and your family from being overwhelmed by the resources that seem to find you. There's no magical set of resources that every homeschooler should master, and a search for resources that are so good that no homeschooler should miss them is more likely to lead to frustration than the perfect education. Really, you don't have to buy anything to homeschool.

• **Spend as little money as possible.** The library is free and you have to take back what you borrow, which keeps the amount of stuff you have to deal with more manageable. Just because you bought something doesn't mean you have to use it. You can use page 3 and throw away the book. Or you can throw stuff away the same week you buy it if it doesn't work for you. Or, if that seems too wasteful, sell it at your support group meeting or the used book sale at the WPA conference. It may be just what some other family is looking for.

• **Keep your sense of humor.** Convince your kids (and yourself) that some things that don't go as planned are great bonding experiences. What seems like a disaster today, if it's not too serious, will make a great story and a wonderful memory someday!

• **Make your relationship with your spouse a priority**. It is one of the foundations of your homeschool and your family life. But you can do small things in the midst of daily life, like a note, a quick phone call, a flower. When the kids are playing outside or asleep, do things that strengthen your relationship. Sometimes this means tackling a major family decision or working together, maybe paying bills or doing the dishes. But often it means relaxing and spending time together, having fun, reminiscing, talking about how amazing the kids are, playing a game, watching a video, sharing a special dessert, or whatever you choose. You can also get time together by taking the family to a place like a playground, where you can talk while the kids play, although it helps to expect to be interrupted.

• **Realize the importance of what you are doing.** One homeschooling mother observed, "Homeschooling is the most wonderfully difficult job I've ever had. But sometimes I think it's too easy, so it doesn't seem to have value. Sometimes, because it's wonderful, I don't think it's difficult."

PART THREE

HOMESCHOOLING WORKS!

Chapter 18

Why Homeschooling Works

Experienced homeschoolers know that homeschooling works. But conventional schooling plays such a prominent role in the lives of the vast majority of children that many people assume such schooling is essential and are surprised to hear that homeschooling works. Therefore, let's consider some of the reasons that it does. This list is only a beginning, the tip of the iceberg. Readers are encouraged to add to it.

The richness and diversity of approaches to learning and living that are available to homeschoolers allow them to try different approaches, to learn from their successes and their mistakes, and to discover or create ways of homeschooling that work for them. There is no one right or best way to homeschool. Each family has to decide for itself which approaches to learning and living work best for the unique, special, and gifted individuals in their family and for their family as a whole, in light of the circumstances in which they live.

Most families use a variety of different approaches, depending on the children's ages and other circumstances, making changes as children's (and parents') ages, interests, needs, and skills change. See Chapter 7.

The flexibility of homeschooling is also one of the main reasons homeschooling should not be unnecessarily regulated by the state. Such regulation would diminish the freedom and flexibility that are essential parts of homeschooling as an approach to education that works well.

Homeschooling offers many different ways of learning. Children learn from reading books, from hands-on experiences, from audiovisual materials, from talking with other people, and in other ways. Children can move around as they are learning, which makes it easier for some children to process information. Children can concentrate on something they find particularly fascinating for several hours or more. This flexibility means that children who had (or would probably have) difficulty learning in a conventional school setting do very well at home. If our society is really committed to meeting the needs of all children and helping each child become educated, homeschools are a critical part of the alternatives that should be available so families can choose an approach to education that works for each child.

Homeschooling works because it is based on one of the most highly respected and recommended approaches to learning: tutorial or one-on-one learning. This allows children to work at their own pace, moving rapidly ahead when they are ready and setting something else aside until later if they're not ready to handle it yet. Children have a chance to discover what interests them and to pursue their special interests.

Homeschooling works because it gives people opportunities to discover things for themselves and to understand why things work. People usually remember what they understand, especially if they have discovered it themselves, because it makes sense. There is much less need to memorize isolated facts that may be hard to remember because they do not make sense.

Homeschooling works because children learn how to learn. No one can learn everything, especially in such a rapidly changing world. But people who learn how to learn can learn what they need to know at any age. It's just a matter of recognizing that you don't know something, being willing to admit it, and then finding out by figuring it out yourself, asking someone, looking in the library or on the Internet, working with a mentor, taking a class, or some other approach.

Homeschooling emphasizes and builds on people's strengths rather than their weaknesses. It starts with what people already know and are interested in and encourages them to learn more by using approaches to learning that work well for them. When people are given a chance to learn in ways that work well for them, at their own pace, they can learn and do not end up being labeled "learning disabled." But what about subjects that people need to learn that are difficult for them, like maybe reading or math? Homeschoolers find that when people are given the opportunity to learn what interests them, using a variety of approaches to learning, including lots of hands-on experiences, and working at their own pace, they increase their ability to learn anything and develop enough confidence and physical, mental, and neurological maturity that they get to the point where they can learn reading, math, or whatever was challenging them before. Emphasizing strengths rather than weakness really works, and it builds strong people.

Homeschooling works because it's fun. Homeschoolers can spend extra time on the subjects and learning activities that they enjoy most. People who are happy about what they're doing are well motivated, have an easier time learning, and absorb and remember more of the ideas and information they're exposed to.

Homeschooling works because people and families are better than institutions at raising children, giving them the love and support they need, and providing a place where they can learn. People are social creatures who do better in small groups than in large institutions. The family is the basic unit of society and provides a safe, secure, supportive place for people to learn. Throughout history, most people have learned at home. It is still the place where most people in our society learn two of the most complex skills, walking and talking.

Children are eager to learn about the world around them, especially when they feel safe and do not have to deal with excessive competition, ridicule, and bullying.

Homeschooling strengthens families. It gives families time together, to share activities and work, to get to know each other better, and to develop strong bonds and meaningful relationships. They also get to be even better at homeschooling.

In a way, every family homeschools. Families whose children attend conventional schools do homeschooling kinds of activities when their children are out of school. Families who decide to homeschool do these things more of the time.

Parents are good at helping their children learn. Parents have the opportunity to work with one child or a small group of children they know well and to whom they are strongly committed. They love their children and are willing to work hard and make sacrifices for them. Parents are consciously and subconsciously tuned in to their children's strengths and the ways they learn well. They understand why their children do some of the things they do. Love gives them extra patience and commitment.

Homeschoolers have time. When homeschooling parents make mistakes, either in helping their children learn or in interacting with them, they have time to think, apologize and make amends if necessary, and move on.

Homeschooling families have more control over their lives. They can eat foods that they prefer, create living and learning spaces that work well for them, and live according to their principles and beliefs.

Homeschooling gives parents opportunities and encouragement to learn what interests them. When parents are unsure about something themselves (how to multiply fractions, for example), they often can learn along with their children and make sense of something they didn't understand when they were in school. Homeschooling encourages whole families, not just children, to learn.

Homeschoolers learn about the world by being in the world, in their homes where all kinds of interesting things happen and in their communities where even more is going on. Homeschoolers are not limited to learning about what can be brought into a classroom and kept there. They have a chance to develop common sense.

Homeschooled children develop the social skills they need to function well in the real world. They have many opportunities to interact with people of different ages. They form strong bonds with members of their family. They learn from and befriend people of all ages, from babies to the elderly. They can make choices and are not forced to spend long hours in relatively large groups of people who are all the same age, an artificial situation that exists only in schools and army boot camp.

Homeschools work because they have one child or a small group of children of different ages. Therefore, homeschools don't need extensive rules for maintaining order or bureaucratic procedures that often fail to respect children and their needs. Homeschools have more flexible schedules, so children can continue working on something they're excited about or take a break to take advantage of an unexpected opportunity.

Homeschooling works because by deciding to homeschool, parents have had the courage to follow their convictions and do something that they feel is right, even though this means doing something different from what most people do. Homeschooling parents are able to take responsibility for their families and to exercise more control over their time, space, and lives. Children who grow up with parents like this usually become strong, confident, and responsible.

Homeschooling works because it has sensible and meaningful goals. Homeschooling parents want their children to learn in ways that work well for them and to grow up to be responsible adults who can do important work, relate well to other people, and learn to understand and fit into life in the world around them. These goals make sense, and they are what our society needs if it is to continue. (Compare these goals with those of most conventional schools, which include things like: to keep the taxpayers happy so they will continue to pass bond issues; to make sure that 25 students are all exposed to instructions on how to add fractions by the end of the month; to respond to pressure from big business that schools prepare students to work at boring and routine jobs for low pay; to rank and label kids so some are on the top and some are on the bottom and no one is too unhappy about where they are; to keep kids out of adults' way and make sure they don't do work that adults could do for pay.)

Homeschooling works because it provides a means by which parents can reclaim some of the rights and responsibilities that have been taken from them by institutions.

Homeschooling families have their own reasons to add. The point is that homeschooling is an approach to learning and living that works. We can trust the process and proceed with confidence.

Chapter 19

Stories from Homeschooling Families

Note: Names have been changed to protect families' privacy. For additional stories, see Chapter 9 and Stories in the Index.

We have three children ages four, six and seven. Our homeschooling journey began a few years ago when, after checking out various preschools, we discovered that we were accomplishing the same activities at home. In the meantime, I began researching homeschooling at our library and was so thankful to read the WPA handbook and many other helpful resources. The decision to homeschool liberated us from many of our concerns. Our children did not want to be separated from the family to go to school. As parents, we wanted a more active role in educating our children than volunteering weekly in the classroom or chaperoning field trips. We felt that homeschooling was a natural extension of our family values.

At the time we began homeschooling, we did not know any other homeschoolers. So our first hurdle was explaining our decision to well-intentioned extended family and friends, who were not familiar with Wisconsin's homeschooling law. Library resources were very helpful in this respect. As time progressed, there was little room for discussion as they could see our children's natural curiosities led to a positive learning environment. We still answer a lot of questions about homeschooling, but as our confidence increases, our answers come easier.

Our next decision was to become WPA members. The first WPA Conference that we attended was informational and inspirational. I'll never forget the emotional graduation ceremony where the graduates could thank their families for their support throughout their homeschooling experience. Each workshop offered us important information that we could use at home. At the second WPA conference that we attended, I met a fellow homeschooler located in my community. Our friendship has provided a wonderful resource for my children so that they know they are not alone on this homeschooling journey. My friend also introduced me to a homeschooling support group in our area that has been a wealth of support for parents as well as children.

Homeschooling has provided us with so many benefits. We have made many Wisconsin, out-of-state (and one international) educational trips, including children's, historical, aviation and science museums, orchards, bakeries, confectioneries, nature trails, insectariums, biodomes, zoos, plays, concerts, art shows, and all kinds of interesting adventures. The library has continued to be a precious resource, and we make regular trips there. It has been an exciting and rewarding experience to work with our children to make learning experiences available to them in all subject areas. Listening to our children read their first book out loud, enjoying their pride as they write their first alphabet, watching their eyes light up after making a scientific discovery, and observing them making healthy nutritional choices have been joyful experiences.

Homeschooling gives us the flexibility to maximize time with their grandparents, who have been natural teachers for the children. With their grandparents, the children have enjoyed building everything from birdhouses and gingerbread houses to an electrical circuit, as well as visiting our state capitol, museums, and zoos. Our children enjoy relationships with a group of friends that span a range of ages, which richly enhances their educational experience and daily life. Homeschooling also provides us an opportunity to focus on each child's specific interests, learning style and preferences so that their learning is a natural, flowing process.

We are thankful for the support we have on this journey through WPA's annual conference, newsletter, and handbook, as well as our community homeschooling support group. Homeschooling has been a rewarding experience for our family.

A mother who was homeschooling before the Wisconsin homeschooling law was passed in 1984 wrote:

In 1979 my husband and I had three small daughters, a newborn, a two year old, and a four year old. We got a letter from our school district inviting our oldest daughter, Theresa, to come for a kindergarten screening. My maternal instincts kicked in 100%. I couldn't bear the thought of trusting my child to total stranger, even if only for a half day. My husband assured me that every mother goes through these feelings and that I'd get over it. I broke the news to him that I wasn't going to send her to school. I had it all figured out—I would teach her everything she needed to know right at home! After I spent a summer of arguing my point and not being willing to accept "no" for an answer, my husband humored me and told me that since our Theresa was only four years old, and since she wasn't required by law to attend school that year, he would allow me to teach her kindergarten at home. He would decide after the year was up if she actually learned anything.

We purchased a structured curriculum from Christian Liberty Academy. All I had to do was present the materials to Theresa, have her do the work, and return it to CLA for grading. They issued report cards showing that our child had straight A's. My husband became a little more supportive of my belief in educating our children at home and gave me the go-ahead to homeschool the following year. First and second grades came and went, again with all A's on Theresa's report card. Our next daughter, Elizabeth, was ready for kindergarten. How would I manage? Two children in school, a toddler, my husband's blind grandmother came to live with us, and I discovered our fourth baby would be due in September.

We forged ahead. Our second daughter was as brilliant as the first and our first few weeks of school held a lot of promise for a great school year. By this time our local school district decided we were truant. We weren't complying with the law! We were served truancy notices and were told that we had three school days to have our girls in school or they would be taken from us and placed in foster care. My sister, who had children the same ages as mine, was sent truancy notices also. Together we hired an attorney from Madison who assured us that our children wouldn't be taken away. But there were a lot of problems we had to deal with.

Our school district had no experience in dealing with anyone who wanted to homeschool their children. They didn't know how to deal with us. They didn't seem to know what, if any, authority they had over us, and all WE knew was that we wanted to continue building our strong family bonds and teach our children at home.

After a year, Grandma went to live with her son. Shortly after, we had our fourth child, a boy. Because there was no specific homeschool law, our attorney did his best to keep the truancy problem very low-key. He told us to continue homeschooling, but we weren't to tell anyone what we were doing. We kept our curtains closed and were as quiet about homeschooling as possible so as not to arouse curiosities. Our children were not to be seen if anyone came to the door. They had their designated hiding spots when the door bell rang. If we had to go somewhere during regular school hours, they sat on the floor of the car so no one would see them.

Then we got a notice from our fire department notifying us that if we felt we were a school we had to have fire drills once a month. I had to record how long it took my students to vacate the building and get to the meeting place and send them monthly reports. We complied.

The fire chief declined my invitation to come to our house during fire prevention week to talk to my students about fire safety, but he did let me know that the street commissioner wanted school zone signs posted a block from our house. When I wrote to the commissioner asking that the signs be placed, he refused saying that he couldn't put school zone signs in a residential neighborhood, even though our property adjoined the elementary school a block away.

The Department of Public Instruction sent us a copy of building codes that apply to private schools. Our lawyer advised us to humor the DPI and comply as much as possible. We were "required" to have two bathrooms, one for boys and one for girls. We had to have EXIT signs over each door leading outside. We had to provide sufficient water bubblers to accommodate our number of students. We were given a "LIST OF SPECIFIC LAWS OF WISCONSIN RELEVANT TO NON PUBLIC SCHOOLS" that we were expected to follow, from displaying a flag, to certifying teachers, to teaching a class called "dairy products," to pledging allegiance once a week. Each employee of our school was required to submit results of a physical exam to the Department of Health and Social Services each year. We complied.

Each September we were served truancy notices. The truant officer and the local sheriff would come to the door (the children were hiding) and read the truancy notice as though I was illiterate. I would quietly accept it. The lawyer advised us that any time public officials asked us questions, we were to ask that their questions be put in writing so we could submit them to our lawyer. We complied.

About this time I was beginning to doubt my sanity. We were informed of a hearing in Madison that had something to do with legalizing homeschooling in Wisconsin. We couldn't believe it! We HAD to go and see that there were really other people out there who had the same ideas as we. If this was true, then other families must be going through the same purgatory of red tape with the public system. We knew that we must attend this hearing and become active with the group fighting for their God-given right to educate their children in the sanctuary of their own home.

We learned that a group of about 80 "secret" homeschoolers had met in Stevens Point a few weeks before the hearing to come up with a strategy of dealing with the upcoming legislation. This group realized a few basic principles, namely, that homeschoolers must become and remain united. All agreed on the basic principle that each family must be free to teach their own beliefs. This was the very beginning of Wisconsin Parents Association. This infant organization busied itself during the next three weeks to inform small

Christian schools of their work on Act 512. They circulated written information and sent articles to newspapers informing people of the hearing.

On January 25, 1984, about 2,500 homeschoolers attended the hearing in Madison. Act 512 was passed and homeschooling as you know it became legal in Wisconsin. We answered people's questions. We explained our positions. We listened patiently to verbal attacks on how we were abusing our poor, unsocialized children. We did what we could to help people understand that homeschooling is an acceptable alternative to public education. But mostly, we thanked God for answering our prayers—that WE could educate the children HE gave us according to our consciences.

Many of you didn't have to work for your right to homeschool. For some, all you had to do was fill out form PI-1206 and begin your 875 hours per year. I cannot stress it enough—please do not abuse this right. If you aren't a member, join Wisconsin Parents Association and help maintain the law we have. We don't want anyone to have to go through what we did prior to the passage of ACT 512. Support WPA and do what you can to preserve Wisconsin's homeschool law. Help us to resist the efforts of DPI and society to erode our rights as parents.—From Opening Remarks, WPA Conference, 1999.

A year ago, just before Christmas, we decided to give in to our discomfort regarding our children's education. Over the years, we had many reasons to be dissatisfied with our children's experiences in school: too little challenge, too much TV ("Popeye"-at school!!), teachers who used *Interview with a Vampire* rather than *The Three Bears* to show a class of first graders how stories have a beginning, a middle and an end. (As Dave Barry would say, I am not making this up!) I was even once accused by a pair of well-meaning and well-qualified teachers of being overprotective of my second-grader: this because, although I never set foot in their classrooms, I spent many days at the school editing the school newsletter, developing a parent volunteer program, running a school-wide recycling program, and serving on the PTA board! I had the nerve to suggest to these teachers that my son, though capable of the challenging work they were giving him, was also frightened by the challenge, and in need of nurturing. They knew all the signs.

We drew the line, however, when our children's elementary school teachers would not come for dinner at our house. Perhaps other parents invite their kids' teachers to butter them up, but we had every confidence that ours didn't need "buttering." We simply felt it was essential to get to know the strangers who had custody of our offspring for the majority of their waking hours. We wanted to have one evening's casual conversation with the people for whom we sent our children to bed early each night, the people into whose care we chastened and hastened them out the door each morning. We were informed that such a meal might jeopardize the teachers' "perspective of [sic] your children as our students." Clearly, gaining perspective on our children, or us, as human beings was not a priority.

So, a year ago, our kids came home, to "school." Yesterday, my husband took our two daughters, ages six and eight, to tell Santa Claus of their Christmas gift wishes. Poor elf: each girl climbed on his lap and told him she wanted a teddy bear. Santa waited politely, and then asked, "What else?" Nothing, especially, just a bear apiece, thanks. Side effects: no TV advertising, no school-based peer pressure for the latest junk, and they find they are mostly happy with just what they have.

Sure, their acquaintances in our immediate neighborhood are fewer, now that they're out of the preselected, intensive society of the classroom, but their current friendships cut across generations and geography. At a recent party for my husband's colleagues at our home, almost all of our guests stopped on their way out the door, especially to comment on their pleasure in holding genuine conversations with our youngsters, who have "never met a stranger," and who would never consider the possibility that they wouldn't be taken seriously by an adult. A novel side-effect, as good for the adults as the children.

Yesterday also included a ride snuggled with Dad on the mall carousel, and a visit to a science store at the same mall, where each child was allowed to purchase one special, polished rock. Then all came home to inquire quietly of various resource books about the specific heritage and characteristics of the rocks, and to read E.T.A. Hoffman's Nutcracker in front of the fire with Mom. A mile-long walk in the falling snow, at about 9:00 pm, ended the day. The remarkable thing about these events is that they took place on a Wednesday-a "school day," a "school night." (No other children were encountered on our magical hike in the pristine, glittering snow!) I found myself grateful that we could share so many of these joyous family moments, in a day and age when magazines and the newspapers seem daily obliged to coach parents in the value of a shared meal, oh, once a week or so.

Another unanticipated side effect of our increased time with our children is a kind of return to comfort in knowing them: Remember when you could tell by the first whimper from your infant's crib whether it was a wet cry or a hungry or an angry or a frightened? I know my kids again, and I can increasingly trust my understanding of them. This means, among other things, that we can trust each other more and experiment with how to express ourselves completely and peacefully to each other, even in angry or otherwise uncomfortable times. It also means that we can be together A LOT (as homeschooling very young children more or less requires) and still give each other plenty of room. I marvel when friends throw up their hands, learning of our choice, and say, "I could never spend that kind of time with my kids-we'd all go crazy!" Surely being apart so much has taught us this false and dangerous thing; for most of history, families have depended on each other, and no one else, for survival! And the children's relationships to each other have taken several more quantum leaps in quality: they know each other better and need each other more.

Our youngest benefited from a side-effect of homeschool that completely surprised us: from the age of five months to the month she left kindergarten for home, at age five and a half, she was never without an ear or sinus infection for more than (if we were lucky) a month or two in the summer. Suddenly, within a few weeks, we noticed that her raspy breathing had disappeared. I thought it a fluke, at first, but her health has held steady. True, homeschooling has added various expenses to our lives-but it has saved us on medical bills and the fear and heartache of having a chronically ill child.

Each day that we slow down to find time to make and do our own work, together, we find more that is sacred in everyday living. We have become more of a family, more blessed and alive, and we find we crave increasingly more of the experience.

I, too, have grown, and have "learned to learn" again by watching my brave children. I have learned new crafts, learned and remembered much about history that had little or no meaning to me in earlier situations, and I, who had few prior political interests, have begun asking questions and speaking up about how to secure our freedoms to homeschool.

Certainly the most central and amazing side effect, though, has been a kind of awakening to the value of our own children as young intellects and human beings. How many questions did we once respond to with a half-hearted grunt? We can no longer afford that complacency, with the result that we feel as if we had only just discovered parenthood. Our children come to us as their guides, and if we cannot help them ourselves, we are obliged to clear a path to those who will pull and push them onward to their self-crafted goals-goals which, we have learned, have as much meaning as any adults'. Taking children seriously-as learners and human beings-was not a goal when we began homeschooling, any more than was the view of the ocean to the first explorers pushing west to the Pacific Coast. But the rewards of our adventure have been, similarly, breathtaking.

We are in our second year of homeschooling. Our children are presently in the sixth and eight grade. We also have a six-month-old baby.

We are so excited about what homeschooling has done for our family.

Our reason for starting homeschooling was to help our oldest child who seemed to be lost in the public school setting. He needed more of a one-on-one way to learn at his own pace. So with the encouragement and blessing of his principal at the time, we decided to try homeschooling.

We have seen such a change in his learning and comprehension. He has gone from reading three books in a school year to one to two books a week. We now have children who watch about one to two hours of TV a week and actually look forward to going to bed because they are allowed to read for one hour before lights out!

As a family we've become a team at getting projects completed, each of us pitching in whatever way we can. Homeschooling has become a learning experience for all of us. Mom and Dad learn things they've forgotten, and baby is watching all of us and learning, too.

As for the social issue, interaction with people of many different backgrounds and ages rather than isolation with age-mates provides our children with adult role models and lessens stress and problems of peer pressure and dependence.

Just last week our oldest was a little long on his paper route. He was stopped by one of his retired customers to hear a few of his poems from a book which will be published soon. The poems tell of his life and military experience. Our son is first on his list for a book, and he's become interested in learning more about World War II and the process of writing and publishing a book.

This is just one example of the daily social and educational experiences our children go through with neighbors, friends, relatives, and other homeschooling families.

Our other child loves working on her own and has advanced greatly in all subjects. She loves to learn, and now there is no stopping her or holding her back.

Our home has become an environment in which our children feel safe and secure, and this fosters exploration, discovery, and independent learning. For this reason, we have accepted homeschooling as a part of our life and love it.

Homeschooling is a big responsibility and a lot of work which we have chosen to do. The state should continue to make it possible for families to homeschool in Wisconsin by not changing the reasonable and workable law which we now have and not adding further regulation which would be restrictive and unnecessary and prevent homeschoolers from doing their best.

Parents who began homeschooling their 15-year-old son after 10 years of conventional schooling wrote:

"What did you consider the most serious problem your child was having in school?"

He was receiving straight A's with very little effort, while really not knowing how to study. Because he was a good student, treated his teachers with respect, and was not an athletic "star," he experienced rejection and ridicule by peers.

"What changes did you notice in your child after you began homeschooling?"

In his years in public school, he went from a talkative, outgoing child to a shy, withdrawn teenager. Upon homeschooling, he gradually began to come out of his shell. He has assumed leadership in our local support group and has been praised by parents as a good role model for the younger ones. His communication, writing, and studying skills have vastly improved. He is **happier!!**

"What have you done while homeschooling that seemed most helpful to your child?"

Removal from negative peers has been the most positive thing for him. We have encouraged him to develop leadership and many outside interests to replace those he had in school. He is learning self-discipline in scheduling his own time.

As a homeschooling parent, I'm convinced that homeschooling is providing our children with the best preparation for their lives as adults. But given my own upbringing and the years I spent in conventional schools, there's a part of my brain that keeps whispering, "People who went to good schools and have prestigious, high-paying jobs are qualified, know what they are doing, and can handle complicated situations." I certainly counted Jane as one of these people. She's a well-paid attorney with a prestigious job while I'm an unpaid mother-at-home.

When a problem came up in an organization Jane and I belong to, I was surprised that she called me to ask what to do. As she was describing her confusion and distress over the situation, I couldn't help wondering, "Why is Jane calling me? Haven't her training and experience prepared her to deal with this?" But the more I listened, the more I realized that she simply didn't know what to do.

I found myself forgetting about Jane's credentials and shifting to the "homemade" approach to solving problems that our family has developed as we've homeschooled together. First I listened to her and responded with brief, empathetic comments like, "That must have been hard." Experience has taught me again and again that it pays big dividends to close my mouth and listen to other people.

Then I used my common sense and described to Jane the situation as I saw it, pointing out some of the reasons the problem had arisen. Yes, she agreed. So far so good; on to the next step. I said, "It seems to me there are two questions we have to deal with: First, what do we need to do to get through the current situation? Second, what can we do to prevent this kind of situation from developing again?" Once I had come up with these questions, Jane was able to respond.

Then I proposed that a few of us meet to talk about how to prevent this problem from developing again. Jane objected, explaining that she did not think a small group should be tackling the problem, that more people should be involved. I explained to her how I view communication and how I think groups work, beginning with the idea that communication has the best chance of happening without misunderstanding when the fewest number of people are involved. (For example, I wouldn't try to solve a tricky problem with one of our children while their sibling was listening.) I couldn't help thinking, "Here I am explaining communication and group process to a prominent attorney, and I'm using what I've learned as a homeschooling mother to do it." Jane soon agreed with me, and then it was easy to figure out the next steps.

Jane thanked me for talking with her. "I knew you'd have good ideas," she said. Interesting-Jane recognizes and acknowledges my "homemade" credentials, even though she may not realize that they come from homeschooling. This is not to say that I'm prepared to take over Jane's job-something I wouldn't want to do anyway. I'm much happier with my family work, which has prepared me to deal with people, communication, and other things that matter to me. I just hope that, as a result of this experience, I'm a step closer to letting go of my school experience and my automatic respect for conventional credentials and a step closer to fully accepting the value of homemade credentials, for parents as well as for children who are homeschooling.

Our family consists of four daughters born in three and a half years, with a son fourteen years later. The girls all went through the public school system. They were excellent students academically, but our family values were disregarded and our relationship with them made distant.

Therefore, the day I heard about the homeschool movement, I pulled our son out of school. He was in his second month of kindergarten. We were living in Minnesota where you need to test your children every year, which basically means you will be bringing "school" home. Of course, I would eliminate the social pressures of the public system, but we weren't free to expand in whatever direction my child wanted to go or learn at our own pace. Therefore, we chose to move to Wisconsin following his first grade year.

Once we were semi-settled in Wisconsin, we found a whole new world opened up to us. Now we could pursue the things that really interested him and have fun doing it. We could attend plays and concerts or spend a day at the nature centers. He became a member of our local 4-H group and there could pursue many of his interests to see what he might enjoy. This was worked in with our bookwork.

Presently, our son has completed his second full year at UW River Falls, receiving scholastic honors for both years. Technically, he is in his junior year, however, as he began his studies there as a junior in high school. When I spoke to the Dean of Admissions concerning his early start, the dean said he had no problems with homeschool students starting early, because he knew they were self-motivated and serious about their studies. However, he did not have the same confidence in public school students. Our son has upheld the dean's expectations and then some.

The one thing I was privileged to experience with this child that I didn't get to with the girls was that I could actually see him blossom. Because he was free to expand into the directions he felt comfortable going, he was able to define his own talents and desires. The girls, on the other hand, were limited by the public system, and are still struggling with who they really are and where can their talents best be used. They're now in their late thirties and he is twenty. What a difference a child's foundation makes!!

The one thing that astounded me all the years I was home educating my son, was the question concerning socialization others seemed so concerned about. All the while I thought it was education that my children were in school for and now I realize that isn't the case at all. When you focus on the total picture, socialization is, indeed, the main theme of our present public education system. What else could it be? Since the public system isn't geared toward each child's unique learning abilities or needs, socialization is all that they can accomplish, isn't it? And it was the socialization that I was unhappy with! Our son is quite comfortable with people of all ages and is a teacher's dream student. He can change diapers for an infant, chat freely with an elderly person, or be a leader among his peers. His sisters, on the other hand, still look to their peers for their leadership and guidance, whereas our son values our wisdom.

Wisconsin Parents Association has made so much of this possible here. A HUGE THANK YOU for all your hard work on our behalf!! Your vision is truly toward a better tomorrow, with a younger generation fully ready for their responsibilities.

Our youngest of three has started college this fall. A landmark in our family history, signaling the official end of our homeschooling days, yet with John living at home, it is emotionally satisfying for me, A.K.A. Mom, not having to leave him to fend for himself away at college in a strange place. We also have another son living at home, which is okay with us for the time being. The oldest is at work on a career in the Navy using his talents working on the electrical systems of jet fighters.

John intends to pursue majoring in electrical engineering. This is not surprising since from about the age of three, we saw he was very interested in how things worked, especially plumbing and electrical systems of houses. All the boys came to prefer real tools to most toys, so John grew up in an enriched environment. As our sons grew, they found it was okay to take things apart; fortunately, they left the telephone and cars alone! Much later I found out this is referred to as "reverse engineering." I often mentioned our "junk curriculum" to fellow homeschoolers, who gave me a blank look and possibly concluded I was one of those "fringe" elements they would occasionally read about. No problem: what we were doing seemed to be what the boys were born to do. My job was to see how we could help nurture their special talents as well as learn the core curriculum through a more loosely scheduled and child-centered plan. I had the opportunity to do a lot of reading research in the last few months before our first son was born, and John Holt (author of *How Children Learn* and others) was a large influence in developing my educational philosophy. After John came along four and a half years later, I was sure I wanted to homeschool. My husband was a bit unsure, but we agreed to take it year by year and see how things developed.

Books and the public library were an important part of our homeschooling life, although for reading material, the boys tended to prefer technical manuals and catalogs rather than fiction. I have memories of bedtime reading to John from a Do-It-Yourself book on making concrete upon his request at three years of age. One of the boys' requests for shopping was to be taken to the local secondhand stores to spend their birthday money on electronic castoffs. Sometimes they even managed to get them working again. One book I was ecstatic to find was the Usborne book, *Introduction to Electronics*. I ended up buying a copy for each child. It was really the only book written to help a child understand how electricity and electronic components work. As my (and my husband's) higher education was in music, I was learning right along with them. Our dining table was often given over to serve as their workbench, laden with exposed parts of radios, VCR's and circuit boards.

One of the WPA conferences I attended helped reassure me that our kids were indeed using the gifts they were given. One of the presenters said that, as a child, his parents thought he was crazy when he kept taking things apart. They were just about at their wit's end when he took apart the grandfather's clock in the front hall. He ended up having a career in a mechanical field and was teaching his sons how to weld in their basement. He also wanted us to know that if any of our children couldn't help themselves from taking things apart and always wanted to know how everything worked, they weren't crazy, just mechanically gifted. I smiled knowingly as he told about his childhood antics and decided to continue as we had been, although the consequences are having to live with a certain amount of messiness and trusting the children with tools. I'm pleased to say we have a nearly perfect safety record with no major injuries.

Another advantage was my husband bringing home cast-off computers from work. This allowed the boys to learn programming and, when a new model came along, they got to see the insides of the old ones. These kids have never known a world without computers. I must say it's nice to have a live-in techie when I have problems!

John continues to be involved in our church choir, of which he has been a member since age nine. He has joined the ceramics club at college and continues his interest in listening to pop music and video gaming. While I know I haven't been entirely 'successful' by my own standards in getting him to know all I wanted him to learn during the homeschooling years, he continues to grow and learn. We all have gaps, no matter what method of education we use or have grown up with. The best part is, we can continue to learn new things and expand on what we already know for the rest of our lives.

Chapter 20

History of Homeschooling In Wisconsin

Working together through WPA, homeschoolers in Wisconsin have reclaimed and maintained basic freedoms in education and family life. We have worked to get and maintain the reasonable homeschooling law that was passed in 1984. We are maintaining this law despite continual pressure from the educational establishment and others to increase state regulation of homeschooling. Our work makes it possible for our families and thousands of other families to choose an approach to homeschooling that works for them and to follow it without unreasonable interference from the state.

If maintaining the law were all that we are doing, it would be a major accomplishment. But through WPA we are doing more.

- We are helping thousands of homeschooling families to discover ways that homeschooling can work for them. We are giving them encouragement, support, suggestions for learning resources, and accurate information about laws (to counter the misleading and inaccurate information from the Department of Public Instruction [DPI]).
- We are educating the general public about homeschooling and developing a climate of opinion that respects homeschooling, so that our homeschooling rights are more secure.
- We are building and maintaining a strong and effective grassroots organization that brings together a widely diverse group of people for the common purpose of maintaining the right of parents to choose for their children an education consistent with their principles and beliefs.
- We are informing ourselves and others of issues outside the homeschooling movement that could threaten our rights as parents as well as our homeschooling rights. We are discovering ways to reclaim and maintain rights of parents, children, and families.

Often knowing the history of something helps us understand it and support it. It is easier to understand homeschooling in Wisconsin today and how we can act to maintain our rights and freedoms if we know how we got here. To promote this understanding, here is our story.

We face obstacles as individual families, but protecting our homeschooling law is a challenge our entire homeschooling community must endure. In the spirit of celebrating our common goal, it is appropriate to dedicate some of our time today in recognition of the people who, 20 years ago, worked so diligently to "get it right."

I am humbled by the unwavering dedication of the few people who started this movement. Regardless of their personal philosophies, economic status, educational approach, or spiritual beliefs, they came together with a vision and a universal passion. Over the course of just a few weeks and through countless phone calls and meetings during the winter of 1984, this small group swelled to over 2,500 homeschooling supporters who went to the Capitol sending a very important message to the legislature. These visionaries focused on a common goal and did not allow their differences to pull them apart. Furthermore, they understood it was their diversity that made their voice strong and their message clear. —From Opening Remarks, WPA Conference, 2004

As you read this, think about where we would be now, what homeschooling rules and regulations we would have to obey, if homeschoolers had not worked together through WPA and stood up to challenges and unreasonable demands, time after time, as individuals and in groups. Remember that when homeschooling laws and regulations are reasonable, homeschoolers have the chance they need to do a good job of homeschooling. On the other hand, when homeschoolers have to deal with unreasonable and unnecessary laws and regulations, homeschooling itself becomes more difficult. Remember, too, that the work described here has been done by Wisconsin homeschoolers, not by "outside experts" coming into the state. In fact, we have worked hard to discourage such people from coming into Wisconsin, realizing that much of our strength comes from working together on the grassroots level in our own state to build a solid foundation for homeschooling here.

Let's begin with some general observations. As homeschoolers, we have a lot going for us.

- Homeschooling is not an isolated activity that we do for only five hours a day, 175 days a year. Homeschooling is part and parcel of the way we view our families, the value and importance of our children, and our roles and responsibilities as parents. It is central to the way in which we live our lives. At stake is more than how our children will learn to do long division or locate Japan on a map. We are fighting for a way of life, for recognition of the primary importance of the family (the basic unit of every known society), for the right to educate our children without unnecessary regulation from the state, for the right to exist as an alternative to conventional schools, for the right of our children to learn in ways that work best for them and according to their own schedules, and for freedom of thought. A lot is at stake. We are a determined, committed group of people.
- We are people of vision. We have learned that most major changes, for good or for ill, take place one small step at a time. We know that our children do not go to bed one night having never looked seriously at a written word and wake up the next morning able to read. We know that reading is a lifelong process that is accomplished one tiny step at a time. Similarly, we know that our basic responsibility for our children and our right to educate them can be taken away from us in the same way, one tiny step at a time. This is why we bother to take the time from our busy lives to work to reclaim and maintain our rights and freedoms.

If we were living in a society that accepted and respected homeschoolers, that viewed parents as the people with primary responsibility for their children, and that trusted parents, then we would not have to be as concerned about small infringements on our rights.

But the bottom line is that we don't live in a society that trusts parents and families. We live in a society in which the government, corporations, and professionals are taking increasing control of people's lives. Not in big, earth-shaking ways. In little bits, just one small piece at a time. So we oppose changes in the homeschooling law that will give others control over our children's educations and then over our families' lives, a little bit at a time. We know this may seem excessive to some who are not homeschooling, but from our perspective it is a reasonable and necessary approach given the developments that are taking place in our society.

Homeschooling in Wisconsin Before the Current Law Was Passed

Homeschooling is the way the vast majority of people have been educated throughout history. By the 1970s and early 1980s, although homeschooling was not illegal (parents have the right to choose an education for their children that is consistent with their principles and beliefs and no state had laws that forbid homeschooling), there were very few homeschoolers in the United States. Families who chose to homeschool in Wisconsin at that time had two options. Either they could declare their home to be a private school and proceed, hoping they would not be challenged by local school officials. Or they could apply to the DPI for approval under the "home tutorial" program.

Homeschoolers who declared their homes to be private schools were on solid legal ground because the statutes governing private schools did not prevent homeschools from being private schools. However, at that time most people were surprised and often distressed by the very idea of homeschooling. "Is that legal?" was a common response to a chance mention of homeschooling. It was challenging to be a pioneer with very little credibility, essentially with no experienced homeschoolers or books on homeschooling to turn to, very few learning resources or published curriculums designed for or marketed to homeschoolers, and children's lives hanging in the balance. "What if homeschooling doesn't work?" wondered some homeschoolers.

Convinced that it was better to stay out of trouble than to have to get out of trouble, the vast majority of homeschoolers maintained a very low profile, mentioning homeschooling as little as possible. Often this required staying indoors at home during "school hours," putting pressure on families and decreasing opportunities to learn in the community. Many children (and parents) found it stressful to be asked common, seemingly simple questions like "What school do you go to?" "What grade are you in?" "Who is your teacher?" In addition, it was difficult to find other homeschooling families, partly because most homeschoolers were so cautious about identifying themselves. There were no homeschooling support groups, no state-wide grassroots organizations, no homeschooling conferences. In an attempt to gain a more secure position, some homeschoolers went to the work and expense of incorporating as a private school, wondering whether this would protect them or simply expose them to school authorities. Vague feelings of not being quite legal and fears of getting caught and taken to court were not uncommon among homeschoolers.

Our family was not one of the "pioneering" homeschooling families. We began homeschooling in 1985, when our oldest son turned six. But as I met homeschoolers with older children and began to hear some of their stories, I started to see how fortunate we were.

One of those stories that gave me a real feeling for what it had been like to homeschool before the current law was in place comes from my friend Jan, whose children are just a few years older than mine. She was a member of a food-buying club, and once a month she and half-a-dozen other women met to unload the truck from the warehouse and divide up 50-pound bags of flour, five-gallon buckets of peanut butter, etc. She was working with another woman in one room of the old schoolhouse where they met, and told her that they were homeschooling. "Oh!" said the other mother, "So are we!" Within a few minutes, five or six other people had heard the word "homeschooling" and come into the room to say "You are homeschoolers? So are we!" These were people who had been working together as part of the buying club for months or years-and none of them knew that any of the others were homeschooling. "At that time you just didn't tell people about it," Jan said.- From Opening Remarks, WPA Conference, 2005

The few homeschoolers who applied to the DPI under the "home tutorial" program often found themselves in even more difficulty. The DPI officials were very difficult to deal with and made ridiculous and impossible demands.

The following stories were among those presented as part of a hearing held by the Wisconsin Senate Health, Education, Corrections and Human Services Committee on March 13, 1984.

• A mother, who happened also to be a certified teacher, felt that the approval process took a long time and the DPI was unreasonable. For example, if at any time during the school day she and her children needed to leave home, she had to notify her local school district. Also, the DPI told her they could visit her home at any time, unannounced, and they did.

• A boy who was having problems in school had a chronic health condition that caused him to miss the equivalent of one year of school over a period of several years. Once he began homeschooling, both his health and his academic standing improved. When he was then tested (at the DPI's request) for learning disabilities, the results were normal. Previous school problems were determined to have been the result of his poor health and resulting absences. However, the DPI ignored this evidence and flatly refused to approve his homeschooling on the grounds that the public school could better provide for him.

• One family was required to hire a certified teacher from five to eight hours a week to work with their children. They were told that their children would have to be tested at the end of the year, and if the test results were satisfactory, they would have no problem being approved the following year. Although the children had had certain remedial problems prior to being homeschooled, all three school-age children tested two years above their respective grade levels at the end of the first year of homeschooling. However, the family was denied approval the following fall because now the DPI was concerned about their physical education, music, and art programs. They were informed that guitar lessons were an unacceptable alternative to owning a piano. When the family agreed to rent a piano, they were told that this was not sufficient even though the mother had studied piano for several years. She was asked if she had ever played in her high school band. She felt that nothing she could say or do would please the DPI.

The testimony presented at the hearing included the experiences of a total of 17 families identified by name who had been harassed or treated unfairly by the DPI during their attempts to get information about homeschooling and/or gain approval of their homeschool from the DPI. A summary was also presented of information from 25 additional families who did not want their names or specific stories included in the testimony because they feared further harassment or denial of approval. Several of these families were required to send the DPI a picture of their children, copies of the floor plan of their house, and the daily personal schedules of both parents from the time they arose in the morning until they retired in the evening, seven days a week. There were even more families who were not contacted due to lack of time before the hearing was held.

For a personal account of homeschooling during this time, see pages 133-135.

Passage of the Current Homeschooling Law in 1984

The situation changed in 1983. A homeschooling family named Popanz had been charged with truancy on the grounds that their home was not a private school. The Wisconsin Supreme Court heard the case and on April 26, 1983, declared that Wisconsin's compulsory school attendance law was "...void for vagueness since it fails to define 'private school.'" (*State v. Popanz*) In other words, the Court ruled that if prosecution of individuals for failure to attend a private school were to be constitutional, the statutes first needed to be changed so people would have a clear definition of a private school. Homeschools were included in this process and definition.

1983 Assembly Bill 887 was drafted by a committee dominated by the educational establishment; no homeschoolers were included on the committee. AB 887 was introduced in December 1983. It defined home-based private educational programs (homeschools) as instruction elsewhere than at school and required that such programs be approved by the DPI as substantially equivalent to a public or private school. It prevented homeschools from qualifying as private schools and made homeschooling unreasonably difficult.

On January 6, 1984, a group of homeschooling parents met in Stevens Point and organized WPA to oppose AB 887 and work for the passage of a more appropriate bill. Homeschoolers worked hard through this new organization to educate legislators and the general public about homeschooling, supply information sheets to people who attended public hearings on the bill, work with others (including small private schools), and build a network of homeschoolers throughout the state who worked together to reclaim their right to homeschool.

The seriousness of the bill and the strength of public reaction to it were demonstrated to the Legislature on January 25, 1984, when 2,500 people, the vast majority opposed to the bill, converged on the capitol for the first public hearing on the bill. Testimony presented the advantages and importance of homeschooling and the need for accountability of homeschooling parents. Further testimony collected by members of WPA was presented before the Wisconsin Senate Health, Education, Corrections and Human Services Committee on March 13, 1984. The testimony clearly showed that having the DPI review and approve homeschools was unacceptable because of the arbitrary and unfair way in which the DPI had dealt with homeschools, as described above.

Several important amendments to AB 887 changed it into a reasonable and workable bill. It was passed by the Legislature and was enacted as 1983 Act 512 on May 10, 1984.

How Homeschoolers Have Worked Since 1984 to Maintain the Law and Develop a Favorable Climate for Homeschooling

Many Wisconsin homeschoolers have worked hard through WPA to maintain the law. WPA has alerted homeschoolers to problems and challenges and provided background information and coordination for much of this effort. Among the accomplishments of homeschoolers working together through WPA are:

August through November 1984—Wisconsin's homeschooling law requires homeschoolers to file a form with the DPI each year. The DPI's first version of form PI-1206 exceeded the law by requiring that homeschoolers have available for review by the local school district attendance officer "materials verifying 875 hours of instruction" and "a course outline listing such items as goals, objectives, instructional activities, printed materials and audiovisuals to document a sequentially progressive curriculum." These requirements clearly are not authorized by law. WPA alerted its members and suggested homeschoolers modify their forms before submitting them to the DPI. In November 1984, WPA initiated and coordinated a meeting among key legislators who supported homeschooling, a representative of small private schools, the State Superintendent of Public Instruction, and a representative of WPA. As a result of this meeting, the illegal requirements were dropped from the form, making it consistent with the law.

January 1986—A resolution requesting legislation to give the DPI authority over homeschools was presented at the Wisconsin Association of School Boards (WASB) Convention. WPA alerted its membership and distributed a fact sheet to convention delegates. The resolution was tabled.

January 1987—A resolution similar to the one from 1986 was again presented at the WASB Convention. This time the factual basis for the resolution was misrepresented, and the resolution passed. WPA defused the resolution by documenting this misrepresentation.

Also in January 1987—The DPI released a report on homeschooling that it had contracted for and that had been written by Henry Lufler. The report was an inaccurate and misleading document intended to discredit homeschoolers. WPA representatives defused the report through radio and TV appearances and press releases. An Associated Press story quoted a University of Wisconsin professor as saying that the Lufler study was flawed and biased against homeschoolers. WPA decided to request that the Wisconsin Legislature audit the report to see whether the researcher followed reasonable management guidelines for oversight and research procedures. Once the Legislature had the audit done, the Lufler report seemed to disappear.

December 1987—WPA suggested ways for its members to react to a case of alleged child abuse involving a homeschooling family. WPA's guest editorial in the Milwaukee Journal stated, "Homeschooling and child abuse are completely separate issues. Attending a public or private school does not protect a child from the tragedy of child abuse, and no homeschooling law based on 'some combinations of pupil testing, teacher certification and curriculum oversight' will either." In a state-wide radio interview, a WPA representative successfully countered an attempt by the State Superintendent of Public Instruction to make a larger issue of this one case.

December 1989—Legislation was proposed that would have increased state regulation of homeschooling in several ways.

1. Homeschoolers would have been placed under the direct control and authority of local public school officials.
2. School district administrators could have taken homeschoolers to court more easily.
3. Homeschoolers alleged to be in need of protection or services (on the basis of a charge of habitual truancy) would have been placed under the jurisdiction of social services.
4. Due process and some civil liberties would have been suspended and families' values, beliefs, life style, and child rearing practices investigated.

WPA developed an accurate and effective analysis of the proposed legislation and published it in the WPA Newsletter. In response, hundreds of homeschoolers and their supporters made reasonable and polite calls to legislators. WPA also made a presentation before an ad hoc legislative committee discussing the proposal, and no legislation was introduced.

May 1990 through January 1991—The continuing attempts to increase state regulation of homeschooling were escalated, despite the fact that the law was working well, there was no evidence that it needed to be changed, and thousands of families were successfully homeschooling. This time it was suggested that the Legislative Council form a special committee to study homeschooling. WPA strongly opposed the formation of such a committee by demonstrating that there was no evidence that such a study was needed and by pointing out that such studies almost automatically lead to the introduction of legislation. Nevertheless, a special committee was formed and spent five months and $100,000 studying homeschooling in Wisconsin. WPA refused to give the committee credibility by sending a WPA representative to serve as a member of the committee, although WPA did provide testimony and information to the committee. Homeschoolers also circulated WPA petitions which over 5,000 people signed to show their support for homeschooling and their opposition to further regulation of private schools, including homeschools. The committee unanimously voted to make no recommendations for changing the homeschooling law, which was highly unusual, since Legislative Council committees such as this almost always recommend legislation. In response, WPA organized a Day at the Capitol (February 6, 1991), attended by over 2,000 homeschoolers and their supporters, to emphasize this important decision and promote communication between homeschoolers and their legislators.

The outcome of the Legislative Council study was especially significant because, at that time, various members of the educational establishment were trying very hard to find evidence of problems with homeschooling. For example:

On March 19, 1990, Anthony J. Kujawa, Administrator of the Baraboo Public Schools, wrote a memo to "WASDA [Wisconsin Association of School District Administrators] Membership" concerning the "Home-based instruction [sic] Survey" of school district members that he had conducted as chairperson of a WASDA committee. Their disappointment in their failure to uncover problems with homeschooling was shown in the comment included in the summary of their study, namely, "I hope that this document will have minimum circulation." Mr. Kujawa refused to make a copy of the study available to the Legislative Council committee studying homeschooling, claiming that the study was a private document.

On June 19, 1990, Herbert Grover, then State Superintendent of Public Instruction, wrote a letter to a local school superintendent in which he said, "I will use the information you have forwarded to me as I continue to do battle with those folks who think that home schooling is a satisfactory alternative to the public schools." (A copy of this letter is included in this chapter.)

On August 8, 1990, the President of the Wisconsin Education Association Council (WEAC), the largest teachers union in Wisconsin with over 75,000 members, issued a memo soliciting evidence of "problems that we have seen with home schooling in Wisconsin. What is needed are concrete examples of students who had a home schooling experience and came back to the public schools with problems that we then had to correct. We are also looking for examples of students who are still in a home schooling situation and not receiving the educational services that every child should expect." (A copy of this memo is included in this chapter.)

The fact that, despite these and other efforts, evidence has not been found to indicate that there are problems with homeschooling is certainly a strong argument against increasing state regulation of homeschooling.

November 1991—WPA informed its members about new "education reform legislation" that would have increased regulation of homeschooling, established portfolios on all three year olds, etc. WPA also coordinated testimony at a hearing on the legislation. About 300 homeschoolers attended. Legislators subsequently agreed to delete all homeschooling proposals from the legislation.

November 1991 through March 1992—WPA informed homeschoolers and other concerned parents about problems with the education reform legislation. Hearings in nine cities were attended by over a thousand people, the vast majority opposed to the legislation. WPA was influential in slowing the passage of the legislation and in having some of the worst provisions removed, including the requirement for portfolios for three year olds.

July 1992—The DPI published a misleading and inaccurate document titled "Frequently Posed Questions and Responses Relating to Home-Based Private Educational Programs" that is sent to local school officials and people who contact the DPI for information about homeschooling. WPA published accurate information in its newsletter. WPA also sent a letter to school officials clarifying information about entry/re-entry, shared services, dual enrollment, and the fact that homeschools are private schools according to Wisconsin statutes.

April 1993—WPA published a fact sheet that outlined problems with outcome-based education (OBE), state goals in education, state-mandated standardized testing, and collaboration. After WPA members and others expressed strong opposition to state goals, the Governor and the State Superintendent of Public Instruction decided not to push to have

Street Address:
125 South Webster Street
Madison, WI 53702
Phone: (608) 266-3390

Mailing Address:
Post Office Box 7841
Madison, WI 53707-7841

Herbert J. Grover
Superintendent of Public Instruction

June 19, 1990

, Administrator
School District of
Route #1
WI

Dear

Thank you very much for submitting the information relative to your experience with home schooled students and home schoolers. I also appreciate you contacting your state representatives so that they will become apprised of the seriousness of this matter. I will use the information you have forwarded to me as I continue to do battle with those folks who think that home schooling is a satisfactory alternative to the public schools.

Any additional information you have gathered, I would appreciate receiving. Thanks again for your help.

Sincerely,

Herbert J. Grover
State Superintendent

HJG:jmh

WISCONSIN EDUCATION ASSOCIATION COUNCIL

Richard W. Collins, President
33 Nob Hill Drive
P.O. Box 8003
Madison, WI 53708-8003
(608) 276-7711 • (800) 362-8034

M E M O

TO: WEAC Board of Directors
Local Presidents
UniServ Presidents

DATE: August 8, 1990

FROM: Richard Collins Dick

Superintendent Grover has, in the last few months, raised the issue of the lack of requirements in the area of home schooling. Bert and other Department of Public Instruction (DPI) employees have received much criticism from home schoolers and their supporters because of the Department's concerns.

It would be helpful if we could provide some examples of problems that we have seen with home schooling in Wisconsin. What is needed are concrete examples of students who had a home schooling experience and came back to the public schools with problems that we then had to correct.

We are also looking for examples of students who are still in a home schooling situation and not receiving the educational services that every child should expect.

Please share this request for information with your members and forward any examples of home schooling problems to me as soon as possible. We will consolidate these examples and share them with legislators and the Department of Public Instruction.

Please feel free to contact me if you have any questions or concerns.

RC:ml

cc: UniServ Directors

the goals enacted into law. WPA members and other parents registered opposition to OBE with the Legislature and at the local level.

June 1993 to 1994—WPA supported legislation which would allow parents of public school students in Wisconsin to have their children exempted from the new state-mandated standardized tests and assessments for fourth, eighth, and tenth graders. Although homeschoolers are not required to take standardized tests, this exemption is consistent with WPA's commitment to reclaiming and maintaining parental rights in education. Also, if testing were ever proposed for homeschoolers, this exemption would be very valuable as a precedent that could be used in claiming that homeschooling parents should be able to have their children exempted from tests as well. The legislation became law in 1994.

January 1994—WPA worked with legislators to ensure that the wording of Senate Bill 89 made it clear that homeschoolers are not subject to the provisions this bill would place on "alternative education programs" in some public schools.

January 1994—The WASB proposed another resolution calling for more regulation of homeschooling. WPA countered this initiative, and it was not adopted by delegates to the annual WASB convention.

February 1994—WPA identified problems with using H. R. 6 (a federal bill) to ask the federal government to protect us since the government doesn't have authority to govern schooling unless we give it to the government by asking for protection.

December 1994—A paper titled "Perspectives on the UN Convention on the Rights of the Child" was written and published by WPA. It pointed out that although this Convention would not become the supreme law of the land in the US, the Convention would still displace families, and it contained other problems.

During 1994—Articles in the WPA newsletter pointed out that the government is not the source of parental rights and that it is dangerous to ask the government to guarantee these rights through state or federal legislation or constitutional amendments.

January through May 1995—WPA brought to light some unreasonable provisions in the Juvenile Justice Code being established by the Wisconsin Legislature and in the recommendations of a Legislative Council special committee studying legislation relating to Children In Need of Protection or Services (CHIPS). WPA held a "Families First" rally at the capitol in March that drew 400 people.

August 1995—WPA alerted members to risks of truancy sweeps authorized by recent legislation.

February 1996—The Library Outreach Program was begun by WPA to make accurate information about homeschooling accessible to more families through public libraries.

February 1996—WPA alerted members to the risks of AB 897, which implied that homeschools are not private schools.

August 1996—WPA informed its members that school districts were sending surveys to homeschoolers and taking other actions that undermine homeschooling freedoms. Suggestions were given for ways homeschoolers can respond.

November 1996—WPA opposed the DPI's proposal for a homeschooling consultant and $10 filing fee for homeschoolers. The proposal was dropped. WPA identified problems with school-to-work programs and academic and performance standards. Members were alerted to problems with the proposed high school graduation test.

March-April 1997—WPA informed members that SB 106, a bill to prohibit habitual truants from homeschooling, would undermine homeschooling freedoms by allowing the government to decide who would be permitted to homeschool. About 400 people attended a hearing on April 9. Sixty people registered to testify against the bill while only the sponsoring senator and one of his constituents spoke in favor. The committee decided not to vote on the bill, which eventually died in committee.

September 1997—WPA informed members of problems with curfews and with surveys and research on homeschooling.

February 1998—WPA sent an open letter protesting a high school mock trial case that presented homeschoolers in a very unfair and negative light. Homeschoolers in Sheboygan were supported by WPA in their fight against truancy sweeps and ID cards.

March 1998—Homeschoolers working through WPA helped defeat a proposed parental rights amendment to the Wisconsin constitution that would have undermined parental rights by asking the government to protect them.

1998—Homeschoolers working through WPA opposed legislation that would have offered homeschoolers small tax credits in exchange for increased government control of homeschooling.

Spring 1998—WPA worked hard to oppose additional truancy legislation. Although the legislation eventually passed, some of WPA's suggestions were adopted.

January—September 1999—Homeschoolers worked through WPA to oppose AB 129, a bill that would have supposedly increased opportunities for the few homeschoolers who want to participate in public school activities, including sports, but that actually would have undermined homeschooling freedoms. A hearing in September was attended by 300 people. Only five people registered in favor of the bill, including its sponsor. AB 129 eventually died.

June 1999—WPA successfully countered the attempt of a Walworth County committee to increase state regulation of homeschooling.

June 1999—WPA members worked to support a much needed increase in state funding for Wisconsin's 17 library systems that handle interlibrary loans and other matters. The funding was increased.

December 1999—Problems with both a report on homeschooling by the Wisconsin Policy Research Institute and a national study of homeschooling were analyzed by WPA as part of its continuing campaign to keep its members and the general public accurately informed.

February 2000—WPA informed its members of problems with a pilot program to supposedly make it easier for homeschoolers to enter the military.

August 2000—In a letter to all school district administrators, WPA provided accurate information on several issues concerning homeschoolers, including truancy laws. Administrators were also reminded that the law requires compulsory attendance, not compulsory education. They were informed that the vast majority of homeschoolers do not want to participate in public schools.

August 2000—WPA corrected a Legislative Reference Bureau (LRB) brief containing inaccurate information on homeschooling and incorrectly stating that homeschoolers supported AB 129. The LRB issued a revision.

February 2000—WPA opposed AB 712, a bill that would have provided a tax deduction of up to $500 for "teacher" supplies bought by a teacher, including a homeschool teacher. The bill died in committee.

February 2001—A national homeschooling organization encouraged homeschoolers in Wisconsin to disobey the provision of Wisconsin's homeschooling law that limits homeschools to "one family unit" and include children from other families in their homeschools. WPA corrected this misinformation by explaining what the law requires. See Chapter 28.

May 2001—WPA worked with other library supporters to get the Legislature to increase funding for library systems that handle interlibrary loans and other matters.

December 2001—At a hearing on providing state funding for four-year-old kindergartens, WPA testified against such funding, arguing that young children benefit from being at home with their families, especially during the early years, the proposal would cost taxpayers significantly, and it could lead to lowering the compulsory school attendance age.

January 2002—WPA led a statewide drive to educate homeschoolers and the general public about the problems with virtual charter schools and to ensure that virtual charter schools were not called homeschools. This would increase the possibility that regulations that virtual charter school students must comply with because they are attending public schools would inappropriately be applied to homeschoolers as well. WPA used postcards and fact sheets, attended meetings, and testified at a legislative information hearing. Responding to WPA's information, hundreds of homeschoolers attended virtual charter open houses to distribute fact sheets, correct misinformation, and report on the meetings. One school district was convinced not to partner with a corporation and run a virtual charter school, but two others agreed. However, very few homeschoolers have enrolled, and homeschoolers working through WPA have convinced people not to call these schools homeschools.

March 2002—WPA again worked to ensure that the Legislature provided needed funds for libraries.

August 2003—WPA opposed the federal Home School Non-Discrimination Act (HoNDA), legislation that would have given the federal government authority over homeschoolers by allowing it to define homeschooling. The legislation was not passed.

December 2003—WPA continued its work to ensure that virtual charter schools were not mistakenly called homeschools. It also helped support groups develop a policy for dealing with virtual charter school students who want to participate in support group activities.

December 2003—WPA further informed its members about the problems with accepting tax dollars, as tax deductions, tax credits, or in other forms, which would give the government a reason and an opportunity to increase state regulation of homeschooling.

December 2003—WPA corrected the DPI's claim that local school districts should be involved in determining grade placement in homeschools.

March 2004—WPA alerted homeschoolers and others to problems with the new public school student identification system that the DPI devised so it could comply with the complex reporting requirements of No Child Left Behind. WPA also explained that homeschoolers should not be included in the database and told homeschoolers how to stay out.

December 2004—WPA researched and informed its members about risks from the increase in mental health screening that is being promoted by drug companies and others and ways to avoid or minimize such screening.

March 2005—WPA corrected inaccurate information about homeschooling from the League of Women Voters and helped prevent adoption of a "Consensus Question" worded to strongly convey the need for increased regulation of homeschooling.

May 2005—WPA added Connections to its annual conference, an area where homeschooling families can gather, learn, play, and meet other homeschoolers. Connections also became a regular feature of the WPA newsletter.

June 2005—Working to help homeschoolers maintain their privacy, WPA gathered resource information and provided a sample letter homeschoolers could send to their local school district administrator explaining that it is illegal for districts to release information about homeschooling students or parents or to use information from homeschoolers' PI-1206 forms, without the parents' written permission, to contact them to gather information or to encourage students to enroll in public school programs. (WPA has posted this sample letter to administrators on its website for homeschoolers to use.)

August 2005—A surprise 4 AM amendment to the Wisconsin budget bill providing tax credits for homeschools and other private schools was adopted by the Legislature as it was hurrying to finish the budget bill. WPA opposed it because accepting money from the government would lead to increased regulation of homeschooling. WPA informed its members through postcards of its problems. Hundreds of homeschoolers called the governor's office asking the Governor to veto the provision, which he did.

December 2005—The federal homeschooling bill called HoNDA was again introduced by the same national homeschooling organization, and again WPA opposed it. As of this writing, the bill has not passed.

Since 1986—WPA has encouraged parents to seriously question the effects of preschool screening and to refuse to have their children screened. (See Chapter 31.) As pressure to have children screened increases, WPA is continuing its efforts to inform and support parents.

Homeschoolers have worked through WPA on the local level and with individuals.

- Numerous local school officials, sometimes apparently misled by information from the DPI, have sent homeschoolers threatening letters that inaccurately claim that they have the right to review homeschool curriculums, visit homeschools, collect personal information from homeschoolers in addition to the information on form PI-1206. WPA has worked with many homeschoolers who have received these threats, resolving issues in favor of homeschoolers and preventing serious problems. In this way, homeschoolers have maintained their rights and freedoms and Wisconsin's homeschooling law.
- Entry/re-entry policies initiated at the local level have often discriminated against homeschoolers. Homeschoolers have worked through WPA to make policies more reasonable.
- A 1988 addition to the truancy law required counties to develop plans for ways in which they planned to deal with truancy. WPA alerted its members who then reviewed many of these plans. Some plans had serious problems, such as the one in Marathon County that would have prohibited homeschooling. WPA members were successful in getting this wording changed. A 1998 law provided a position for homeschoolers on county truancy committees. WPA has provided information and support to homeschoolers serving on these committees.
- Since 1997, WPA has worked with homeschoolers throughout the state to oppose local curfew ordinances and truancy sweeps.
- WPA continues to remind homeschoolers not to comply with demands from officials that exceed the law, whether they be sending surveys to homeschoolers, asking for information in other ways, or imposing new requirements on homeschoolers.

How WPA Gets Things Done

WPA is a grassroots organization whose strength comes from its membership. Its impressive record of accomplishments would not be possible without the hard work of members who have done an outstanding job of homeschooling themselves, provided support and information for new homeschoolers and parents considering this option, communicated with legislators and school boards, appeared in positive media coverage of homeschooling, organized support groups, participated in WPA conferences, made financial donations, and contributed in other ways.

On legislative matters and policy issues, WPA monitors developments in the Wisconsin Legislature and other educational policy making bodies so it can uncover potential problems. WPA then puts the problems in context, informs its members, and provides leadership and direction for needed action.

WPA informs, supports, strengthens, and brings homeschoolers together in the following ways:

- By laying careful groundwork and gathering, analyzing, and publishing background information, WPA prepares its members for challenges or crises before they develop. This information is reported in WPA's quarterly newsletter, which also includes stories of members' homeschooling experiences, in special bulletins, and on its website. WPA also coordinates action during a crisis.

Behind each newsletter and each grassroots action initiated and coordinated by WPA are countless hours of gathering and analyzing proposed legislation, studies, and reports;

working with legislators, Regional Coordinators, and allies; and maintaining a network to provide support and information.

• Since 1984, WPA's Executive Director, Corresponding Secretary, Board of Directors, Regional Coordinators, speakers at conferences and many members have responded to countless inquiries and requests for help from homeschoolers and the general public. WPA has helped many people make the decision to homeschool, overcome difficulties with local officials, and address other questions and concerns.

• WPA has studied various topics such as truancy, accountability, standardized testing, shared services, Outcome-Based Education (OBE), state and national goals in education, collaboration among agencies, tax credits, curfew ordinances, virtual public charter schools, student ID numbers, privacy, mental health screenings, etc. It has provided fact sheets and guidelines for dealing with issues before school boards, legislators, and the general public.

• WPA has emphasized what all homeschoolers have in common, namely, the commitment to maintaining the freedom to choose for their children an education consistent with their principles and beliefs. By refusing to mix causes, become involved in issues not related to homeschooling, or recommend one particular approach to learning, education, or curriculum, WPA has enabled Wisconsin homeschoolers to remain united and work together to protect the freedom of each family to make its own decisions.

• A state-wide conference held in each spring gives information, inspiration, and an opportunity to meet other homeschoolers. Recent conferences have been attended by well over a thousand people.

• Communication among homeschoolers is facilitated through WPA's network of Regional Coordinators.

• WPA works with local support groups. When people join WPA through a support group, part of their WPA membership fee stays with the support group. In this way, homeschoolers can contribute to their local support group at the same time that they become full members of WPA.

PART FOUR

MAINTAINING RIGHTS AND RESPONSIBILITIES

Chapter 21

Eight Principles for Keeping Our Homeschooling Freedoms

Why Work for Homeschooling Freedoms?

Homeschooling is complicated enough when we just focus on our own families. It takes time, energy, and experience to organize our lives around the fact that we are homeschooling, choose an approach that has a reasonable chance of working for each child, gather materials we need, defend our sanity when questioned by friends and relatives, and keep our own doubts under control. Add to this the mid-course corrections that need to be made because we discover a better approach or our children outgrow what we've been doing. It sometimes seems like focusing on our own family is all we have time or energy to do.

But we make a big mistake if we don't put some time and energy into working to maintain our homeschooling freedoms. Unless we work to ensure that state regulation of homeschooling is not increased, critics and opponents of homeschooling (such as some school officials, teachers, judges, social workers, legislators, teachers unions, etc.) are likely to increase it. If this happened, our own homeschooling would be much more difficult. We'd be more limited in what we could do. For example, if we were required to submit our curriculum for review and approval, have our children take standardized tests, or send periodic reports to public school officials, such requirements would no doubt undermine our confidence in our ability to choose an approach to homeschooling that will work for our family and follow it. We would be handicapped and might have to spend more time complying with state requirements and figuring out ways to homeschool according to our principles and beliefs despite the requirements. To be sure, some families homeschool successfully in states that have such requirements, but it is more difficult for them and impossible for others. Homeschoolers who have to comply with public school standards (by adopting a curriculum that public school officials approve, reporting to public school officials, or taking tests based on conventional school curriculum, etc.) often have a more difficult time discovering and creating approaches to homeschooling that will allow their children to interact with the real world and prepare for adult life than they would have if they were free of such regulations and could simply concentrate on their children's education. So it's much better to include plans to work to maintain our homeschooling freedoms with our other activities as homeschoolers. It's a good idea, if we are experienced homeschoolers, to review what we are doing to maintain our freedoms from time to time or, if we are new to homeschooling, to begin working to maintain our freedoms.

But, you may be thinking, isn't maintaining our freedoms dull, onerous, difficult, sometimes hopeless work? Not at all! Most of the time, all that we have to do is to be alert and make sensible choices as we homeschool our families. The few specific steps we need to take, outlined below, are relatively quick and easy, provide great learning opportunities, increase our confidence, and help us learn to take responsibility for ourselves. The work is especially manageable if every homeschooler does their part. The only major time- and energy-consuming work is dealing with a crisis, like countering legislation that undermines our freedom. Fortunately, such crises are much less likely to occur if we (and other homeschoolers) have followed the basic points outlined below.

By following the principles below, we can:

- Ensure that our family can make as many decisions as possible about the approach to homeschooling we choose, the curriculum we use, what we do each day, and what principles and beliefs we share with our children.
- Make important contributions to homeschooling both now and in the future.
- Learn more about taking responsibility for our own lives and activities, lessons we can apply to other areas of our lives.

Perspectives from a Homeschooling Father

Raising a child is a huge responsibility, and we all look for assurances that we are doing the right thing. One way to achieve peace of mind is to hire acknowledged experts to take over some of this task. When it comes to education, these experts are called teachers, administrators, and counselors. But in the name of efficiency, a large group of children is assigned only a few of these experts, so the school's mission is seriously compromised right from the start. The school is like a large and efficient greenhouse, with rows and rows of pots and a carefully set schedule of light, warmth, water, and just the right kind of fertilizer. The problem is that the whole setup assumes that only one kind of plant will be put in all the pots-all tomatoes. So all the pots are the same size and shape and the amount and timing of everything needed for growth has been designed to be optimum for just this one kind of plant. Now some of the plants do turn out to be tomatoes, so they thrive. But others are different: they are daisies or roses, broccoli or watermelon. These are all plants, so they all grow to some extent, but not as much as they could, and some are left permanently stunted.

The homeschooling greenhouse, by contrast, is small and has just a few plants, so each can receive exactly what it needs, when and how it needs it, and so the homeschooled plants grow and flourish and .... But wait a minute, isn't this analogy getting a bit ridiculous? It's too cute and convenient, and applying labels is the mistake schools make. My daughter is not a daisy and my son is not a watermelon. (Sometimes I wish they were, because then I would know exactly what to do to help them grow.) But no, they are much more complicated and interesting. They are mystery plants, unfolding to become something unique in all of history, a one-specimen species never seen before that will never be seen again. And therein lies the challenge: how do I guide the growth of a plant that has no label, does not come with a tag telling its requirements, and, moreover, sometimes changes its requirements without any notice? To properly guide my children, I must be wholly open to their unique set of talents and interests as those grow and change day by day, guiding, responding, suggesting, and even demanding in the ways that will help them realize their potential. . . .

For me, homeschooling is one of life's great truths, the kind of truth that everyone should rejoice in knowing but most seem unable to risk opening their eyes to see. I know that the freedom it gives us, while often daunting, is also a spur to supremely satisfying achievements, both for my children and for me.

But like most valuable freedoms, the freedom to homeschool is fragile and under nearly constant siege. I have not always appreciated this fact. When I first joined the WPA, about 9 years ago, I remember receiving my first issue of the WPA newsletter with excitement. As a neophyte homeschooler, I was hungry for guidance, advice, and reassurance. To my dismay, the newsletter had little of that. Instead it had articles with exciting titles like "Impact of DPI's Inaccurate Document on Home Schooling" and "Effects of Collaboration Plans on Families, Schools, and Society." At that time I knew nothing about the WPA's role in creating our current homeschooling law, and I remember thinking that the WPA seemed practically paranoid in the way it saw threats to homeschooling around every corner.

Over time, my ignorance has turned to appreciation. Gradually, I came to realize that the defining characteristic of homeschooling is not that our children are at home when others are at school, or that our children can study nuclear physics at age 9, or learn to read at age 11, or study creationism, atheism or any other topic that seems worthy and interesting. The essence of homeschooling is not in these particular choices, important though they may be to some families. The essence of homeschooling is in the freedom to make our own choices, the freedom from any state regulation telling us when, where, how, or what in particular we must learn. Protecting this freedom is absolutely essential for us to realize the full benefits of homeschooling. Anything that diminishes that freedom, however slightly, turns me, to that extent, into an unpaid agent of the state, carrying out someone else's directives as to how my children should learn. For example, if I want to have my children take a standardized test, I can do so. But if the state requires me to do so, our freedom is diminished. If the state then labels my son a watermelon based on his test score, our freedom is significantly undermined. If the state then specifies what exactly I must do to turn him back into a tomato, then our precious freedom is largely gone.

So I now see that the WPA's vigilance, which is to say, our vigilance, in protecting this freedom is the most important work it-and we-can do. And, yes, unfortunately, threats to that freedom are around every corner. Having worked as a lawyer, I know how quickly a law, even a seemingly well-established one, can change or even disappear if the powerful are against it and those who rely on it stay silent. I also have seen how an apparently unrelated or innocuous law can be twisted and put to quite different purposes if that suits those who have the power to enforce it. We are fortunate to have this great freedom called homeschooling, but we must keep in mind that we are not lucky to have it. Luck has nothing to do with it. This freedom was won by hard work on the part of many, and it can only be maintained with help from all of us.—From Opening Remarks, WPA Conference, 2002

Eight Essential Principles for Maintaining Homeschooling Freedoms

1. Know what is required of homeschoolers in Wisconsin. Read the explanations of the law in Chapters 3 and 28 so you clearly understand what the law requires and, perhaps more importantly, what it doesn't require. If you don't understand, you will put yourself, your family, and others at risk. If you don't know your rights and exercise them, you will not have them, just as people who don't understand history are doomed to repeat it. No one else, including lawyers, will make sure your rights are respected and protected; you have to take responsibility for them yourself. Finally, if you don't know what the law does and does not require, you will not be able to follow some of the other principles. Have a copy of the homeschooling statute available for reference when you need it. (See Appendix A for the wording of the statutes.) Don't ask school officials or the Department of Public Instruction (DPI) for information about statutes, regulations, or what is required. They often do not know, have been misinformed, misunderstand, or have purposely misconstrued what the statutes or regulations say. Be careful about information from books or websites that cover the laws in all 50 states. They sometimes provide only the text of the statutes without essential information about how they are interpreted or enforced.

2. Do ONLY the minimum required by statute or regulation. If a school official asks or tells you to do more than is required, politely refuse and explain what is required. If they persist, ask them to show you the statute or regulation that gives them the authority to make such a request. Occasionally, it may be tempting to take what seems like the easy way out and do more than the minimum requirements of the law by showing school officials our curriculums, samples of our children's accomplishments, test scores, etc., even though these are not required by statute in Wisconsin. Perhaps we are proud of our children's accomplishments or want to educate officials about homeschooling or show them how well it works. It is very important to resist such temptation. Any action that exceeds statutes or regulations sets a precedent. It's likely to increase demands officials make of us and other homeschoolers in the future. It also may increase the questions, doubts, concerns, and criticisms that officials have about our homeschooling.

3. Don't ignore violations of your rights, even if they seem too small to matter. Major freedoms are often lost one small step at a time. Our failure to respond also encourages those who are limiting our freedoms to continue the process. For example, suppose a school district requires that homeschoolers submit their curriculums for review and approval, even though Wisconsin's homeschooling statute does not give districts the authority to require this. If homeschoolers do not object, in a while the district may ask for periodic reports in addition to the curriculums. On the other hand, if homeschoolers object strongly the first time the district exceeds its authority (either by mistake or in a deliberate attempt to increase its power and authority over homeschoolers), school officials will probably be more reluctant to take on homeschoolers in the future. Responding to small infringements on our freedoms not only prevents loss of freedom in the specific situation in question. It also prevents future, perhaps more serious, challenges. People who think that homeschoolers shouldn't complain as long as no one declares homeschooling illegal greatly misunderstand the importance of choosing an approach to education and a curriculum, allowing children to pursue their interests and learn at their own pace, and offering our children an education consistent with our principles and beliefs rather than those of the public school system.

4. Do not seek or accept benefits from the government, including direct funding, tax deductions, or tax credits, even though it is very tempting to think about benefits for our children or having money to pay for some of the many wonderful but expensive learning resources and opportunities that are available. Benefits or money is especially tempting since most homeschoolers give up income and make a financial sacrifice so parents can be home more with the children. Work to prevent the government from offering money or favors to any homeschoolers. There is no such thing as a free lunch. Such benefits are likely to be followed by increased regulation, especially since the government is accountable for how tax dollars are spent. Even benefits that seem quite safe, like allowing homeschoolers to play on public school sports teams, open the door for increased regulation of homeschooling. Such regulation would apply to all homeschoolers, not just those accepting the benefits. Families could not refuse the benefit and avoid the increased regulation. It is important to remember that there are people and organizations (for example, some school officials, social workers, legislators, teachers unions, etc.) who are looking for opportunities to increase state regulation of homeschooling.

5. Do not push for new homeschooling legislation. Small minorities generally have difficulty getting legislation passed. In addition, once a bill has been introduced, it is very difficult to control. It can be changed so much through amendments that it actually ends up working against the minority that introduced it rather than in their favor. (For example, Wisconsin's good homeschooling law resulted from legislation that was introduced by opponents of homeschooling and then changed through amendments so it ended up supporting homeschooling.) It is easier for a small minority like homeschoolers to gain support from non-homeschoolers when we are a beleaguered minority being put upon by a large interest group like a teachers union than to find support for legislation we initiated ourselves. (This is why we would be unlikely to succeed in getting favorable homeschooling legislation passed if we initiated it, even though we were successful in turning harmful legislation around in 1984.)

6. Stay out of court if at all possible. It is almost always better for homeschoolers to try to reach settlements through negotiation or arbitration than to take cases to court. Rulings in court cases having to do with any topic, not just homeschooling, generally uphold the status quo and support the dominant culture. This means that rulings concerning small minorities such as homeschoolers tend to be biased in favor of conventional education rather than alternatives. We are much better off without any court rulings than with rulings that go against us. Evidence to support this idea can be found in a 1990 report written by Jane Henkel of the Wisconsin Legislative Council titled *Recent Court Cases Examining the Constitutionality of Other States' Laws Regulating Home Schools.* Her report showed that court cases uphold the constitutionality of increased state regulation of homeschooling. The report states, "Special care was taken to attempt to find reported cases striking down state regulations. With the limited exception of cases which found regulations to be unconstitutionally vague, that effort was unsuccessful, which tends to indicate that there are few, if any, such cases." The report is available at www.homeedmag.com/HEM/185/henkel/info_memo90-23.html or from the Wisconsin Legislative Council, One East Main Street, Suite 401, Madison, WI 53703, (608) 266-1304.

7. Understand and apply the distinction between compulsory school attendance and compulsory education. Basically, remember and remind school officials and others that the law requires that young people attend school, but it does not require that they receive an education while doing so. Therefore, it is discriminatory for school officials, judges, court commissioners, and others to insist that homeschoolers demonstrate that their children are receiving an education that is equivalent to the education that children supposedly receive in public schools or that they are at grade level or to penalize them for failing to achieve specific educational goals. For more information on this distinction, see Chapter 22.

8. Work with other homeschoolers. Some of homeschooling's greatest strengths come from the fact that it is a grassroots movement. It becomes even stronger as we communicate with each other, share information and experiences, support each other, and work together to maintain our freedoms.

A good way to work with other homeschoolers is through WPA. WPA is strong because it includes all homeschoolers, regardless of their approach to learning, homeschooling, lifestyle, religion, etc. WPA is strong because it relies on people like you knowing their rights and responsibilities. Our homeschooling freedoms depend on our working together to maintain our homeschooling freedoms. Renew your membership when it expires, make donations, buy copies of this handbook for friends, homeschoolers you know, libraries, etc.; and attend the conference held each spring. It is very important to be organized and prepared before challenges to our freedoms arise.

Also consider joining a local homeschooling support group. If none exists in your area, start one yourself. See Chapter 14.

My homeschooling friend Miranda wrote at age eleven: "Freedom means you can have your own thoughts without having to tell anyone what they are . . . But freedom also means that every choice you make has a consequence . . ."—From Opening Remarks, WPA Conference, 2000

Homeschooling Laws in Other States

Some homeschoolers find it helps them appreciate Wisconsin's homeschooling law and understand why it is important to work to maintain that law if they consider homeschooling laws and regulations in other states. The comments below from homeschooling parents make this point strongly.

From a mother homeschooling in Wisconsin:

The Green Mountains of Vermont call me. They whisper in my ear with watery voices like the mermaids who call sailors to the sea. I am enchanted and cannot resist following.

Yet, as I consider answering their chorus, I realize that Vermont poses formidable challenges for me.

Trying to find some practicality, some tangible reason to go to Vermont, I decided to research the homeschooling laws. The Department of Education sent me a 47-page packet entitled "Guidelines for Home Study in Vermont," which included four forms to fill out and an enrollment checklist. Under General Information, the page begins with this paragraph:

During the 1999-2000 school year, over 1,700 Vermont children received their education at home. Parents or guardians who decide to educate their children at home assume a great responsibility. In effect, they take on the roles of ***teacher, administrator, resource coordinator, librarian, curriculum supervisor and performance evaluator.*** *All this, combined with the everyday tasks of good parenting, presents a formidable challenge, which can be successfully met only by dedicated, concerned parents, willing and able to devote the time and effort necessary to make home schooling work well.* [bold in original]

I am utterly dumbfounded. How dare the government use such a patronizing, and suspicious, tone to describe what I do? But the affront does not stop there. Page after page describes the rules. A homeschooling family must fill out forms. If this is their first year filing, they must fill out a Pre-assessment on which their child is screened to determine whether the child has a disability that would affect the child's learning. They file a Minimum Course of Study describing how they intend to have learning experiences in six fields. Later in the year, the family submits a Progress Assessment on which a child's progress in the six fields is documented in one of six ways. The options include submitting a portfolio of work to the Department of Education, having a certified Vermont teacher assess your child, or completing a standardized achievement test which tests skills in all six fields. Vermont is vigilant for its children!

Next, the packet continues with the consequences and threats. If the Commissioner has significant doubt about whether the Minimum Course of Study is comprehensive enough, s/he may call a hearing. During this time, if your child is not already enrolled in a home study program, enrollment will not occur until after the hearing. This means that your child may be required to enroll in a public or private school.

All of this is shocking to those of us who live in a state with a wonderful homeschooling law. Yet, when I spoke to Vermont homeschooling families, they often told me what a good law they had. Good compared to what? Good compared to having a Department of Education officer visiting once a week to observe?!

Through my research, I feel deep admiration and gratitude for the people who worked so hard to pass this law (and have continued to work to maintain it). These visionaries had wisdom which has benefited me, years later. Their work makes a wonderful environment for homeschooling families, no judges or evaluations or tedious paperwork, only the free joy of growing. I am very, very thankful.

The Vermont mountain nymphs continue to call, but the sensible freedom of Wisconsin's rolling corn fields also has its appeal. As homeschoolers, Wisconsin is the only choice.

From a Wisconsin Homeschooler:

We were living in Minnesota when I learned about homeschooling. In Minnesota you need to test your children every year, which basically means you will be bringing "school" home. Of course, I would eliminate the social pressures of the public system, but we weren't free to expand in whatever direction my child wanted to go or learn at our own pace. Therefore, we chose to move to Wisconsin following his first grade year.

From a Wisconsin Homeschooler:

Meeting families from other states, I am continually struck when people speak of having evaluators look over portfolios as "not much interference" or having to test "only" every other year.

The mother that has made the deepest impression is from New York state. That state has some of the most intrusive laws in the US, AND the county AND the local school district can add to these. The NY family has to supply quarterly reports in each of up to 12 subject areas for each child. Testing is mandatory at certain grades. Detailed descriptions of curriculum and lesson plans must to be submitted for approval-approval that has been withheld for such infractions as not including her telephone number. Tears welled up as she explained that she spent more energy complying than she did working with her children. The decision to submit to such a drain made each year's decision to homeschool a struggle. To think that I frequently grumble about our official attendance record!

My children were not yet born when the fight for Wisconsin's laws was fought in 1984. I thank each of the families who forged a group that could work together no matter why or how each family chose to homeschool. I greatly appreciate the patient hours they spent enabling our homeschooling law to pass. The legacy given my family allows us to proceed in the ways most meaningful to our needs and beliefs. Thank you.

But we cannot rest on their laurels. The New York law replaced an older and now easier law. We need to continue to monitor our local school boards and our legislature. Each of us is able to contribute information about our local situations to the WPA newsletter: articles from our local newspapers about truancy or copies of letters the local officials send to homeschoolers in their districts. Meeting with our state senators and assembly members to explain how well the law serves us is best done when there are no fires raging. We can always take the easiest way out and contribute money so that WPA can work up to a budget on a shoestring.

We must never forget: "Eternal vigilance is the price of freedom."—From Opening Remarks, WPA Conference, 2000

From a mother homeschooling in Minnesota:

Thank you for the WPA newsletters that are part of my WPA membership. I enjoy reading them. Although our family is originally from Minnesota, we were living in Wisconsin when we started homeschooling. We have since moved back to Minnesota but are hoping to move to Wisconsin soon. There is just so much less pressure on homeschoolers in Wisconsin. It really makes a big difference.

Chapter 22

Foundations of Homeschooling Rights and Responsibilities

The following list of foundations of homeschooling rights and responsibilities is based on principles that support reasonable homeschooling laws and oppose unreasonable ones. Many of these ideas also support other important family rights, and the list itself provides a model for ways in which rights can be maintained. A wide range of ideas is presented so that the most appropriate and compelling ones can be selected for a given situation. It is important to understand that we have inalienable rights. These rights are not given to us by the state. We should not look to the state as the source of these rights, we should not give them over to the state, and we should not ask the state to protect them for us through laws or constitutional amendments.

Many of these ideas are based on common sense and a willingness to question assumptions and practices that are widely accepted. They are organized into categories for convenience, but in reality they overlap and interrelate. Some basic ideas are repeated so each category is nearly self-contained and so subtle points can be included.

Legal foundations are listed first because homeschoolers and other parents must deal with them so often. However, legal arguments are often not the most compelling or effective way to support and maintain family rights and responsibilities and should not be heavily relied on. See Chapter 23.

Legal Foundations

(1) Constitutional provisions. The U.S. Constitution does not specifically mention education. This was not an oversight. The idea of including education was discussed and rejected. However, the several amendments to the Constitution guarantee rights that are important to homeschoolers and others.

• **The First Amendment** covers freedom of religion, speech, and the press, and the rights of assembly and petition.

• **The Fourth Amendment** states, "The right of the people to be secure in their persons, houses, papers, and effects, against unreasonable searches and seizures, shall not be violated, but upon probable cause." In other words, the state must have reasonable cause or evidence before officials can enter the houses of citizens or threaten their persons or insist that they answer questions.

• **The Fifth Amendment** protects citizens from being compelled to testify against themselves. It guarantees the right to trial by jury and the right not to "be deprived of life, liberty, or property, without due process of law." The right to due process has been used to protect personal liberties. It is strengthened and given more authority under the Fourteenth Amendment.

• **The Ninth Amendment** says that there are some rights that are retained by the people even though they are not listed in the Constitution. This amendment is important for people who want to reclaim rights that the state has usurped by custom and even by statute, since they can argue that the state had no constitutional basis for taking away these rights in the first place. On the basis of this amendment, courts have recently upheld parental rights in education and rights to privacy.

• **Section 1 of the Fourteenth Amendment** provides civil rights that are very important to individuals, especially minorities.

> **First,** "no state shall make or enforce any law which shall abridge the privileges or immunities of citizens of the United States." In other words, state laws may not take away fundamental privileges (rights and liberties) guaranteed by the U.S. Constitution.
>
> **Second,** "nor shall any state deprive any person of life, liberty, or property, without due process of law." While this provision seems to repeat the language of the Fifth Amendment, here it is establishing that a state government may not do this. For example, a state may not pass laws that deny parents' constitutional rights to choose for their children an education consistent with their principles and beliefs.
>
> **Third,** the section continues, "nor deny to any person within its jurisdiction the equal protection of the laws." Each individual has equal rights and liberties under the law. Homeschoolers can use this in dealings with public school officials. For example, officials cannot legally deny homeschoolers the opportunity to participate in public school programs and activities merely because they are homeschoolers. They cannot legally require more of former homeschoolers who are entering public schools than of students transferring from other schools.

(2) Case law. Rulings by the U.S. Supreme Court and federal, state, and local courts interpret and expand on the Constitution. Important for homeschoolers are the U.S. Supreme Court cases *Pierce v. Society of Sisters* (268 U.S. 510 [1925]) and *Farrington v. Tokushige* (273 U.S. 284 [1927]) in which the court ruled that parents have a right to secure for their children an education consistent with their principles and beliefs and that the state may not have a monopoly in education.

Homeschoolers involved in serious legislative or court battles are strongly encouraged to study the Constitution and case law in greater depth. More detailed information is in John Holt and Patrick Farenga's *Teach Your Own* and John W. Whitehead and Wendell R. Bird's *Home Education and Constitutional Liberties*. Of course there is no substitute for reading the original documents themselves.

(3) Common law. This is a system based on practice, court decisions, and customs and usage rather than on statutes. Some of the legal maxims or principles that are so widely accepted that they do not need to be written down and can be applied to homeschooling in the United States are:

• **"Innocent until proven guilty."** In other words, the state must prove an individual is guilty; individuals do not have to prove they are innocent. Although the state has an interest in ensuring that children do not grow up to be a burden on the state, courts have confirmed that parents have rights in education which the state may not violate. Homeschooling parents should not need to prove themselves innocent (by meeting certification requirements or showing that their curriculum is substantially equivalent to that of a public school or having their children tested) as a condition for exercising their parental rights in education.

• **Rights of minorities.** People cannot be prosecuted or forced to abandon their principles or practices just because the majority of the people do not agree with them or choose their approach. Homeschoolers should not be prosecuted simply because they have chosen an approach to education that is different from that of the majority of Americans today.

• **Civil liberties**. Everyone, including homeschoolers, is entitled to fundamental civil liberties, some of which are described in the Bill of Rights.

• **"Hard cases make bad law."** In other words, a law designed to take care of the worst possible hypothetical case is almost certain to be long, difficult to enforce, and more likely to prevent good people from doing good than bad people from doing bad. It is unfair and solves nothing to punish conscientious homeschoolers by passing an unnecessarily restrictive law that does not solve the problem of high risk children anyway. Such a law would damage the effectiveness of good homeschools.

(4) Limitations of the compulsory school attendance law. Homeschooling laws are based on compulsory school attendance laws. (If there were no attendance laws, the state would have no basis for regulating homeschooling. People who wanted to homeschool would simply not attend school.) However, it is extremely important to realize that compulsory school attendance laws require attendance, not education. See below.

Compulsory Attendance, Not Compulsory Education

Compulsory school attendance laws require that children of certain ages attend school. Wisconsin's law (s. 118.15) reads in part: "Any person having under control a child who is between the ages of 6 and 18 years shall cause the child to attend school regularly." Other laws define what schools must do that is educational, such as having a curriculum that covers basic subjects, but they do not require that students become educated. Additional requirements are placed on public schools that want to receive state tax dollars (which, of course, all public schools do). They often include ensuring that curriculums meet state standards and that students take standardized tests. In addition, schools in states that want to receive federal tax dollars for education (which all states do) are required to meet additional criteria that have recently been greatly increased under the new federal No Child Left Behind law. Private schools that accept state or federal tax dollars or both are also required to meet extra criteria. These extra requirements are not part of the basic definition of a school. Private schools (including homeschools) that do not accept tax dollars do not have to meet them.

The fact that laws require attendance can also be seen in the definition of truancy, which is clearly understood as failure to attend school and is independent of education. Laws don't say, "If you can come up with a better way to learn what you need to know than attending classes, you may be excused today." Laws do say, "If you're not in school and don't have what school officials consider a 'good excuse,' which pretty much means a serious illness, YOU ARE TRUANT, regardless of how smart you are, how much you already know about what's being taught, how meaningless or irrelevant or wrong it is, or how much more you could be learning some place else."

Generally speaking, laws do not require compulsory education. Among the reasons:

- There's no common agreement about what it means to be "educated." Can you dislike math and still be considered educated? What if you have outstanding mechanical or musical abilities but are not drawn to the printed word? Or if you're smart enough to see through the phoniness and artificiality of school and strong enough to protest?
- Even if we could agree on what one needs to know to be "educated," we lack the means to determine what people know. Tests can only cover a tiny fraction of a subject. They measure how well a person performed on a given test on a given day, not how much a person knows. Some know a lot more than tests show; in fact, they know so much that they realize many questions oversimplify and distort things, and they have difficulty choosing a "right" answer because, really, all the possible choices are usually at least a little bit wrong. Some people have different perspectives and life experiences from the test makers, so the questions don't make sense to them. Some excel at things that are not covered on tests (such as creativity, mechanical ability, musical ability, compassion, justice) but not on the things that are included. Some have good test-taking skills even though they don't know much about the material being covered, so they score "too high."
- Perhaps most important, schools apparently aren't capable of educating many students. Obviously, many people don't learn what they need or want to know in school. Assuming schools would educate people if they could, we have to conclude that they can't. Passing compulsory education laws that require education would not change this. Instead, such laws would show schools' failings without providing realistic solutions.

So laws wisely require attendance, not education. If you don't measure up to the schools' idea of what education should be, you and your parents don't have to pay a fine or go to jail. The worst that can happen is that you're not allowed to move on to the next grade, although many, many children keep moving along even though they haven't learned what they were supposed to. Further evidence that laws do not require education appears when parents get really fed up and sue schools for failing to educate their children. In such cases, courts rule in favor of the schools. This is not surprising; in fact, the courts have to rule that way. Think of the chaos and the number of lawsuits that would result if courts allowed parents to sue schools for failing to educate their children!

It is important to note that the lack of laws requiring education plays a major role in maintaining freedom of education for everyone, not just homeschoolers, and thus in maintaining freedom of thought. If laws did require education, the government would directly control education and indirectly control people's thinking, since education has a strong influence on thought and belief.

At this point, the distinction between compulsory attendance and compulsory education may seem obvious. After all, people generally refer to the laws under discussion as "compulsory attendance laws" or "compulsory school attendance laws." Why then aren't these points obvious to legislators, judges, the general public, and even some homeschoolers? Why don't legislators and the general public realize that it is inappropriate to require compulsory education of homeschoolers (or anyone else)? One reason is the wide acceptance of the notions that "real learning" takes place in a conventional school and that the most important things people learn are what they study in school between the ages of 6 or 5 or 4 and 18 or 22 or 26. We homeschoolers have done a lot to reclaim learning, but the task is far from complete.

In addition, our society gives moral authority to people who have important positions in education, such as teachers, principals, school superintendents, etc. Many people look to such officials for the answers to questions about education and trust their responses. However, we need to remember and explain to others that, although these school officials may have moral authority, they do not have legal authority either to define education or to require compulsory education. We can ensure our freedoms by not confusing the moral authority ascribed to them by the larger society with legal authority.

As homeschoolers, we can use the distinction between compulsory attendance and compulsory education in a variety of situations.

• When legislators or others claim that laws are needed to ensure that homeschoolers are being educated, we can explain that compulsory education is not required of students who attend conventional schools, so it would be discriminatory to require it of homeschoolers. We can also explain that requiring compulsory education of homeschoolers would set a dangerous precedent for students in conventional schools and for our society as a whole.

• In situations where social workers, judges, or court commissioners insist that homeschoolers demonstrate that they are being educated and/or are at grade level, homeschoolers can oppose such compulsory education on principle. If authorities threaten to require that homeschoolers attend conventional schools because they are not learning enough or may not learn enough through homeschooling, a similar argument can be used.

• When someone challenges our homeschooling on the basis of our children's failure to learn something important, we can point out that, although we want very much for our children to be educated, the laws do not require education, people don't agree on what it means to be educated, and we don't have a good way to determine what people know. These points may seem formal and stilted, but using them in this way reminds us of their importance and helps other people understand them.

Logical Foundations

1. Laws regulating homeschools are basically unnecessary. The experiences of hundreds of thousands of parents and children have shown that parents are very capable of educating their children at home. In addition, thousands of formerly homeschooled children have entered or re-entered conventional schools without problems, showing that their homeschooling experience did not handicap them or make them unable to handle the work done in conventional schools.

2. Homeschooling laws and regulations do not improve homeschools. Homeschooling works because children and adults are good at learning if given a chance. Homeschools are small enough and flexible enough to meet the needs of individual children and allow them to use their strengths. They work because parents care about their children and want what is best for them. People do not become loving and caring parents or conscientious homeschoolers because there are laws that require them to do this. (See Chapter 18.)

3. Regulations can be harmful to homeschools and limit their effectiveness. Regulations frequently interfere with the alternative nature of homeschools, limit their flexibility, and make it more difficult for homeschools to be effective and meet the needs of families.

4. It is commonly understood and widely accepted by people who think seriously about it that decisions about children's educations should be made by parents. Some parents choose to delegate part of the responsibility for their children's education to a conventional school while others (called homeschoolers) decide to fulfill this responsibility directly themselves.

5. Some proposed homeschooling laws and regulations imply that parents cannot be trusted to homeschool their children. However, parents can be trusted because:

• Homeschooling is a big responsibility and a lot of work. It is not something parents undertake lightly. Free public schools are a readily available alternative for parents who do not want to be strongly involved with their children through homeschooling.

• Children and adults are good at learning if given a chance.

• Homeschooling families regularly interact with other people. Some critics of homeschooling argue that homeschooled children are too isolated and too strongly influenced by their parents. However, rather than being isolated, homeschoolers are active in their neighborhoods, communities, and other groups. Homeschooled children interact with a wide variety of people of differing ages and backgrounds. Also, children are strongly influenced by their parents whether they are homeschooled or not.

6. It is widely held that parents have a stronger influence on children who attend schools than do the schools. For example, when schools are criticized for not educating children, school officials often defend themselves by saying that they are unable to overcome the influence of the children's families and home life.

Writing in the *Journal of Economic Literature* (September, 1986), Eric A. Hanushek critiques 147 studies that sought to correlate student achievement with a wide variety of school-related factors including teacher certification and advanced degrees, curriculum, time on task, quality of the facility, expenditures, class size, etc. The single variable that consistently correlated positively with student achievement was family background. (Most if not all of such research is highly questionable, especially since it relies on standardized tests to measure achievement and equates achievement with learning. However, it is worth noting that much of what passes for the soundest educational research indicates that the family rather than the school correlates positively with academic achievement.)

Historical Foundations

Throughout history, most people have been educated at home. In fact, many people, unfortunately labeled "primitives," have had the good fortune to live rich and full lives without anyone telling them they were being "educated." The first compulsory school attendance laws in the United States were not passed until after 1850, and it was not until after World War II that all states required people of high school age to attend school. Although homeschooling is often labeled "new and different," it is really a very old, traditional, tried-and-true approach to education that works very well.

Some people argue that "times have changed" and that formal education is required in today's highly technological society. However, times are changing so fast that it is most important that people learn how to learn, how to be flexible and handle change, and how to solve problems. Homeschools are especially good environments for this learning.

Unfortunately, the historical foundations of homeschoolers were undermined by a paper by Scott Somerville, an attorney for the Home School Legal Defense Association (HSLDA), a national organization claiming to represent homeschoolers. Somerville presented a paper titled "The Politics of Survival: Home Schoolers and the Law" before the American Educational Research Association on April 11, 2001. The opening sentence was "Twenty years ago, home education was a crime in almost every state." (In response to severe criticism, Somerville has since changed this statement so that the current version on the Internet reads, "…home education was treated as a crime…")

Among the serious problems with this statement:

• The statement is incorrect. Actions are crimes when laws prohibit them. No state had a law outlawing homeschooling. Some had strict requirements for homeschooling, but that did not make it illegal. Most did not have homeschooling laws. An activity is not a crime just because no law specifically gives citizens permission to do it. If that were the case, most of what we do everyday would be a crime, because there are no laws that give us permission to do most of what we do.

• Saying homeschooling was a crime before the 1980s gives the government too much power and weakens our position as homeschoolers. It implies that the right to homeschool comes from the government when it is based on the sources discussed in this chapter. They give homeschooling a much broader and more solid foundation than laws giving parents permission to homeschool.

• Various media pieces on homeschooling have picked up the catchy idea that "homeschooling was illegal," spreading misinformation and undermining the true foundations of our homeschooling freedoms.

Practical Foundations

1. Homeschooling works. See Chapter 18.
2. Homeschooling provides a wide range of learning opportunities and ways of learning. Because of this, homeschools prevent the development of learning difficulties in many children and are good places for children who learn better by doing than through reading and writing, the main approaches to learning offered by conventional schools.
3. Homeschools provide an excellent opportunity to learn about how children learn. By their nature, homeschools can focus on learning and do not need to deal with classroom management and discipline, often the first concerns of conventional teachers. (If teachers cannot control a class, how can they teach?) The flexible, many-faceted, alternative character of homeschools means that they offer a rich opportunity for children to learn in many different ways, and for professional educators to learn from homeschoolers' experiences.
4. Homeschools save taxpayers money. Children who do not attend public schools reduce the schools' expenses.
5. Parents learn a great deal from homeschooling, which is an educational experience for the whole family.
6. Neither lay persons nor professional educators can agree on the best way to educate a child. In the absence of such agreement, a range of alternatives, including homeschooling, must be permitted and ought to be encouraged.

Moral Foundations

1. Our society has an obligation to provide children the education best suited to them as individuals. Since children vary widely in their needs, abilities, interests, and talents, a wide range of alternative approaches to education, including homeschooling, must be available. Families must be able to choose the best alternative for each child. For homeschools to function as true alternatives, they must be free from unreasonable restrictions, some of which would force them to become similar to conventional schools. They would then cease to be alternatives, and children who have difficulty learning in conventional schools would not have as good an alternative.
2. A society that believes in freedom of thought and freedom of belief must allow parents to choose for their children an education consistent with their principles and beliefs and must allow people to choose alternative approaches to education without unreasonable regulation.
3. The family is the fundamental unit of any society. Homeschooling strengthens families. Opposition to homeschooling and unreasonable regulation of homeschooling weaken families. Parents who choose to homeschool are choosing one way of taking seriously their responsibilities for their children. They deserve the support of the larger community.

Religious Foundations

Religious beliefs and arguments are very important to many homeschoolers and provide very strong support for homeschooling. Under our federal and state constitutions, the state may not pass any law or engage in practices that would either establish a religion or interfere with the free exercise of religion, including parents instructing their children in religion.

Specific religious arguments that support homeschooling are not presented here because they are understandably personal and vary widely.

Chapter 23

The Role and Limitations of Laws in Maintaining Rights

Note: Nothing in this handbook is intended or should be taken as the giving of legal advice. This handbook is not intended to substitute for privately retained legal counsel.

Laws matter to us as homeschoolers. Reasonable laws can make homeschooling much more manageable; unreasonable laws can make life more complicated and difficult. Homeschoolers worked hard through WPA in 1984 to gain a good homeschooling law and have worked hard since to maintain it. (See Chapter 20.) As a result, homeschooling in Wisconsin is in a much better position than it would be if the law were less reasonable.

However, it is important to realize that any law, including Wisconsin's homeschooling law, is less than ideal, a compromise, perhaps even a last resort. Ideally our communities and our society as a whole would give families the support they need and would trust parents and children to learn together. Then homeschooling laws would not be needed. Families who chose to homeschool would simply do so, without even filing a form with the state. In addition, having a reasonable law is not enough.

Understanding these points is important, not so we will feel overwhelmed or pessimistic or paranoid, but so we can be realistic about what we need to do to maintain our rights and responsibilities. We need to understand the limitations of laws, even reasonable laws like Wisconsin's homeschooling law. We need to realize that a good homeschooling law is not enough to maintain our rights and responsibilities. It would be nice if we could simply concentrate on our families and our homeschooling activities and assume that Wisconsin's law is all we need. But if we do that, we will lose our rights and responsibilities.

The more we understand about laws in general, as well as the specifics of Wisconsin's homeschooling law, the better prepared we will be to use laws in ways that benefit our families and our communities and that minimize the chances of our losing our rights and responsibilities or getting into legal difficulties. Therefore, this chapter will present general information about how laws work followed by suggestions for ways in which we can deal with the law.

Understanding the Role and Limitations of Law

Laws can occasionally be helpful tools, but they are not an effective way to protect our rights and freedoms, and they can get us into trouble. To retain our rights and freedoms, two things are required. First, we need to recognize the strength we have through homeschooling and communicate to others in our communities how well homeschooling works. (This represents most of the work that needs to be done to keep homeschooling alive, healthy, dynamic, and secure.) Second, we need to work to prevent laws that would increase regulation of homeschooling from being passed in Wisconsin.

Here are some perspectives on how laws work and what limitations they have:

- **Laws do not give us anything we did not already have in nature or under God.** Laws are merely a way of trying to shore up what otherwise might become worse. For example, the homeschooling movement has developed not because of laws but in spite of them. In general homeschoolers have more freedom in states that have not changed their education laws to include homeschooling and in states that have merely clarified their laws to include homeschools with other private schools. Homeschoolers have less freedom in states that have specific laws that supposedly give parents the right to homeschool and at the same time require that parents have their curriculum approved, have their children tested, or submit portfolios or other evidence that their children are learning. Homeschoolers in these states have not gained homeschooling freedoms as a result of these laws. They have lost freedoms and rights that should be theirs as parents. Similarly, the strength of the homeschooling movement does not depend on homeschooling laws. It rests on the rights and responsibilities inherent in being parents.
- Laws give order to a society, but they represent a compromise rather than the best way for people to organize themselves and get along. Ideally people figure out a way to interact based on communication, consensus, cooperation, and trust. However, when a society becomes too large or takes wrong turns, laws become necessary. Therefore, **laws are not a sign of strength, although they can be a protection for those who would have even less standing without them.**
- **The law is a process, not a finished product.** A law sets a direction, but it does not make a once-and-for-all final decision. It is not "set in stone." In a very real sense, a law is only worth the value of the paper it is printed on, because the way a society interprets and enforces a law determines its real meaning and value. A law does not have much effect until someone enforces it or exercises the rights it guarantees. There are laws which are meaningless because they are not enforced. On the other hand, sometimes a law is passed which is unconstitutional or violates a basic right. If no one objects, this law can be enforced and become accepted practice. It is part of our responsibility as citizens to make sure that laws that are passed are fair and consistent with basic rights. The law can be a great ally, but it is just a tool which cannot do anything for us unless we use it.
- Laws are limited in what they can achieve. **Laws can only govern behaviors that can be described, observed, and evaluated.** Laws do not simply state that people should "drive

safely." Such a law would require continual subjective judgments on the part of drivers, and enforcing it would require similar judgments by the police. However, determining the right of way at intersections can help prevent accidents. Therefore, signs and signals are used to increase safety, and violations are punished.

However, some things that cannot be controlled by law can definitely be encouraged and made easier by passing supporting laws. For example, it would not make sense to pass a law requiring that homeschooling parents "do a good job." But it is much easier for parents to do a good job when homeschooling laws allow them the flexibility they need to meet their children's needs, and allow children to learn at their own pace and in their own way. It is harder for parents to do a good job when laws require that they have their children tested.

• **Laws cannot protect parental rights.** Parental rights do not come from the state. But if a law were passed in which the state supposedly protected parental rights, it would inevitably imply that those rights came from the state. In other words, parents have to surrender their parental rights to the state before the state can pass a law that supposedly protects them. In the process, parents lose more than they gain. See Chapter 34.

• **Laws are made by the most powerful segments of a society and reflect their values and goals.** It is very difficult for a small minority that does not have much money or power (like homeschoolers) to get favorable laws passed, especially if that minority is seen as a threat to a larger, more powerful group (like the educational establishment). The few laws that guarantee the rights and freedoms of minorities and less powerful people come about only because these people get fed up. Then they work together to secure such laws.

Therefore, it is better to work not to have laws that seem to benefit homeschoolers introduced in the legislature. It is difficult to get enough support to pass such laws, and they often backfire because additional homeschooling requirements are added to the bills. Homeschoolers in Wisconsin have maintained our freedom since the reasonable homeschooling law was passed in 1984 by resisting any change in that law and by resisting the temptation to seek legislation that would give us supposed benefits like vouchers and tax credits at the cost of our freedom. See Chapter 24.

Reading and Interpreting Laws Ourselves

One of the best ways to increase our ability to use laws in ways that are as positive and constructive as possible is to read and interpret the texts of laws. Among the reasons this is important:

• **Usually the best way to understand a law is to read it ourselves.** Then we can present ourselves, and if necessary defend ourselves, with greater confidence. If we are in a conflict, our confidence makes a big difference in how we act and how our adversary reacts.

• **We may be in a better position to find the most important parts of a law than anyone we could hire or turn to.** Self-interest is an excellent motivator. It takes time, careful attention to detail, and creative thinking to interpret a law. The people most directly affected may be the most willing and strongly motivated to do this. Also, doing at least part of our own research may be the only affordable option, given the cost of attorneys' time. Experience and legal training may sometimes be useful. But in reading homeschooling laws, for example, our experience with and commitment to homeschooling may be as valuable as (or perhaps even more valuable than) the experience of an attorney who has read a lot of other laws. (If you are considering working with an attorney, see "Working with an Attorney" below.)

• **If we don't know what our rights are, we cannot be sure we are getting the protection we are entitled to.** We are literally "at the mercy of the court." For example, the Wisconsin law that requires that children have certain immunizations before entering school, also specifies that this requirement can be waived if parents object to immunizations "for reasons of health, religion or personal conviction." However, schools often do not tell parents this. If parents are not familiar with the law, that right does not exist for them. The phrase "exercise one's rights" is very appropriate. Like muscles, rights must be exercised or they become weaker. Before we can exercise our rights, we have to know what they are.

• Few laws are so simple that there is no question as to their intent or application. Most laws need to be interpreted before they can be obeyed or enforced. (This is more often a result of the inherent complexity of life, including political compromises made in passing laws, than a reflection on the verbal skills of those who draft laws.) Our familiarity with issues, details, and nuances increases our ability to apply a law to our particular circumstances. **To ensure that the interpretation given to a law will be most beneficial to us, we must read and interpret it ourselves.**

In short, in a government based on law, citizens are the custodians of the law. If we simply accept legal experts' interpretations of laws or if we allow school officials to enforce their interpretations (which undoubtedly will be different from ours), we will lose our rights and responsibilities.

In reading laws, it helps to accept the fact that laws are not designed to be as accessible as possible to ordinary citizens. They are not written in the vocabulary that most people use for casual conversation, but they are written in English. A good place to start reading laws is in Appendix A to this book, which contains Wisconsin statutes that are important to homeschoolers. It is also good to read proposed legislation (see Chapter 30) and court cases that have interpreted and thus shaped laws. More detailed and extensive legal research is based on a logical system and does not require that one be a trained lawyer.

Two books on locating and reading laws are Stephen Elias's *Legal Research: How to Find and Understand the Law* (Berkeley, CA: Nolo Press, 1982) and *Using a Law Library,* published in 1983 by HALT, Inc. Two books that have excellent information on homeschooling laws and their foundations are John Holt and Patrick Farenga's *Teach Your Own* and John W. Whitehead and Wendell R. Bird's *Home Education and Constitutional Liberties: The Historical and Constitutional Arguments in Support of Home Instruction.*

A word of caution: Don't use your confidence in working with the law to jump into a court case. See "Avoiding Couirt Cases" below.

Participating in a Grassroots Organization

Developing and maintaining a strong grassroots organization like WPA is one of the most effective ways for a minority to deal with laws. Through such an organization, a variety of people can come together to work toward their common goal of maintaining rights and responsibilities. By making it clear that the organization is based on the work and commitment of its members, and not on the actions of a few key leaders, a grassroots organization has a solid foundation. Sometimes the presence of a strong grassroots organization that is recognized and respected by the legislature is enough to discourage the introduction of unfavorable legislation that might otherwise be introduced.

Members can watch for developing legislation that would affect them negatively and work to defeat or change it. They can develop interpretations of laws that are as favorable to them as possible and work together to have their interpretations accepted by others. Members can anticipate upcoming issues and problems and stay one or two steps ahead of the opposition by having an effective network of active grassroots members who pick up issues long before they become widely known in the state capitol or in the media. Members can support each other, exchange information, plan strategies, and work to foster a positive climate of opinion in their state.

Watching Developing Legislation and Acting When Appropriate

The more favorable laws are in the first place, the easier they are to work with. Therefore, it makes sense to review legislation being considered by the legislature and work when appropriate to support, change, or oppose it. One of the most effective ways to monitor legislation is through a grassroots organization. For example, WPA tracks legislation in Wisconsin that will affect homeschoolers and reports to members in its quarterly newsletter. Minorities like homeschoolers are also more likely to be effective when they work together through an inclusive statewide organization like WPA.

Using Our Own Abilities Instead of Relying on Outside Experts

It is important to realize that we homeschoolers are our own best experts. We rely on our own knowledge and abilities, which are considerable. We do our own careful ground work, we watch for new developments, we fight our own battles, and we live with the results.

Of course this kind of "stubborn independence" can be carried too far. There is a lot we can learn from the ideas and experiences of other homeschoolers around the country. WPA is in regular contact with many homeschooling organizations with a wide variety of perspectives, and we regularly exchange information with them.

This kind of communication is positive and helpful and benefits us all. But we need to be careful not to become dependent on people (or organizations) working on the national level who would come in and "solve" our problems for us. Such reliance would be unwise and would not work in Wisconsin because:

- Using outside experts decreases the commitment and energy that members of a grassroots organization put into the work that must be done, thus weakening the organization.
- Much of WPA's success depends on the reputation we have established in Wisconsin. We are seen as a responsible, informed, and committed group of people. We have many contacts throughout the state with whom we can work on a personal basis. Outside experts simply don't have the time or ability to do this kind of careful groundwork.
- We can sometimes work with legislators who strongly disagree with us because, underneath our differences, we all live in Wisconsin and we all care about its future. (Of course our commitment to Wisconsin is not our highest commitment, but it is important.) Obviously outside experts cannot have this kind of a bond with legislators, simply because they don't live here.
- Legislators view outside experts differently than they view us, their constituents. Once experts are called in, a legislator's role shifts from that of a champion of minority-interest constituents to a judge of claims made by experts in response to other experts.
- Outside experts who emphasize one particular perspective or belief can seriously divide a movement. Once a minority grassroots movement has been divided, it loses the best chance it had to achieve and maintain its goals.
- Sometimes outside experts' personal experiences (such as the way they handled a similar problem in another state), training, or self-interest give them a perspective that may be inappropriate to another state.
- When outside experts come into a state, the result is generally more restrictive laws than when outside experts are kept out of a state. Experts often have a vested interest in creating controversy and restrictive laws because then they will have more clients and more business.

Avoiding Court Cases

WPA strongly recommends that homeschoolers stay out of court whenever possible for several reasons:

- Court cases are often long, very costly, usually require trained legal help to handle logistics and technicalities, and can have very serious outcomes. People involved in court cases are in vulnerable positions and are open to attack by adversaries. It is better not to initiate a court case than to present one poorly and lose. Before voluntarily getting involved in a court case, homeschoolers should take a long hard look at questions such as: Do we have the resources necessary to undertake this case and handle it well? Is there any other way this question or difficulty could be resolved? Is the case worth the time, energy, and stress involved? Is there a reasonable chance of success? Similarly, if we find ourselves in a situation in which we may be taken to court, we may want to work for an out-of-court settlement (unless, of course, this would require compromising important principles).

• It is unrealistic to expect courts to make clear-cut, black and white, once-and-for-all decisions that will resolve complicated issues and be fair to everyone involved. To be sure, courts can sometimes be helpful in protecting innocent people and resolving conflicts without bloodshed. But we cannot protect homeschooling from unnecessary and unreasonable regulation by the state by working through the courts or through the legislature when the courts fail us. This leads to the mistaken idea that lawyers and other professional experts can solve our problems and protect our rights.

A much better approach is for citizens to take responsibility for solving their own problems in ways other than by taking cases to court. Citizens understand clearly what is at stake, are strongly committed to getting the best possible outcome, and will be in a position to do the necessary work to follow up and maintain the gains that have been made and the positive agreements that have been worked out. In other words, informed citizens can do a much better job of protecting their rights and freedoms than can lawyers working for pay.

Lawyers and courts have an adversarial approach to resolving conflicts. Sometimes it works well, but the vast majority of conflicts that arise in our lives are resolved outside of courts. People explain their positions to each other and reach a consensus or work out a compromise or agree to disagree. We need to move homeschooling issues out of the courts and work harder to deal with them in other ways such as through grassroots organizations and educating the general public about homeschooling.

• Courts reflect the prevailing opinion of the community, which often is not supportive of homeschooling. Because the idea of homeschooling is relatively new to many people and homeschooling is not well understood, homeschoolers often encounter prejudice and misunderstanding when their case is heard.

• Courts operate to protect the status quo and the power structure in our country, as well as protecting the innocent. Since homeschoolers are not part of the current power structure and in fact are often seen as a threat to it, we cannot expect many court cases to be decided in our favor.

• The consistency with which homeschooling court cases have been lost during the past 20 years should serve as a strong indicator that the courts are not the place to win or maintain basic homeschooling freedoms. (Note: Some lawyers have claimed "victory" in cases which many homeschoolers feel have clearly been lost. Some claim victory in nearly any case in which the court does not jail the parents and/or strictly forbid the family's homeschooling, while many homeschoolers consider a case lost if it upholds unreasonable and unnecessary state regulation of homeschooling.) Except for a few state supreme court cases around 1980-86 that ruled that state laws were too vague, federal district courts, federal courts of appeals, and state courts of appeals (including state supreme courts) have all upheld the constitutionality of state laws regulating homeschooling. Arguments concerning the right of free exercise of religion, the right of equal protection and due process, and against self-incrimination and unreasonable searches have all been unsuccessful in convincing the courts to rule against state laws regulating homeschools.

As a result, we now have a body of precedent-setting case law that says that it is constitutional for the state to review and approve homeschooling programs or to require instructor qualifications and/or standardized testing. This collection of cases does not help the cause of homeschooling in the courts, legislatures, the media, or the general public.

(Note: More information about court cases involving homeschooling is available in a 62-page document *Recent Court Cases Examining the Constitutionality of Other States' Laws Regulating Home Schools,* by Jane R. Henkel, Senior Staff Attorney for the Wisconsin Legislative Council, November 21, 1990. Copies are available at no charge from the Wisconsin Legislative Council, Post Office Box 2536, Madison, WI 53701-2536; 608-266-1304. This report states: "Special care was taken to attempt to find reported cases striking down state regulations. With the limited exception of cases which found regulations to be unconstitutionally vague, that effort was unsuccessful, which tends to indicate that there are few, if any, such cases." [page 2].)

In addition, it generally does not work to try to overcome the negative effects of unfavorable court decisions by introducing new legislation. In states such as Pennsylvania, New York, and New Hampshire, this strategy backfired, resulting in very demanding state laws that regulate homeschooling unreasonably. This strategy seldom advances homeschooling freedoms and often leads to further restrictions, more court cases, and more business for lawyers.

• States that have unfavorable homeschooling laws are those that also tend to have more court cases, and so the vicious circle continues. The way to stop it is to work at the grassroots level, avoid going to court, avoid introducing legislation, learn to live with ambiguity, and find quiet and effective ways of maximizing freedom by interpreting the laws ourselves and helping other homeschoolers do the same.

• An individual or a court case may become a pawn of more powerful individuals or institutions that have a very different agenda than ours. This is a risk especially for people who have gotten involved in a case to prove a point. Sometime their efforts backfire as the issue for which they were fighting is lost or becomes distorted or is used to support an end very different from the one they envisioned.

Civil Disobedience

People who find that their principles and consciences will not allow them to comply with a given law and who therefore choose to practice civil disobedience can greatly reduce the change that they will end up in court. Some people get others to also practice civil disobedience. In this way, they show that their action is not that of a single misguided individual and that if the state is going to prosecute, it will have to deal with more than one or two people. Some people develop strong, easily understood reasons to justify their action. Then they increase their base of support by sharing these reasons with the media and in their community. Some people ensure that their act of civil disobedience draws public attention and is structured to win public support.

Alternatives to Working With an Attorney

Many homeschoolers have been pleased to discover that they could handle situations that they at first thought would require an attorney. They have been able to gather information from other homeschoolers, often working through WPA to find the people and information they needed. They have learned from the experiences of other homeschoolers and gained confidence from their support. For example, many homeschoolers have used the sample letters in this handbook to respond to demands from school officials that exceeded the authority these officials have been given under the law. Homeschoolers who resolve potential problems with officials in this way gain confidence, set a good example for other homeschoolers, and save on legal bills. Often they end up in a more secure position as well, because officials are generally less likely to bother people who are working from a position of strength and can defend themselves.

Mediation: Alternative Dispute Resolution

Increasingly people are choosing to resolve conflicts or settle disputes through mediation. Mediation involves disputing parties working together toward a resolution by listening to each other, trying to understand each others' perspective, and reaching an agreement everryone accepts. The discussion is facilitated by a neutral third party called a mediator. While mediation is not litigation, it is recognized by the courts in Wisconsin.

For more information on the process of mediation and ways to find a mediator, contact the Wisconsin Association of Mediators, P.O. Box 44578, Madison, Wisconsin 53744. Phone 608-848-1970. www.wamediators.org

Working With an Attorney

If you are thinking about working with an attorney, the following suggestions may be helpful:

- Consider the alternatives above.
- **It is important to find an attorney who accepts and is willing to work for your principles, beliefs, and premises.** For example, if your major concerns are protecting parental and family rights and preserving the unity of the family, make sure your attorney will work with you for this. It is also very important that your attorney accepts and is prepared to defend your approach to homeschooling. This may be especially important if the attorney has experience with homeschooling, either personally or professionally or both. Homeschoolers have many different approaches based on their beliefs, philosophy of education, educational methods, etc. It may be a real problem to try to work with an attorney whose approach to homeschooling differs from yours. For example, some homeschoolers think standardized testing is a reasonable way to evaluate children, while others strongly oppose testing. It might not work well to have an attorney who accepted standardized testing defending homeschoolers who were fighting a court order to have their children tested.
- **The attorney needs to understand your local community.** Judges consider community practice in making their decisions, and the climate of opinion within a community can influence the outcome of a case. This is why local attorneys often are a better resource than "outside experts."
- **Make sure the attorney will listen to you, accept your input, and let you make decisions.** You are looking for an attorney who will work with you, not an expert who will simply take over the whole case and run it for you. Your involvement is crucial because you are the one who is most directly involved in the case and its outcome and because you are the one who knows what direction you want to go.
- **It is not essential that you find an attorney who has been personally involved in homeschooling** or who has read homeschooling law or worked with homeschooling cases. Your ideas and understanding of the law, plus this handbook and the resources it cites, are what an attorney needs to get started. (In fact, this handbook could save you significantly on legal fees if you were involved in a court case. Without it, an attorney would need to search for the information and develop the legal interpretations and strategies presented and referenced here.)
- Consider giving your attorney a copy of this handbook. Point out sections that are particularly important to you.

The information in this chapter about the complications, limitations, and risks of relying on laws may leave readers wondering what we can do to maintain our homeschooling rights and freedoms. In addition to taking responsibility for ourselves and working with other homeschoolers through WPA, we can work to gain support for homeschooling by educating the general public about homeschooling, working to win the hearts and minds of the people. Ways to do this are discussed in the following chapters.

Chapter 24

Issues Homeschoolers Need to Know About

These issues have been simmering for varying lengths of time. When they become active, front burner issues, you will need up-to-date information from WPA newsletters, special bulletins, fact sheets, and the website. Meanwhile, your help is needed to prevent them from becoming more serious. With the information below, you will be prepared to respond promptly whenever one of these issues comes up in casual conversation, at a support group meeting, on a radio talk show, in a media piece, in a speech by a public official, or wherever. If we all do what we can to educate other homeschoolers, legislators, the media, and the general public, we will have a better chance of preventing or at least minimizing problems from these threats to our homeschooling freedoms.

Background Information

• For our society to remain free, we citizens need to be alert for threats to our freedom. "Eternal vigilance is the price of liberty." We homeschoolers need to be especially concerned about the potential loss of our homeschooling freedoms because opponents of homeschooling are looking for opportunities to increase government regulation of homeschooling. We have to work to maintain our freedoms in the face of one of the most powerful interest groups in the US: the education establishment, which includes teachers, school administrators, teachers unions, textbook publishers, school boards, and others. Some issues discussed here might not be problems if we did not have active adversaries. But because of our position, we need to be extra alert, some people might even say paranoid. We need to bend over backward to make sure we don't give opponents of homeschooling opportunities to increase regulation of homeschooling.

• Parents have the right to educate their children according to their principles and beliefs. This right comes from nature or God, not from the state. We do not need laws to give us this right. We do need to prevent laws from being passed that would take this right away or significantly decrease it. And we need to educate the general public about homeschooling. In the long run, we must win the hearts and minds of the people in order to maintain our homeschooling freedoms. We need to be able to explain issues clearly and convincingly. Also, some of the points below include discussion of potential harmful backlash against homeschoolers.

• The general public is accustomed to public schools being regulated by the state, so they tend to assume that homeschools should be regulated as well, "just to be sure kids are getting a good education." They think homeschoolers who are doing a good job should have nothing to fear and should be willing to comply with regulations and have the state check up on them. Non-homeschoolers don't usually stop to think about all the reasons why public school standards should not be applied to homeschools, which are very different from public schools. (Homeschools have few students, so they can have a more flexible curriculum and allow children to learn at their own pace. The teacher knows them all well, so there is less need for testing. Homeschools don't receive tax money, so they don't have to answer to taxpayers.)

• Increased regulation by the state would affect what we homeschoolers do each day. It would force homeschools to be more like public schools in what knowledge, skills, and attitudes children are expected to learn, how they are expected to learn, what principles and beliefs they are expected to choose, etc. It would be a blow, especially to families who chose to homeschool because they wanted something different from the atmosphere, values, beliefs, and approaches to learning of the public schools.

• Avoiding or preventing state regulation of homeschooling is difficult to do, but it is much easier than getting rid of existing regulations. As pointed out above, the general public thinks that state regulation of homeschooling is not unreasonable, making it very difficult for homeschoolers as a small minority to find enough power and support to eliminate or improve existing regulations. New York and Pennsylvania have had very difficult homeschooling regulations since the 1980s; homeschoolers have been unsuccessful in getting them changed.

• The legislative process is very difficult, if not impossible, to control. Once a bill is introduced, it can be drastically changed through amendments. Politics is messy. An old saying goes something like, "Two things you don't want to watch being made are sausage and legislation." Homeschooling legislation is especially risky because homeschoolers are a small minority that is opposed by large and powerful interest groups.

Several points are given in response to each issue so you can pick the one or ones that are most likely to be understood by the person with whom you are talking.

At the end of this chapter are suggestions for what we can do to minimize the problems caused by any or all of the issues discussed below. Although homeschoolers are a small minority, we have considerable strength when we work together on the grassroots level through WPA. Two examples: First, we managed to get one of the best homeschooling laws in the country in 1984, and we have managed to maintain it despite numerous challenges since then. (See Chapter 20.) Second, when corporations and school districts began marketing virtual charter schools in 2002, they referred to the schools as "homeschools." Homeschoolers working together through WPA countered this, and soon marketers were saying, "These are not homeschools."

Tax Credits and Other "Favors" From the Government

The problem: If the federal or state government used tax credits to reimburse homeschoolers for certain educational expenses approved by the government, it would be able to increase government regulation of homeschooling, force homeschools to become more like public schools, and decrease our homeschooling freedoms. Unfortunately, some individual homeschoolers and the Homeschool Legal Defense Association (HSLDA), a vocal national organization whose members are a small minority of the homeschooling population, support tax credits.

• At first glance, the idea of having more money for our homeschooling expenses may sound tempting. What homeschooling family wouldn't welcome more money to spend on learning resources, classes, travel, and other educational opportunities? But recipients of government money are held accountable by the government. (For example, taxpayers want assurance that recipients of road contracts build satisfactory roads.) Therefore, government money would mean increased regulation of homeschools. There is no such thing as a free lunch.

• Experience shows tax credits don't work well for homeschoolers. As of March 2006, only two or three states had tax credits for homeschoolers. One of them, Minnesota, already had very demanding homeschooling regulations, including required standardized testing and reporting to school officials. In Illinois, homeschoolers receive little benefit from the tax credits and face the threat of regulation because of them.

• Governments use money to gain authority they don't otherwise have. For example, during the 1970s the federal government wanted states to reduce the speed limit to 55 miles per hour, but it did not have the constitutional authority to order them to. So it threatened to deny federal highway construction funds to any state that did not reduce its speed limit. Similarly but on a much smaller scale, governments could use money in the form of tax credits to get homeschoolers to become more like conventional schools by only allowing tax credits for educational expenses approved by the government. This would be a subtle and clever way for the government to gain control of homeschools.

• Tax credits are only reimbursements. They are not a means by which the government gives money to families so they can spend it on education. To receive tax credits, homeschoolers must first have money available and choose to spend it on expenses the government has approved.

• Tax credits mean the government collects less tax money, so they indirectly cost the government and taxpayers money. Therefore, they are designed to sound like a good deal but limit what anyone can receive, to prevent the government from losing too much money. Usually only people whose income is below a certain level can qualify for them. Often these people don't have enough money to spend in the first place so they can get a tax credit. People who can afford to spend a significant amount of money on education in the first place usually have incomes that are too large for them to qualify for tax credits.

• Religious materials generally do not qualify for tax credits. Therefore, religiously based curriculums in basic subjects such as reading and math undoubtedly would not be eligible for tax credits. This could include such popular curriculums as A Beka, Alpha Omega, Bob Jones, Christian Liberty Academy, Christian Light, etc.

• Some supporters of tax credits argue homeschoolers are entitled to tax credits because we pay taxes that support public schools our children do not attend. However, citizens pay taxes to make services available to people who need or choose to use them. As homeschoolers, we pay for many services that we don't plan to use in addition to public schools, like jails, fire departments, police departments, etc.

• Some supporters of tax credits claim that homeschoolers do not need to be concerned because tax credits are not mandatory, so homeschoolers can decide not to claim the tax credits. Our concern is not being forced to pay lower taxes! Experience in other states and countries has shown that when homeschoolers become eligible for benefits, the benefits open the door to increased regulation of homeschooling, the regulations are applied to all homeschoolers, not just those who accept the benefits. In other words, if tax credits led to increased regulation of homeschooling, we would not be able to avoid the new regulations by refusing to accept the tax credits.

Sports

The problem: Some homeschooling athletes want to play on public school sports teams. Their desire is understandable, but their participation in public school sports would jeopardize the homeschooling freedoms of all of us.

• Wisconsin Interscholastic Athletic Association (WIAA) rules limit participation in school sports to students who are enrolled full-time as defined by the Department of Public Instruction (DPI). If homeschoolers were allowed to play on public school sports teams, they and other homeschoolers would be forced to comply with the DPI's definition of a full-time student, which would give the DPI authority over homeschoolers.

• Allowing homeschoolers to play on public school sports teams would offer a golden opportunity to increase regulation of homeschooling. Athletes who attend public school are required to maintain a certain grade point average, study a curriculum that meets state standards, and take state-mandated tests. To be fair, homeschoolers would undoubtedly be required to do the same. Also, if they weren't, public school athletes who could not meet the academic requirements could simply start homeschooling and continue to play sports.

• Because of the pressure to increase state regulation of homeschooling, the regulations devised for homeschoolers playing on public school sports teams would be applied to all homeschoolers and not just to athletes.

• Backlash against homeschooling could result from homeschoolers playing on public school sports teams. Making the team and being a starter are highly competitive. Some people would resent having kids who didn't even attend the school filling prime and highly desired spots on sports teams.

See the section on Sports in Chapter 32.

Media Reports of Alleged Child Abuse

The problem: Once in a great while, a media report of a tragic case of child abuse in a family who claims to be homeschooling may prompt a call for legislation to increase regulation of homeschooling.

• Child abuse is not a homeschooling issue. In most, if not all, cases, serious problems preceded homeschooling, and the family had not been homeschooling for long. In some cases, it is unclear whether they were officially homeschooling or only claimed to be. Some may have been pushed into homeschooling.

• If a homeschooling family is suspected of child abuse, the problem can be handled as any other abuse case. Wisconsin already has statutes that provide for prosecution of parents who are charged with abusing their children. Child abuse and homeschooling are separate issues. No public, private, or homeschooling law can protect children from the tragedy of child abuse.

• Some people claim that if state regulation of homeschooling were increased, state officials would be able to identify homeschooling families with serious problems and prevent tragedy. However, in most cases, the family had already been reported to social services. If the family was officially homeschooling, this had not prevented them from being reported. School officials are not the only people who can and do report potential problems to social services. Family members, neighbors, members of the community, health care workers, etc., make such reports, and some professionals, such as physicians, are required by statute to do so. Increased regulation of homeschooling would not prevent child abuse, just as regulation of public schools does not prevent child abuse.

• Increased regulation would undermine the effectiveness of many homeschools that are now helping children learn and strengthening families.

• Any group is likely to have a very few members with serious problems. An old legal maxim states, "Hard cases make bad law." In other words, a statute designed to take care of the worst possible case is almost certain to be long, difficult to enforce, and more likely to prevent good people from doing good than bad people from doing bad. It is unfair and solves nothing to punish conscientious homeschoolers by passing statutes that do not solve the problem of high-risk families anyway.

• Homeschoolers continue to be a target of the mainstream media. Most articles on homeschooling are positive, which is not surprising since the vast majority of homeschoolers do very well. However, we can expect this kind of sensational reporting from time to time. It highlights the importance of homeschoolers' continuing to be well informed and positive and active in our communities.

Federal Homeschooling Legislation

The problem: Homeschoolers have very little if anything to gain and a lot to lose from federal legislation. Unfortunately, HSLDA has repeatedly introduced such legislation.

• Any federal homeschooling legislation would require the government to define homeschooling so it's clear what is being discussed. Because legislators and other non-homeschoolers think of conventional schools when they think of education, and because they don't understand how different homeschools are from public schools, such a definition would inevitably force homeschools to become more like the public schools that many families wanted to avoid and so chose to homeschool.

• Federal legislation would be an especially big mistake because the federal government has very limited authority in education, which is governed by the states instead. Federal homeschooling legislation would introduce a new source of homeschooling regulation (the federal government) and make it more difficult than ever to maintain our homeschooling freedoms.

• In 2003 and again in 2005, HSLDA introduced the Home School Non-Discrimination Act (HoNDA), a complicated bill they claim is intended to ensure that federal laws don't discriminate against homeschoolers. A detailed analysis shows that the bill is unnecessary and inaccurate. It is also unwise because it would open the door for a federal definition of homeschooling and federal regulation of homeschooling. For details about the problems with HoNDA, see the WPA website.

• If federal legislation were passed that the media and/or the general public thought granted special favors to homeschoolers, there would easily be a backlash against homeschoolers. Backlashes are especially hard for small minorities that lack broad support, like homeschoolers.

Virtual Charter Schools

The problem: Virtual charter schools are public schools that loan students computers, give them assignments to do at home, and monitor their progress by computers. Because they are public schools, they are regulated by the state and must comply with public school standards and testing requirements. Because students stay at home, extra monitoring (sometimes using cameras through the computers) is required to make sure they are complying with the regulations. Also, because students stay at home, many people assume they are homeschools, which they are not. We homeschoolers need to maintain the distinction between homeschools, which are private, and virtual charter schools, which are public, so virtual charter school requirements are not placed on private homeschoolers.

• In 2002, two out-of-state corporations began trying to find a school district that would work with them to set up a virtual charter school. Homeschoolers working together through WPA educated the school boards and the general public about the problems with such schools. We were successful in convincing the Lake Mills School District not to offer such a school, but Appleton and Northern Ozaukee School Districts agreed. For details, see the WPA website.
• Despite corporate marketers' promises of rapid growth and big profits for school districts, the growth has not been impressive.
• We have done a very effective job of convincing both virtual charter school personnel and the general public that these schools are public schools, not homeschools.
• WPA is continuing to watch virtual charter schools to make sure that changes do not occur that would undermine our homeschooling freedoms.
• Families whose children are enrolled in virtual charter schools sometimes ask to join homeschooling support groups and participate in their activities. When groups ask WPA for suggestions about how to respond, WPA suggests that groups ask questions like: How would our group change if we allowed virtual charter school families to join? Do members of our group feel more free to raise concerns, discuss issues, and ask for support if they do not have to wonder if the person with whom they are talking is a homeschooler or a virtual charter schooler? With virtual charter schoolers in our group, would it be united and strong enough to take a position as a group, if need be, on homeschooling issues that come before the local school board or the Wisconsin Legislature?

One possibility is to treat virtual charter schoolers as we would other public schoolers. A support group could agree to welcome them as long as they are there to explore homeschooling. But if it becomes clear that they only want to participate in the activities, we could ask them to leave. The group's leaders are responsible for protecting it, looking out for its best interests, and taking action. If the virtual charter schoolers try to shift the group's orientation toward virtual charter schools (asking that activities be scheduled at their convenience, suggesting topics for parents' meetings that have more to do with virtual charter schools than homeschooling, etc.), it would be even more important to act. Consider suggesting that they form their own group.

Testing

The problem: Both the federal and the state government are increasingly using standardized tests to punish, reward, and hold accountable the schools they give money to. Homeschoolers need to be alert to ensure this practice is not applied to us. See Chapter 34.
• To prepare for and pass required tests, students need to follow a curriculum similar to those used in public schools and to adopt, at least temporarily, the test-makers' values and attitudes, which means giving up the opportunity to pursue an education consistent with their principles and beliefs. Testing homeschoolers would force homeschools to become more like the conventional schools many of us have chosen to avoid by homeschooling.
• Standardized tests are biased and unfair. They do not measure what a person knows; they only measure how a person performed on a given test on a given day. They are unfair to minorities, women, and anyone whose values, beliefs, and experiences differ from those of the test makers. They do not measure or give credit for physical skills, mechanical ability, creativity, integrity, etc. Creative thinkers and people who know a lot about a subject often have more difficulty because they see the complexities in supposedly simple questions.
• Standardized tests interfere with learning in a wide variety of ways. Any test is basically a vote of "no confidence." Taking such a test can be a frightening, intimidating experience for children. Tests force test takers to focus on oversimplified answers instead of questions and problem solving. Tests encourage students to focus on learning to take tests. This reduces

children's interest in learning since simple answers are not as interesting or mentally rewarding as problems. In emphasizing "right" and "wrong" answers, tests imply a kind of certainty that does not exist or cannot be measured. The learning process is much more complex, non-linear, and dynamic than tests can measure.

• Despite the severe limitations, defects, and unfairness of standardized tests, the results are taken seriously by schools, parents, and students and used to label children, justify additional testing, and control the choices parents have in where and how their children will be educated. Too often, one unfair and erroneous test leads to a child's being labeled "learning disabled" or seriously limited in some other way. Effects can be lifelong in terms of lost opportunities, self-confidence, and self-esteem.

• Government-mandated standardized testing means that the state, rather than parents, will decide when children are ready for tests, what tests will be used, how and where tests will be administered, and what action will be taken based on the results.

• Wisconsin's homeschooling law is reasonable and holds parents accountable. Since 1984, thousands of homeschoolers have entered conventional schools, gone to college, or entered the work force. Homeschools in Wisconsin have been successful in part because they have not been required by either the state or the federal government to take tests. They have been free to choose or develop a curriculum that works well for their family. There is no evidence that homeschoolers need to be required to take tests.

• If homeschoolers were required to take standardized tests, the tests would inevitably become high stakes tests with more potential problems for homeschoolers than conventional school students. This is because homeschoolers who supposedly do not score well enough could be forced to attend a conventional school, while conventional school students with low scores will not be forced to homeschool.

• If homeschoolers accept tax credits or other money from the federal or state government, they will voluntarily and unnecessarily give the government an opportunity to require testing of homeschoolers.

• Homeschoolers who ask to take state-mandated tests or who cite research based on homeschoolers' test scores send the misleading signal that homeschoolers are willing to be tested. It is much safer if homeschoolers who want to take tests use private testing services; this also allows parents to control what happens to test scores. Stories of homeschoolers who are doing well are better and more convincing evidence that homeschooling works than test scores are.

Growth of Homeschooling

Problem: Inaccurate media reports claiming homeschooling is still growing rapidly have regularly caused concern within the educational establishment and among some legislators and fueled proposals for increased regulation of homeschooling.

• Actually, as of March 2006 when this book was written, the rate of growth of homeschooling in Wisconsin has declined over the past seven years. Wisconsin had fewer homeschoolers in June 2004 than in June 2003. Homeschooling has leveled off at about two percent of the school age population or about 21,000 students. The media and others have been slow to recognize this change and have continued to report that homeschooling is growing rapidly.

• The decline in the rate of growth is a national trend, not something that's happening just in Wisconsin.

• Homeschoolers can use the fact that we are a small number of students and are not growing rapidly to assure the educational establishment, legislators, and the media that they do not have to be concerned about us and do not need to further regulate us. If teachers, teachers unions, school administrators, school boards, the DPI, and other members of the educational establishment think homeschooling is still growing rapidly, they are likely to be more concerned about losing students, money, and jobs and to press for increased regulation of homeschooling. If they were convinced that homeschooling was growing slowly or possibly beginning to decline, they would probably be less intent on getting homeschoolers to enroll in public school programs and on trying to increase government regulation of homeschooling.

• Several factors may account for the decrease in the rate of growth. Some people speculate that, given the alternative nature of homeschooling, the work involved, and the responsibility parents must assume, homeschoolers are unlikely to ever represent more than about two percent of the school age population, which is where we are now. In addition, the US economy has declined over the past several years, with middle and lower income families being most affected. This may mean that fewer families can afford to homeschool, which usually requires families to make a financial sacrifice so parents spend more time with their children.

• Although Wisconsin now has several virtual charter schools, they are not the cause of the decrease in the rate of growth, which began before the schools opened. The schools have remained relatively small, and the percentage of their applicants who were former homeschoolers has declined.

• An often cited but inaccurate government study reported that there were 850,000 homeschoolers in 1999 and 1,096,000 in 2003. Although the methodology and validity of the study are questionable, the publicity it has gotten makes it more difficult to convince people that the rate of growth of homeschooling has leveled off in recent years.

Research on Homeschooling

The problem: Many homeschoolers do not use homeschooling research and do not participate in surveys of homeschoolers and other research. Research and surveys could diminish our freedoms in several ways.

• Research and surveys could contribute to increased state regulation of homeschooling. For example, research based on homeschoolers' scores on standardized tests could be used as evidence that homeschoolers consider such tests an acceptable way to measure and document learning. It could support arguments that homeschoolers should be required to take state-mandated standardized tests.

• The right of families to homeschool has a solid foundation. (See Chapter 22.) But by agreeing to be the subjects of research, homeschoolers would be implicitly agreeing that they need to be judged and assessed, that the foundations of homeschooling freedoms are not enough.

• Research and surveys promote the values of conventional education at the expense of the strengths of homeschooling. The way educational research and surveys are structured and organized, the variables they choose to measure, and the background and biases of researchers themselves are all heavily weighted in favor of conventional approaches to education. Such research and surveys are not an effective way to educate the public or legislators about homeschooling.

• Research weakens grassroots movements by promoting the idea of using quantitative measurements to convince others. A much more effective way to educate people about homeschooling is by telling our stories. See Chapters 9, 19, and 26.

• Research quantifies and dehumanizes people. It is an invasion of privacy. The emotional impact of filling out a survey is often much like that of taking a standardized test. The implication is that someone, somewhere knows what we should be doing, that there are right answers, or at least better answers, and that we might not be doing what we should.

Rational, logical, legal, constitutional, moral, and practical arguments can be given to support homeschooling, along with the more intangible reasons of the heart. It is much better for homeschoolers to provide such reasons and tell their stories than to participate in research or surveys on homeschooling.

Legislation to Prevent "Unqualified" Families From Homeschooling

The problem: Legislation to prevent "unqualified" families from homeschooling would give the government the power to decide who will be allowed to homeschool and who will not.

• There is no evidence of significant numbers of "unqualified" families or habitual truants escaping to homeschooling.

• Allowing the state to determine who can homeschool would undermine parental rights and responsibilities and homeschooling freedoms. It would also interfere with all the thriving homeschools.

• "Hard cases make bad laws." In other words, a law designed to take care of the worst possible hypothetical case is almost certain to be long, difficult to enforce, and more likely to prevent good people from doing good than bad people from doing bad.

What We Can Do In Response to These Issues

• We can inform other homeschoolers about the issue in question. The more homeschoolers who understand the importance of a given issue, the better chance we have of minimizing the damage it could do. We can bring up issues in casual conversations, plan support group meetings to discuss them, etc.

• We can contact our state and federal legislators and inform them that we do not want favors from the government. This may surprise them, because they are accustomed to people asking for favors, not refusing them. We can share some of the points above and explain that we value our homeschooling freedoms and do not want to sacrifice them in exchange for favors.

• We can support WPA by being members, encouraging others to join and purchase a handbook, attending the annual conference held each spring, and making donations. This support makes it possible for WPA to continue watching for challenges to our homeschooling freedoms, researching issues that arise, planning strategy, informing members, communicating with legislators when necessary, and other work that is necessary to maintaining homeschooling freedoms.

Chapter 25

Maintaining Unity and Respecting Diversity Among Homeschoolers

To maintain our rights and freedoms, we need to work together and remain united. Therefore, WPA is a group of people united to affirm parents' responsibility for their children's education and to protect the right of parents to educate their children at home if they so choose. WPA has avoided, and will continue to avoid, taking a stand on potentially divisive issues such as what approach to learning is best; what specific techniques should be used in homeschooling; whether a purchased curriculum should be used and if so, which one; and similar issues.

Wisconsin homeschoolers have many different loyalties and commitments. Our families are extremely important to us. That is one of the main reasons we are homeschooling. We feel strongly about our right to choose for our children an education consistent with our principles and beliefs. We have strong ideas and convictions about the particular approach to education that we have chosen for our families.

Sometimes our loyalties and commitments seem to conflict with each other. We have to figure out a way to order them so they don't interfere with one another. WPA has always been clear about how it approached these conflicting loyalties: We believe that political questions in general are not the most important questions in life. We don't think that the legal right to homeschool without undue state regulation is the most important issue we will ever face. But to be able to deal with the questions that really matter, questions of approaches to education and even larger questions of principles, beliefs, religious faith,and moral values and principles, we must have the political freedom and right to choose an education consistent with our principles and beliefs without undue interference from the state. So WPA was organized and has always operated on the premise that we will all work together to maintain our right to homeschool, regardless of the reasons any of us as individuals has for exercising this right or the approach to education we choose. WPA has steadfastly refused to take any position on approaches to education, religion, and moral values. Instead it has fought for the rights of its members and others to make these decisions for themselves.

It seems backwards, but by putting a less important question first in time (that is, by first assuring our right to homeschool before dividing up into smaller groups whose members agree about approaches to education, religion, and moral values), we are really giving the most important questions the emphasis and priority they deserve. If we took the other approach, if we first split into smaller groups that agreed about educational and religious questions, we would not be able to withstand the political pressures from those who oppose homeschooling. We would soon be living under repressive legislation which would place unnecessary regulations on homeschoolers. (Look at states that have experienced this situation and the laws they have.) We all need time and energy to decide about educational and religious questions and act on them. But we would have to spend much of that time and energy fighting the results of repressive legislation, meeting ridiculous requirements that we "prove" to school officials that we are truly educating our children. (This would, of course, have to be according to their standards, and too bad for us if we happen to disagree with them!) Or we would be trying to stay out of court and possibly even jail.

In addition to the practical need to remain united, there is a more fundamental reason why WPA does not take an official position on curriculums, approaches to education, learning techniques, and related questions. We believe there is no one right answer for everyone. Each family must decide for itself what is most important and works best when it comes to the specifics of homeschooling. One of our objections to conventional schools is that they do not allow enough flexibility to meet the widely varying needs of different individuals. This is also why we are concerned about the increasing standardization and centralization of the public schools. So let's welcome diversity, respect our differences, learn from each other, and remain united on the one principle that ensures our freedom, namely, the right of families to choose an education consistent with their principles and beliefs.

Another key to unity among homeschoolers is remembering that we need to work to maintain the right of all parents to homeschool if they choose to do so. It is not our responsibility as homeschoolers to ensure that all other homeschooling parents are doing a "good job" and that all homeschooling children are learning well. In fact, it is our responsibility to work to ensure that parents are not denied the right to homeschool because they are not high school graduates, or because their children have been labeled "learning disabled" by the schools, or because their children have been truant, or because they are single parents or have a low income, or for any other reason. A law or regulation that prevents any parent from homeschooling diminishes the rights and freedoms of all homeschooling parents.

Of course the possibility exists that the behavior of a few irresponsible homeschooling parents could diminish our rights and freedoms. However, instead of seeking laws or regulations that would prevent such parents from homeschooling, we would be much better off if we offered these parents support and accurate information about homeschooling. We can invite them to our support group meetings, tell them about resources we have found helpful, and share this handbook with them.

Although we come together with many different views on education and personal beliefs, we have a common bond and a common goal. Just as a quilt has a variety of textures, interesting shapes, and vibrant colors, our homeschooling community is rich in diversity. But there is a common thread that draws us together, nurtures us, and provides warmth. Today, we honor what brings us together so that we may celebrate as a community.-From Opening Remarks, WPA Conference, 2004

Chapter 26

Winning Support and Dealing with Critics

The Importance of Public Opinion

In some ways public opinion can be more important than the law in determining what rights and responsibilities a group of people will have. If there is strong public opinion in support of a group, officials will be reluctant to take action against them, even if the law would allow it. On the other hand, if a large or vocal segment of the general public is prejudiced against a group, it will probably be difficult for that group to receive fair treatment, even though such treatment is legally required. The more understanding, acceptance, and support homeschoolers have from the general public, the more secure our rights and freedoms will be.

Dealing with Critics

As homeschoolers we need to deal with skeptics and critics of homeschooling both in public settings and in our personal lives. The following suggestions might help in either of these situations:

- Generally we are better able to deal with critics calmly, without becoming defensive, when we are feeling confident. It often helps to remind ourselves about what our children are doing and what they are learning in addition to academics, such as how to get along with others, take responsibility, and talk with people of different ages. It might help to review records we are keeping and remind ourselves about how well homeschooling works (see chapters 10 and 18). It is better to share our doubts with people who are strong supporters of homeschooling than with critics.
- Homeschooling is a relatively new and different idea. People who have not had such experience often have a difficult time imagining how homeschooling could possibly work, especially in a culture dominated by conventional schools.

• We can try to make homeschooling seem reasonable and similar to experiences that non-homeschoolers have had personally or can relate to. Saying homeschools are like one room schools helps some people understand. It sometimes helps to point out to non-homeschooling parents that they do many learning activities (like reading aloud, playing games, and visiting parks and museums) with their children when they are not in school. Homeschoolers just do them more.
• We can explain that children learn in many different ways. We can translate what our children are doing into conventional school terms. For example, interlocking building blocks are "math manipulatives," learning to cook is "home economics," and curling up with a picture book before bed is "learning to read."
• We can emphasize that each family needs to make its own decisions about education (and other aspects of family life and parenting). Homeschooling works well for our families, but we are not trying to convince other families that they should homeschool.
• If we avoid attacking the public schools or other conventional schools, non-homeschoolers are less likely to feel angry or defensive.
• Sometimes it helps to try to find out what critics are most concerned about and address those specific concerns. For example, many people say they can understand how children could easily learn basic subjects at home, but they don't see how they can learn to get along with a lot of other people. Once we have heard that, we can focus our comments on how homeschooled children gain social skills.
• It may help if we and our family appear as conventional as possible without compromising important principles.
• The mention of homeschooling or not having to attend school often raises very strong feelings. Without realizing it, people who ask about our homeschooling may really want to talk about themselves. With genuine interest, we can ask what school was like for them or what they think it would have been like if their parents had homeschooled them.

Dealing with Critics in Public Settings

• Generally speaking, the calmer we homeschoolers remain, the more positive the audience's response will be to us. It often helps to say, "Families have to make their own decisions about what approach to education will work for them."
• Regardless of what critics say, it helps to try to get across to the audience that we know from our own experience and from that of thousands of other families that homeschooling works. Increased state regulation of homeschooling is unnecessary and could be detrimental to homeschools. If we have made those points, we can feel good and not worry about the fact that we did not explain in detail things like what the law requires, how homeschooling children learn, or how they develop social skills. If we have convinced a few people that homeschooling might not be such a bad idea after all, we have accomplished a lot. We cannot expect to turn people into supporters of homeschooling overnight.

Dealing with Critics in Our Personal Lives

Criticism from friends, relatives, and acquaintances is frustrating for parents who are putting a lot of time and energy into their children's education. However, many families manage to homeschool and feel good about it despite criticism and lack of support. These families may begin by deciding that it is more important to choose an approach to education that works well for their children than to please other people and gain their approval. They realize that people can be good friends, neighbors, or relatives without understanding or agreeing with homeschooling.

When their homeschool is criticized, many parents listen carefully to try to understand the critic's real objections. Critics often fit into one of three groups. Some are open-minded enough to listen to information about homeschooling and possibly change their minds once they understand it better. In this case, it may help to share personal experiences and ideas and possibly articles and books.

A second group of critics has their minds definitely made up and is simply not interested in learning more about homeschooling. However, they may be willing to agree to disagree. They will continue their approach to education and will accept homeschoolers' decision to homeschool. This approach avoids a lot of pointless discussion and makes it possible to continue a relationship on relatively good terms.

Unfortunately a third group of people seems unable to accept the idea of homeschooling. Some homeschoolers find that they just have to give up, ask these people to stop talking about homeschooling, and, if they refuse, possibly even stop seeing them. It can be very frustrating to have a relationship end this way, but sometimes it seems the only choice. Many parents feel strongly that it is important to protect their children from undue criticism, teasing, ridicule, negative comments, lack of confidence, or informal testing. ("Can you read this word?" "Haven't you learned to multiply yet?" "How are you ever going to learn algebra?") Sometimes this means that parents have to speak very firmly to critics and possibly limit their children's contact with them.

Many homeschoolers find that time spent making connections with people who support homeschooling and trying to help others understand homeschooling is time well spent.

Telling Our Stories

Why Tell Homeschooling Stories

Telling our stories is important for a number of reasons, including the following:

- Stories are a dramatic, easily understood way to convey to others why we chose to homeschool and how well it works. The stories in Chapters 9 and 19 say that what happens to children in conventional schools does matter, even when they are things that some people might consider "not that important" or "things that happen to every kid growing up." They also show how well homeschooling works for children who had trouble learning in a conventional school. Sometimes skeptics can be shown that homeschooling does work by giving them specific examples.
- Homeschooling stories show the indispensable role of parents in children's lives and education, a point that is particularly important to make these days as more people are turning to experts and specialists rather than to parents as the people who know most about raising children. As the stories in this book show, it is not usually school personnel who say, "Things are happening in this school that are harming your child. We need to do something about it." Instead it is usually parents who say, "We have to do something."
- Stories give us an opportunity to give ourselves and our families the credit we deserve for what we are doing. They help children realize how much they are learning and doing and how important and legitimate it is.
- Stories are an effective way to educate legislators about homeschooling and the effects of both reasonable and unreasonable laws and regulations. For example, Wisconsin's current reasonable homeschooling law was passed in part because legislators listened when homeschoolers described the arbitrary and unfair ways in which they had been treated by Department of Public Instruction (DPI) officials to whom they had applied for approval of their homeschools. (See Chapters 19 and 20.) As a result, the Legislature decided not to give the DPI authority over homeschools.
- Some families find that telling stories helps them recover from difficult experiences they have had. It also helps if stories prevent others from having similar experiences or show them how they, too, could solve problems.

• Stories sometimes make it possible for listeners to understand how strongly they themselves have been influenced by their own personal school experiences and to begin finding ways to overcome negative ones. Few people question the power and influence that conventional schools have in our society. However, homeschooling stories help people realize that they can make choices and learn things outside conventional schools that they thought or were told they were unable to learn in school.

• Stories are an effective way to convey information about homeschooling without risking the problems of research and surveys. See Chapter 24.

Suggestions for Telling Homeschooling Stories

As homeschoolers we need to tell our homeschooling stories, or they will not be heard. However, we also have to be careful to protect our children's feelings and privacy. Making sure we have our children's permission before telling a story is important. Sometimes even then it is often better to say, "I know (or heard about) a nine-year-old homeschooler who..." instead of "When my son John was nine, he..."

When and where can we tell our stories? Among the possibilities are informal conversations, public meetings about homeschooling, radio talk shows, newspaper interviews, and at our place of worship. Also, send your stories to WPA. They are included as a regular part of the quarterly newsletter.

Some points to consider when telling stories:

• Concentrate on the positive aspects of homeschooling rather than the negative parts of conventional schools. Sometimes a story only makes sense if it includes something negative about a conventional school, but such details should be used only to make larger constructive points and only with caution because they may put listeners on the defensive.

• Stories that may be particularly helpful are those that show how much fun learning can be and how children learn in many different ways. Listeners frequently feel more comfortable with homeschooling after they have heard that children can learn science by studying bugs in their backyard, math and nutrition by planning menus and shopping, and history by listening to grandparents talk about their childhood. Stories can also show how good parents are at helping their children learn, how well socialized homeschooling children are, how well children who have been labeled "learning disabled" can learn at home, how often children simply need the opportunity to learn at their own pace, how homeschooling strengthens families, what a wonderful opportunity homeschooling provides for parents to simply be with and understand their children, and how homeschooling builds confidence for families to take responsibility in other important areas of life.

• Whenever possible, relate homeschooling to experiences that listeners have had or are familiar with. Some people seem to understand better when homeschools are compared to one room schools. Sometimes it helps to point out that every family homeschools (in the sense that they do things together when children are not in school from which children learn); homeschoolers simply do this full-time.

• It may help if homeschoolers appear as conventional as possible without compromising important principles. Generally it works best to concentrate on one issue at a time, and not try to convince an audience of the importance of both homeschooling and, for example, good nutrition.

• If we have doubts about homeschooling or about our children's learning, it is usually better to share them with people we know who support homeschooling than to include them in stories we are telling to help skeptics or critics understand homeschooling.

For examples of homeschoolers' stories, see Chapters 9 and 19 and Stories in the index.

Holding Public Meetings

Public meetings to introduce the general public to homeschooling have been helpful in many communities. Such meetings increase the general public's understanding and acceptance of homeschooling. They also provide information and support for parents who are considering homeschooling and help new homeschoolers get accurate information so they can comply with the law, show others that homeschooling works, and thereby help maintain Wisconsin's reasonable homeschooling law.

Here are some suggestions.

• Hold the meeting in a public library or other public place where people will feel welcome and comfortable.

• It works well to schedule such a meeting just before or soon after conventional schools start in the fall.

• Design a poster. Consider listing topics or questions that will be covered at the meeting. For example:

—Am I qualified to teach?
—What about socialization?
—What are the legal requirements for homeschooling in Wisconsin?
—How do I get started?

• Make copies of the poster (perhaps on eye-catching colored paper). Post them in libraries, churches, children's book and clothing stores, and other logical places. If you are willing to receive phone calls about homeschooling, you can add your name and phone number to the poster.

• Send information about the meeting to your local newspaper. Sometimes it can be included in the community calendar at no charge. Some homeschoolers purchase an ad. Some newspapers are willing to write an article about the meeting. Such contacts with the newspaper might lead to a good feature article about homeschooling.

• Use information from WPA newsletters and this handbook to respond to questions. WPA brochures can be used to encourage people to become members and to contact WPA for more information. Call the WPA Voice Mail to request brochures.

• Consider inviting people who attend the public meeting to your support group.

Send ideas that work well in your community to WPA.

Chapter 27

Working with the Media

Responding to or Contacting the Media

Positive articles in the press and appearances on radio and television can educate the general public about homeschooling and win support. Therefore, it is usually a good idea to consider seriously and discuss with others any requests from the media, even though the idea of an interview might seem a bit overwhelming, especially the first time. On the other hand, it may be best to refuse to be interviewed if, for example, the publication is very radical (either left or right) or if the reporter is known to be very negative about homeschooling or has a reputation for quoting people out of context or being difficult to deal with.

It helps to figure out the reporter's objective or goal. Most articles and programs about homeschooling are either (1) human interest stories about a particular family, (2) general background pieces about homeschooling as an educational alternative, (3) explorations of one or more controversial issues that seem to involve homeschooling, or (4) a combination of these. Reporters often try to emphasize controversy because it makes stories seem more exciting. However, this may be more challenging to handle smoothly. If the reporter is focusing on controversy, you may prefer to respond to questions only in writing, so you have more time to consider your answers and less chance of being misunderstood and misquoted.

As in other areas, however, don't act hastily on your own, particularly on an important issue. Discuss your approach and strategy with other homeschoolers, including your WPA Regional Coordinator. Without this kind of communication, homeschoolers could make mistakes or work at cross purposes.

Preparing for an Interview

Keep in mind the background and perspectives of the reporter and the publication or station involved. Try to select homeschoolers from your area whose background, perspectives, and abilities would enable them to communicate effectively with the reporter, such as someone who regularly reads the publication or watches the program involved. Decide whether to include children and how you will respond if the reporter asks to include children. (Many children benefit from practice before an interview.)

Gather background information. Review your own experiences and talk with other homeschoolers. Make a list of the most important points you would like to try to include, such as:
• Homeschooling works. Children learn well at home, especially since they can follow their own interests and learn at their own pace. Homeschooling strengthens families.
• Homeschooled children participate in community groups and get along well with their peers and with people who are older and younger than they are.
• The current law works well and holds homeschoolers accountable. Increased regulation of homeschooling by the state (including testing children or reviewing and approving homeschoolers' curriculums) is not necessary and could be harmful to homeschools.
• Homeschoolers are just over two percent of the school-age population and are not a threat to public schools.
• Homeschoolers are a diverse group who choose to homeschool for many different reasons and use a wide variety of approaches to learning. There is no "typical" homeschooling family.

If possible, find out what kinds of questions the reporter is planning to ask. Commonly asked questions include:
• Why are you homeschooling? Is it for religious reasons? Do you use a curriculum? Describe a typical day in your homeschool. What makes you qualified to teach?
• Do you plan to continue homeschooling when your children are high school age? How will they get a high school diploma or get into college? Will they be able to get jobs?
• What about socialization? Aren't peer group experiences important? Shouldn't children meet people from different ethnic groups? Are your children going to be able to deal with the real world? What do your friends and relatives think of your homeschooling?
• What does Wisconsin law require of homeschoolers? Don't you think it would be a good idea for homeschoolers to be required to take standardized tests to be sure they are learning? If your children decided to go to school, how would the school figure out what grade they should be in? Doesn't the state have a responsibility to ensure that all children are receiving a good education? It sounds like your family is doing a good job, but what about the homeschoolers who aren't? What about child abuse among homeschoolers? What's so bad about the public schools?
• May I ask your children some questions? Questions children may be asked include: Do you think you are learning as much as children who go to school? Are you ever bored? Do you like having your mom and dad for teachers? Won't you be sorry not to be able to go to the prom?

Review pertinent sections of this book and other materials. Consider choosing some quotes to share with the reporter. If you quote others, the reporter can't argue with you personally on that particular point.

Give the reporter articles from the local, state, and national press on homeschooling, and background information from homeschooling authors, newsletters, magazines, and publishers. Read over the material first to be sure it doesn't make points that will work against homeschoolers. Think through how the material is likely to be used by the reporter.

During the Interview

Relax. As a homeschooler you have many reasons to feel confident. Try to be brief in your answers and make the most important points before going into detail. Remember that your comments will probably be condensed before they are printed or broadcast. Be polite and courteous, no matter how heated the discussion. Rudeness does not win friends, no matter how just the cause.

Speak only for yourself or the group you are specifically authorized to represent. (Being a member of an organization like WPA does not authorize you to speak for the organization.) Avoid making sweeping statements or speaking for all homeschoolers. Try to convey that homeschoolers have a wide variety of reasons for homeschooling.

Match your presentation to your audience. Think in terms of most people's ideas about conventional education and try to translate your ideas and experiences into terms they can understand. Keep your answers as basic and simple as possible, so you will be less likely to be misunderstood or misquoted.

Avoid negative comments about public schools, legislators, school boards, superintendents, etc. Reporters are often interested in advancing controversy, but this rarely helps our cause or public image and often hurts both.

Don't jeopardize relations with allies or potential allies by speaking for them or presenting a position that might embarrass them, forcing them to deny what you said or decreasing their trust in you and other homeschoolers.

Don't rely on or overemphasize our constitutional rights, which are very important but also complex and seldom accurately presented in the media. It may be better for homeschoolers to emphasize that we are a small minority, that we act responsibly, that our children do well academically and socially, and that the current law is working well.

Remember that you can refuse to answer a question and change the subject. You can also repeat an answer if you don't want to say more on a topic or be drawn into controversy.

Following Up

Few (if any) articles or news reports are perfect, and many people find it especially frustrating to try to convey anything substantive via television. If the article or program is basically accurate and positive, thank the reporter. Keep in touch with the reporter, sending articles that may be of interest, sharing information on further developments, etc. A reasonable reporter who is willing to listen can be a valuable ally.

If the article is inaccurate, unfair, or negative, write a letter to the editor and ask others to do the same. State your objections and counter-arguments clearly, but be polite. If possible, continue to send the reporter information about homeschooling.

Send WPA a copy of the article and your response (if any).

Responding to Negative Reports by the Media

If homeschoolers do not respond to negative and inaccurate reports about homeschooling, the public and the media get the facts wrong. Uncorrected information can be harmful. If the reporters and editors are not told about their errors, they are likely to assume that their reporting is accurate or at least acceptable, repeat their errors, and perhaps become emboldened to do more and worse reporting.

Some suggestions that may help when responding:

- Share your concerns with other homeschoolers. If possible, develop strategies that involve more than one person. Make sure that the people with the greatest likelihood of being heard are among those who respond.
- Respond as promptly as possible. The news media is most interested in and likely to publish or broadcast what it considers to be current information.
- Be as calm and polite as possible. Support your response with facts and logical statements. Consider using the index of this handbook to find facts and ideas that can be included.
- Consider talking with the reporter and editor to see how much they really know about what they wrote about. If they seem open to your ideas and perspectives, ask for an opportunity to write a guest column (rather than writing a letter to the editor) or appear on radio or television.
- Send WPA copies of the original publication or a report about the program and your response. They may be included in the WPA newsletter and other publications.

PART FIVE

UNDERSTANDING AND WORKING WITH LAWS

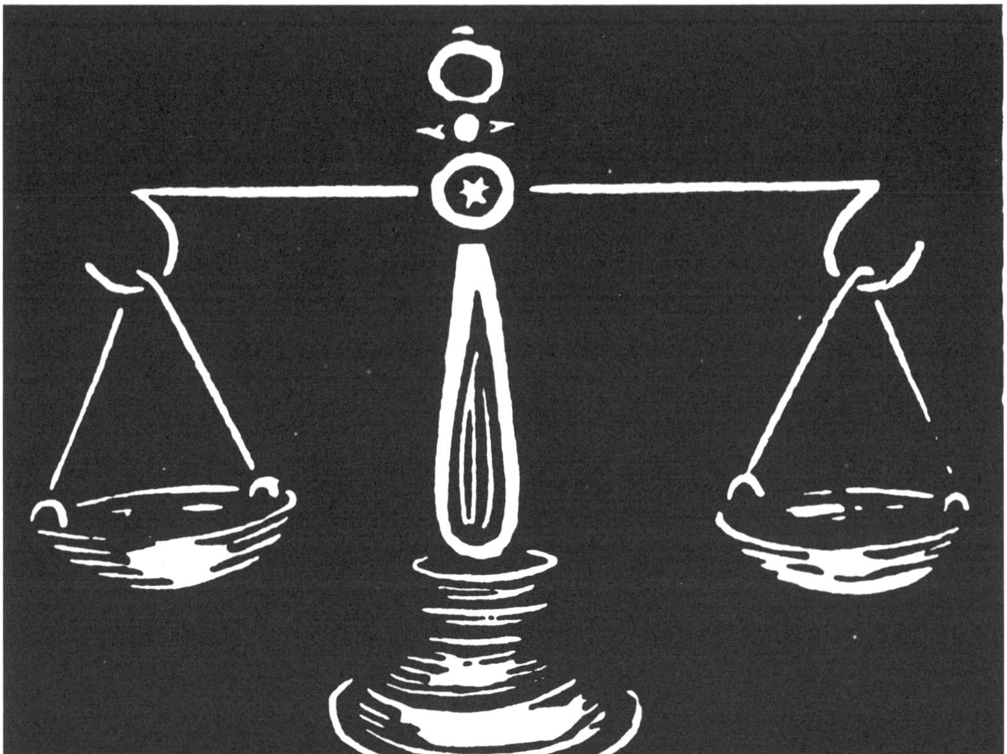

Chapter 28

Understanding Wisconsin's Homeschooling Law

History and Legislative Intent

In interpreting a law and deciding how it will be enforced, judges, public officials, and others often give serious consideration to the intent of the law. If it can be shown that one particular interpretation of the law conforms to the intent of the law, that interpretation is more likely to be accepted. Wisconsin's homeschooling law is intended to be a reasonable, workable law that protects the interests of the state and the rights of parents, children, and families. This is clearly different from the apparent intent of the educational establishment, including the Department of Public Instruction (DPI), now and in the past, to exercise control over private education, including homeschools, and to make private schools as much like public schools as possible. Fortunately for homeschoolers, the Legislature, not the educational establishment, passes laws. But if we don't keep in mind the intent of the legislation, we could lose valuable and important support for our reasonable homeschooling law.

The intent and meaning of Wisconsin's homeschooling law becomes clearer when it is seen in an historical context. Before May 1984, some homeschoolers in Wisconsin applied to the DPI to have their homeschool officially approved as part of the state's "home tutorial" program. (Many more homeschoolers declared their homes to be private schools and thereby operated legal homeschools independent of the DPI.)

On April 26, 1983, the Wisconsin Supreme Court declared Wisconsin's compulsory school attendance law "...void for vagueness since it fails to define 'private school.'" (*State v. Popanz*) In other words, the Court ruled that in order for prosecution of individuals for failure to attend a private school to be constitutional, the statutes first needed to be changed so people would have a clear understanding of what the law required of homeschools. This meant, according to the court, that the state should first legislate a definition of a private school. In fact, the Popanz family had been charged with truancy although they considered their homeschool a private school.

1983 Assembly Bill 887 was drafted by a legislative committee that was dominated by the educational establishment and included no homeschoolers. It was introduced in December 1983. It defined home-based private educational programs (homeschools) as instruction elsewhere than at school and required that such programs be approved by the DPI as substantially equivalent to a public or private school. It prevented homeschools from qualifying as private schools and would have made homeschooling unreasonably difficult.

The seriousness of the bill and the strength of public reaction were demonstrated to the Legislature on January 25, 1984, when 2,500 people, the vast majority opposed to the bill, converged on the capitol for the first public hearing on the bill. Testimony presented the advantages and importance of homeschooling. Further testimony was presented before the Wisconsin Senate Health, Education, Corrections and Human Services Committee on March 13, 1984. It clearly showed that having the DPI review and approve homeschools was unacceptable because of the arbitrary and unfair way in which the DPI had dealt with homeschools. See Chapter 20.

Through amendments, AB 887 was changed into a reasonable and workable homeschooling law that was enacted as 1983 Act 512 on May 10, 1984. It includes the following provisions.

- The Legislature did not give the DPI review and approval authority over homeschools.
- The Legislature did not place the burden of proof on homeschoolers to show that they are in compliance with the law. Instead, the burden of proof is on the state, to show that homeschoolers are not doing an adequate job. (When there is reasonable evidence that a homeschool is not in compliance with the law, the local truant officer can initiate actions leading to prosecution of the parents if necessary.)
- For reasons of privacy, the Legislature voted not to require parents to submit the names and ages of their children either to the DPI or to their local school district.
- A memo dated March 28, 1984, from Senator Marvin Roshell to all senators addressed the question of how the compulsory school attendance law would apply to private school students including homeschoolers. This was a central issue in the debate leading to this law, and the Legislature took special care to ensure that Wisconsin reinstated the compulsory school attendance law for private school students, including homeschools as private schools.

What Wisconsin's Homeschooling Law Does

Wisconsin's homeschooling law balances and protects the interests of the state and the rights of parents, children, and families.

1. The interests of the state: The state has an interest in seeing that children do not grow up to become a burden on the state. The US Constitution does not give the federal or state governments authority in the area of education. However, the US Supreme Court has ruled that because of the policing powers granted to the states by the Constitution, states can pass and enforce compulsory school attendance laws. Wisconsin's homeschooling law was passed to ensure that the state could enforce the compulsory school attendance law.

As an additional way of protecting the state's interests, private home-based educational programs in Wisconsin are subject to the same standards and requirements as all other private schools. Parents are held accountable and are subject to prosecution and fines and/or imprisonment if they fail to comply with the law.

2. Rights of parents, children, and families: Parents have the right to secure for their children an education consistent with their beliefs and principles. The state may not have a monopoly in education and may not demand a uniform education for all. This right is guaranteed by the First, Fourth, Fifth, Ninth, and Fourteenth Amendments to the US Constitution. It has been upheld by US Supreme Court cases such as *Pierce v. Society of Sisters* and *Farrington v. Tokushige.* Wisconsin's homeschooling law protects parental rights by requiring that the information reported to the DPI, while sufficient to protect the state's interests, is not too burdensome; does not violate constitutional, parental, and religious rights; and does not violate the principle of innocent until proven guilty.

Children have the right to attend a quality educational program consistent with their needs and abilities. This means a range of alternatives must be available. Children should also have the right

- to learn at their own pace, free from harmful competition and comparisons;
- not to be forced to take standardized tests (which dictate curriculum and can be unfair, biased, inaccurate, and inappropriate);
- not to be labeled as "learning disabled," "hyperactive," or other such terms and tracked, especially at an early age;
- to be a member of a family which is supported by the larger community and not torn apart by it; and
- to be helped and supported by parents and others.

Wisconsin's homeschooling law protects the rights of children by allowing homeschools enough flexibility that they can be true alternatives and thereby meet the educational needs of the children attending them.

Wisconsin's homeschooling law holds parents accountable. It provides for the enforcement of the compulsory school attendance law. On form PI-1206 which is submitted to the DPI, parents attest that, "The Program is not operated or instituted for the purpose of avoiding or circumventing the compulsory school attendance requirement under s. 118.15 (1)(a)." Homeschools must meet the same criteria as other private schools, including "875 hours of instruction" and "a sequentially progressive curriculum." Under the truancy law, s. 118.16 (c), the attendance officer may take action based on evidence of "intermittent attendance carried on for the purpose of defeating the intent of s. 118.15." In other words, although the statutes are quite clear that an attendance officer lacks authority for routine attendance checks on students attending home-based private educational programs, if there is reasonable evidence of truancy, the officer may request information concerning attendance from administrators of home-based private educational programs. Homeschooling parents who fail to comply with Wisconsin law are subject to prosecution for truancy, which is a criminal offense punishable by fines and/or imprisonment.

Wisconsin's homeschooling law defines homeschools as private schools. A major decision by the Legislature was to define homeschools by exactly the same criteria that define all other private schools, rather than defining them as "instruction elsewhere than at school," as the committee dominated by the educational establishment that drafted the initial legislation had proposed.

Statutes 115.01 (1g), 115.01 (1r), and 118.165 (1) clearly state that an educational program that meets all of the criteria under 118.165 "is a private school." Administrators of home-based private educational programs attest that they are meeting these criteria when they send form PI-1206 to the DPI.

Homeschools are called "home-based private educational programs" in the law only to satisfy concerns that if homeschools were formally identified as schools, they might be eligible for federal or state funds that are paid directly to schools to cover the cost of things like school lunch programs and school bus service. However, private school students, including homeschoolers, are eligible for services provided by public schools, including courses in special education and other subjects. (See Chapter 32.) The other distinguishing features of a home-based private educational program, namely, that instruction is provided by a parent or guardian and that the school is limited to one family unit, could be applied as well to "homeschools" as to "home-based private educational programs."

It is clear that the Legislature intended that homeschools be defined as private schools. The Legislature was responding to a court decision involving a homeschooling family who had defined their homeschool as a private school. The court called for a definition of a private school. The DPI committee offered a definition that prevented homeschools from being defined as private schools. The Legislature, on the other hand, after four months of deliberation and debate, rejected the DPI definition of a homeschool and instead passed into law a definition that defines home-based private educational programs (homeschools) as private schools. This is an important point to understand since the DPI continues to disregard the fact that homeschools are in fact and in law private schools. Instead the DPI supports efforts to separate homeschools from other private schools and has proposed legislation that would regulate homeschools differently from other private schools. This is contrary to the intent and language of Wisconsin's homeschooling law.

Wisconsin's homeschooling law appropriately limits the state's role in regulating homeschools. There are important reasons why the Legislature acted well when it limited the DPI's role in relation to homeschools. First, according to Article X of the Wisconsin Constitution, "The supervision of public instruction shall be vested in a state superintendent and such other officers as the Legislature shall direct." Therefore, the DPI has authority over public education but not over private education. Private schools (including homeschools) exist and operate as separate and distinct from public schools. The DPI's role in homeschooling is to collect the required forms. It does not have direct authority over or direct involvement in any private schools, including homeschools. It does not have authority to review and approve private schools, including homeschools.

Children vary widely in their strengths, abilities, interests, and needs. To ensure that children have access to educational programs that are well suited to them, a variety of programs must be available. Some children don't or can't learn well in a conventional school. Private schools, including homeschools, need flexibility so they can meet the needs of a wide variety of children. Regulation by the state makes it very difficult to be flexible. The state's commitment to increasing centralization and standardization demonstrates that it neither understands nor can fairly assess educational alternatives such as homeschools.

The homeschooling law places the burden of proof on the state, not on homeschoolers. The state must prove that homeschoolers are not complying with the law. It is not the responsibility of homeschoolers to prove that they are complying. This is consistent with the fundamental principle of common law that people are "innocent until proven guilty."

One Family Unit

Wisconsin's homeschooling statute states that "'Home-based private educational program' means a program of educational instruction provided to a child by the child's parent or guardian or by a person designated by the parent or guardian. An instructional program provided to more than one family unit does not constitute a home-based private educational program." (S. 115.01 [1r]) If a family wants to include children from other families in their homeschool, they need to organize a private school that is not a homeschool. (Remember that homeschools are private schools.) This is not difficult to do under Wisconsin law.

This statute was written to prevent people from organizing small private schools that are attended by children from more than one family and calling them homeschools. At the same time, the statute does not prevent homeschooling families from getting together to share resources or a homeschooling parent from organizing an activity such as a math club for kids from different families. Homeschooling parents are unlikely to be considered in violation of this statute if they provide children from other family units with instruction (such as music lessons) that is independent of the homeschooling program they provide their own children.

So-called 'homeschooling cooperatives' (in which children from more than one family unit are provided with a significant portion of the required 875 hours of instruction by some of the parents or guardians or by people they hire) are not legally considered to be homeschools in Wisconsin, and therefore participants should not file form PI-1206 with the Department of Public Instruction. (However, such families can form a small private school that is not a homeschool.) At the same time, "co-ops" that provide only a small number of hours of primarily extracurricular activities would not seem to be in violation of the statute.

The question could be raised: Is this part of the statute necessary? It maintains the important distinction between homeschools and conventional small private schools. It is needed to maintain a common understanding of homeschooling.

If you have questions, call WPA's Voice Mail. WPA can provide general guidelines based on our interpretation of the statute, but there is no guarantee as to what precisely would result in a court case. In general, it seems safe to assume that the more an activity looks like a conventional school, with kids from more than one family attending classes for a significant period of time, the more likely it is to be seen as a conventional private school and to cause trouble.

Foundations of Wisconsin's Homeschooling Law

The foundations of our homeschooling rights and freedoms (and other rights and freedoms) are discussed in detail in Chapter 22. Here is a brief discussion of some of the most important foundations of Wisconsin's homeschooling law.

Wisconsin's current homeschooling law is based on important fundamental rights, legal principles, and legislative intent. As homeschoolers we need to keep this point firmly in mind so that we remember that our rights and freedoms exist independently of the state and are not given to us by the state, the educational establishment, or the schools. Therefore, we need to take responsibility for maintaining our rights and responsibilities. It is a big mistake to ask the state to protect our rights for us.

Although the US Constitution does not specifically mention education, parental rights in education are strongly supported by US Supreme Court cases such as *Pierce v. Society of Sisters* (268 US 510 [1925]) and *Farrington v. Tokushige* (273 US 284 [1927]). The court has ruled that parents have a right to secure for their children an education that is consistent with their principles and beliefs and that the state may not have a monopoly in education. Recent rulings by courts in various states have reaffirmed this.

The US Constitution does guarantee rights that are important to homeschoolers (as well as all other citizens, of course). The First Amendment guarantees freedom of religion, speech, and the press, and the rights of assembly and petition. The Fourth Amendment protects us from "unreasonable searches and seizures." The Fifth Amendment prevents us from being compelled to testify against ourselves, and protects our right not to "be deprived of life, liberty, or property, without due process of law." The Ninth Amendment says that certain rights are retained by the people even though they are not listed in the Constitution. This amendment is important for people who want to reclaim rights that the state has usurped by custom and even by statute, since they can argue that the state had no constitutional basis for taking away these rights in the first place. Under this amendment, courts have recently upheld parental rights in education and rights to privacy. The Fourteenth Amendment provides civil liberties that are important to homeschoolers.

More detailed information about these constitutional amendments is in Chapter 22. Other foundations of Wisconsin's homeschooling law include the legal principle of "innocent until proven guilty," the old legal maxim, "Hard cases make bad law," and the compulsory attendance law, all of which are discussed in Chapter 22.

Chapter 29

Other Wisconsin Laws That Affect Homeschoolers

Compulsory School Attendance Law

Every state has a compulsory school attendance law. These laws have been upheld by numerous state and US Supreme Court cases, generally on the grounds that the state has an interest in seeing that citizens do not grow up to become a burden on the state. Enforcement authority comes from the policing powers granted to the states by the US Constitution. However, these laws require attendance, not education. This is a very important distinction. See Chapter 22.

Wisconsin's current compulsory school attendance law covers children from age 6 through 18, or until a diploma is earned. (See Appendix A for the text of this law.) This requirement has been tightened in two ways. First, it is now much more difficult for 16 and 17 year olds to gain exemption from the law. (See the text of the statute for ways in which this can be done.) Second, to earn a General Educational Development (GED) certificate or a High School Equivalency Diploma (HSED), people must be at least 18 1/2, or the class with which they entered ninth grade must have graduated. (See Chapter 12 for more on the GED and HSED.) Therefore, young people cannot meet the requirements of the compulsory school attendance laws by earning an equivalency diploma. The current law is narrow, rigid, and offers few options.

Truancy Laws

Truancy laws follow logically from compulsory school attendance laws. Wisconsin homeschoolers are subject to truancy laws and penalties. Unfortunately, truancy laws as of this writing are rigid and punitive. (See Appendix A for texts.) Truancy is a criminal offense punishable by a fine and/or imprisonment. A recent law defines a "habitual truant" as a student who is absent from school without an acceptable excuse for part or all of five or more days during a semester. Other recent legislation requires each county to establish a truancy committee that includes, among other people, a homeschooling parent. The committee is to draft a truancy plan and submit it to each school board. Truancy sweeps have also recently been authorized by law. See Chapter 31.

It may be helpful to homeschoolers to know that in Wisconsin local school boards are responsible for enforcing truancy laws. Local school superintendents do not enforce them unless the school board happens to select them as the attendance/truant officer. Homeschoolers engaged in discussions with local public school officials concerned about truancy questions should identify the district's attendance/truant officer. In certain situations it may be better to discuss truancy questions with the local school board than with the superintendent.

Public School Records of Homeschooled Children

See Chapter 32 for information on this statute (118.125) and suggestions for ways homeschoolers can obtain these records. The text of the law is in Appendix A. As part of increases in government collaboration, recent legislation allows freer exchange of records among agencies, which diminishes our privacy and increases prejudice that public officials have toward people who are already in one agency's data base. Therefore, it is a good idea for parents to get their children's records when they begin homeschooling.

School Census and Homeschools

School districts often contact homeschoolers to request information for the school census. See Chapter 31.

Wisconsin's Open Records Law

When dealing with state and local school officials and other public officials, Wisconsin homeschoolers may sometimes find it helpful to use Wisconsin's open records law, which is found under Public Records and Property, s. 19.21-19.39. (See Appendix A.) This law guarantees public access to public documents on the state level similar to the way the federal freedom of information act does on the federal level.

The Wisconsin law states that any document sent to or produced by a public employee is a public document unless it is specifically protected under the confidentiality provisions of the statutes. Since public school officials are obviously public employees, homeschoolers could use this law when necessary to get copies of documents these officials have produced or received. This might be important to do if public officials are doing research or surveys that affect homeschoolers, or collecting stories or anecdotal evidence about homeschoolers, especially if there is reason to think that these stories may be one-sided and present only negative evidence. In cases such as these, homeschoolers can use the open records law to gain access to the files, to documents produced by public officials (including reports they have written) and to letters sent to them (such as reports from neighbors). Then homeschoolers can work to correct incorrect or misleading information, to provide balance or clarification, or to plan other strategies for dealing with the situation.

However, even though homeschoolers have a legal right to these public documents, they should remember that public officials may react negatively or be resistant to giving the information. They are not accustomed to being subject to these statutes and may not even be aware of the openness the statutes require. Therefore, in requesting public documents, it may help if homeschoolers are polite but firm and cite or quote the statutes on which their request is based. Also, certain working drafts of documents are not subject to this law, and names and addresses may need to be removed from some documents before they are released.

Immunization

Wisconsin law requires that children admitted to an elementary, middle, junior or senior high school or into any day care center or nursery school present evidence that they have received certain immunizations. However, this requirement is waived if parents object to immunization "for reasons of health, religion or personal conviction." (See Appendix A.) Home-schoolers who are asked about immunization can explain that their homeschool is the school of record and has the evidence of immunization or the waiver on file.

Child Abuse and Neglect

Homeschooling and child abuse and neglect are two separate issues. Homeschooling laws do not, and should not, cover child abuse. (See Chapter 24.) Under Chapter 48 of the Wisconsin Children's Code, complaints of child abuse and neglect can be brought against parents and legal guardians of children, including homeschoolers, and others. However, Wisconsin statutes do not allow prosecution of parents and others for educational neglect. WPA has worked over the years to help ensure that a vague term like "educational neglect" is not added to Wisconsin statutes, especially when the law requires compulsory school attendance, not compulsory education, and provides ways parents can be charged with truancy.

People who have a complaint filed against them should be familiar with the statutory definitions of abuse and neglect and also be aware of how much power social service workers have. A family that is being investigated by social services because of their choices in education can point out that the law does not allow prosecution for educational neglect. (However, homeschoolers who are not complying with the homeschooling law can be charged with truancy.) See Chapter 31 for suggestions on how to respond if you are contacted by a social service worker and Appendix A for the text of the statutes on child abuse and neglect, truancy, and homeschooling.

Legal Rights of Wisconsin Parents

Parents in Wisconsin have important legal rights that we should be aware of, so we can use them and work to maintain them. (See Chapter 21.) Here are some of them.

• We have exemptions from certain requirements. For example:

—Parents can have children who are attending public schools exempted from state-mandated standardized tests.

—Parents who object to immunizations can have the immunization requirement waived for their children. See above.

• We have the legal right not to participate in a screening, a program, or a discussion, even though many people expect us to. It is important to remember that many of our strongest rights are those that we have retained and never given over to the government. This is especially important in education. The only real authority the government has in education is based on compulsory school attendance laws. Here are some examples of educational programs that we are not required to participate in:

—Preschool screening is voluntary. Parents are not required to have their children screened. See Chapter 31.

—Attending kindergarten is also voluntary. Children do not come under the compulsory school attendance law until the year they are six by September 1.

—Answering many of the questions asked by school officials and other educators, medical personnel, social service workers, etc. is voluntary.

—Some screening, testing, and assessment of children requires parental permission. By refusing to give their permission, parents can prevent their children from being screened.

• We have important legal rights based on the fact that the compulsory school attendance law requires attendance but not education. See Chapter 22 for an explanation of this important distinction.
• Parents have access to information and records held by the government, including school districts. See Chapter 32 for information on pupil records and ways homeschoolers can obtain records from when their children attended public schools.
• Our right to privacy is protected by the federal Family Educational Rights and Privacy Act (FERPA). This act is the basis for the DPI's appropriate policy, "The DPI does not release the names of families who are currently providing a home-based private educational program." ("Questions and DPI Responses Relating To Home-Based Private Educational Programs") Homeschoolers can use FERPA to object to the release of the names of homeschooling families by their local school districts and other similar actions.

Chapter 30

Working with the Legislature

If we have a reasonable working relationship with our legislators, or at least know who they are and how to get in touch with them, we will be in a stronger position when we want to support or oppose a piece of legislation that is important to us or if we need to resolve a problem with a government agency or official. This chapter provides basic information on how a bill becomes a law, how to contact legislators and develop a working relationship with legislators, and how to testify at a legislative hearing.

Identifying Federal and State Legislators

State legislatures and the US Congress have jurisdiction over fairly distinct although somewhat overlapping areas of the government. The role of the federal government in education is very limited; the vast majority of laws concerning education are passed by state legislatures. It does not work well to ask the federal government to pass laws to take care of us or solve our problems, such as those that are supposed to protect parental rights. See Chapter 34.

Wisconsin citizens are represented in the Wisconsin Legislature by one representative who is a member of the Assembly and serves a two-year term and one senator who serves a four-year term. For their names, addresses, and phone numbers, call your local library or call the Legislative Hotline at 800-362-9472 (in Madison, 266-9960). Or visit: www.legis.state.wi.us

In case it is needed, here is information about the US Congress. American citizens are represented by one representative who is a member of the US House of Representatives and serves a two-year term, and two senators who are members of the US Senate and serve a six-year term. There are eight congressional districts in Wisconsin (at the time of publication), each represented by one US Representative. Everyone in Wisconsin is represented by the same two Senators. To find the names of your US Representative and Senators, call your local library, use a computer service that lists such information, or look in the government section of the phone book under United States Government.

Because we often contact legislators so we can share our ideas and concerns about legislation currently before the Legislature, this book presents a brief review of the legislative process before discussing ways of contacting legislators.

How a Bill Becomes a Law

Remember that laws are not the only (or even necessarily the best) means of maintaining rights and responsibilities (as discussed in Chapter 23). Also, it is seldom, if ever, a good idea for a small minority that does not have much money or power (such as homeschoolers) to try to initiate legislation and get it passed. It is difficult for a minority to get the necessary support for legislation. The process often backfires as the initial legislation is amended and the law that passes ends up working against, rather than for, its initial sponsors. Initiating legislation in one area can easily serve as a catalyst that opens other areas of the law to change, areas we do not want changed. In addition, much of the legislation that might be proposed regarding homeschooling would undermine our homeschooling freedoms. See Chapter 24.

Keeping these points in mind, let's consider the process by which a bill becomes a law in Wisconsin. A similar process is followed in passing federal legislation.

1. When legislators have an idea for a new law or a change in an existing law, they have it drafted as a bill. The Legislative Reference Bureau (LRB) drafts most bills, although the Legislative Council Service (LCS) does some.
2. One or more legislators introduces the bill by having the Chief Clerk of the Assembly or Senate, or both, record it, assign it a number, and, usually, assign it to a legislative committee. At this point the bill must become available to the general public; before this it can be kept a secret.
3. Hearings are not required, but at least one is held on most bills. The chairperson of the appropriate committee schedules the hearing, so chairpersons have considerable power in deciding whether a bill gets a hearing, how quickly this happens, and whether the full committee votes on it. Hearings are open to the public, and anyone may speak and/or register for or against the bill. The committee goes into executive session (closed to all but the committee) to amend and vote on the bill. This may happen on the same day as the hearing or later. If the bill is controversial or the hearing draws a large number of people, the chairperson will often delay the executive session. Amendments to the bill made by legislators during executive session or later can result in a much different bill than the one considered at the public hearing.
4. The Committee on Rules schedules the bill for floor debate in the Assembly or the Senate. A bill can die in this committee if it is not scheduled. Toward the end of a legislative session, this happens fairly often.
5. The bill is debated and voted on by the full Assembly or Senate and passed or defeated with or without amendments.
6. The bill goes to the other house of the Legislature and steps three, four, and five are repeated. If the bill is amended further in the second house, either it goes back to the first house so the new amendments can be considered or it goes to a conference committee to resolve the differences between the versions from the two houses. Once the same version of the bill passes both houses, it goes to the governor for signature.
7. The bill becomes law when signed by the governor. If the governor vetoes the bill, both houses of the Legislature must override the veto by a two-thirds majority for the bill to become law.

Making Initial Contacts with Legislators

Among the ways to contact a legislator are the following:

- Many legislators have open meetings with their constituents. Call the legislator's office in your district to find out when and where such meetings are held.
- A letter of introduction can be written. If you send your letter by e-mail, mention in the subject that you are a constituent and include your street address and city or town in the message.
- Make an appointment to meet legislators at their offices either in your district or in the capitol in Madison.
- Invite legislators to speak to your support group. Groups that include more than one district sometimes invite a senator and several representatives.

Whatever approach is chosen, legislators will be more likely to support good homeschooling laws if they have had positive encounters with homeschoolers as real people, not just as statistics. A particularly good time to get to know legislators is while they are candidates for election or re-election. (Representatives are elected in November of even-numbered years. Senators from odd-numbered districts will be elected in 2006 and 2010, those from even-numbered districts in 2008 and 2012, etc.) But if there will not be an election within the next few months, don't wait for the next one to get to know your legislators.

Among the topics you may want to discuss with your legislators are the following.

- Wisconsin's homeschooling law is working very well. (Consider sharing some personal experiences and reasons you appreciate having such a reasonable law.)
- Thousands of homeschooled children in Wisconsin enter or re-enter conventional schools each year with no problem. This gives concrete evidence that the homeschooling law is working well.
- The law balances the state's interest in ensuring that children do not grow up to become a burden on the state, parents' rights to choose an education for their children that is consistent with their principles and beliefs, and children's rights to a quality education consistent with their needs and abilities. See Chapter 28.
- The law holds homeschooling parents accountable. See Chapter 28. Homeschools need to meet the same standards and criteria as other private schools. Each year they must submit a signed form to the Department of Public Instruction (DPI), attesting that they are in compliance with the law, are providing 875 hours of instruction and a sequentially progressive curriculum in the required subjects, and are not attempting to circumvent the compulsory school attendance law. Homeschoolers can be prosecuted for truancy, a criminal offense punishable by fines and/or imprisonment.
- There is no evidence that the homeschooling law needs to be changed. Further regulation would be harmful and would unnecessarily restrict the flexibility that homeschools need to operate effectively. Despite these facts, the DPI and other parts of the educational establishment try to gain greater control over homeschools, sometimes through legislation that would serve their self-interests at the expense of homeschoolers.
- Share with your legislator the information in Chapter 24. Explain the kinds of legislation that homeschoolers don't want. This will probably surprise many legislators and aides, because most people who contact legislators want them to do something, often introduce legislation. However, homeschoolers do not want government money because they realize that money would be accompanied by increased regulation by the government, a price they are not willing to pay.

Other sections of this handbook give more detail and support for these points and ideas for other topics to discuss. You may also find it helpful to ask your legislators whether they have questions or concerns about homeschooling. This book will help you be better prepared to answer questions. Offer to find answers to questions you can't answer and to send them more information if they are interested. Ask your legislators for their support in maintaining the current homeschooling law without change. Ask them what their position is on homeschooling and on Wisconsin's homeschooling law.

Contacting Legislators to Discuss a Specific Bill

When you hear about a bill relating to homeschooling or another topic that concerns you, it is time to act, whether or not you have previously contacted your legislators. The first step is to make sure that you have accurate information about the bill and what it will and will not do. Do not act quickly on the basis of rumors or scanty information, even if you hear there is a legislative emergency. Take time to make sure the information you have received is accurate and it comes from a reliable source. If possible, get a copy of the bill from www.legis.state.wi.us. Read and interpret the bill yourself and discuss it with others. Check with other homeschoolers in your district to be sure you are working together and not at cross purposes. Give information that you gather to your WPA Regional Coordinator so that it can be shared with others.

When you are confident that you have accurate information about the bill and know where you stand on the issues involved, contact your legislators. If you use email, mention in the subject that you are a constituent and include your street address and city or town in the message. In writing, you can begin by identifying yourself, your work, community, position, etc. State your concern or request, identifying the bill by number and general subject. Thank your legislators for any previous help. Briefly and factually state the main arguments to support your position. Choose arguments that your legislator is most likely to agree with even if they are not the most important points to you. It is fine to indicate how the bill would affect your family but even better if you can indicate how it would affect others as well. Assume that your letter will be read and acted upon. Be reasonable and courteous, and do not use threats. Do not use exaggerated or misleading information. Ask your legislators to tell you their views on the bill in question and to notify you when a hearing is scheduled. Close with a note of thanks and your full name

If your legislators respond favorably, send a letter of appreciation.

If you want to talk with your legislators, you can call their offices or call the Legislative Hotline (800-362-9472; in Madison, 266-9960) and ask to have them call you. Plan your call before you dial by listing the issues you want to cover and rehearsing if you like. When you call, identify yourself. If your legislators are busy or not available, you may talk with an aide, which is fine. Be friendly and courteous. Give the specific reason for your call, and say you would like your legislator to work for (or against) the bill. Stick to the facts. If your legislators or their aides disagree, listen carefully to determine their real objection. Explore disagreements but don't argue. If they ask a question you can't answer, offer to find out and call back. Ask your legislators if they will work and vote for (or against) the bill. Close with a thank you.

How to Participate in a Legislative Committee Hearing

Hearings are held to provide information and perspective on pending legislation for legislators and for the public record. Your attendance is very important, whether you speak or not. You can simply register for or against the bill on a form provided at the hearing. The following suggestions are for people who want to testify at a hearing.

- Learn as much as you can about the bill as soon as it is introduced. You can get a copy from your legislator or through the Legislative Hotline (800-362-9472; in Madison, 266-9960) or from the Documents Room (608-266-2400) or from the Wisconsin Legislature's website. Find out the name(s) of the committee(s) that are holding the hearing. Legislator's websites have helpful information on their backgrounds, including their occupations, volunteer work, affiliations, interests, and the geographical area they represent.

• Contact your WPA Regional Coordinator and other homeschoolers for their ideas. Find out who else is testifying and coordinate the subjects each of you will cover or select a few representatives from your group to testify. Review your draft testimony with others.

• Verify the date, time, and place the hearing will be held by calling the Legislative Hotline.

• When you arrive at the hearing, fill out a registration form indicating that you are speaking or registering "for" (if you support the bill), "against" (if you oppose it), or "for information only" (if you will be providing testimony and will not take a position either for or against the bill).

• Address the chairperson and committee members as "Mr./Ms./Mrs./Miss Chairperson and Members of the Committee." Thank them for holding the hearing and for the privilege of speaking. Be polite and respectful. Make your points briefly but with enough detail and emphasis to be understood and remembered. Time limits for speakers will be determined by the number of people who want to speak and the length of the hearing. Plan to speak for three to five minutes, but be prepared to shorten your presentation if requested.

• State that you are speaking for yourself only, unless you have been explicitly authorized to speak for a support group or another organization. Being a member of an organization such as WPA does not authorize you to speak for that organization or to claim to represent it. To promote unity among homeschoolers and to help ensure that unnecessary changes are not made in the current homeschooling law, avoid highlighting either your personal "credentials" (degrees, teacher certification, etc.) or your use of standardized tests or other standards of acceptability related to public schools. Such references may lead committee members to conclude that all homeschoolers should have these credentials or follow these practices and/or that homeschoolers would not object to the state's requiring such credentials or practices.

• Be prepared to answer questions from committee members and to respond to testimony from speakers who disagree with you and are critical of homeschooling. It may help you prepare for such questions to talk with other homeschoolers and read this book.

• Since hearings are public meetings, the information you give, including answers to questions, becomes a matter of record and may be used by the committee and others in developing a position on an issue. Therefore, it is a good idea to give a written copy of your testimony to the chairperson before or after your presentation and also to keep a copy for your records. It may prove useful if your testimony later becomes a matter of debate or is forgotten or not used. Include on the written copy the name of the committee holding the hearing; the bill number and topic; the date, time, and location of the hearing; and your name and contact information.

PART SIX

HOMESCHOOLING IN A NON-HOMESCHOOLING WORLD

Chapter 31

What to Know and Do When Public Officials Contact You

As homeschoolers we may be contacted by public officials for a number of reasons. These encounters are most likely to proceed smoothly if we understand what the law requires of us and what our rights are, and if we act in ways that help maintain our rights and responsibilities. Read Chapter 21 for important information on maintaining our rights. Chapters3 and 28 have information on Wisconsin's homeschooling law, and Chapter 29 covers other Wisconsin laws that affect homeschoolers.

An Ounce of Prevention

It is worth thinking of ways we as homeschoolers can reduce the chances of being contacted by officials and strengthen our position if we are contacted. Some suggestions:

• Be thoroughly familiar with Wisconsin laws concerning homeschooling, compulsory school attendance, and truancy. Have a copy available for quick reference. See Chapters 3, 28, and 29 for detailed discussions of these laws and Appendix A for texts of the laws. Many homeschoolers feel more confident and better able to deal with school officials once they understand the broader legal context for homeschooling, so see Chapter 22 for the foundations of Wisconsin's homeschooling law.

• Comply with the law, including filing form PI-1206 with the Department of Public Instruction (DPI).

• Document your compliance with the law. Keep attendance records as required by Wisconsin law. (See Chapter 10.) Plan a calendar and schedule to ensure 875 hours of instruction per school year. For yourself, keep records; see Chapter 10 for suggestions.
• Meet your legislators. See Chapter 30 for suggestions.
• Promote a positive image of homeschooling in your community. See Chapter 26.
• Be discreet. As far as you can, without compromising important principles, appear as conventional as possible. WPA's goal is to secure the best possible education for children, not to reform our whole society. We know that children learn outside the home, for example, during field trips and regular visits to the library. But most non-homeschoolers expect children to be in school during conventional school hours. It may be prudent to make sure children are supervised during those hours. This of course does not require sitting at a desk for five hours without a break; students in conventional schools don't do that.
• Think before responding to questions responding to questions from others, including neighbors, relatives, and school officials. As homeschoolers, we need to be able to translate what we are doing into terms that others will understand. For example, we can say that we have a curriculum because that is really an educational plan, and we all have a plan for our children's education. This plan may be a detailed course of study we have purchased; or it may be a detailed plan we have written ourselves; or it may be a more general plan we are following as we watch our children learn and encourage and support them. Whatever option we have chosen, we can and should say that we have a curriculum. To say, "We don't use a curriculum" would make us appear to be failing to comply with Wisconsin's homeschooling law, when in fact we are complying because we do have an educational plan that we have chosen to meet our family's needs.

Translating what we are doing into conventional terms like "school" and "curriculum" is part of our responsibility as homeschoolers. We are the ones who understand homeschooling and know from experience how much our children are learning and how well homeschooling works. Sometimes we may get tired of having to explain what we are doing. But we will be much better off, and we will be much less likely to get into difficulty with concerned neighbors and relatives and with school officials if we are translate what we are doing into terms they understand.

Understanding the Perspectives of Public Officials

The more we understand the positions, responsibilities, and perspectives of officials, the more we will have a sense of what we are up against and be to be able to communicate effectively and work things out so our needs are met and our principles and rights maintained.

As bureaucrats, public officials are parts of large, inflexible institutions that they depend on for their jobs and feel some loyalty to. Some officials are well intentioned and genuinely try to be helpful. (However, because of their experiences with and commitment to large institutions, they are unlikely to share our perspectives on many things. Also, it is their job to look out for the interests of the institution, which may very well conflict with what is best for our families or what we are trying to do.) However, many officials are just doing a job and are unlikely to stick their necks out for us. Some may not even care very much about us and our requests or problems. Most often, officials do not have final authority; sometimes they have very little authority. Their world is very proscriptive. Their job is to make up and/or enforce rules. By contrast, requests from homeschoolers often involve basic issues of freedom, rights, and gaining exceptions from arbitrary rules. This makes it difficult for us to find a common ground on which we can work with officials. Also, unfortunately, some officials who are very nice people when they are off the job can be difficult to deal with in their official capacities. In addition, many officials, especially ones with inaccurate or incomplete information regarding homeschooling, fear the officials or boards above them. They may say or think, "If I don't get this from you, I might be reprimanded or fired."

Screenings: Newborn, Birth to Three, Preschool, Mental Health, and Others

Types of Screenings

Screenings have increased tremendously in the last decade. Children are screened in many ways, including the following:

• Newborns are routinely screened at birth.

• Screenings of children under three are done under programs such as Birth to Three and Child Find. The federal Individuals with Disabilities Education Act (IDEA) is used to justify many screenings, even though the law only requires that officials make screenings available and does not require that parents have their children screened. These programs were originally designed for children with disabilities. However, they have expanded to include children who do not have disabilities but only have developmental delays or even only potential developmental delays. The expansion seems strongly motivated by the fact that professionals, schools, and other institutions get more money from the government if they can find and treat more children. Some children who do not have real problems and some who would outgrow their so-called problems themselves given time, love, and support are no doubt being misdiagnosed by screenings and then subjected to treatment that may do more harm than good. Some parents choose to retain direct responsibility for their children rather than submitting them to screening and treatment, especially knowing that money is one of the motivations behind the screening.

• Formal preschool screenings are conducted by school districts on children who the districts expect to enroll in the public schools. They are a scheduled one-on-one encounter with an evaluator who asks the child to do various tasks and reports on problems or potential problems the child supposedly has. They are discussed in detail below.

• Letters inviting parents to bring their children to informal preschool screenings make them sound like relaxed, informal get-togethers. However, during the events, evaluators observe children and decide what problems they have. Much of the information below about formal preschool screenings applies to informal ones as well.

• Drug companies and others are pushing for increased mental health screening. Informal, unannounced screenings are conducted by health care workers on people of all ages, many of whom do not realize they are being screened.

Problems With Screening

• Numerous articles and books have been written on the problems with the diagnostic methods and techniques used to identify children with special needs and learning disabilities. Gerald S. Coles' *Learning Mystique: A Critical Look at "Learning Disabilities"* is a comprehensive study of the research and literature on learning disabilities. Dr. Coles, a psychiatrist, concludes that there is no reliable method or technique for identifying learning disabilities. Thomas Armstrong's *In Their Own Way: Discovering and Encouraging Your Child's Personal Learning Style* and Frank Smith's *Insult to Intelligence: The Bureaucratic Invasion of Our Classrooms* demonstrate the severe limitations of the learning theory that supports most special education and programs for learning disabled children.

• Reports from screenings are often misleading and inaccurate. Inaccuracies arise from several sources. Any test or assessment inevitably reflects the values, background, and experience of its creators. Members of ethnic minorities and people who have chosen values different from the dominant culture are unfairly handicapped when assessed by mainstream standards. Is it really fair or accurate to say that children who don't do well on tests biased in favor of white, middle-class boys are abnormal?

Most people do not do their best in stressful situations. Young children who are appropriately shy around strangers and in unfamiliar settings often fail to perform tasks during preschool screening that they frequently do at home, leading assessors to underestimate their abilities.

To make matters worse, inaccurate assessments can become self-fulfilling prophecies when children conclude they are dumb.

• Many evaluators are biased, sometimes unintentionally. They focus on finding problems, not on identifying the few children who need and would benefit from available help and encouraging the rest of the families to continue what they are doing. Evaluators' training, mindset, and worldview tend to be dominated by the notion that many, many children need the help that their profession can offer. In addition, evaluators' prestige, salary, and job security depend on their finding new clients.

• Screening undermines children's confidence. It is a search for weaknesses, not strengths, and a vote of no confidence. To enable assessors to rank and label children, screenings include questions and tasks that few if any children will be able to handle in the time allowed. This increases some children's sense that "something must be wrong with me," that they have failed or at least done poorly.

• Screening interferes with children's learning and development. Each of us learns best at our own pace, quickly in some areas, more slowly in others. Learning happens much more easily and effectively when we discover things for ourselves instead of trying to follow a teacher's explanations that may not make sense or that we aren't ready to understand. But screening imposes arbitrary, one-size-fits-all standards that really don't fit anyone. Attempts to correct supposed deficiencies often make the situation worse. Supporters of screening often argue that early detection is necessary so problems can be corrected promptly. This leads to children being diagnosed with problems they would have outgrown given more time.

• Screening undermines parents' confidence in their children, themselves, and their ability to raise children. It says that parents are not competent and that experts are needed to assess children and tell parents what to do. In addition, parents know more about their children than people conducting screenings do. When parents are intimidated by screenings and give up on their own ideas and observations, we lose a very valuable resource for helping children grow and learn.

Although screenings are biased, unfair, and sometimes inaccurate, even parents and children who are skeptical of screening have a very hard time not being influenced by results, especially negative ones. People who think they need information from screenings are even more strongly influenced. For example, everyone encounters difficulties when trying to learn. People with self-confidence usually figure out how to resolve or get around the difficulty, or they seek help. But people who have been labeled learning disabled tend to give up much more quickly, saying, "The tests were right; I can't learn."

• By undermining confidence of both parents and children, screening makes it less likely that children will be able to develop their strengths and abilities Ironically, it interferes with and hinders children's development, rather than giving them the help proponents claim it does.

• Screening can lead to legal difficulties now and in the future. Parents who allow screening surrender a great deal of control. It is often harder to prevent additional screening once a child has been screened. Schools and other agencies may claim the initial screening shows that formal evaluations are necessary as a follow-up to the screening. As a result of screening, children are often diagnosed as having problems and labeled as learning disabled, etc. Such labels give schools legal authority they don't have if children have not been labeled. Even if children are not officially labeled, difficulties or potential difficulties that are supposedly found during screening and noted on children's records might cause problems in the future.

Because of recent increases in collaboration and sharing of information among government agencies, information from screenings can easily spread and be used in numerous ways.

Even parents who really want to have their children screened should seriously consider whether the information from public school screening is worth the risk of legal difficulty. It is less risky to pay for a private assessment and consider the expense a relatively small price to pay for maintaining privacy and control of their lives and minimizing the risk of intervention by the state. However, parents must select private evaluators carefully to ensure that they will not submit results of the screening to the state, as some evaluators now do. And, of course, the basic risks of screening, such as inaccurate results and loss of confidence, apply to private assessments as well as public ones.

• Screening can lead to labels and treatments that damage children. Often the cure is worse than the disease. If there are areas in which children could use support and encouragement, the response of trained professionals may delay development by undermining children's self-confidence, increasing the pressure and embarrassment children feel, trying to make them learn in ways that are more difficult for them, and interfering with their natural learning style. For very dramatic information about the damage that can be done by special education, see Lori and Bill Granger's *Magic Feather: The Truth about "Special Education."*

What do screenings really accomplish? Educational bureaucracies and professional special interest groups decide what qualities, abilities, and skill levels are important and must be demonstrated by young children for them to be labeled normal. But what about families who value qualities different from those chosen by the government? What about children who are developing well but on a schedule different from the one prescribed? Sensitive children who are too overwhelmed by strangers in strange surroundings to demonstrate their real abilities? Geniuses who just don't fit the expected patterns?

Similar questions can be raised about the wisdom of using professional experts to assess children's strengths and limitations when parents have a wealth of information and are the real experts and know their children well. Although a big mystique has developed around the process of diagnosing and labeling all sorts of alleged disorders, most diagnoses are based on either common sense or unsubstantiated theories. Serious problems are pretty obvious, and some less serious problems that are diagnosed turn out, on closer examination, to be ridiculous.

• Some parents may say, "What if we don't have our children screened and we miss a problem that could have been corrected? If the kids are normal, the screening will confirm this, right?" Wrong. The likelihood that screening will turn up a serious but previously unidentified problem is slim and has to be weighed against the much greater chance that the screening will damage a child's natural development. Parents know a lot about their children, especially when they take responsibility for their children and don't turn them over to experts. Screenings, on the other hand, can be inaccurate and often claim to identify problems that children would naturally outgrow given more time.

Preschool Screening

Parents are not required by state or federal law to have their preschoolers screened. However, federal law states that public or private schools that receive federal funding for special education must make their programs, including testing and screening, available to all children. This does not mean that children must participate in these programs or screenings. It would be helpful to parents if screening announcements said something like, "We are required to inform you that free preschool screening is available for all children ages __ to __. Your child's participation in this screening is voluntary. If you are interested, please contact..." But this might jeopardize the jobs of testers and school personnel who often have a strong self-interest and financial interest in finding children with special needs.

If you receive a letter from your school district announcing or telling you to report for preschool screening, you can respond in one of several ways.

• You can continue to retain direct responsibility for your preschooler's development. To do this, observe your child, which you are no doubt already doing. Serious problems are generally obvious. If you feel you need more background information, try a book like Frank Smith's *Reading Without Nonsense.* He points out that: "Children who have learned to comprehend spoken language (not necessarily the language of school, but some language that makes sense in the world they live in) and who can see sufficiently well to distinguish a pin from a paper clip on the table in front of them have already demonstrated sufficient language, visual acuity, and learning ability to learn how to read." (page 9)

Many parents find it helpful to keep records of their children's learning and activities so they can see progress more clearly. A discussion with someone who knows your children and shares your values, perspectives, and approach to education can also be helpful.

• You can then ignore a letter telling you to bring your children in for screening, since you know the law, your rights under it, and your children's abilities.

• You can let others in your community know the facts in this matter.

• You can also ask the author of such a letter to document it with legal references or issue a retraction or clarification.

Mental Health Screening

Increased mental health screening for children and adults is being encouraged by the federal government in response to strong marketing and lobbying by the pharmaceutical industry. Screenings can be done by school counselors and officials, doctors and other health care providers, employees of clinics and hospitals, social service workers, juvenile justice authorities, etc. People may not be told that the questions they are being asked are part of a mental health screening. The questions may sound reasonable, sometimes even complimentary.

For example, here are some questions from a widely used questionnaire designed to be answered by parents of children ages 27 through 32 months or roughly 2 1/2 years old.

- Does your child cling to you more than you expect? Does your child seem too friendly with strangers? [Note that it's not easy to get these questions right. Children can't be either too clingy or too outgoing.]
- Does your child seem more active than other children her age?
- Can your child settle himself down after periods of exciting activity?
- Does your child follow routine directions? For example, does she come to the table or help clean up her toys when asked?
- Can your child move from one activity to the next with little difficulty, such as from playtime to mealtime?

Scoring on this screening makes it easy for a child to be referred for a mental health assessment. For example, there are 28 questions like the ones listed above. A score of 5 points is assigned each time a parent answers the question "sometimes." A score of 57 (in other words, a response of "sometimes" on 12 or more of the 28 questions) or higher leads to a referral.

Open-ended questions are also included, such as:

- Has anyone expressed concerns about your child's behaviors? If you checked "sometimes" or "most of the time," please explain.
- Do you have concerns about your child's eating and sleeping behaviors or about her toilet training? If so, please explain.
- Is there anything that worries you about your child? If so, please explain.

A questionnaire to be completed by parents of children ages 6 to 18 and widely used in schools includes questions such as the following:

- About how many close friends does your child have? (Do not include brothers & sisters)
- Do any of the following describe your child now or within the past six months?
  –Clings to adults or too dependent

–Daydreams or gets lost in his/her thoughts
–Doesn't seem to feel guilty after misbehaving
–Feels too guilty
–Fears going to school
–Feels or complains that no one loves him/her
–Bites fingernails
–Not liked by other kids
–Overweight
–Prefers being with older kids
–Prefers being with younger kids
–Showing off or clowning
–Too shy or timid

Problems Raised by Mental Health Screening

• Those who define mental illness and decide who is mentally ill have enormous power. Unlike physical illness where symptoms are often clear and uncontroversial, the definition of mental illness depends on one's approach to life, self-interest, history, and belief system. In other words, essentially anyone could be labeled mentally ill depending on the definitions chosen.

• Labeling people as mentally ill is a way of blaming individuals, parents, and families rather than social service agencies, schools, the economy and financial inequalities, racism, etc.

• These mental health screening programs are set up so that drug companies, public school districts, social service agencies, prison systems, some professionals in the mental health field, etc., stand to gain financially. Such financial incentives obviously make it more likely that people will be misdiagnosed and unnecessarily labeled and treated.

• Screening preschoolers and children in elementary schools is justified by the argument that early detection will prevent more serious problems from developing. However, sometimes early detection catches a person in a weak moment or makes a mountain out of a mole hill, turning a behavior that a child would have outgrown given some time, support, and love into an emotional disturbance, undermining the confidence of the child and their family, and becoming a self-fulfilling prophecy.

• Much controversy surrounds the treatment of mental illness. The use of drugs is promoted by drug companies to increase their profits. Drugs are chosen by some patients, families of patients, and professionals because they seem easier to use and seem to give faster results than therapy or other approaches. They are promoted by HMOs and insurance companies because they are sometimes cheaper than other approaches. However, many people question whether drugs really work and are concerned about their safety. Many of these drugs have not been tested thoroughly. Many consumers do not like taking drugs and object to their side effects. Many people object to drugging people.

• The groundwork for labeling many people mentally ill has been laid in the fourth edition of the *Diagnostic and Statistical Manual of Mental Disorders* (DSM-IV), an 886-page book published in 1994 by the American Psychiatric Association. According to the DSM-IV, a very wide range of behavior can be defined as abnormal and indicative of mental illness. For example, in an article in *Harpers,* L. J. Davis reviewed the DSM-IV's description of several adolescent disorders (including Attention-Deficit/Hyperactivity Disorder and Oppositional Defiant Disorder) and concluded, "A close reading of the text reveals that the illnesses in question consist of failure to listen when spoken to, talking back, annoying other people, claiming that somebody else did it, and (among a lot of other stuff familiar to parents) failure to clean up one's room. According to the DSM-IV, adolescence is a mental disorder." ("The Encyclopedia of Insanity-A Psychiatric Handbook Lists a Madness for Everyone" by L. J. Davis, *Harpers*, February, 1997).

• Mandatory mental health screening would provide a legally sanctioned way for professionals to interfere with homeschooling or possibly prevent some families from homeschooling. Some children have, quite understandably, reacted to difficulties in school (such as problems with teachers, bullying, and labeling) by becoming anxious or developing other behaviors that are listed in the DSM-IV. Many parents have found that simply removing their children from school and homeschooling them has solved the problem and was far superior to labeling the children mentally ill and treating them with drugs.

Sharing Our Concerns With Others

It's worth considering several points that may be raised by people who either support increased screening or feel that they do not need to be concerned about it, including legislators and their aides.

• Some may claim that mentally ill people really do need help. It's true that there are people who need or want help, and they should certainly get it. However, they are far more likely to be harmed than helped by a program of mental health screening strongly influenced by drug companies intent on increasing their profits, supported by professionals who have received money and other favors from drug companies, and promoted by lawmakers who have received lots of money from drug companies.

• Some people may argue that they aren't afraid to be screened because neither they nor their children are mentally ill. But as pointed out above, the symptoms listed in the DSM-IV are general, broad, and widespread. It may be difficult to get through a screening, especially one conducted by someone who has a strong financial incentive to label as many people mentally ill as possible.

• Other people may argue that the current screenings are only demonstration projects aimed at marginal groups like prisoners, young people in the juvenile justice system, and families involved with social services. In April 2002, President Bush launched the New Freedom Commission on Mental Health. The commission conducted a "comprehensive study of the United States mental health service delivery system" and developed six goals "as the foundation for transforming mental health care in America." The report states, "The early detection of mental health problems in children and adults-through routine and comprehensive testing and screening-will be an expected and typical occurrence."

Experience has shown that many programs are started with assurances that they are only for a small group in need and then spread to a much wider group. For example, IDEA, originally for children with disabilities, has resulted in the screening of nearly all preschool children, the labeling of 10% of the school age population, and the wide use of Ritalin and other drugs. These drugs are now being seriously questioned, but they continue to be used, despite their obvious costs to children, families, and taxpayers, largely because professionals and institutions are committed to the program and the drugs.

• When we are asked questions like those above or asked to complete questionnaires, we can find out what our rights are. We can ask which questions or questionnaires are mandatory, which we can refuse to answer, and how the information we provide will be used. If the person asking us the questions cannot answer our questions in this regard, or if they insist that we have to answer questions we don't feel comfortable answering, or if we are told that information is mandatory but we don't want to provide it for reasons of privacy or anything else, we can ask to see the statute that requires that we provide such information.

• See Appendix C for the WPA resolution on mental health screening adopted on May 7, 2005.

School Census

Wisconsin law (s. 120.18, in Appendix A) requires school districts to report to the DPI each year the total number by age of people between the ages of 4 and 20 who live in the district, regardless of where they attend school. Therefore, along with other residents of their school district, homeschoolers often receive a letter, phone call, or personal visit from public officials requesting information for the school census. Sometimes the district asks for the names and ages of everyone between the ages of 4 and 20. When this happens, the following points should be considered:

• In amending the bill that eventually became the 1984 homeschooling law, the Legislature decided that homeschoolers should not be required to report to the DPI the names and ages of their children. Therefore, form PI-1206 requires the number of children by sex and grade level, including the options to report children as "ungraded, 1-8" and "ungraded, 9-12." This is consistent with the intent of the Legislature and the specific requirements of the homeschooling law and is reasonable.

• School districts do not need to know children's names and ages. They report the gender and grades and/or ages of children, but ages can be estimated from grade levels. (Parents of homeschooled children listed as "ungraded" can either provide the child's grade or grade range.) Anyway, it would be more helpful for school districts and the state to know children's grades, rather than their ages, since planning for school facilities and finances is based on the number of children in each grade.

• We are in a much better position to maintain our rights and freedoms if we make it a practice not to give the state any more information than is necessary for the orderly functioning of the government. This protects families' rights to privacy and is consistent with the Fifth Amendment to the U.S. Constitution. It helps to ensure that the government has enough power to govern but does not unreasonably interfere with people's lives. Voluntarily providing a bureaucracy with more information than is required by law sets a precedent and may lead to this information eventually being required.

• Two laws are in conflict here. The homeschooling law tells parents they do not have to report their children's names and ages. The school census law requests numbers and ages. Since the homeschooling law was specifically designed for homeschoolers and determines what requirements they must meet, it seems logical that they should obey the homeschooling law rather than the census law, which only involves homeschoolers in a minor way. Moreover, the census law allows school districts to do surveys and make estimates, so they can easily complete their reports without having the names and ages of homeschooled children.

• The number of children by age is only one part of the report each district sends to the DPI. Also included are the names and monthly salaries of teachers, an itemized account of money received and expended by the school district, and the amount and type of school district debt. The law also states, "If the school district clerk neglects to make the annual report, the clerk shall be liable to the school district for the whole amount of money lost by the school district because of such neglect." Clearly the report deals primarily with finances of public school districts. Information about privately educated homeschoolers is a very small part of it.

In addition to requesting names and ages of homeschooled children, some school districts use the school census as an opportunity to request additional personal information about homeschooled children and their families. Such requests clearly exceed the districts' legal authority and the intent and purpose of the school census. Providing such information could set unwise precedents, invade families' privacy, and diminish their rights.

WPA therefore suggests that homeschoolers respond to school districts' requests for school census data by providing the same information they provided on form PI-1206, adding a grade or range of grades for children identified as ungraded on the form. Parents can simply give a copy of the form to the census taker. Homeschoolers who think a problem or battle is going to develop over this approach might prefer simply to give names and ages of their children, realizing that such action may contribute to the bureaucracy's beginning to require such information. This approach is consistent with WPA's general approach of cooperating with school districts and the DPI whenever there is clearly a need and legal requirement for such cooperation and of acting on principle to protect homeschoolers' rights as private educators whenever necessary.

Consider this example from a WPA member who received a census form from her school district. The form requested for "ALL Children (age 19 and under): Name, Male/Female, Date of Birth, Race, Social Security #, School, Grade, Homeroom." Accompanying the form was a letter which read,

> We are aware that you home teach your children. However, we do need their names, gender, race and date of birth for our records. The Department of Instruction [sic] requires us to complete several reports each year and many of them require information on the total number of students living in the District as well as students enrolled in the schools in the District.

The mother shared her response with WPA:

> I responded to this letter and census. At first I wasn't sure what to do. I knew something wasn't quite right with these questions. The WPA handbook was a real help. I wrote a nice letter explaining the law, Act 512, the school census law, and the Fifth Amendment right to privacy. I sent them a copy of PI-1206 for their reference. I said I was sorry, but all I could supply them with was gender and grades, and that they had my permission to estimate my children's ages. If I hadn't had all this wonderful information, I probably would have filled out the form and sent it back, just to keep the peace.

Other Forms from Local School Districts

Occasionally school districts send various other forms to homeschoolers. WPA strongly encourages homeschoolers not to fill out any forms except PI-1206 (which is sent to the DPI) and not to supply local school officials or other public officials any information (except information for the school census, discussed above) unless they are sure that the form and the information are required by law. This is important because:

- Providing information sets a precedent. Any time citizens give a bureaucracy more information than is required by law, the bureaucracy's power and control are increased. By their nature, bureaucracies grow and spread. One of the most effective ways they do this is by repeatedly asking for small, seemingly harmless pieces of information. If citizens comply without giving the matter much thought, before long the bureaucracy may have gathered an impressive amount of information. It is important for citizens to resist this encroachment on their rights and liberties.
- Officials frequently request information although they do not have the legal authority to do so. When people refuse to supply this information, they are acting in a way that helps maintain their rights and freedoms. See Chapter 21.
- Although the information seems innocent and insignificant, it may be used to support a claim by local public school officials or the DPI that they should have (or actually do have) authority to require this information. Sometimes supplying a piece of information can legally be construed as an indication that a bureaucracy has authority over the individual supplying the information. Or it can be used as a justification for the bureaucracy's demanding such authority.

WPA also recommends that homeschoolers exercise caution in responding to requests for information about their homeschool from researchers working for the DPI, a university, or any other organization. Such information can end up being distorted, misinterpreted, quoted out of context, and misused. See Chapter 24 for more information on research.

If you have questions about a form or other request for information that you have received from a public official, or if you need help dealing with such a request, contact your WPA Regional Coordinator or call the WPA Voice Mail.

For information and suggestions on responding to offers made to homeschoolers by public school officials, see "Offers from Public Schools to Homeschoolers" in this chapter.

Unauthorized Requests from School Officials

Occasionally school officials request a copy of homeschoolers' curriculums, school calendars, etc., either to review or to file. Such requests can often be handled by letter. See the sample letter below.

As an example, consider the experience of a Wisconsin family who had been homeschooling for more than ten years when they received the following letter from the assistant principal of their local school district.

> September 11, 1995
>
> Parent of XXXXXXXXXXXX
>
> Please remember that requests with the DPI for Home Based instruction need to be filed each year. According to our records, we do not have a cur rent request on file. Until we receive this form, your son/daughter is required to be in school.
>
> If we do not hear from you within the next week, we will consider him/her truant and will be filing a truancy referral with Social Services.
>
> If you have moved out of our school district please let us know so we can remove him/her from our roll.
>
> Please contact us at the high school, to let us know your plans. We would be glad to assist you in this matter in any way we can.
>
> Sincerely,
> XXXXXXXXXXXXXXXX
> Assistant Principal

At first glance this might seem like a reasonable request: the school district simply wants homeschoolers to notify them at the beginning of the school year that they are homeschooling. (Even so, the threat of truancy charges is harsh and impolite.) However, the letter contains several significant errors.

• Under Wisconsin law, it is the truant officer's responsibility to prove that students are truant. It is not up to parents or students to prove that they are innocent.

• Form PI-1206 does not request anything. It is designed to report enrollment as of the third Friday of September.

• The school district presumably does not contact all private school students and all students who were enrolled during the previous year but have not enrolled this year. Therefore, this action is clearly discriminatory and does not treat homeschools as the private schools that they are.

Consider, too, the consequences that would result if homeschoolers voluntarily complied with this request which exceeds the school district's legal authority.

• Compliance with the request would place homeschools under the authority of public schools by setting the precedent that they have the authority to direct the timing and reporting of homeschools.

• Compliance would separate homeschools from other private schools. Homeschools would then be more vulnerable to school district power in the community and in the legislature.
• Other school districts would follow suit and require that homeschools report to them at the beginning of the school year.
• School districts might claim additional authority that they have not been given by law. They might set rules about when students can begin homeschooling or other such matters.

In other words, if parents don't know the law and their rights and don't take action to protect their rights, rights and freedoms can be diminished, even though Wisconsin has a reasonable homeschooling law.

Fortunately in this case the situation was resolved. The family realized the official was exceeding their legal authority and called WPA. Both the assistant principal and the DPI were contacted. A DPI official agreed with WPA's assessment of the situation and interpretation of the law. The assistant principal complied with the family's request for a written statement that the matter had been resolved by sending the following letter.

September 25, 1995

Dear XXXXXXXXXXXXX

Thank you for your understanding when we spoke this morning. I want apologize again for any misunderstanding. It is not our intent to file truancy on your son.

The letters that went out were intended to simply verify which students are being home-schooled or are enrolled elsewhere. In the future, we will not contact students who were home-schooled the previous year before the October 15 deadline for filing with the DPI.

Thank you for your understanding on this issue. If we can be of any assistance in the future, please feel [sic] to call.

Sincerely,
XXXXXXXXXXXXXXXX
Assistant Principal

This letter does several important things. First, it states in writing that the school does not intend to file truancy charges against the family, thus resolving the threat. Second, the school district agreed not to do something like this in the future. The district also refers to filing the form rather than making a "request" of the DPI.

As homeschoolers we need to be prepared to use this information with our school districts, if necessary; to share it with other homeschoolers; and to encourage homeschoolers not to set precedents by complying with demands from school officials that are not required by law.

Sample Letter to a School Official Who Requests Documents

Your street address
City, state, zip code
Date

Dr. or Mr. or Ms. (full name of official)
_______ School District
Street address
City, state, zip code

Dear Dr. or Mr. or Ms. (last name):

I am writing in response to your letter dated _______, in which you requested ____.

This is to advise you that in accordance with the laws governing a home-based private educational program, I have completed, signed, and sent form PI-1206 to the Department of Public Instruction and am in compliance with the laws referenced above. Further, there is no provision within the laws that grants to local public schools or the DPI monitoring responsibility or authority with regard to a home-based private educational program. This is clear from the laws themselves; from the legislative discussion and debate leading to the passage of the laws; from the Legislative Council's memorandum on the law; and from meetings and correspondence involving the DPI, public school officials, legislators, and homeschoolers, concerning the administration of the laws.

We are aware that the attendance officer has authority under the truancy statute to initiate action when there is reasonable evidence of "intermittent attendance carried on for the purpose of defeating the intent of S. 118.15." However, your request does not concern a truancy matter.

After much discussion, the Wisconsin Legislature passed the "Definition of a Private School" law to ensure that home-based private educational programs were not subject to review or approval by public school officials. This is consistent with parental rights in education, provisions of the U.S. and Wisconsin Constitutions, and the distinction between public and private schools.

Therefore, I respectfully decline your request for _________________.

Sincerely,
Your signature
Your full name
Home-Based Private Educational
Program Administrator

It is in educating ourselves about the complicated legal issues that arise and then speaking out that we will maintain our easy-to-live-with law. The school district administration in my own town has an individual who dislikes homeschoolers and whose actions try to erode our rights. This spring, he sent a registered letter to a new member of my homeschool group, a family that has just moved here from out west. In it he said that the application to homeschool needed additional information before it could be approved. They needed to call his office immediately. The parents were not rattled, much.

The mother consulted the WPA handbook to see just what they needed to report for a school census. Then she read the law itself. No, it was not fun to read. Yes, it takes a while to read and understand. Yet the more she read, the more clearly she knew her legal foundation, the angrier she got at this upstart. She wrote back, not phoned. She corrected that the PI-1206 form is a notification of intent and not an application, that no approval was needed, that some of the information will come on the annual school district census, and that most of it is not required by any law or regulation. Another member of the group is checking to see what letter, if any, is sent to families who enroll in one of the conventional private schools midyear. Conserving our rights continues each day and in a thousand places. —From Opening Remarks, WPA Conference, 2000

Offers from Public Schools to Homeschoolers

Public school officials are increasingly making special offers to homeschoolers. Some request meetings with homeschoolers to discuss ways public schools could serve homeschoolers. Some offer use of school computers, libraries, and other facilities. Some even offer to supervise families' homeschooling programs, providing curriculum, conferences with parents, testing, resources, and perhaps money to cover educational expenses.

These offers may sound tempting, but it is important to be aware of problems they raise.

• The offers are sometimes motivated by school officials' desire to gain more control over homeschoolers. Their goal is to make homeschools more like conventional schools, thereby reducing the competition and threat that they see coming from homeschools.

• Most offers are motivated by money. Some school officials think that they can increase both their enrollments and their budgets by offering special programs to homeschoolers that will draw them into public schools so they can be counted as enrolled students.

• Homeschoolers who accept offers from public schools also have to accept the schools' requirements, approaches to education, value systems, etc. Money and services have strings attached. There's no such thing as a free lunch. Officials will use this opportunity to require things like review and approval of homeschoolers' curriculums, testing (including state-mandated testing), and documentation of what students have learned. So homeschoolers who accept these offers are surrendering some of their homeschooling freedoms.

• The freedom of other homeschoolers is undermined when some homeschoolers accept offers from public schools. First, their compliance with increased regulation sets a precedent that other homeschoolers are likely to be expected to follow. Second, the general public begins to think of these homeschoolers as typical, especially since they are more visible and easy to locate, so they are more likely to be the subject of media stories and research studies. This promotes the idea that homeschooling should be an arm of the public schools, rather than part of private education and therefore independent.

If school officials invite you to a meeting to discuss ways the school district could help you and other homeschoolers or send you a survey to get ideas for programs they could offer that would draw homeschoolers into the public schools, think before you respond. Most homeschoolers do not want to participate in public schools. They prefer to maintain the flexibility they have when they don't have to attend classes every day. They don't want their children to be required to take the state-mandated tests that are required of public school students. They don't want their children strongly influenced by the culture and values of public school. They also realize that the more homeschoolers participate in public schools, the more opportunity the schools have to increase their power and authority over homeschoolers.

Many homeschoolers who are invited to a meeting with their school district administrator decide to go to the meeting to explain clearly that they don't want public school services. This is important. If the only people who attend such meetings are the few homeschoolers who do want to participate in such activities or are new to homeschooling and don't understand the consequences, school officials will assume that most homeschoolers want such "opportunities" and will increase their efforts to provide them. If you receive such an invitation, please seriously consider attending to explain your opposition to public school control of homeschooling. If you receive a survey asking for ideas for services your school district could provide homeschoolers, you can send it back with a letter explaining that you do not want such services and that school districts' use of the names and addresses of parents for purposes other than record keeping is a violation of the federal Family Educational Rights and Privacy Act (FERPA).

Contact by a Social Service Worker

Homeschoolers are very seldom contacted by social service workers. However, because such contacts can have serious consequences, the following comments and suggestions are included.

In Wisconsin, as in most other states, county or state social service workers have legal authority to intervene in the lives of families on the basis of a complaint. (The family will not necessarily know the source of the complaint. In fact, the identity of the people who make complaints is protected by law.)

Social service workers have a lot of power and authority. Some common civil liberties and parts of due process are suspended in situations where they are investigating complaints against families. Social service workers do not need to have formal evidence or an indictment in order to be legally authorized to question parents and children. Results of questioning by social service workers can be serious, too, including removing children from their families. Therefore, contacts from social service workers need to be taken seriously and handled carefully.

Usually if homeschoolers are suspected of failing to comply with the homeschooling law, the case is handled by truant officers, as described below. However, social service workers who are investigating families for other reasons may begin asking questions about their homeschool. It is usually best for homeschoolers to try to keep homeschooling separate from whatever other investigations are being conducted. They can explain that Wisconsin statutes do not allow parents to be charged with "educational neglect." (See Chapter 29.) They can also remind the social service worker that parents whose children are attending public schools are not questioned about curriculum, hours of attendance, testing, etc. These are questions about education and should not enter into complaints of abuse or neglect. Homeschoolers who are contacted by social service workers often find it helpful to discuss the situation with other homeschoolers or their WPA Regional Coordinator or call the WPA Voice Mail.

Generally, any complaints that are received by social services need to be investigated, regardless of their source or credibility. If a social service worker contacts you by letter or phone or comes to your house, you can usually explain that you are busy with your children and ask that an appointment be scheduled to discuss the questions. This gives you a chance to prepare for the interview by thinking about questions you might be asked and how you want to respond. You can also schedule the appointment outside school hours and find someone to be with your children while you talk.

More Serious Situations

Even if you have received threatening letters from your school district or the district attorney, have been investigated by social services, have been scheduled to appear in court on truancy or other charges, are involved in a custody dispute, or are involved in another serious situation, you still have choices and can make decisions that will help the outcome of your difficulty be as satisfactory as possible. Suggestions include the following:

- Don't panic. Staying as calm as possible will improve your chances of working things out.
- Review key chapters in this book, including Chapter 29. Texts of many important laws are in Appendix A and interpretations of laws can be found by consulting the index.
- Make a written record of what has happened so far, if you have not already done so. Be as specific as possible about dates, names and titles of people involved, what they have said and what you have said, etc. The form titled "Record of Discussions Concerning Homeschooling" in this chapter can be copied and used and will give you ideas for what to write down.
- Ask for help from people you know, your WPA Regional Coordinator, and your support group, or call the WPA Voice Mail. It often helps to seek help as soon as you realize there is

RECORD OF DISCUSSIONS CONCERNING HOMESCHOOLING

For use with public school officials, DPI, District Attorney, the media (newspapers, radio, TV), etc.

This form filled out by:

Name ______________________________

Address ______________________________

____

Phone (___) ___________ Date __________

Email ______________________________

Support person(s) with me at time of contact (spouse, friend, attorney, etc.):

Name ______________________________

Address ______________________________

____

Phone (___) ___________ Date __________

Email ______________________________

I was contacted about homeschooling by or I contacted:

Name ______________________________

Title ______________________________

Agency ______________________________

Address ______________________________

____

Phone (___) ___________Date __________

Email ______________________________

Name ______________________________

Title ______________________________

Agency ______________________________

Address ______________________________

____

Phone (___) ___________ Date __________

Email ______________________________

Contact was made by [ ] phone [ ] letter [ ] email [ ] in person [ ] other ___________

Contact took place on (date) ____________ at (time) ______________AM/PM

at (location) ____

Reason for contact ____

____

Summary of what happened ____

____

____

Attach letters, longer summaries, media coverage, etc.

a problem rather than waiting or allowing threats, claims, or court dates to go unanswered or become pressing before preparing yourself and taking action.

• Don't expect to be able to simply turn your case over to attorneys or rely on them to be well prepared to defend you, especially if you have little or no money and must rely on court appointed attorneys. But even if you do have money to hire an attorney, be prepared to educate your attorney yourself and help plan how your case will proceed. Consider giving your attorney a copy of this book. See Chapter 23.

• In most cases, don't agree to have your children screened, tested, or evaluated. See Chapter 24 for problems with testing and section on screening in this chapter.

• Read the law yourself and think about possible solutions, even if you think you don't have time or wouldn't understand it.

• Find character witnesses who can testify on behalf of you, your children, and your family, if necessary. Develop a local support system of people who agree with what you are trying to do.

• These more serious problems tend to have long histories of conflicts and often a good bit of emotion. Homeschooling is often not the real issue but only a convenient lightning rod. In such a situation, discussions about homeschooling are often not only a waste of time but also provide an opportunity for the other party to hear your arguments and build a case against you and your homeschooling.

Recording Contacts with Public Officials

Whatever the outcome of your contact with truant officers or other public officials, it is a good idea to make a record, using the form on the next page (which can also be used for contacts with the media, etc.) or something similar. Readers may copy this form as needed. This documentation is important for several reasons. First, if the contact develops into a conflict, documentation will be important. Second, documentation will help others who are assisting you. (These may include friends, other homeschoolers, the media, your legislator, an attorney, etc.) Third, documentation lets the people who are contacting you know that they are dealing with someone who knows what rights people have under the law and who will be thorough in dealing with officials and agencies. This may deter officials who might otherwise try to take advantage of a situation without due cause, but it does not threaten officials who are on solid, professional footing.

How Truancy Laws Affect Homeschoolers

Truancy affects homeschoolers in several very different ways. Despite the differences, these ways are discussed together here because they all center around truancy issues. Following an overview and some general comments about truancy, each situation is discussed in detail.

1. Individual homeschooling families can be charged with truancy.

1a. If a family is starting homeschooling and local school officials think the family has not complied with the law, including submitting form PI-1206, they sometimes threaten to charge the family with truancy.

1b. Sometimes when children were so unhappy with school that they became truant, families decide to homeschool. (This can work well when the family is serious about taking on the responsibilities involved in homeschooling.) After they begin homeschooling, they can still be prosecuted for truancy that was allegedly committed before they began homeschooling. In other words, families can't escape truancy charges simply by beginning homeschooling.

1c. If a school truant officer has substantial evidence that a family is not complying with Wisconsin's homeschooling law, the officer can charge them with truancy. It is important to remember that the state must prove that the family is not complying. Consistent with the

principle of "innocent until proven guilty," homeschoolers do not have to prove their innocence by demonstrating that they are complying.
2. Some truancy issues undermine the freedoms of all homeschoolers.
2a. Curfews threaten civil liberties and homeschoolers' ability to work and learn outside their homes during school hours.
2b. Truancy sweeps also threaten civil liberties and homeschoolers' ability to work and learn outside their homes during school hours.
2c. Legislation has been considered that would prohibit habitual truants from homeschooling. Such a law would undermine the freedoms of all homeschoolers.
3. Some homeschoolers serve on county truancy committees.

Background Information on Truancy

To deal effectively with all these concerns, it helps to have some general background on aspects of truancy that have nothing to do with homeschooling, so we can make better decisions on how to respond to each of the above situations.

• Truancy laws tend to reflect our society's negative attitude toward young people and the legislation that has been passed as part of the war on crime. Some violate young people's civil liberties. (This is partly because the juvenile justice system was set up a hundred years ago with an emphasis on rehabilitation rather than punishment. Young people were not guaranteed the same civil liberties as adults. This has not been corrected even though the juvenile justice system is now used much more for punishment.)

• Truancy may be caused by:
—Many different kinds of stress, from a variety of sources, that many families and children face today.
—An educational system that tries to force parents and children to comply with mandates rather than offering them choices and incentives.
—Lack of alternative educational programs that would allow students to make maximum use of their widely varying talents, abilities, and learning styles.
—Labeling students with demeaning terms and self-fulfilling prophecies that they are "learning disabled" and require "special education," and then tracking them.
—Lack of parental participation in their children's education caused in part by the widespread but mistaken notion that professionals and institutions know better than parents do what children need and by the attitudes of many school personnel toward parents.
—Wisconsin statutes that force students to remain in school until age 18.
—The redefinition of truancy in strictly quantitative terms. Now a habitual truant is anyone who misses part or all of five days of school in a semester without an acceptable excuse. Some school districts count someone who is ten minutes late to class absent. Truants could include children who went on a five day trip with their family, or those who were injured and unable to afford a doctor's visit to get an official and valid excuse. Until this law was passed, truancy was decreasing. After the law was passed, some districts reported an 300% increase in "truancy." This redefinition also makes it easier to prosecute truants.
—Other legislation eliminated the possibility of legally dropping out of school at age 16 with the agreement of parents and the local school board. Since students cannot earn a GED certificate or an HSED until they are 18 1/2 or until the class with which they entered ninth grade has graduated, there is no legal way to get out of school before a student turns 18 or graduates. Therefore, teens who refuse to attend school become truants.

• Forcing reluctant young people to attend school does not work. It make things more difficult for the school personnel and other students. Fines and denying truants drivers licenses or hunting licenses don't turn them into willing students, either. Do we really want to send teens or their parents to jail for truancy?

• Approximately 85,000 Wisconsin students are reported to the DPI by school districts as "habitual truants" each year. However, very few are prosecuted for truancy, partly because prosecutors have more important cases to deal with and neither punishment nor trying to force kids to go to school works.
• One solution to truancy would be to offer young people constructive alternatives to school, such as on-the-job training, volunteer service programs, independent study, and college classes.

Specific Truancy Situations

1. Individual homeschooling families can be charged with truancy.

1a. If you are starting homeschooling and local school officials are threatening to charge you with truancy because your children are not attending school any more and the officials think you have not complied with the homeschooling law, read Chapter 2. If you are not in compliance, do what is required now. If you are in compliance, explain that to officials, show them the appropriate pages in Chapters 2, 3, and 4. Or if you prefer, send a letter like the example in Chapter 4.

1b. If you are being charged with truancy because your children did not attend classes before you started homeschooling, read Chapter 2 and follow the instructions to make sure they are not still truant. Since truancy charges are seldom prosecuted, you have a reasonable chance of not being taken to court, especially if officials see that you know what the homeschooling law requires and are complying with it.

1c. If a truant officer is threatening to charge you with truancy because they claim that you are not complying with Wisconsin's homeschooling law:
• Don't panic. Take time to think. Remember that the state has to prove that you are not complying with the law. You do not have to prove you are innocent.
• Be polite.
• If the truant officer comes to your home, talk with them at the door. It is generally better not to invite the officer into your home, at least at first.
• Either on the phone or at the door, explain that you are busy teaching your children and that you know the law and are in full compliance. If the truant officer has further questions, ask them to write to you or make an appointment to talk with you at a convenient time. Whatever approach to homeschooling you are using, remember you do not have to prove that you are complying with the law. You do not have to show your curriculum, school calendar, or other materials. The only record you might have to show a truant officer is your attendance record. (See Chapter 10.)

If the truant officer insists on talking with you right then, you will have to decide what seems best to do. Among the alternatives:
• If you have done the preventive work outlined above and know you have at least some support (from the local school superintendent, for example) and perhaps even know the truant officer, it may be best in the long run to cooperate by inviting him or her in and showing your daily attendance records (which will show that you are complying with the compulsory school attendance law). Perhaps the truant officer is under pressure from other people and will be able to satisfy their concerns with this kind of cooperation from you. If the officer wants a copy of your attendance record and you are willing to cooperate, offer to make a copy yourself and send it; don't give them the original.
• As another alternative, if the truant officer seems somewhat less than friendly, you can refuse to talk and refuse to allow them in your home.
• If the officer is not satisfied with just seeing your attendance records, it may be very tempting to talk further about your homeschooling program. However, this approach should only be used as a last resort for several reasons.
—Sharing more information very seldom solves the problem. Often officials respond by making still further requests. Before the current homeschooling law was passed in 1984,

some homeschoolers tried to gain approval of their homeschools from the DPI. They found the DPI difficult to deal with, arbitrary, and unreasonable. Often when they cooperated with the DPI's requests for more information, officials then demanded even more. See Chapters 19 and 20.

—Truant officers are usually looking for problems rather than successes. They have been trained to behave in a bureaucratic and legalistic manner. They often do not understand the law, parental rights in education, or the principles of due process. Curriculums different from those used in public schools tend to raise more questions in a truant officer's mind than they answer.

—Giving the truant officer more information sets a dangerous precedent. It is another example of the way in which we can diminish our rights and freedoms by doing more than the minimum that the law requires.

If you do decide that it is worth taking these risks and talking further with the truant officer, remember that legally you don't have to prove anything or gain approval. You are talking in a spirit of cooperation. It generally is better not to discuss areas that are not mentioned in the law. For example, if the truant officer asks about your educational background, you could refuse to discuss that. Don't be intimidated. Feel free to stick with an answer you want to give, no matter how many times you have to repeat it. Silence can also be effective if you don't want to discuss something.

You may want to tape the conversation. Begin the tape by having everyone present identify themselves and acknowledge that a tape is being made. You may want to have a witness present, a neighbor, for example.

If the truant officer sends you a follow-up letter, respond but remember you don't have to give more information than the law requires. The law does not require a certified teacher, a curriculum equivalent to that used in the local public schools, school hours at any set time, or many other things that truant officers often expect because of their experience with public schools.

If an interview with the truant officer is set up, the above suggestions may be helpful.

See the example earlier in this chapter for the way one family dealt with the threat of truancy charges.

2. Truancy issues that undermine the freedoms of all homeschoolers

2a. Curfews

Daytime and nighttime curfews that prohibit young people from being in public places may at first glance seem like one possible approach to problems of truancy and juvenile crime. However, further thought shows that curfews undermine civil liberties, are difficult to enforce fairly, and promote submission of citizens to the power of the state. Therefore, people from every political persuasion oppose curfews.

2b. Truancy sweeps

Be prepared for the possibility of truancy sweeps in which police take into custody young people who are not in a school building during regular school hours and do not appear to have a valid excuse for being out of school. Recent truancy legislation in Wisconsin allows the use of these sweeps.

Truancy sweeps present homeschoolers with challenging, complex, and contradictory issues. The very idea of police taking children into custody simply because they are not in a specific building during school hours is an appalling demonstration of fundamental problems within our society. On one hand, the idea of cooperating in any way with such actions may feel like too great a moral compromise. On the other hand, the specter of children undergoing the traumatic experience of being taken into custody is very troublesome.

As homeschoolers we have several options, all of which have drawbacks.

• Children can stay with their parents or other adults or in safe places during school hours, thereby minimizing their chances of being included in a truancy sweep. In the past WPA has suggested that parents minimize the chances of getting into difficulty over truancy questions by generally accompanying their children during conventional school hours. However, legalizing truancy sweeps changes such parental action from voluntary to potentially mandatory. It limits children's independent learning opportunities during conventional school hours. And it implies acceptance of the loss of the freedom to choose where we will be during school hours, a freedom that should be ours and our children's.

• Some homeschooling families think carefully about where their children are during conventional school hours and tell neighbors, librarians, and others that they are homeschooling.

• Children can carry a copy of form PI-1206 and the letter of acknowledgment from the DPI and present such evidence to any official who questions them, thereby hopefully avoiding the experience of being taken into custody. However, it is inconvenient for children to have to carry these papers. Much more serious, carrying papers implies we are willing to comply with requirements for registration and identification and risk losing important freedoms.

• Parents can help their children learn how to act in ways that do not attract negative attention or arouse suspicion and how to respond in ways that are likely to minimize difficulty if they are questioned by officials for not being in school. Often the best approach may be to answer questions directly and politely and offer a phone number at which a parent or another responsible adult can be reached to confirm the information supplied by the young person.

2c. Legislation that would prohibit habitual truants from homeschooling

Early in 1997, SB 106 was introduced to prohibit habitual truants from homeschooling. WPA strongly opposed this bill for several reasons, including the following:

• SB 106 was unnecessary. Wisconsin's homeschooling law has worked since 1984. Evidence has not been presented that truants are flocking to homeschooling and should be prevented from doing so. Under existing law, people who have been charged with truancy and who then begin homeschooling can still be prosecuted for those truancy charges. Homeschoolers who do not comply with the requirements of the homeschooling law can be prosecuted. In addition, there are already a wide range of truancy laws.

• By giving the state the authority to determine who is eligible to homeschool, SB 106 would have seriously threatened homeschoolers' independence of the state educational bureaucracy. It does not make sense to undermine the thousands of homeschools that are working well in the hopes of keeping out a few families for whom homeschooling might not work well.

• SB 106 violated two fundamental principles of American jurisprudence that the homeschooling law is based on. One is parents' right to choose for their children an education consistent with their principles and beliefs. The second is "innocent until proven guilty." If homeschoolers do not comply with the law, they can be charged with truancy and prosecuted. To give the state the authority to determine who is eligible to homeschool would violate both these principles. It would give the state more authority than parents in determining how children should be educated.

Over 400 homeschoolers attended a legislative hearing on SB 106 on April 9, 1997. The bill died in committee.

3. County truancy committees

Legislation passed in 1988 and 1998 established county truancy committees, each of which is to include one homeschooling parent, to draw up a truancy plan and submit it to the school board. See Appendix A. These committees influence the policies that are adopted by their county and can make recommendations to the Legislature for new truancy legislation.

Here are some important points that homeschoolers and others can use in trying to develop reasonable truancy policies and in issuing minority reports when they disagree with their committees.

- See the points made above.
- Schools play a role in why students are truant and this should be factored into determining both the causes of truancy and what can be done to prevent and deal with truancy.
- According to Wisconsin statutes, school districts may provide alternative programs for students who can demonstrate that they want and need one. (See Appendix A.)
- The Fourth Amendment to the US Constitution protects citizens from unlawful search and seizure. Truancy policies should be consistent with this civil liberty.
- Truancy policies should be consistent with the fundamental idea that people are innocent until proven guilty.
- Compulsory school attendance laws require attendance but not compulsory education. See Chapter 22.
- Students cannot legally be forced to homeschool.
- "Hard cases make bad law." Truancy policies designed to catch and punish a few serious offenders are much more likely to prevent good young people from being fairly treated than they are to solve serious hard-core truancy problems.

Send WPA information you get about your county's truancy committee and reports of your experiences if you get involved with your committee.

In sum, when dealing with truancy issues,

- Protect yourself from truancy charges by filing form PI-1206 with the DPI at the appropriate time. See Chapter 4.
- Oppose curfews and truancy sweeps because they unnecessarily limit freedom of movement and, more importantly, violate civil liberties of young people.
- Prepare your children for possible truancy sweeps. Talk with them. Consider having them carry a copy of form PI-1206 with letter of acknowledgment on the back.
- Oppose legislation that would prevent habitual truants from homeschooling because it sets a dangerous precedent of allowing government to decide who can homeschool and is unfair to people in trouble.
- If you are the homeschooling representative on your county's truancy committee, get information from WPA, and issue minority reports when appropriate.

Chapter 32

Dealing with Public Schools

Problem Solving Through Effective Communication with Public School Officials

Most homeschoolers find homeschooling in their homes and communities works very well, and they do not want to be involved in conventional public schools. However, some homeschoolers choose to become involved in public schools, through shared services, because their children are entering or re-entering the public schools, or for other reasons. They often work easily and cooperatively with their local public schools. Here are some suggestions for developing good working relations with public schools, for homeschoolers who are interested in doing so.

• Do background research. Find out what your local school's or school district's current policy is concerning entry/re-entry, shared services, or whatever you are interested in. Be prepared to talk with several different people before you find someone who can answer your questions. Try to track the policy to its source. If it is a written policy, get a copy. If it is not written, find out as much as you can from the people responsible for enforcing it. If you are told that something is "required by law," get the number of the statute and then get a copy of the statute itself, from either the person you are talking with, your local library, or the Internet.

If you are working to change existing policy or if the problem you are working on is covered by statute, be sure to read and interpret these policies or statutes yourself. Often, people with the most at stake in an issue have the clearest, most reasonable perspective, despite the commonly held notion that they aren't objective. Do not accept anyone else's interpretations, even if they are the basis for years of practice. Just because people are getting paid to interpret or enforce a policy doesn't mean they are right. One of our greatest strengths as homeschoolers is our experience with alternative perspectives and practices. Use your expertise in this area.

• Talk with other homeschoolers to answer the following questions:

–What is your goal? What policy or outcome do you want?
–What factual evidence and supporting arguments can you use?
–In what ways would your proposal benefit the other party (such as the public school)?

The more you can convince them that your proposal will benefit them, or solve problems for them, the better your chances.

- Present your policy or approach and have it accepted.
- Present your proposal and supporting arguments. If you need the approval of a group, such as your school board, consider meeting with individual members first, beginning with the one you expect to be most supportive of your ideas, before asking to make a presentation before the whole group.
  - –Include in your presentation factual information that will help other people feel comfortable about homeschooling. Share positive articles. Be polite, reasonable, and as conventional as possible. Stick to the issue.
  - –If you reach an impasse before you reach agreement, ask yourself and your adversary what other alternatives exist that might be acceptable. Don't be afraid to suggest new ideas that may at first seem impossible.
  - –Once a positive policy is in place, work to see that you and other homeschoolers act responsibly in accord with it.

Developing a good working relationship with your local school board can pay big dividends. An example of this is described in Mary Penn's article "Board nixes homeschool monitoring," which appeared in the *Sauk Prairie Star* on October 26, 1989. Ms. Penn reported on the discussion that followed the introduction of a resolution "which would have enabled school district personnel to visit and evaluate local homeschooling situations."

> Board member Tony DeGiovanni said, "Personally I do not think we need to take on that responsibility. I don't know how a person would evaluate a home school. If the state wants them to follow guidelines, I think that is their problem. I think we are ill prepared to measure what is going on in a home school."
>
> Board member Walter Dickey said the philosophy of home schooling is not to educate so students can pass certain tests, so standardized testing could prove meaningless in a home schooling situation. "If the state feels it is a problem they should legislate it," Dickey said.
>
> "If it is not a big problem, say four to five students go to the high school and are not at grade level, I think they should leave it alone," DeGiovanni said.
>
> Val McAuliffe objected to what she sees as the "inflammatory" wording of the resolution. McAuliffe said any movement to regulate home schooling means the district has its own education problems to deal with.
>
> The resolution died for lack of a motion. [Reprinted with permission.]

Entry/Re-Entry into a Conventional School

Many public schools in Wisconsin deal with entry/re-entry in a common sense manner, on an individual basis, without formal written policies. This approach has worked well, and homeschoolers who have used a variety of curriculums and approaches to learning have successfully entered public schools thanks in part to good communication among parents, students, teachers, principals, and/or superintendents.

However, the question of entry/re-entry sometimes causes concern.

- Parents of homeschoolers who are considering entering or re-entering a conventional school want to be sure they are prepared and make a smooth transition.
- School officials who are critical or skeptical of homeschooling sometimes allude to problems homeschoolers may cause if they enter conventional schools. These concerns are vague

and undocumented. There have been no significant problems, despite the fact that over 70,000 homeschooled students in Wisconsin have entered conventional schools since 1984.

• School districts sometimes pass entry policies that discriminate against homeschoolers by requiring that they meet requirements not placed on transfer students from other public and private schools. These requirements may include testing, a trial period, or a demonstration of social maturity. They have been judged discriminatory by attorneys working for local school districts, by an attorney working for the Wisconsin Association of School Boards, and by local school officials. For example, many of these requirements were included in a February 1986 proposed entry/re-entry policy in the Sparta school district. Homeschoolers in that district pointed out the discriminatory nature of the policy. A local newspaper reported:

> The [Sparta school] board requested a legal view of their proposal which [Ralph] Osborne [a Sparta attorney] presented at the March meeting. He said the policy could be considered discriminatory and was asked to prepare another policy for Tuesday's meeting. Osborne said the new policy treats all students equally. He added that he thinks it would meet any tests of constitutionality. To create the proposal, he consulted with an attorney of the Wisconsin School Board Association and studied the policies incorporated in other school systems. (*Monroe County Democrat,* April 24, 1986, page 2.)

Many parents whose children have entered school have found the following suggestions helpful:

• At least several months before your children will enter school, begin establishing a good working relationship with school personnel. Visit the school with your children, sit in on classes, and talk with teachers and the principal. Being familiar with the facilities is often reassuring to children, and you can ask about policies concerning records, credits, tests, and psychological counseling and screening. You can also request further information from the district superintendent and the school board. It is particularly important to find out how children's grade placement will be determined. Among the questions to ask: What criteria will be used? (Among the possibilities are age, test results, curriculum, review of the children's records and credits, interviews of children and parents, assessment of social maturity.) Which criteria are most important and/or mandatory? Which could be waived or deemphasized? Who makes the final decision?

• Are the criteria reasonable, non-discriminatory, and acceptable to you? If not, try to change them or have them waived. For suggestions, see below.

• Wisconsin law requires that public schools administer standardized tests to students who are attending public schools. (Parents of public school students can have them exempted from the state-mandated standardized fourth, eighth, tenth, and twelfth grade tests.) Although state law does not require that entering students take tests, some school districts do require tests. This is a discriminatory policy if it is not applied to all students; see below for more details. Some parents object to standardized tests for entering students and work hard to prevent their children from having to take them. (See Chapter 24 for information on standardized tests.) If tests are unavoidable, some parents arrange to have them administered in a setting in which their children are comfortable and stay with younger children. Sometimes the tests can be postponed until the children have been in school for several months. Many parents also find it beneficial to have their children practice taking sample tests of the same type from the same company as those they will take at school.

• Be careful about signing any authorizations or waivers, especially concerning psychological testing and screening. Some controversial tests cannot be administered without parental permission. It is important to find out exactly what test will be administered, why, and what will be done with the results before signing away your rights and your children's.

• Many parents work hard to give their children extra support while they are adjusting to school. They communicate frequently with the teacher(s), are available to help with homework, and act as their children's advocates whenever necessary. Extra time and effort often pay big dividends in a smooth transition and good adjustment for their children.

The following questions are sometimes asked about entry/re-entry policies.

On what basis should homeschoolers evaluate proposed entry policies?

If homeschoolers cannot convince their local school board that a formal entry policy is unnecessary, they need to be sure that any policy that is adopted does not discriminate against homeschoolers. The only valid requirements for entry of homeschoolers are those which are also required of other transfer students (whether from public or private schools) and for promotion of students from one grade to the next within the school. Examples of specific requirements which are sometimes placed exclusively on homeschoolers are:

• Achievement of a certain score or percentile on a standardized test in order to be placed in a specific grade.

• Completion of a probationary period during which former homeschoolers must prove themselves.

• Demonstration of social maturity, including a certain degree of socialization or appropriate interaction with one's peers.

• Completion of a certain number of semesters at the school to be eligible for a diploma.

What arguments can be used against discriminatory policies?

• There is no concrete evidence that such discrimination against homeschoolers is warranted. Thousands of former homeschoolers have entered or re-entered conventional schools without problems.

• The Wisconsin Constitution requires that public schools provide services for all children, and it states that children may not be denied on the basis of discriminatory practices.

• The Fourteenth Amendment of the U.S. Constitution guarantees equal treatment under law and protects citizens against discrimination. (See Chapter 22.)

• Such policies violate the principle of "innocent until proven guilty" by assuming there is something wrong with homeschoolers until they have proven otherwise. The policies also disregard due process.

Shared Services: When Homeschoolers Participate in Public Schools

The term "shared services" refers to situations in which students from other public school districts or from private schools, including homeschools, participate in classes or activities at a public school. WPA supports homeschoolers' right to shared services, even though the vast majority of homeschoolers do not want them.

Homeschoolers' right to shared services is founded on Article X (pronounced Article 10), Section 3 of the Wisconsin Constitution. It reads, "The legislature shall provide by law for the establishment of district schools, which shall be as nearly uniform as practicable; and such schools shall be free and without charge for tuition to all children between the ages of 4 and 20 years." There are no restrictions. Neither the Constitution nor the statutes say that students who want to receive shared services from a given public school must be full-time students in that or any other public school. Neither say students can only have shared services if the public schools have enough money. Neither say shared services are only available for students that the school district or DPI approve of. Neither say that homeschoolers do not qualify for shared services. Therefore, none of these is a valid reason for denying homeschoolers access to shared services.

On the basis of this constitutional guarantee, homeschoolers have participated in public school classes and activities. Homeschoolers who want shared services find it works well to begin with the general steps in "Problem Solving Through Effective Communication With Public School Officials" earlier in this chapter. Find out your local school's policy.

Taking courses in a public high school

Homeschoolers who want to take courses at their local high schools can cite s. 118.145(4). It states that school boards "shall allow" homeschoolers living in the district to take up to two courses each semester provided they meet "the standards for admission to high school," This phrase is generally understood to mean that they have to meet prerequisites for courses they want to take. In other words, they could not take German II without German I or its equivalent. The law also says that the school board has to determine that "there is sufficient space in the classroom." The board can refuse homeschoolers on the basis that there is not enough room.

Taking courses and receiving services from elementary and middle schools

The DPI's position on homeschoolers' taking courses in elementary and middle schools is outlined in a six-page document they mail with PI-1206 forms and give to school districts called "Questions and DPI Responses Relating to Home-Based Private Educational Programs." According to the 2005-2006 version of this document:

While the part-time attendance option applies specifically to pupils attending high school, a school district may choose to provide services, including courses, to resident elementary and middle school-aged children enrolled in home-based educational programs. However, the school district may not claim state aid on behalf of those elementary and middle school students.

If you want your children to take a course or two in an elementary or middle school, begin with the person who seems most likely to support your request, perhaps the person teaching the class you are interested in, the principal, a counselor, or someone on your local board. Use the points above about Article X of the Wisconsin Constitution. Explain that some homeschoolers have taken courses in other districts. It will be easier and makes more sense to simply try to make arrangements for your family than to go to the work and potential problems of trying to get your local school board to adopt a policy covering shared services for homeschoolers in elementary and middle school.

Receiving special education and related services from public schools

Some of the greatest need for shared services comes from families who want speech or other therapy for their children and have decided the therapy offered by the public schools would be helpful. Private therapy can be very expensive and too often is not covered by insurance.

Final decisions about shared services are made by local school districts, but the DPI advises them, and many districts follow the DPI's advice. Unfortunately, the DPI has written in its document cited just above and titled "Questions and DPI Responses..." that

16. What responsibilities does a school district have to provide special education and related services to a student enrolled in a home based private educational program?

> The Individuals with Disabilities Education Act (IDEA) does not require public school districts to provide individualized special education and related services to children with disabilities enrolled by their parents in private schools. However, the IDEA does require public school districts to provide services to children with disabilities in private schools as a class. Because the statutory definition of private schools does not include home-based private educational programs, school districts are not required to provide for the similar participation of home schooled children. However, neither federal nor state law prohibits districts from providing special education and related services to children with

> disabilities enrolled in home based private educational programs. Therefore, school districts may provide any special education and related services to these children that they deem appropriate. If a public school district chooses to provide these services, the costs are not aided by DPI under federal or state categorical aids. Public school districts are required to identify and evaluate all children in the district who may have a disability. If a child is found to have a disability, the district must offer a placement that would provide the child a free appropriate public education. Generally, this placement means the child would be enrolled in a public school. If the parents of a child in a home-based private educational program suspect that their child may have a disability, they can refer the child for an evaluation at the public school. The district will then perform a publicly funded evaluation of the child and, if found to be a child with a disability, offer the child a placement to meet the child's educational needs.

However, families who want shared services for special needs children can still request them from local school officials, supporting their request with the following information.

- Homeschools are private schools, so homeschoolers should have the same access to shared services that other private school students have. Unfortunately, the DPI claims that homeschools are not private schools. You may need to use the information in "What Wisconsin's Homeschooling Law Does" in Chapter 28 to try to convince officials that homeschools are in fact private schools.
- School officials should take seriously both Article X of the Wisconsin Constitution and their responsibility to make their own decisions about what is right, regardless of what the DPI advises them.
- School districts that want to be reimbursed for providing services to homeschoolers can get the money they are due by including homeschoolers in the district's annual plan for providing services to private school students. Because homeschools are private schools, as explained in the first point above, homeschoolers can be counted as private school students. Of course, if the district identifies the students as homeschoolers, or asks the DPI if it is all right to include homeschoolers as private school students, the DPI will most likely refuse. This is why it is important that the district realize that the DPI can only give advice, and the district has final responsibility for complying with the Wisconsin Constitution and the statutes.

Some families decide it is worth their effort to contact their school district, even though officials may not be very receptive and some can be vengeful. Few are as vengeful as the district that ended the speech therapy they had been providing for a family's oldest child when she turned six and began homeschooling and also refused to provide therapy for their three year old because "you probably will homeschool her when she turns six."

WPA is opposed to working to get legislation requiring districts to offer shared services either to homeschoolers who want them from elementary or middle schools or those who want them for special needs children. Introducing legislation on shared services (or any other topic related to homeschooling) would raise the possibility of increased regulation of homeschooling. The Wisconsin Constitution and current statutes already allow shared services, as explained above. The problem is not that we don't have appropriate statutes. The problem is that the DPI and school officials do not follow them. Therefore, even if we were successful in getting a law passed, it would not necessarily prevent powerful agencies from disobeying it just as they are disobeying current statutes. In addition, the roadblock in getting services for special needs children is the DPI's refusal to acknowledge that homeschools are private schools, even though legislation passed in 1984 makes it clear that they are. Getting powerful agencies to abide by the 1984 statute is another matter. Also see Chapter 23 for general information on avoiding legislation and court cases if at all possible.

A Homeschooling Mother's Perspectives on Shared Services:

Public schools are required by statute to offer up to two courses per semester to homeschooled students in the 9th through 12th grades. Friends assume that I think that this is a wonderful opportunity. I do not agree.

Homeschooling is more than just a choice of location for learning. Homeschooling is family life. Homeschooling is learning all the time, in all places and under all conditions. Homeschooling is about family control of our family life.

Our experience with high school came several years ago when we had exchange students live as part of our family. We wanted to continue to have a close family life, but the institutional schedule the exchange student had to follow drove our family's schedule-when we woke and ate and slept, or when we had to be home from an outside activity to meet the one returning from school. We certainly could not leave town to visit the Smithsonian for a few weeks if school were in session. Everyone was affected by just one person involved in the school.

We chose to homeschool in the first place because we felt that we wanted our children to have more control over when, how or on what to spend time and effort learning. In school, tests are used to evaluate what was learned and then, mistakes or not, holes in understanding or not, the class moves on. In our homeschool, we can spend as much or as little time as needed to master any particular subject to our standards. Outside of school I have learned that success comes not from avoiding failure or getting it all right on the first try. I triumph from continuous, successive actions, picking myself up from mistakes and working onward.

The subjects taught in a high school are subjects that have been useful in some way to the larger society-and those subjects still exist in that larger society. Short conversations with a commercial artist give my son insight into his drawing, but he must draw to improve. A college student majoring in Spanish gives a homeschooler I know refinements to her accent, but she must use her Spanish to continue to improve. The high school physics lab may have a $400 air table to study friction, but only one day is scheduled for thirty students to use it; the oil and ice my youngest uses to examine friction is inexpensive enough to allow him to think about the process and play around with it until he can understand it thoroughly.

There might be some things which we cannot do, but there are so many more benefits to controlling our learning, it is no sacrifice to give them up. I do not intend to ever send my children to a conventional school.

Sports

A few homeschoolers occasionally ask whether they can play on public school sports teams. The question is not unreasonable; public school sports are important to some people. However, a complex set of reasons, including Wisconsin Interscholastic Athletic Association (WIAA) regulations, make it difficult and risky for homeschoolers to do this. Fortunately, homeschoolers can participate in sports in a number of other ways, some of which have significant advantages over public school sports.

First, consider high school sports. At present, high school sports are governed by the WIAA. WIAA rules limit participation in school sports to students who are enrolled full-time as defined by the DPI. (Even homeschoolers who took two courses under the shared services law discussed above would not qualify to participate in sports.) The question has been raised: Could WIAA rules be changed? However, a closer look reveals that WIAA rules are not the major factor that prevents homeschoolers from playing public school sports. Instead, there is a complex set of reasons.

If homeschoolers played on public high school teams, they would undoubtedly be required to demonstrate their eligibility by taking tests, providing evidence of academic work they have done, etc. One reason is that all other team members are required to have a certain grade point average or in some other way prove they meet academic standards. Why should homeschoolers be an exception? In the second place, it would undoubtedly be argued that without such requirements for homeschoolers, athletes who did not meet the high school's academic standards could begin homeschooling as a way to get around the academic standards and continue playing.

In addition, it would probably be argued that some oversight of homeschooling athletes would be needed to prevent misuse of the situation. For example, a young person could homeschool for one year, claim that homeschooling had not worked out, and re-enter the public schools to repeat that grade. This would give them the advantage of being a year older and more mature than others in their grade. (This is not a far-fetched scheme. It happened in Fond du Lac, Wisconsin.)

The major problem for homeschoolers is that setting such a precedent for public school regulation of homeschoolers is very likely to lead to increased regulation of all homeschoolers. Once a mechanism has been established for determining whether homeschoolers meet the academic standards required for athletes, whether that is standardized testing or review and approval of curriculum and records or some other approach, there will be pressure to apply the same process to all homeschoolers. Some school officials and others want to increase state regulation of homeschoolers. Homeschoolers working through WPA have countered this pressure since 1984. If a way were worked out for homeschoolers to demonstrate their academic competence so they could play sports, it would set a dangerous precedent of public school regulation of homeschoolers. With such a precedent and a way of judging homeschoolers' academic achievement in place, it would then be much more difficult to continue to prevent school officials from requiring that all other homeschoolers also prove that they are meeting public schools' academic standards.

In addition, there is a great deal of pressure, competition, and status surrounding positions on teams. If homeschoolers became prominent athletes, they might generate a backlash against homeschooling, with people feeling that it isn't fair for homeschoolers to get to do the fun parts of school without (as they see it) having to do all the less fun parts.

In a few states, such as Maine, homeschoolers have made arrangements to play sports. However, homeschoolers in these states were already under much greater government regulation than we are in Wisconsin, so procedures were already in place for them to demonstrate their academic competence through review of their curriculum and in other ways. (See Chapter 21 for comparison of Wisconsin's freedoms with those in other states.) In other words, homeschoolers in these states had already lost a great deal of the freedom that we in Wisconsin have. We have much more to lose than they did, and it is important for us to work to maintain our freedoms.

The situation is somewhat different for homeschoolers who want to play on public elementary or middle school teams. Most elementary and middle schools are not members of WIAA, although increasing numbers of middle schools are joining. Therefore, a few homeschoolers have made arrangements to play on elementary and middle school teams without having to comply with WIAA's rule that they meet the DPI's definition of a full-time student in that school and without having to prove to the school that they meet academic requirements for team participation.

However, even here homeschoolers need to be careful. A recent story from a Wisconsin family is not unusual. A fifth grader was invited to play on the local school's basketball team. The venture started well. But soon parents of other girls on the team began pressuring school officials who requested a report card as proof that the girl had the required grade point average. The family complied. Then they requested copies of the family's curriculum and school calendar. The family refused.

Homeschoolers who are strongly committed to sports can develop their interest and skills in ways other than being on public school teams. Among the possibilities:

- Some communities have sports teams and programs homeschoolers can join. Where teams don't already exist, homeschoolers can participate in organizing them. The Amateur Athletic Union (AAU), which provides a multi-sport program for all ages and organized athletic competition, may be contacted at 407-934-7200 or: www.aausports.org
- Informal sports are another possibility. Examples are neighborhood softball games, groups of homeschooling teens who gather to play sports, and a foursome that plays tennis regularly.
- Some private schools will allow families to homeschool and pay a fee just to play sports.
- Playing sports in college without having played them in high school is another option.
- Homeschoolers can participate in sports camps.
- Homeschoolers can choose individual sports that do not require a team, such as running and swimming.
- To be sure, none of these alternatives is the same as strongly competitive high school team sports. If that is what is most important to homeschoolers, they can simply attend high school and consider it part of the cost of playing sports. Homeschoolers and their families need to make their own decisions and balance the advantages and disadvantages. However, people who dream of being a star on the high school team, winning an athletic scholarship, and going on to play professional sports may want to think about how realistic these goals are. How many stars are there on the team, and how many athletic scholarships are there? There are 50 million students in kindergarten through twelfth grade and only 8,500 professional athletes in all sports in this country.

In considering ways in which homeschoolers can play sports outside public schools, it may help to remember that homeschooling does offer tremendous advantages to young people who are very serious about sports. Because of their more flexible schedules, homeschoolers have good opportunities to develop their talents. For young people whose long range goal is to become an outstanding athlete, rather than simply to play high school sports, homeschooling offers rich possibilities. For young people whose goal is to develop healthy minds and bodies through positive, supportive physical activity without overwhelming competition and pressure, homeschooling also offers a great deal.

Nonetheless, some people may argue that it is not fair to ask homeschoolers who really want to play high school sports not to pursue this option. One logical response is that homeschoolers who want to play sports can find other ways to do so, such as those mentioned above. They can even enroll in public school if sports are that important. But if the participation of a few homeschoolers in public school sports leads to increased government regulation of all homeschoolers, those who want to homeschool without unnecessary regulation would not be able to do so.

Therefore, WPA asks homeschoolers who may want to try to change WIAA regulations so they can play high school sports to think seriously about the cost to themselves, their families, and other homeschoolers in Wisconsin. Obviously, it is not easy to give up something that is very important, but as we have pointed out above, other good alternatives exist. And many, many homeschoolers have made sacrifices to gain and maintain our homeschooling freedoms. We will need to continue to make sacrifices, some of us more than others, to continue to maintain them.

Public School Records of Homeschooled Children

Parents who begin homeschooling after their children have attended a conventional school should get either the original set or a copy of their children's records, especially in light of recent legislation that has weakened provisions that protect the privacy of pupil records. In addition, collaboration among government agencies has increased the kinds of records that can be released to government agencies. Parents who obtain the original set of records are protecting their family's privacy and reducing the chances that information from their children's time in conventional schools will be transferred to other agencies and used against the family. Parents who obtain a copy of their children's pupil records at least know most of what is contained in the records and can take action to have inaccurate and unfair records corrected and to do as much as the law allows to protect their privacy and prevent the records from being released to individuals or agencies.

In requesting original pupil records or copies of them, it helps to understand that Wisconsin statute 118.125 defines several different categories of records, including behavioral records, directory data, progress records, and pupil phsyical health records. Some records are included in more than one category. See Appendix A for the text of this statute which defines these types.

When children withdraw from a school, the original set of pupil records is usually transferred to another school or school district within five days of a written notice from the school of record that the pupil intends to enroll in that school or district. See statutes 118.125(3) Maintenance of records and 118.125(4) Transfer of records in Appendix A..

Local school boards are required to have rules and regulations concerning the maintenance and confidentiality of pupil records. Parents who want to get their children's records might find it helpful to get a copy of these from their school district to see how they could be used by the parents.

There appear to be two different ways that homeschooling parents can obtain pupil records. The first, simplest, and most straightforward is to write to the school superintendent as a parent and request a complete copy of your children's records. Requests from parents are supported by three provisions in the statutes:

118.125(2)(a) A pupil, or the parent or guardian of a minor pupil, shall, upon request, be shown and provided with a copy of the pupil's progress records.

118.125(2)(b) An adult pupil or the parent or guardian of a minor pupil shall, upon request, be shown, in the presence of a person qualified to explain and interpret the records, the pupil's behavioral records. Such pupil or parent or guardian shall, upon request, be provided with a copy of the behavioral records.

118.125(2)(e) Upon the written permission of an adult pupil, or the parent or guardian of a minor pupil, the school shall make available to the person named in the permission the pupil's progress records or such portions of the pupil's behavioral records as determined by the person authorizing the release. Law enforcement officers' records obtained under s. 48.396 (1) or 938.396 (1) or (1m) may not be made available under this paragraph unless specifically identified by the adult pupil or by the parent or guardian of a minor pupil in the written permission.

Copies of "directory data" records are not specifically provided for in the statutes, but given the language of the statutes, the intent is clearly that parents are to have copies of these records as well. What is not as clear is how and where the personal notes and records used for psychological treatment by certain teachers and school personnel are maintained, or how parents could obtain either the original set or copies. Due to recent amendments to this statute, it is also unclear what happens to health records. Furthermore, confidentiality of records is no longer protected unless parents take action and formally deny access to the records. Even then courts and agencies now have access to information that until recently parents could prevent from being released.

The second way, and the way to get the original set of records (rather than getting a copy and leaving the originals with the school), is to write to the local school superintendent as the administrator of a home-based private educational program, including a copy of PI-1206 for the current school year and a copy of the DPI letter acknowledging receipt of your form. Request that the original and complete set of records be transferred to your home-based private educational program, since statute 118.165 defines such a program as a private school, and since your homeschool is now the school of record as shown on the enclosed PI-1206 form you signed as administrator.

The school district may be more willing to give you your children's original records if you request them in a formal letter you have signed as "Administrator." You could point out to the district that the law says they need to send the records within five days of receipt of your request.

School districts may hesitate to transfer original records to administrators of home-based private educational programs. They may claim that administrators of home-based private educational programs may not be qualified to interpret or use certain behavioral records. For these and/or other reasons, school districts may claim that they cannot transfer the original set of records to homeschools because they are not "schools." However, homeschools in Wisconsin are private schools. They are subject to the compulsory school attendance law and carry out the functions of a school. Therefore, administrators of these private schools may request the original set of pupil records, and public and other private schools should provide them.

Public School Student ID Numbers

In response to the federal No Child Left Behind Act of 2001, the DPI has created a statewide system for assigning ID numbers to public school students and using them to collect, store, sort, and use more personal data about students than the state has ever collected before. Called the Wisconsin Student Number Locator System (WSLS), this system undermines privacy and freedoms by allowing government officials and others access to personal information about students and families. Because of collaboration statutes passed during the 1990s, the data can be shared with other government agencies such as public health departments, law enforcement agencies, the courts, social service agencies, etc. An innocent adult applying for a job that requires a background check, a motorist charged with a traffic violation, or a parent reported to social services by an anonymous tipster could all find information collected during their years in public school included in materials being used against them.

The DPI has assured WPA that homeschoolers should not be assigned public school student ID numbers, even if they take one or two courses in a public school. The DPI has also informed school districts that private school students, including homeschoolers, are not to be included. It has posted on its website as one of the questions and answers dealing with the ID system the following: "Which students count as enrolled for WSLS purposes?" The answer: "A student is 'enrolled' in your district if the student receives his/her primary PK-12 educational services either (1) directly from district employees or (2) from a third party (not another Wisconsin district) under the direct supervision of your district." It is clear that since homeschoolers receive their primary PK-12 educational services from their homeschools and not from a public school district, they should not be included. However, because school officials are often misinformed or uninformed, we need to take responsibility for ensuring that our children are not wrongfully assigned a student ID number and included in the statewide ID system. It is easy to imagine a well-intentioned clerk who thinks that every student in the building should be in the system and therefore makes sure that homeschoolers taking one or two courses in the public school or participating in a program sponsored by the district (such as a summer recreation program) are included.

If your children are involved in any public school courses or programs, during the process of registering them you can send a letter of understanding to the school district administrator with a copy to the principal or program director. Give the names of the children involved, explain that they should not be included in WSLS, and state that it is your understanding that they will not be. Request that the district notify you within 10 days if your children are already included.

If homeschooled children have already been assigned an ID number, perhaps because they attended a public school at some point or they were assigned one by mistake, it is important to get them out of the system. Call the WPA Voice Mail for suggestions.

Inform other homeschoolers, especially those taking public school courses or participating in public school activities. If homeschoolers are included in the statewide database, it will set a precedent and make it more difficult to maintain the current policy.

Parents of public school students can reduce damage from their inclusion in the database by formally notifying their school district in writing that none of the directory data for their children may be released. Such notification requires the school district to activate the No-Release Indicator in the WSLS. The WSLS will then restrict access to the student's directory data, but it will not totally prevent it from being released to certain people. For more information, contact the DPI official responsible for administering the WSLS and/or visit the DPI web pages dealing with WSLS.

Chapter 33

Protecting Your Family's Privacy

We strengthen our position as homeschoolers when we act in ways that protect our privacy. Developing the habit of not giving away information about our family pays big rewards, especially if many of us do it. We are not paranoid, and we don't have anything to hide. We simply want to maintain as much control as we can over our lives and our personal information.

Why Privacy Is Important

• The more people and institutions know about us, the more power they have over us. Privacy is especially important for homeschoolers because homeschooling itself is sometimes a red flag. The more red flags we have, the greater the chance we will be regarded with suspicion and/or investigated. Thanks to legislation on collaboration passed in the 1990s, government agencies (including law enforcement, social services, county health, and courts) can share much more information than was previously allowed, so all those flags could end up in one file.
• Our children's futures may be influenced by the information about them that is in databases.
• Prevention is much, much better than cure. Once you have released information, it is very difficult, if not impossible, to get it back.
• Computers sort, use, misuse, flag, and spread information at frightening speed. If any incorrect information about your family gets into the system, it is very difficult to catch up with it and correct it.
• Protecting your privacy helps prevent identity theft. It also reduces annoying marketing calls and junk mail.
• As citizens of a democracy, we need to take responsibility for maintaining our freedoms and our privacy. When citizens do so, it helps keep the government in check.

Developing the Habit of Protecting Privacy

Developing the habit of refusing to give information, and teaching your children to do so, will make a big difference. Here are some suggestions.

• Be aware of the many ways information about your family is being collected through birth certificates, preschool and mental health screenings, social security numbers, medical records, drivers licenses, taxes, mortgages, credit cards, Internet use, etc.
• Ask the following questions before providing any information:
1. Is this information absolutely necessary? Some is legally required, like that on form PI-1206. Some is necessary for your own safety and well-being, like telling a doctor what medications you are taking. Some is simply on a form and not required, like giving your phone number when you buy something.
2. How will the information be used?
3. Is it likely to be spread or shared with companies and organizations?
4. Can I really trust the organization, institution, or business I'm giving the information to? It's not usually enough to trust the individual you are communicating with. They probably are just doing their job and don't have a real understanding of how the information will be used.
• Know your rights and exercise them. Refuse to give information that is not required. Otherwise, if people voluntarily give information, we don't even need laws to allow the government and other organizations to collect, store, sort, use, and misuse information about us and other families.
• Read privacy notices that banks, insurance companies, and other institutions are required by federal statute to send every year. If they offer a way you can restrict the information they share, do so.
• Have only the minimum information printed on personal checks. Do not include your phone number, social security number, drivers license number, or other information.
• Ask unwanted telemarketers to put you on their "do not call" list.
• Tell your federal and state legislators that you oppose legislation that allows the government and/or other institutions access to people's private information and that you favor legislation that protects privacy.
• Don't just say, "What's the point? They could get my address, phone number, or whatever other information is being requested from the Internet or some other source." If you don't give them the information, they will have to work to get it, which they may not bother to do, so they may not get the information. You also send the message that privacy is important, which may build a basis for protecting it further.
• Try to keep private information off the Internet. Occasionally do a search for your name and then for your phone number. Try to have as much personal information removed as possible.
• Carefully dispose of papers that have private information.

Specific Ways to Protect Our Privacy

Newborns

When getting a birth certificate and requesting a social security number for her newborn in Wisconsin, a mother is asked for personal information about herself and her husband, including things like their social security numbers, employment a year before the birth, the highest grade each of them completed in school, the month that the mother's prenatal care began, cigarette and alcohol use, weight gain or loss during pregnancy, etc. This information is certainly not needed to record a birth or issue a social security number for the baby. The fact that it is asked for just after a birth makes it easier to collect-what new parent feels like worrying about a form at such a special time?

WPA recommends that new parents ask which of the questions are optional, since the person requesting the information is unlikely to inform parents that many of the questions are optional, and refuse to answer any optional questions.

Immunization Records

We can have information about members of our family removed from the Wisconsin Immunization Registry (WIR). The WIR can be accessed by health professionals, insurance companies, schools, hospitals and clinics, and state and county agencies dealing with health and human services. To have records removed, we need to file a separate Wisconsin Immunization Registry Exclusion form (HCF 5102) for each person. To request forms, write to the Wisconsin Immunization Program, 1 W. Wilson, P. O. Box 2659, Madison, WI 53701-2659. Parents who do not want their children's records included in WIR in the first place can indicate this when they provide information for their children's birth certificates. For more information, see www.dhfs.state.wi.us/vitalrecords/index.htm.

Screenings

Preschool screenings, informal mental health screenings by professionals, and other screenings give the government a lot of information about our families. Parents are not legally required to take their children to preschool screenings, even though the letters that announce such events often say they are "required by law." (School districts are required by law to provide them; families are not required to participate.) We can avoid them by refusing to participate. More difficult to avoid are informal mental health screenings by health care providers and others. Often they do not announce that they are screening us. It is worth our while to be alert for such screenings and to refuse to answer the questions. See "Screenings" in Chapter 31.

Social Security Numbers

Be especially careful of your social security number, given its importance and the amount of information that is connected to it. Unless you have very, very good reason, do NOT give it to anyone except an employer for whom you are working, a financial institution from whom you will be getting interest which may be taxable (which means your social security number is required by statute), or, if you want a drivers license, the Department of Motor Vehicles. (Wisconsin statutes require that people getting drivers licenses give their social security number or sign a form stating they are withholding it for religious reasons.) Do not put your social security number on a job application, even if there's a blank for it or a clerk asks you for it. Do not have it printed on your checks. (If it's on checks you don't want to waste, cross the number out before using the checks.) Do not use it as a student ID number. (Many institutions request it because it's an easy way to keep track of you. However, if you explain that you don't want it used that way, they will usually assign or let you choose an alternative number.)

Drivers Licenses

The Wisconsin Department of Motor Vehicles (DMV) releases personal information about licensed drivers. For example, for $250, anyone can purchase a computerized file with the name, date of birth, address, gender, license type, license number and expiration date of the four million licensed drivers in Wisconsin (except those who have opted out of the database). The DMV receives several requests a month for this information. The only way to prevent the release of this information is to file form MV 3592 with the DMV. Forms are available at DMV locations or at www.dot.wisconsin.gov/drivers/optout.htm.

Conventional School Records

If your children have attended a conventional school and are now homeschooling, it's a good idea to get the originals of their school records or at least copies of them, especially if there were problems. Negative school records can follow children into adulthood. See "Public School Records of Homeschooled Children" in Chapter 32.

Public School Student ID Numbers

To comply with the reporting requirements of the federal education law called No Child Left Behind (NCLB), Wisconsin public schools now have an extensive and elaborate statewide database of students. Homeschoolers are not supposed to be included, but this does not guarantee that we won't be. Homeschoolers who take one or two classes at a public high school or participate in a public school program need to be especially careful that they are not put in the database. See "Public School Student ID Numbers" in Chapter 32.

Family Educational Rights and Privacy Act

Our right to privacy is protected by the federal Family Educational Rights and Privacy Act (FERPA). This act is the basis for the DPI's appropriate policy, "The DPI does not release the names of families who are currently providing a home-based private educational program." ("Questions and DPI Responses Relating To Home-Based Private Educational Programs") Homeschoolers can use FERPA to object to the release of the names of homeschooling families by their local school districts and other similar actions. The code reference for the statute is Title 20, Chapter 31, Subchapter III, Part 4, Section 1232g. See Appendix A for the text.

Department of Defense Database

The Department of Defense announced in May 2005 that it was creating a database of young people ages 16-25 for military recruiting and other "routine" purposes. Many homeschoolers do not want to be included. They prefer to contact the military themselves if they are interested. If you want, you can try to stay out of the database by writing a letter to your local school district explaining that they do not have the authority to release contact information about homeschoolers and you do not want them to release any information about you that they might have.

If you are already in the database, the best you can do is contact JAMRS (the company that manages it) and ask to "opt out," which means requesting that your data not be released. (It will be moved to a "suppression file;" it will not be deleted from the database.) However, this presents a dilemma. If you are not already in the database, you will be providing more information than the database managers have in order to opt out. Unfortunately, WPA has been unable to find an effective way to determine whether someone is in the database. However, people who are being contacted by military recruiters probably have been included. When a young person turns 18, they are required to register and therefore information about them is probably in the database. Requesting suppression, however, is still possible.

To opt out of the database, write to Joint Advertising and Marketing Research & Studies Office (JAMRS), Attention: Opt Out, 4040 North Fairfax Drive, Ste. 200, Arlington, VA 22203

Telemarketers

To prevent telemarketers from contacting you, contact Wisconsin's No Call List at 866-966-2255 or complete a form at https://nocall.wisconsin.gov/web/registration.asp. Call the National Do Not Call Registry at 888-382-1222. The website is www.ftc.gov/donotcall.

Privacy Resources

For comprehensive information about privacy, your rights, laws, and effective measures to take to protect your privacy, contact Privacy Rights Clearinghouse at www.privacyrights.org or 3100 5th Ave., Suite B, San Diego, CA 92103; 619-298-3396 or Electronic Privacy Information Center (EPIC) at www.epic.org.

Chapter 34

Current Developments That Affect Homeschoolers

Developments occurring outside homeschooling affect homeschoolers. Some are discussed here so that we homeschoolers can better understand changes that are happening and act in ways that will minimize the negative effects they have on us. Sometimes we can have a significant effect on what is happening. More often, unfortunately, the changes are too large and powerful and beyond our control. Then our best response is to work to maintain the rights and freedoms we have, perhaps also trying to secure exemptions from laws and regulations so that parents and families will still have as much choice as possible. It sometimes seems that the magnitude of these changes and the swiftness with which they are occurring make it more important than ever that we continue to homeschool and work to maintain our homeschooling rights and freedoms, which offer a way to make our own decisions, maintain greater control over our lives, and live according to our principles and beliefs.

Increases in State-Mandated Testing and Assessment

Use of state-mandated standardized tests is increasing, partly because recent federal education legislation, No Child Left Behind (NCLB), requires that schools test students to qualify for federal funds.

Among the problems with federal testing of students, including homeschoolers:

• Standardized tests are biased and unfair. They do not measure what a person knows; they only measure how a person performed on a test on a given day. They are unfair to minorities, women, and anyone whose values, beliefs, and experiences differ from those of the test makers. They do not measure or give test takers credit for physical skills, mechanical ability, creativity, integrity, etc. Creative thinkers and people who know a lot about a subject often have more difficulty because they see the complexities of supposedly simple questions.

• Tests dictate curriculum and how subjects are covered. To prepare students, schools need to teach what is on the tests. This means that tests required by the federal government will lead to federal control of the curriculum in schools throughout the country. Federal testing of homeschoolers would force homeschools to become more like the conventional schools many of us have chosen to avoid by homeschooling.
• Federal testing erodes local control of education and the role of local school boards, communities, and individual states in education. It moves the US toward federal control of education, something that is inconsistent with freedom of education.
• Compulsory attendance laws require attendance, not education. This distinction is crucial. If the government were to require compulsory education, we would lose our freedom of education and learning and even our freedom of thought. However, testing required by either the federal or state governments increases the government's role in education and moves us closer to compulsory education because tests dictate what students must learn.
• Testing required by the federal government represents a major increase in federal control of education. According to the US Constitution, the states, not the federal government, have the policing authority to make laws that govern schools. But through No Child Left Behind and other legislation, the federal government is claiming it has the authority to require testing to ensure that students in schools that accept money from the federal government meet federal standards and goals.
• The bipartisan support for and lack of opposition to federal testing requirements indicate that the general public either supports testing or does not care enough to oppose it. It is unsettling, to say the least, to observe the readiness with which people are sitting by while the federal government ties a noose around the neck of America's schools.

In Wisconsin, as in other states, state-mandated tests are now required of public school students in the fourth, eighth, and tenth grades plus a twelfth grade graduation test. Such tests have a strong effect on children's futures and give the state increased power and authority over education. Fortunately, parents worked hard through WPA to have included in the legislation a provision that allows parents to have their children exempted from these tests.

Vouchers and School Choice Programs

At first glance, a voucher system appears to have many advantages: the government would give each family the money it would have spent on a public school education for the family's children, and the family could use this money to educate their children in the way they choose. It sounds like a homeschooler's dream-to actually get paid for homeschooling. However, in reality it is clear that vouchers would not be allowed to be used for homeschooling unless the government had strong control over homeschools, unless strong regulations were strictly enforced, and unless homeschoolers could prove that their children were getting an equivalent education. Therefore, many homeschoolers conclude that the only way we could participate in a voucher system would be to pay for it with our freedom, and they are very wary of submitting to further regulation in order to participate in a voucher program.

Collaboration

Legislation has increased collaboration among government agencies, allowing them to exchange confidential information and records. This undermines the privacy of individuals and families. It also may cause officials to be prejudiced against families who are already on record with other agencies for doing things that the officials consider to be questionable, like homeschooling. WPA recommends that families try to minimize the records that are kept on them. For example, when parents do not take their children to preschool screening, they prevent the establishment of a record with screening and test results in it. See "Screening" in Chapter 31 and "Privacy" in Chapter 33.

Legislation Supposedly Designed to Protect Parental Rights

In recent years, legislation has been introduced in the US Congress and many state legislatures that attempts to protect parental rights and responsibilities in education, health care, religion, and other areas. To be sure, parental rights and responsibilities need to be maintained, especially in light of recent attempts to protect children by increasing the power and authority of the government, particularly in the areas of education and social services. Unfortunately, either state or federal legislation to protect parental rights is a serious mistake that will not only fail to protect our rights but will also cost parents and families an enormous amount of freedom and contribute to the current erosion of the legal, social, and moral position of families in our society.

Parental rights and responsibilities in education are basic and fundamental and do not come from the government. If we allow the government to pass a law or a constitutional amendment which gives the government authority in education, we will be diminishing the rights we have independent of the state and increasing the control the state has over our children's education.

One of the important lessons from these initiatives is that it is virtually impossible to write a law that protects parental rights in areas that are considered fundamental, such as education and health care, without first passing laws that require parents to take responsibility for their children. (To be sure, parents are responsible for their children. However, they do not want or need to have the government grant this responsibility to them and then check to make sure that they are doing the right thing.)

Even more serious, if the government passed legislation that required that parents assume responsibility for their children, then parents would have to demonstrate to the government that they were being responsible by acting in ways that were consistent with the beliefs, standards, and choices of those people who have the most power in our society. Therefore, the government would decide what kind of education and health care would be required, how families would be monitored to ensure that they were complying with the law, and how they would be dealt with if a government official decided that they were not complying. These legislative initiatives, supposedly designed to protect parental rights, actually diminish basic freedoms that are the foundations of a democratic society.

Offers from Public Schools to Homeschoolers

See Chapter 31.

Increases in Programs Targeted at Children from Birth to Three

Child development specialists, social workers, medical personnel, and professional educators are focusing increased attention on children from birth to age three. Some of these "experts" are well-intentioned, but many are influenced by the fact that their prestige, careers, job security, and salaries all benefit from the increased emphasis. Government involvement in this area is also increasing. One prime example is the 1986 reauthorization of the federal Individuals with Disabilities Education Act (IDEA). Part H of this program covers "Early Intervention Programs for Infants and Toddlers With Disabilities." The programs are designed to find and treat children from birth on who

> (1) Are experiencing developmental delays...in one or more of the following areas: (i) Cognitive development, (ii) Physical development, including vision and hearing, (iii) Communication development, (iv) Social or emotional development, (v) Adaptive development; or (2) Have a diagnosed physical or mental condition that has a high probability of resulting in developmental delay. (b) The term may also include, at a State's discretion, children from birth through age two who are at risk of having substantial developmental delays if early intervention services are not provided.

These criteria would give the state grounds for intervening in just about any family with young children. Among the people who are to report suspected problems are parents and families, medical personnel (including those attending births), and employees of social service agencies, mental health programs, WIC, day care centers, preschools, Head Start, and public school programs.

In addition, government records would be established for children identified under such programs. Since collaboration increases the exchange of information among government agencies, once a file is established on children in a family, the chances increase that the file will be expanded with other information about the family.

These programs could cause problems for families that have young children and are considering homeschooling, including the following:

• The programs undermine families by decreasing parents' confidence. The programs often take so-called problems that don't really exist, that are really a normal part of development for many children who outgrow them if given time and support, and turn them into self-fulfilling prophecies. In addition, they increase the power and authority of the state and professionals in families' lives by increasing the extent to which they are taking over the traditional roles of the family.

• If children are diagnosed as having disabilities or labeled as being at risk, officials may pressure parents not to homeschool, claiming that these children need the expert help that is available only through specialists and conventional schools. Of course, many families have shown that such children certainly can be homeschooled. In fact, they often learn better at home than in conventional schools. See Chapter 9.

WPA recommends that families be alert for ways in which they could get drawn into such programs and seriously consider not having their children screened or tested unless there is a very clear need. For more information, see "Screening" in Chapter 31.

What We Can Do To Counter These Developments

• Be informed. We need to choose our sources of information carefully. The mainstream media reports and reflects the views of the government, professional interest groups, and big corporations. Therefore, much of the information we receive from mainstream radio, television, newspapers, and magazines is strongly biased in favor of the very developments we oppose and is unlikely to be helpful to us. Many people prefer to get their information from independent sources such as the WPA newsletter.

• Share our concerns with others. We need to help as many people as possible understand what is happening and decide what they want to do in response to the direction in which our society is moving.

• Act in ways that support and communicate to others what we believe. We can refuse to have our children tested at preschool screenings or in other situations.

• Act in ways that will maintain our rights and responsibilities. See Chapters 20 and 21.

• Continue to homeschool. By homeschooling we are living according to our principles, maintaining strong families, strengthening an important educational alternative, living meaningful lives, and preparing our children and ourselves for the future.

Conclusion: Strengthening Homeschooling

Among the ways you can strengthen both your own homeschool and the homeschooling movement are the following.

• Relax and enjoy learning with your family.

• Find approaches to learning that work well for everyone in your family and encourage family members to develop their strengths, talents, and special interests.

• Make connections with other homeschoolers.

• Make sure your own house is in order. Comply with Wisconsin law, including filing Form PI-1206. Act in ways that reflect positively on homeschooling. Be discreet. Whenever possible, without compromising important principles, appear as conventional as possible.

• Know your rights and responsibilities under the law. Understand the basic foundations of homeschooling freedoms, including the difference between compulsory school attendance and compulsory education.

• Comply with only the minimum requirements of the law. Don't set dangerous precedents by agreeing to officials' requests that are not required by law.

• Resist the temptation to use personal credentials ("I'm a certified teacher") or status ("I'm recognized as an exemplary homeschooler"), even to get out of difficult situations with school officials, reporters, and others. Using credentials or status may make it difficult for other homeschoolers who do not have the same credentials or status, which are not necessary for homeschooling anyway.

• Join with other homeschoolers in WPA, an inclusive statewide grassroots homeschooling organization that encourages all homeschoolers to work together to protect the right of every family to choose for their children an education consistent with their principles and beliefs. Send information to WPA on developments in your local community and on your experiences both homeschooling your children and working to maintain rights and responsibilities. Support WPA with participation, membership, and donations. Attend the WPA conference each spring. Encourage other homeschoolers to join.

• Respect diversity among homeschoolers.

• Help new homeschoolers and people considering homeschooling get accurate information so they can comply with the law and act in ways that will help maintain our rights and responsibilities. Encourage them to get a copy of this book.

• Get to know your legislators. It is important that legislators get to know homeschoolers as individuals and families, not just names and statistics. The outstanding work we do in educating our children and our commitment to homeschooling are best communicated through personal contact. Legislators who know homeschoolers as individuals are less likely to view homeschoolers merely as a political faction.

• Take responsibility for developments in your local community and the state. It is better not to assume that someone else is going to identify and solve problems. Each of us needs to be alert to what is happening that affects or could affect homeschooling at the community and state level. WPA learns of important events from individual homeschoolers, not through a top-down chain of command. Establish and use communication channels, including WPA Regional Coordinators, to help us all be informed.

• Avoid acting hastily on your own. Before making a move, particularly on an important issue, discuss your concerns and proposed strategy with other homeschoolers, including your WPA Regional Coordinator. Without this kind of communication, we could easily make serious mistakes or work at cross-purposes, threatening each other's effectiveness.

• Promote a positive image of homeschooling through public meetings about homeschooling, newspaper articles, letters to the editor, calls to radio talk shows, etc. Telling our stories is also an important part of gaining support for homeschooling.

• Accentuate the positive. Celebrate who your children are and what they do.

Appendix A
Wisconsin Laws Relating to Homeschooling

DESCRIPTION	STATUTE HEADER	STAT. #	PAGE
Compulsory school attendance	Compulsory school attendance	118.15	266
	School attendance enforcement	118.16	266
Homeschooling law	Private schools	118.165	268
	Private school determination by state superintendent	118.167	268
	Definitions	115.001 (3g)	268
	Definitions	115.001 (3r)	268
Age of pupils	Age of pupils	118.14	266
Immunization	Immunization	252.04	269
Open records law (freedom of information)	Public records and property	19.21--19.35	262
Courses in public schools	Admission to high school	118.145	266
Public school ID system	Pupil identification numbers	118.169	268
Public school assessment and exemption	Pupil assessment	118.30	268
Public school graduation	Public school graduation standards criteria for promotion	118.33	268
School census	Annual school district report	120.18	268
Student discrimination	Pupil discrimination prohibited	118.13	266
Student records	Pupil records	118.125	263
Wisconsin State Constitution	Article X. Education	Article X	269
Homeschool graduate	Military enlistment statute (US)	Sect. 591	269

NOTES:

(1) Selected parts of the statutes are printed on the following pages.

(2) The Wisconsin statutes included here were amended or enacted through January, 2005. Many statutes are revised each year. Major changes in these and related statutes will be reported in the WPA newsletter. (Actually, important proposed changes will be discussed there before they become law.) If you need to be sure that you have the most recent version of the statutes, get a current copy from the Legislative Reference Bureau, the Legislative Council, or through the Internet.

(3) The sections of the law that relate most directly to the content of this book are printed in a larger type. Also, bold type was added for emphasis.

*Wisconsin's homeschooling law, 1983 Act 512, when put into statute form became s.118.165, s.118.167, s.115.001 (3g), and s.115.001 (3r). It appears on page 268.

PUBLIC RECORDS AND PROPERTY

19.21 Custody and delivery of official property and records. (1) Each and every officer of the state, or of any county, town, city, village, school district, or other municipality or district, is the legal custodian of and shall safely keep and preserve all property and things received from the officer's predecessor or other persons and required by law to be filed, deposited, or kept in the officer's office, or which are in the lawful possession or control of the officer or the officer's deputies, or to the possession or control of which the officer or the officer's deputies may be lawfully entitled, as such officers.

19.31 Declaration of policy. In recognition of the fact that a representative government is dependent upon an informed electorate, it is declared to be the public policy of this state that all persons are entitled to the greatest possible information regarding the affairs of government and the official acts of those officers and employees who represent them. Further, providing persons with such information is declared to be an essential function of a representative government and an integral part of the routine duties of officers and employees whose responsibility it is to provide such information. To that end, ss. 19.32 to 19.37 shall be construed in every instance with a presumption of complete public access, consistent with the conduct of governmental business. The denial of public access generally is contrary to the public interest, and only in an exceptional case may access be denied.

19.32 Definitions. As used in ss. 19.33 to 19.39: **(1) "Authority"** means any of the following having custody of a record: a state or local office, elected official, agency, board, commission, committee, council, department or public body corporate and politic created by constitution, law, ordinance, rule or order; a governmental or quasi-governmental corporation except for the Bradley center sports and entertainment corporation; a local exposition district under subch. II of ch. 229; a family care district under s. 46.2895; any court of law; the assembly or senate; a nonprofit corporation which receives more than 50% of its funds from a county or a municipality, as defined in s. 59.001 (3), and which provides services related to public health or safety to the county or municipality; a nonprofit corporation operating the Olympic ice training center under s. 42.11 (3); or a formally constituted subunit of any of the foregoing. (1b) **"Committed person"** means a person who is committed under ch. 51, 971, 975 or 980 and who is placed in an inpatient treatment facility, during the period that the person's placement in the inpatient treatment facility continues. (1bg) **"Employee"** means any individual who is employed by an authority, other than an individual holding local public office or a state public office, or any individual who is employed by an employer other than an authority. (1c) **"Incarcerated person"** means a person who is incarcerated in a penal facility or who is placed on probation and given confinement under s. 973.09 (4) as a condition of placement, during the period of confinement for which the person has been sentenced. (1d) **"Inpatient treatment facility"** means any of the following: (a) A mental health institute, as defined in s. 51.01 (12). (c) A facility or unit for the institutional care of sexually violent persons specified under s. 980.065. (d) The Milwaukee County mental health complex established under s. 51.08. (1de) **"Local governmental unit"** has the meaning given in s. 19.42 (7u). (1dm) **"Local public office"** has the meaning given in s. 19.42 (7w), and also includes any appointive office or position of a local governmental unit in which an individual serves as the head of a department, agency, or division of the local governmental unit, but does not include any office or position filled by a municipal employee, as defined in s. 111.70 (1) (i). (1e) **"Penal facility"** means a state prison under s. 302.01, county jail, county house of correction or other state, county or municipal correctional or detention facility. (1m) **"Person authorized by the individual"** means the parent, guardian, as defined in s. 48.02 (8), or legal custodian, as defined in s. 48.02 (11), of a child, as defined in s. 48.02 (2), the guardian, as defined in s. 880.01 (3), of an individual adjudged incompetent, as defined in s. 880.01 (4), the personal representative or spouse of an individual who is deceased or any person authorized, in writing, by the individual to exercise the rights granted under this section. (1r) **"Personally identifiable information"** has the meaning specified in s. 19.62 (5). **(2) "Record"** means any material on which written, drawn, printed, spoken, visual or electromagnetic information is recorded or preserved, regardless of physical form or characteristics, which has been created or is being kept by an authority. "Record" includes, but is not limited to, handwritten, typed or printed pages, maps, charts, photographs, films, recordings, tapes (including computer tapes), computer printouts and optical disks. "Record" does not include drafts, notes, preliminary computations and like materials prepared for the originator's personal use or prepared by the originator in the name of a person for whom the originator is working; materials which are purely the personal property of the custodian and have no relation to his or her office; materials to which access is limited by copyright, patent or bequest; and published materials in the possession of an authority other than a public library which are available for sale, or which are available for inspection at a public library. (2g) **"Record subject"** means an individual about whom personally identifiable information is contained in a record. (3) **"Requester"** means any person who requests inspection or copies of a record, except a committed or incarcerated person, unless the person requests inspection or copies of a record that contains specific references to that person or his or her minor children for whom he or she has not been denied physical placement under ch. 767, and the record is otherwise accessible to the person by law. (4) "State public office" has the meaning given in s. 19.42 (13), but does not include a position identified in s. 20.923 (6) (f) to (gm).

19.34 Procedural information. (1) Each authority shall adopt, prominently display and make available for inspection and copying at its offices, for the guidance of the public, a notice containing a description of its organization and the established times and places at which, the legal custodian under s. 19.33 from whom, and the methods whereby, the public may obtain information and access to records in its custody, make requests for records, or obtain copies of records, and the costs thereof. The notice shall also separately identify each position of the authority that constitutes a local public office or a state public office. This subsection does not apply to members of the legislature or to members of any local governmental body. (2) (a) Each authority which maintains regular office hours at the location where records in the custody of the authority are kept shall permit access to the records of the authority at all times during those office hours, unless otherwise specifically authorized by law. (b) Each authority which does not maintain regular office hours at the location where records in the custody of the authority are kept shall: 1. Permit access to its records upon at least 48 hours' written or oral notice of intent to inspect or copy a record; or 2. Establish a period of at least 2 consecutive hours per week during which access to the records of the authority is permitted. In such case, the authority may require 24 hours' advance written or oral notice of intent to inspect or copy a record. (c) An authority imposing a notice requirement under par. (b) shall include a statement of the requirement in its notice under sub. (1), if the authority is required to adopt a notice under that subsection. (d) If a record of an authority is occasionally taken to a location other than the location where records of the authority are regularly kept, and the record may be inspected at the place at which records of the authority are regularly kept upon one business day's notice, the authority or legal custodian of the record need not provide access to the record at the occasional location.

19.345 Time computation.

In ss. 19.33 to 19.39, when a time period is provided for performing an act, whether the period is expressed in hours or days, the whole of Saturday, Sunday, and any legal holiday, from midnight to midnight, shall be excluded in computing the period.

19.35 Access to records; fees.

(1) RIGHT TO INSPECTION. (a) Except as otherwise provided by law, any requester has a right to inspect any record. Substantive common law principles construing the right to inspect, copy or receive copies of records shall remain in effect. The exemptions to the requirement of a governmental body to meet in open session under s. 19.85 are indicative of public policy, but may be used as grounds for denying public access to a record only if the authority or legal custodian under s. 19.33 makes a specific demonstration that there is a need to restrict public access at the time that the request to inspect or copy the record is made. (am) In addition to any right under par. (a), any requester who is an individual or person authorized by the individual, has a right to inspect any record containing personally identifiable information pertaining to the individual that is maintained by an

authority and to make or receive a copy of any such information. The right to inspect or copy a record under this paragraph does not apply to any of the following:
1. Any record containing personally identifiable information that is collected or maintained in connection with a complaint, investigation or other circumstances that may lead to an enforcement action, administrative proceeding, arbitration proceeding or court proceeding, or any such record that is collected or maintained in connection with such an action or proceeding.
2. Any record containing personally identifiable information that, if disclosed, would do any of the following: a. Endanger an individual's life or safety. b. Identify a confidential informant. c. Endanger the security, including the security of the population or staff, of any state prison under s. 302.01, jail, as defined in s. 165.85 (2) (bg), secured correctional facility, as defined in s. 938.02 (15m), secured child caring institution, as defined in s. 938.02 (15g), secured group home, as defined in s. 938.02 (15p), mental health institute, as defined in s. 51.01 (12), center for the developmentally disabled, as defined in s. 51.01 (3), or facility, specified under s. 980.065, for the institutional care of sexually violent persons. d. Compromise the rehabilitation of a person in the custody of the department of corrections or detained in a jail or facility identified in subd. 2. c.
3. Any record that is part of a records series, as defined in s. 19.62 (7), that is not indexed, arranged or automated in a way that the record can be retrieved by the authority maintaining the records series by use of an individual's name, address or other identifier. (b) Except as otherwise provided by law, any requester has a right to inspect a record and to make or receive a copy of a record which appears in written form. If a requester appears personally to request a copy of a record, the authority having custody of the record may, at its option, permit the requester to photocopy the record or provide the requester with a copy substantially as readable as the original. (c) Except as otherwise provided by law, any requester has a right to receive from an authority having custody of a record which is in the form of a comprehensible audio tape recording a copy of the tape recording substantially as audible as the original. The authority may instead provide a transcript of the recording to the requester if he or she requests. (d) Except as otherwise provided by law, any requester has a right to receive from an authority having custody of a record which is in the form of a video tape recording a copy of the tape recording substantially as good as the original. (e) Except as otherwise provided by law, any requester has a right to receive from an authority having custody of a record which is not in a readily comprehensible form a copy of the information contained in the record assembled and reduced to written form on paper. (em) If an authority receives a request to inspect or copy a record that is in handwritten form or a record that is in the form of a voice recording which the authority is required to withhold or from which the authority is required to delete information under s. 19.36 (8) (b) because the handwriting or the recorded voice would identify an informant, the authority shall provide to the requester, upon his or her request, a transcript of the record or the information contained in the record if the record or information is otherwise subject to public inspection and copying under this subsection. (f) Except as otherwise provided by law, any requester has a right to inspect any record not specified in pars. (b) to (e) the form of which does not permit copying. If a requester requests permission to photograph the record, the authority having custody of the record may permit the requester to photograph the record. If a requester requests that a photograph of the record be provided, the authority shall provide a good quality photograph of the record. (g) Paragraphs (a) to (c), (e) and (f) do not apply to a record which has been or will be promptly published with copies offered for sale or distribution. (h) A request under pars. (a) to (f) is deemed sufficient if it reasonably describes the requested record or the information requested. However, a request for a record without a reasonable limitation as to subject matter or length of time represented by the record does not constitute a sufficient request. A request may be made orally, but a request must be in writing before an action to enforce the request is commenced under s. 19.37. (i) Except as authorized under this paragraph, no request under pars. (a) and (b) to (f) may be refused because the person making the request is unwilling to be identified or to state the purpose of the request. Except as authorized under this paragraph, no request under pars. (a) to (f) may be refused because the request is received by mail, unless prepayment of a fee is required under sub. (3) (f). A requester may be required to show acceptable identification whenever the requested record is kept at a private residence or whenever security reasons or federal law or regulations so require. (j) Notwithstanding pars. (a) to (f), a requester shall comply with any regulations or restrictions upon access to or use of information which are specifically prescribed by law. (k) Notwithstanding pars. (a), (am), (b) and (f), a legal custodian may impose reasonable restrictions on the manner of access to an original record if the record is irreplaceable or easily damaged. (L) Except as necessary to comply with pars. (c) to (e) or s. 19.36 (6), this subsection does not require an authority to create a new record by extracting information from existing records and compiling the information in a new format.

(2) FACILITIES. The authority shall provide any person who is authorized to inspect or copy a record under sub. (1) (a), (am), (b) or (f) with facilities comparable to those used by its employees to inspect, copy and abstract the record during established office hours. An authority is not required by this subsection to purchase or lease photocopying, duplicating, photographic or other equipment or to provide a separate room for the inspection, copying or abstracting of records.

(3) FEES. (a) An authority may impose a fee upon the requester of a copy of a record which may not exceed the actual, necessary and direct cost of reproduction and transcription of the record, unless a fee is otherwise specifically established or authorized to be established by law.

118.125 Pupil records.

(1) DEFINITIONS. In this section:

(a) "Behavioral records" means those pupil records which include psychological tests, personality evaluations, records of conversations, any written statement relating specifically to an individual pupil's behavior, tests relating specifically to achievement or measurement of ability, the pupil's physical health records other than his or her immunization records or any lead screening records required under s. 254.162, law enforcement officers' records obtained under s. 48.396 (1) or 938.396 (1) or (1m) and any other pupil records that are not progress records.

(b) "Directory data" means those pupil records which include the pupil's name, address, telephone listing, date and place of birth, major field of study, participation in officially recognized activities and sports, weight and height of members of athletic teams, dates of attendance, photographs, degrees and awards received and the name of the school most recently previously attended by the pupil. (be) "Law enforcement agency" has the meaning given in s. 165.83 (1) (b). (bL) "Law enforcement unit" means any individual, office, department, division, or other component of a school district that is authorized or designated by the school board to do any of the following: 1. Enforce any law or ordinance, or refer to the appropriate authorities a matter for enforcement of any law or ordinance, against any person other than the school district. 2. Maintain the physical security and safety of a public school. (bs) "Law enforcement unit records" means records maintained by a law enforcement unit that were created by that law enforcement unit for the purpose of law enforcement.

(c) "Progress records" means those pupil records which include the pupil's grades, a statement of the courses the pupil has taken, the pupil's attendance record, the pupil's immunization records, any lead screening records required under s. 254.162 and records of the pupil's school extracurricular activities. (cm) "Pupil physical health records" means those pupil records that include basic health information about a pupil, including the pupil's immunization records, an emergency medical card, a log of first aid and medicine administered to the pupil, an athletic permit card, a record concerning the pupil's ability to participate in an education program, any lead screening records required under s. 254.162, the results of any routine screening test, such as for hearing, vision or scoliosis, and any follow-up to such test, and any other basic health information, as determined by the state superintendent.

(d) "Pupil records" means all records relating to individual pupils maintained by a school but does not include any of the following: 1. Notes or records maintained for personal use by a teacher or other person who is required by the state superintendent under s. 115.28 (7) to hold a certificate, license, or permit if such records and notes are not available to others. 2. Records necessary for, and available only to persons involved in, the psychological treatment of a pupil. 3. Law enforcement unit records. (e) "Record" means any material on which written, drawn, printed, spoken, visual, or electromagnetic information is recorded or preserved, regardless of physical form or characteristics.

(2) CONFIDENTIALITY.

All pupil records maintained by a public school shall be confidential, except as provided in pars. (a) to (p) and sub. (2m). The school board shall adopt regulations to maintain the confidentiality of such records.

(a) A pupil, or the parent or guardian of a minor pupil, shall, upon request, be shown and provided with a copy of the pupil's progress records.

(b) An adult pupil or the parent or guardian of a minor pupil shall, upon request, be shown, in the presence of a person qualified to explain and interpret the records, the pupil's behavioral records. Such pupil or parent or guardian shall, upon request, be provided with a copy of the behavioral records.

(c) 1. The judge of any court of this state or of the United States shall, upon request, be provided by the school district clerk or his or her designee with a copy of all progress records of a pupil who is the subject of any proceeding in such court.
2. Names of dropouts shall be provided to a court in response to an order under s. 118.163 (2m) (b).

(cg) The school district clerk or his or her designee shall provide a law enforcement agency with a copy of a pupil's attendance record if the law enforcement agency certifies in writing that the pupil is under investigation for truancy or for allegedly committing a criminal or delinquent act and that the law enforcement agency will not further disclose the pupil's attendance record except as permitted under s. 938.396 (1) to (1x). A school district clerk or designee who discloses a copy of a pupil's attendance record to a law enforcement agency for purposes of a truancy investigation shall notify the pupil's parent or guardian of that disclosure as soon as practicable after that disclosure.

(ch) The school district clerk or his or her designee shall provide a fire investigator under s. 165.55 (15) with a copy of a pupil's attendance record if the fire investigator certifies in writing that the pupil is under investigation under s. 165.55, that the pupil's attendance record is necessary for the fire investigator to pursue his or her investigation and that the fire investigator will use and further disclose the pupil's attendance record only for the purpose of pursuing that investigation.

(cm) If school attendance is a condition of a child's dispositional order under s. 48.355 (2) (b) 7. or 938.355 (2) (b) 7., the school board shall notify the county department that is responsible for supervising the child within 5 days after any violation of the condition by the child. (d) Pupil records shall be made available to persons employed by the school district which the pupil attends who are required by the department under s. 115.28 (7) to hold a license and other school district officials who have been determined by the school board to have legitimate educational interests, including safety interests, in the pupil records. Law enforcement officers' records obtained under s. 938.396 (1m) shall be made available as provided in s. 118.127 (2). A school board member or an employee of a school district may not be held personally liable for any damages caused by the nondisclosure of any information specified in this paragraph unless the member or employee acted with actual malice in failing to disclose the information. A school district may not be held liable for any damages caused by the nondisclosure of any information specified in this paragraph unless the school district or its agent acted with gross negligence or with reckless, wanton or intentional misconduct in failing to disclose the information.

(e) Upon the written permission of an adult pupil, or the parent or guardian of a minor pupil, the school shall make available to the person named in the permission the pupil's progress records or such portions of the pupil's behavioral records as determined by the person authorizing the release. Law enforcement officers' records obtained under s. 48.396 (1) or 938.396 (1) or (1m) may not be made available under this paragraph unless specifically identified by the adult pupil or by the parent or guardian of a minor pupil in the written permission.

(f) Pupil records shall be provided to a court in response to subpoena by parties to an action for in camera inspection, to be used only for purposes of impeachment of any witness who has testified in the action. The court may turn said records or parts thereof over to parties in the action or their attorneys if said records would be relevant and material to a witness's credibility or competency.

(g) 1. The school board may provide any public officer with any information required to be maintained under chs. 115 to 121.
2. Upon request by the department, the school board shall provide the department with any information contained in a pupil record that relates to an audit or evaluation of a federal or state- supported program or that is required to determine compliance with requirements under chs. 115 to 121.The department shall keep confidential all pupil records provided to the department by a school board.

(h) Information from a pupil's immunization records shall be made available to the department of health and family services to carry out the purposes of s. 252.04.

(hm) Information from any pupil lead screening records shall be made available to state and local health officials to carry out the purposes of ss. 254.11 to 254.178.

(i) Upon request, the school district clerk or his or her designee shall provide the names of pupils who have withdrawn from the public school prior to graduation under s. 118.15 (1) (c) to the technical college district board in which the public school is located or, for verification of eligibility for public assistance under ch. 49, to the department of health and family services, the department of workforce development or a county department under s. 46.215, 46.22 or 46.23.

(j) 1. Except as provided under subds. 2. and 3., directory data may be disclosed to any person, if the school has notified the parent, legal guardian or guardian ad litem of the categories of information which it has designated as directory data with respect to each pupil, has informed the parent, legal guardian or guardian ad litem of that pupil that he or she has 14 days to inform the school that all or any part of the directory data may not be released without the prior consent of the parent, legal guardian or guardian ad litem and has allowed 14 days for the parent, legal guardian or guardian ad litem of that pupil to inform the school that all or any part of the directory data may not be released without the prior consent of the parent, legal guardian or guardian ad litem.
2. If a school has notified the parent, legal guardian or guardian ad litem that a pupil's name and address has been designated as directory data, has informed the parent, legal guardian or guardian ad litem of the pupil that he or she has 14 days to inform the school that the pupil's name and address may not be released without the prior consent of the parent, legal guardian or guardian ad litem, has allowed 14 days for the parent, legal guardian or guardian ad litem of the pupil to inform the school that the pupil's name and address may not be released without the prior consent of the parent, legal guardian or guardian ad litem and the parent, legal guardian or guardian ad litem has not so informed the school, the school district clerk or his or her designee, upon request, shall provide a technical college district board with the name and address of each such pupil who is expected to graduate from high school in the current school year.
3. If a school has notified the parent, legal guardian or guardian ad litem of the information that it has designated as directory data with respect to any pupil, has informed the parent, legal guardian or guardian ad litem of the pupil that he or she has 14 days to inform the school that such information may not be released without the prior consent of the parent, legal guardian or guardian ad litem, has allowed 14 days for the parent, legal guardian or guardian ad litem of the pupil to inform the school that such information may not be released without the prior consent of the parent, legal guardian or guardian ad litem and the parent, legal guardian or guardian ad litem has not so informed the school, the school district clerk or his or her designee, upon request, shall provide any representative of a law enforcement agency, district attorney, city attorney or corporation counsel, county department under s. 46.215, 46.22 or 46.23 or a court of record or municipal court with such information relating to any such pupil enrolled in the school district for the purpose of enforcing that pupil's school attendance, investigating

alleged criminal or delinquent activity by the pupil or responding to a health or safety emergency.
(k) A school board may disclose personally identifiable information from the pupil records of an adult pupil to the parents or guardian of the adult pupil, without the written consent of the adult pupil, if the adult pupil is a dependent of his or her parents or guardian under 26 USC 152, unless the adult pupil has informed the school, in writing, that the information may not be disclosed.
(L) A school board shall disclose the pupil records of a pupil in compliance with a court order under s. 48.236 (4) (a), 48.345 (12) (b), 938.34 (7d) (b), 938.396 (1m) (c) or (d) or 938.78 (2) (b) 2. after making a reasonable effort to notify the pupil's parent or legal guardian.
(m) A parent who has been denied periods of physical placement with a child under s. 767.24 (4) does not have the rights of a parent or guardian under pars. (a) to (j) with respect to that child's pupil records.
(n) For the purpose of providing services to a pupil before adjudication, a school board may disclose pupil records to a law enforcement agency, district attorney, city attorney, corporation counsel, agency, as defined in s. 938.78 (1), intake worker under s. 48.067 or 938.067, court of record, municipal court, private school, or another school board if disclosure is pursuant to an interagency agreement and the person to whom the records are disclosed certifies in writing that the records will not be disclosed to any other person except as permitted under this subsection.
(p) A school board may disclose pupil records to appropriate parties in connection with an emergency if knowledge of the information is necessary to protect the health or safety of any individual.
(2m) CONFIDENTIALITY OF PUPIL PHYSICAL HEALTH RECORDS.
(a) Except as provided in par. (b), any pupil record that relates to a pupil's physical health and that is not a pupil physical health record shall be treated as a patient health care record under ss. 146.81 to 146.84.
(b) Any pupil record that concerns the results of a test for the presence of HIV, antigen or nonantigenic products of HIV or an antibody to HIV shall be treated as provided under s. 252.15. In this subsection, "HIV" has the meaning given in s. 252.01 (1m).
(3) MAINTENANCE OF RECORDS. Each school board shall adopt rules in writing specifying the content of pupil records and the time during which pupil records shall be maintained. No behavioral records may be maintained for more than one year after the pupil ceases to be enrolled in the school, unless the pupil specifies in writing that his or her behavioral records may be maintained for a longer period. A pupil's progress records shall be maintained for at least 5 years after the pupil ceases to be enrolled in the school. A school board may maintain the records on microfilm, optical disk or in electronic format if authorized under s. 19.21 (4) (c), or in such other form as the school board deems appropriate. A school board shall maintain law enforcement officers' records obtained under s. 48.396 (1) or 938.396 (1) or (1m) separately from a pupil's other pupil records. Rules adopted under this subsection shall be published by the school board as a class 1 notice under ch. 985.
(4) TRANSFER OF RECORDS. Within 5 working days, a school district shall transfer to another school or school district all pupil records relating to a specific pupil if the transferring school district has received written notice from the pupil if he or she is an adult or his or her parent or guardian if the pupil is a minor that the pupil intends to enroll in the other school or school district or written notice from the other school or school district that the pupil has enrolled or from a court that the pupil has been placed in a secured correctional facility, as defined in s. 938.02 (15m), a secured child caring institution, as defined in s. 938.02 (15g), or a secured group home, as defined in s. 938.02 (15p). In this subsection, "school" and "school district" include any secured correctional facility, secured child caring institution, secured group home, adult correctional institution, mental health institute or center for the developmentally disabled, that provides an educational program for its residents instead of or in addition to that which is provided by public and private schools.
(5) USE FOR SUSPENSION OR EXPULSION. (a) Except as provided in par. (b), nothing in this section prohibits a school district from using a pupil's records in connection with the suspension or expulsion of the pupil or the use of such records by a multidisciplinary team under ch. 115. (b) Law enforcement officers' records obtained under s. 48.396 (1) or 938.396 (1) or (1m), records of the court assigned to exercise jurisdiction under chs. 48 and 938 obtained under s. 938.396 (7) (a), (am), (ar), (b), or (bm), and records of a municipal court obtained under s. 938.396 (7) (ar) may not be used by a school district as the sole basis for expelling or suspending a pupil or as the sole basis for taking any other disciplinary action, including action under the school district's athletic code, against a pupil.
(6) APPLICATION TO EXISTING RECORDS. Any records existing on June 9, 1974 need not be revised for the purpose of deleting information from pupil records to comply with this section.
(7) DISCLOSURE OF LAW ENFORCEMENT UNIT RECORDS. A school board shall treat law enforcement unit records of juveniles in the same manner as a law enforcement agency is required to treat law enforcement officers' records of juveniles under s. 938.396 (1) to (1x) and (5). History: 1973 c. 254; 1977 c. 418; 1979 c. 205; 1981 c. 20, 273; 1983 a. 189; 1985 a. 218; 1987 a. 27, 70, 206, 285, 337, 355; 1987 a. 399 s. 491r; 1987 a. 403 ss. 123, 124, 256; 1989 a. 31, 168; 1989 a. 201 s. 36; 1989 a. 336; 1991 a. 39, 189; 1993 a. 27, 172, 334, 377, 385, 399, 450, 491; 1995 a. 27 ss. 3939, 3940, 9126 (19), 9130 (4), 9145 (1); 1995 a. 77, 173, 225, 352; 1997 a. 3, 27, 205, 237, 239; 1999 a. 9, 149; 2003 a. 82, 292. A public school student's interim grades are pupil records specifically exempted from disclosure under s. 118.125. A failure to specifically state reasons for denying an open records request for records that are specifically exempted from disclosure does not compel disclosure of those records. State ex rel. Blum v. Board of Education, 209 Wis. 2d 377, 565 N.W.2d 140 (Ct. App. 1997), 96-0758. Pupil information that local education agencies are required to release to the department of public instruction under the reporting provisions of ch. 89, laws of 1973, may be provided, with or without permission, without violation of the state or federal confidentiality statutes. 65 Atty. Gen. 1. "Pupil records" are "public records" under 19.32 (2) but are subject to special statutes that limit access and direct maximum and minimum periods of maintenance before destruction. 72 Atty. Gen. 169. Access to student records in Wisconsin. 1976 WLR 975.

118.126 Privileged communications. (1) A school psychologist, counselor, social worker and nurse, and any teacher or administrator designated by the school board who engages in alcohol or drug abuse program activities, shall keep confidential information received from a pupil that the pupil or another pupil is using or is experiencing problems resulting from the use of alcohol or other drugs unless: (a) The pupil using or experiencing problems resulting from the use of alcohol or other drugs consents in writing to disclosure of the information; (b) The school psychologist, counselor, social worker, nurse, teacher or administrator has reason to believe that there is serious and imminent danger to the health, safety or life of any person and that disclosure of the information to another person will alleviate the serious and imminent danger. No more information than is required to alleviate the serious and imminent danger may be disclosed; or (c) The information is required to be reported under s. 48.981. (2) A school psychologist, counselor, social worker or nurse, or any teacher or administrator designated by the school board who engages in alcohol or drug abuse program activities, who in good faith discloses or fails to disclose information under sub. (1) is immune from civil liability for such acts or omissions. This subsection does not apply to information required to be reported under s. 48.981. History: 1979 c. 331; 1985 a. 163; 1987 a. 188, 339. 118.127 Law enforcement agency information. (1) Upon receipt of information from a law enforcement agency under s. 48.396 (1) or 938.396 (1) or (1m), the school district administrator or private school administrator who receives the information shall notify any pupil named in the information, and the parent or guardian of any minor pupil named in the information, of the information. (2) A school district or private school may disclose information from law enforcement officers' records obtained under s. 938.396 (1m) only to persons employed by the school district who are required by the department under s. 115.28 (7) to hold a license, to persons employed by the private school as teachers and to other school district or private school officials who have been determined by the school board or governing body of the private school to have legitimate educational interests, including safety interests, in that information. In addition, if that information relates to a pupil of the school district or private school, the school district or private school may also disclose that information to those employees of the school district or private school who have been designated by the school board or governing body of the private school to receive that information for the purpose of providing treatment programs for pupils enrolled in the school district or private school. A school district may not use law enforcement officers' records obtained under s. 938.396 (1m) as the sole basis for expelling or suspending a pupil or as the sole basis for taking any other disciplinary action, including action under the school district's athletic code, against a pupil. History: 1991 a. 39; 1995 a. 77, 173, 352; 1997 a. 27, 205.

118.13 Pupil discrimination prohibited.
(1) No person may be denied admission to any public school or be denied participation in, be denied the benefits of or be discriminated against in any curricular, extracurricular, pupil services, recreational or other program or activity because of the person's sex, race, religion, national origin, ancestry, creed, pregnancy, marital or parental status, sexual orientation or physical, mental, emotional or learning disability.
(2) (a) Each school board shall develop written policies and procedures to implement this section and submit them to the state superintendent as a part of its 1986 annual report under s. 120.18. The policies and procedures shall provide for receiving and investigating complaints by residents of the school district regarding possible violations of this section, for making determinations as to whether this section has been violated and for ensuring compliance with this section.
(b) Any person who receives a negative determination under par. (a) may appeal the determination to the state superintendent.
(3) (a) The state superintendent shall:
1. Decide appeals made to him or her under sub. (2) (b). Decisions
of the state superintendent under this subdivision are subject to judicial review under ch. 227.
2. Promulgate rules necessary to implement and administer this section.
3. Include in the department's biennial report under s. 15.04 (1) (d) information on the status of school district compliance with this section and school district progress toward providing reasonable equality of educational opportunity for all pupils in this state.
(b) The state superintendent may:
1. Periodically review school district programs, activities and services to determine whether the school boards are complying with this section.
2. Assist school boards to comply with this section by providing information and technical assistance upon request.
(4) Any public school official, employee or teacher who intentionally engages in conduct which discriminates against a person or causes a person to be denied rights, benefits or privileges, in violation of sub. (1), may be required to forfeit not more than $1,000.

118.14 Age of pupils. (1) Except as provided in s. 120.12 (25): (a) No child may be admitted to a 4-year-old kindergarten unless he or she is 4 years old on or before September 1 in the year that he or she proposes to enter school. (b) No child may be admitted to a 5-year-old kindergarten unless he or she is 5 years old on or before September 1 in the year he or she proposes to enter school. (c) No child may be admitted to the 1st grade unless he or she is 6 years old, on or before September 1 in the year he or she proposes to enter school. (2) A resident over 20 years of age may be admitted to school when in the judgment of the school board the resident will not interfere with the pupils of school age. History: 1977 c. 418, 429; 1983 a. 36; 1985 a. 29; 1997 a. 240.

118.145 Admission to high school.
(1) The school board of a district operating high school grades shall determine the minimum standards for admission to high school.
(2) A certificate or diploma or other written evidence issued by a school board showing that the pupil has completed the course of study in the elementary grades of the school district in which the pupil resides shall entitle the pupil to admission to high school. Such certificate or diploma or a certified copy thereof or a certified copy of a list of graduates shall be filed with the school district clerk of the school district operating the high school.
(3) If the superintendent of a private school files with the department the course of study for elementary grades prescribed by such school and if such course of study is substantially equivalent to the course of study prepared for elementary grades by the department, a certificate or diploma or other written evidence issued by the superintendent of the private school showing that the pupil has completed such course of study shall entitle the pupil to admission to a public high school. The certificate or diploma or a certified copy thereof or a certified copy of a list of graduates shall be filed with the school district clerk of the school district operating the high school.
(4) The school board of a school district operating high school grades shall allow a pupil enrolled in a private school or a pupil enrolled in a home_based educational program, who has met the standards for admission to high school under sub. (1), to take up to 2 courses during each school semester if the pupil resides in the school district in which the public school is located and if the school board determines that there is sufficient space in the classroom.
History: 1975 c. 39, 199; 1995 a. 27 s. 9145 (1); 1997 a. 27, 240.

118.15 Compulsory school attendance. (1) (a) Except as provided under pars. (b) to (d) and sub. (4), unless the child is excused under sub. (3) or has graduated from high school, any person having under control a child who is between the ages of 6 and 18 years shall cause the child to attend school regularly during the full period and hours, religious holidays excepted, that the public or private school in which the child should be enrolled is in session until the end of the school term, quarter or semester of the school year in which the child becomes 18 years of age.

118.16 School attendance enforcement. (1) In this section:
(a) "Habitual truant" means a pupil who is absent from school without an acceptable excuse under sub. (4) and s. 118.15 for part or all of 5 or more days on which school is held during a school semester.
(b) "School attendance officer" means an employee designated by the school board to deal with matters relating to school attendance and truancy. "School attendance officer" does not include an individual designated under sub. (2m) (a) to take into custody a child who is absent from school without an acceptable excuse under s. 118.15 unless that individual has also been designated by the school board to deal with matters relating to school attendance and truancy.
(c) "Truancy" means any absence of part or all of one or more days from school during which the school attendance officer, principal or teacher has not been notified of the legal cause of such absence by the parent or guardian of the absent pupil, and also means intermittent attendance carried on for the purpose of defeating the intent of s. 118.15. (1m) The period during which a pupil is absent from school due to a suspension or expulsion under s. 120.13 or 119.25 is neither an absence without an acceptable excuse for the purposes of sub. (1) (a) nor an absence without legal cause for the purposes of sub. (1) (c).
(2) The school attendance officer:
(a) Shall determine daily which pupils enrolled in the school district are absent from school and whether that absence is excused under s. 118.15.
(b) Annually, on or before August 1, shall determine how many pupils enrolled in the school district were absent in the previous year and whether the absences were excused under s. 118.15 and shall notify the state superintendent of the determination.
(c) Except as provided under pars. (cg) and (cr), shall notify the parent or guardian of a child who has been truant of the child's truancy and direct the parent or guardian to return the child to school no later than the next day on which school is in session or to provide an excuse under s. 118.15. The notice under this paragraph shall be given before the end of the 2nd school day after receiving a report of an unexcused absence.

The notice may be made by personal contact, mail or telephone call of which a written record is kept, except that notice by personal contact or telephone call shall be attempted before notice by mail may be given.

(cg) Shall notify the parent or guardian of a child who is a habitual truant, by registered or certified mail, when the child initially becomes a habitual truant. **The notice shall include all of the following:**

1. A statement of the parent's or guardian's responsibility, under s. 118.15 (1) (a), to cause the child to attend school regularly.

2. A statement that the parent, guardian or child may request program or curriculum modifications for the child under s. 118.15 (1) (d) and that the child may be eligible for enrollment in a program for children at risk under s. 118.153 (3).

3. A request that the parent or guardian meet with appropriate school personnel to discuss the child's truancy. The notice shall include the name of the school personnel with whom the parent or guardian should meet, a date, time and place for the meeting and the name, address and telephone number of a person to contact to arrange a different date, time or place. The date for the meeting shall be within 5 school days after the date that the notice is sent, except that with the consent of the child's parent or guardian the date for the meeting may be extended for an additional 5 school days.

4. A statement of the penalties, under s. 118.15 (5), that may be imposed on the parent or guardian if he or she fails to cause the child to attend school regularly as required under s. 118.15 (1) (a).

(cr) After the notice required under par. (cg) has been given, shall notify the parent or guardian of a habitual truant of the habitual truant's unexcused absences as provided in the plan under s. 118.162 (4) (a). After the notice required under par. (cg) has been given, par. (c) does not apply.

(d) May visit any place of employment in the school district to ascertain whether any minors are employed there contrary to law. The officer shall require that school certificates and lists of minors who are employed there be produced for inspection, and shall report all cases of illegal employment to the proper school authorities and to the department of workforce development.

(e) Shall have access to information regarding the attendance of any child between the ages of 6 and 18 who is a resident of the school district or who claims or is claimed to be in attendance at a private school located in the school district.

(2m)

(a) A school district administrator may designate any of the following individuals to take a child who resides in the school district and who is absent from school without an acceptable excuse under s. 118.15 into custody under s. 938.19 (1m):

1. An employee of the school district who is directly involved in the provision of educational programs to the truant child.

2. An employee of the school district who is directly involved in the provision of a modified program or curriculum under s. 118.15 (1) (d), a program for children at risk under s. 118.153 or an alternative educational program under s. 119.82 or any other alternative educational program to children who attend the school attended by the truant child, if the school district administrator believes that the program or curriculum may be appropriate for the truant child.

3. A school social worker employed by the school district who provides services to children attending the school attended by the truant child, if the school district administrator believes that the services provided by the social worker may be appropriate for the truant child.

4. An employee of a social services agency who is directly involved in the provision of social services to the truant child or the child's family.

5. A school attendance officer, but only if the school attendance officer meets the criteria specified in subds. 1., 2. or 3.

(b) A designation under par. (a) shall be in writing and shall specifically identify the child whom the individual is authorized to take into custody.

(c) A school district administrator may not designate an individual under par. (a) unless the individual agrees to the designation in writing.

(d) A school district administrator who makes a designation under par. (a) shall provide each individual so designated with an identification card of a form determined by the school board. The designee shall carry the identification card on his or her person at all times while the designee is on official duty under s. 938.19 (1m) and shall exhibit the identification card to any person to whom the designee represents himself or herself as a person authorized to take a child into custody under s. 938.19 (1m).

(e) A school district administrator who makes a designation under par. (a) or the individual designated under par. (a) shall immediately attempt to notify, by personal contact or telephone call, the child's parent, guardian and legal custodian that the designation has been made and that the child may be taken into custody under s. 938.19 (1m). The school district administrator, or the designee, is not required to notify a parent, guardian or legal custodian under this paragraph if the parent, guardian or legal custodian is the person who requested that the child be taken into custody under s. 938.19 (1m).

(3) All private schools shall keep a record containing the information required under ss. 115.30 (2) and 120.18. The record shall be open to the inspection of school attendance officers at all reasonable times. When called upon by any school attendance officer, the school shall furnish, on forms supplied by the school attendance officer, the information required under ss. 115.30 (2) and 120.18 in regard to any child between the ages of 6 and 18 who is a resident of the school district or who claims or is claimed to be in attendance at the school.

(4) (a) The school board shall establish a written attendance policy specifying the reasons for which pupils may be permitted to be absent from a public school under s. 118.15 and shall require the teachers employed in the school district to submit to the school attendance officer daily attendance reports on all pupils under their charge.

(b) No public school may deny a pupil credit in a course or subject solely because of the pupil's unexcused absences or suspensions from school. The attendance policy under par. (a) shall specify the conditions under which a pupil may be permitted to take examinations missed during absences, other than suspensions, and the conditions under which a pupil shall be permitted to take any quarterly, semester or grading period examinations and complete any course work missed during a period of suspension.

(c) The school board may establish policies which provide that as a consequence of a pupil's truancy the pupil may be assigned to detention or to a supervised, directed study program. The program need not be held during the regular school day. The policies under this paragraph shall specify the conditions under which credit may be given for work completed during the period of detention or assignment to a supervised, directed study program. A pupil shall be permitted to take any examinations missed during a period of assignment to a supervised, directed study program. (cm)

---

(5) Except as provided in sub. (5m), before any proceeding may be brought against a child under s. 938.13 (6) for habitual truancy or under s. 938.125 (2) or 938.17 (2) for a violation of an ordinance enacted under s. 118.163 (2) or against the child's parent or guardian under s. 118.15 for failure to cause the child to attend school regularly, **the school attendance officer shall provide evidence that appropriate school personnel in the school or school district in which the child is enrolled have, within the school year during which the truancy occurred, done all of the following:**

(a) Met with the child's parent or guardian to discuss the child's truancy or attempted to meet with the child's parent or guardian and received no response or were refused.

(b) Provided an opportunity for educational counseling to the child to determine whether a change in the child's curriculum would resolve the child's truancy and have considered curriculum modifications under s. 118.15 (1) (d).

(c) Evaluated the child to determine whether learning problems may be a cause of the child's truancy and, if so, have taken steps to overcome the learning problems, except that the child need not be evaluated if tests administered to the child within the previous year indicate that the child is performing at his or her grade level.

(d) Conducted an evaluation to determine whether social problems may be a cause of the child's truancy and, if so, have taken appropriate action or made appropriate referrals.

(5m) Subsection (5) (a) does not apply if a meeting under sub. (2) (cg) 3. is not held within 10 school days after the date that the notice under sub. (2) (cg) is sent. Subsection (5) (b), (c) and (d) does not apply if the school attendance officer provides evidence that appropriate school personnel were

unable to carry out the activity due to the child's absences from school.
(6) (a) If the school attendance officer receives evidence that activities under sub. (5) have been completed or were not required to be completed as provided in sub. (5m), the school **attendance officer may do any of the following:**
1. File information on any child who continues to be truant with the court assigned to exercise jurisdiction under chs. 48 and 938 in accordance with s. 938.24. Filing information on a child under this subdivision does not preclude concurrent prosecution of the child's parent or guardian under s. 118.15 (5).
2. Refer the child to a teen court program if all of the following conditions apply:

____

(7) Any school district administrator, principal, teacher or school attendance officer who violates this section shall forfeit not less than $5 nor more than $25.

118.165 Private schools.
(1) An institution is a private school if its educational program meets all of the following criteria:
(a) The primary purpose of the program is to provide private or religious-based education.
(b) The program is privately controlled.
(c) The program provides at least 875 hours of instruction each school year.
(d) The program provides a sequentially progressive curriculum of fundamental instruction in reading, language arts, mathematics, social studies, science and health. This subsection does not require the program to include in its curriculum any concept, topic or practice in conflict with the program's religious doctrines or to exclude from its curriculum any concept, topic or practice consistent with the program's religious doctrines.
(e) The program is not operated or instituted for the purpose of avoiding or circumventing the compulsory school attendance requirement under s. 118.15 (1) (a).
(f) The pupils in the institution's educational program, in the ordinary course of events, return annually to the homes of their parents or guardians for not less than 2 months of summer vacation, or the institution is licensed as a child welfare agency under s. 48.60 (1).
(2) An institution may request the state superintendent to approve the institution's educational program as a private school. The state superintendent shall base his or her approval solely on the criteria under sub. (1). History: 1983 a. 512; 1989 a. 336; 1995 a. 27; 1997 a. 27.
118.167 Private school determination by state superintendent. If an association that regulates or accredits private educational institutions in this state submits an affidavit to the state superintendent attesting that the institution meets or exceeds all of the criteria under s. 118.165 and the state superintendent finds that the institution does meet or exceed all of the criteria under s. 118.165, the state superintendent shall determine that the institution is a private school. If at any time the state superintendent finds that an institution determined to be a private school under this section no longer meets the criteria under s. 118.165, the state superintendent may withdraw the determination. History: 1983 a. 512; 1995 a. 27; 1997 a. 27.
115.001(3g) Home-based private educational program.† "Home-based private educational program" means a program of educational instruction provided to a child by the child's parent or guardian or by a person designated by the parent or guardian.† An instructional program provided to more than one family unit does not constitute a home-based private educational program.
115.001(3r) Private school.† "Private school" means an institution with a private educational program that meets all of the criteria under s. 118.165 (1) or is determined to be a private school by the state superintendent under s. 118.167.

118.169 Pupil identification numbers. A school board, and the governing body of a private school, may assign to each pupil enrolled in the school district or private school a unique identification number. The school board or governing body shall not assign to any pupil an identification number that is identical to or incorporates the pupil's social security number. This section does not prohibit a school board or governing body from requiring a pupil to disclose his or her social security number, nor from using a student's social security number if such use is required by a federal or state agency or private organization in order for the school district or private school to participate in a particular program. History: 1997 a. 128.

118.30 Pupil assessment. (1) The state superintendent shall adopt or approve examinations designed to measure pupil attainment of knowledge and concepts in the 4th, 8th and 10th grades. [Does not apply to private school students, including homeschoolers.]

______

118.30(2)(b)3. Upon the request of a pupil's parent or guardian, the school board shall excuse the pupil from taking an examiniation administered under sub. (1m) [that is, the state-mandated 4th, 8th, and 10th grade examinations].

118.33 High school graduation standards; criteria for promotion.
(1) (a) Except as provided in par. (d), a school board may not grant a high school diploma to any pupil unless the pupil has earned:
1. In the high school grades, at least 4 credits of English including writing composition, 3 credits of social studies including state and local government, 2 credits of mathematics, 2 credits of science and 1.5 credits of physical education.
2. In grades 7 to 12, at least 0.5 credit of health education.
(am) The state superintendent shall encourage school boards to require an additional 8.5 credits selected from any combination of vocational education, foreign languages, fine arts and other courses. [These standards do not apply to private school students, including homeschoolers.]

120.18 Annual school district report.†
120.18(1) Annually at such time as the department prescribes but after the end of the school year and no later than September 1, the school district clerk of a common or union high school district shall file a verified annual school district report with the department, on forms supplied by the department.† The school district clerk shall send a copy of the annual school district report to the school district administrator and shall notify the person in charge of each school in the school district that the reports are on file in the school district clerk's office.†† Accounting and financial information provided by the school district in the annual report shall be prepared from the system of accounts prescribed by the department.† If the school district clerk neglects to make the annual report, the clerk shall be liable to the school district for the whole amount of money lost by the school district because of such neglect.† The annual report shall contain:
120.18(1)(a) The school count, showing the numbers and ages of persons who are at least 4 years old but not yet 14 years old and who reside in a school district operating only elementary grades, showing the number and ages of persons between the ages of 14 and 20 residing in a union high school district and showing the number and ages of persons between the ages of 4 and 20 residing in any other school district.† Children cared for at a charitable or penal institution of this state may not be included in the report.† The school district clerk may employ a competent person to take the school count.† **The count may be determined by using any of the following methods:**
120.18(1)(a)1. **†Conducting a school census** on the preceding June 30.
120.18(1)(a)2. †Adding the number of persons under this paragraph who were residents of the school district and were enrolled in the school district on the 3rd Friday of September of the previous school year; plus the number of persons under this paragraph who were residents of the school district and who were **enrolled in private schools, home-based private educational programs** or other school districts on the 3rd Friday of September of the previous school year; **plus the number or an estimate of the number** of those persons under this paragraph who were residents of the school district and not enrolled in the school district, private schools, home-based private educational programs or other school districts on the 3rd Friday of September of the previous school year.
120.18(1)(b) †The number of children between the ages of 4 and 20 taught in the schools of the school district during the school year.

120.18(1)(c) †The number of children attending the schools of the school district during the school year under the age of 4 and over the age of 20 years.

120.18(1)(d) † The number of school days taught, including holidays, by teachers legally qualified to teach.

120.18(1)(e) The names of all teachers employed by the school district during the school year; the number of days taught by each, including holidays; the monthly salary paid to each; and the time allowed each teacher for attendance at an educational convention for which no wages were deducted.

120.18(1)(f) † The amount of money received during the school year, designating separately the amount received from the school fund income, from taxes levied by the county board, from taxes voted by the school district and from all other sources and the manner in which such money was expended, showing separately the expenditure of school money received from the state.

252.04 Immunization program.

(1) The department shall carry out a statewide immunization program to eliminate mumps, measles, rubella (German measles), diphtheria, pertussis (whooping cough), poliomyelitis and other diseases that the department specifies by rule, and to protect against tetanus.† Any person who immunizes an individual under this section shall maintain records identifying the manufacturer and lot number of the vaccine used, the date of immunization and the name and title of the person who immunized the individual. These records shall be available to the individual or, if the individual is a minor, to his or her parent, guardian or legal custodian upon request.

(2) Any student admitted to any elementary, middle, junior or senior high school or into any day care center or nursery school shall, within 30 school days, present written evidence to the school, day care center or nursery school of having completed the first immunization for each vaccine required for the student's grade and being on schedule for the remainder of the basic and recall (booster) immunization series for mumps, measles, rubella (German measles), diphtheria, pertussis (whooping cough), poliomyelitis, tetanus and other diseases that the department specifies by rule or shall present a written waiver under sub. (3).

(3) The immunization requirement is waived if the student, if an adult, or the student's parent, guardian or legal custodian submits a written statement to the school, day care center or nursery school objecting to the immunization for reasons of health, religion or personal conviction. At the time any school, day care center or nursery school notifies a student, parent, guardian or legal custodian of the immunization requirements, it shall inform the person in writing of the person's right to a waiver under this subsection.

Wisconsin State Constitution

ARTICLE X. EDUCATION [Selected sections] Superintendent of public instruction. SECTION 1. [As amended Nov. 1902 and Nov. 1982] The **supervision of public instruction** shall be vested in a state superintendent and such other officers as the legislature shall direct; and their qualifications, powers, duties and compensation shall be prescribed by law. The state superintendent shall be chosen by the qualified electors of the state at the same time and in the same manner as members of the supreme court, and shall hold office for 4 years from the succeeding first Monday in July. The term of office, time and manner of electing or appointing all other officers of supervision of public instruction shall be fixed by law. [1899 J.R. 16, 1901 J.R. 3, 1901 c. 258, vote Nov. 1902; 1979 J.R. 36, 1981 J.R. 29, vote Nov. 1982] District schools; tuition; sectarian instruction; released time. SECTION 3. [As amended April 1972] The legislature shall provide by law for the establishment of district schools, which shall be as nearly uniform as practicable; and such schools shall be free and without charge for tuition to all children between the ages of 4 and 20 years; and no sectarian instruction shall be allowed therein; but the legislature by law may, for the purpose of religious instruction outside the district schools, authorize the release of students during regular school hours. [1969 J.R. 37, 1971 J.R. 28, vote April 1972]

House Report 109-360 - **NATIONAL DEFENSE AUTHORIZATION ACT FOR FISCAL YEAR 2006 SEC. 591. RECRUITMENT AND ENLISTMENT OF HOME-SCHOOLED STUDENTS IN THE ARMED FORCES**

(a) Policy on Recruitment and Enlistment-

(1) POLICY REQUIRED- The Secretary of Defense shall prescribe a policy on the recruitment and enlistment of home-schooled students in the Armed Forces.

(2) UNIFORMITY ACROSS THE ARMED FORCES- The Secretary shall ensure that the policy prescribed under paragraph

(1) applies, to the extent practicable, uniformly across the Armed Forces.

(b) Elements- The policy under subsection (a) shall include the following:

(1) An identification of a graduate of home schooling for purposes of recruitment and enlistment in the Armed Forces that is in accordance with the requirements described in subsection (c).

(2) A communication plan to ensure that the policy described in subsection (c) is understood by recruiting officials of all the Armed Forces, to include field recruiters at the lowest level of command.

(3) An exemption of graduates of home schooling from the requirement for a secondary school diploma or an equivalent (GED) as a precondition for enlistment in the Armed Forces.

(c) Home School Graduates- In prescribing the policy under subsection (a), the Secretary of Defense shall prescribe a single set of criteria to be used by the Armed Forces in determining whether an individual is a graduate of home schooling. The Secretary concerned shall ensure compliance with education credential coding requirements.

(d) Secretary Concerned Defined- In this section, the term `Secretary concerned' has the meaning given such term in section 101(a)(9) of title 10, United States Code.

Appendix B
About Wisconsin Parents Association

Wisconsin Parents Association (WPA), a statewide inclusive grassroots organization, was founded in response to a crisis. Late in 1983, legislation designed by the Department of Public Instruction (DPI) and other members of the educational establishment was introduced in the Wisconsin Legislature. Homeschoolers were about to be put under the DPI's control and authority.

On January 6, 1984, a diverse group of 70 homeschoolers founded an organization to include all homeschoolers. Its mission was to support and defend the right of families to choose an education consistent with their principles and beliefs. The organization decided to work for legislation that made no compromises: no state-mandated standardized testing, no review and approval of homeschoolers' curriculum, no progress reports to school districts, no special qualifications required of parents. Parents would be held accountable in a reasonable way, and the interests of the state would be respected.

Members of the new organization quickly encouraged homeschoolers to attend a legislative hearing on January 25th. When 2,500 people came, nearly all opposed to the bill, legislators took note. At a March 13th hearing, WPA presented information from homeschoolers who had had difficulty with the DPI. Amendments turned the legislation around. After much effort by homeschoolers working together through WPA, one of the best homeschooling laws in the country was created. Since then, WPA has maintained its strong reputation in the Legislature.

But WPA's work was just beginning. The DPI quickly exceeded its authority by putting more requirements on the first PI-1206 form than the law allowed. WPA's meeting with DPI representatives and legislators forced a correction that made the form consistent with the new law.

To meet homeschoolers' need for support and information, WPA opened a post office box. Later Voice Mail was added. WPA's first annual conference was held in June, 1984 so homeschoolers could meet, celebrate, and learn from each other. The first edition of this handbook, a slender, 35-page, typed volume, was published in 1985. Over the years, the courage and work of thousands of homeschooling families have turned it into the book you are holding. WPA has also educated the general public and the Legislature about homeschooling and established a favorable climate for homeschooling in Wisconsin.

Since 1984, WPA has had to counter numerous challenges, including resolutions introduced by the Wisconsin Association of School Boards (WASB), an inaccurate study of homeschooling by the University of Wisconsin (the "Lufler Report"), and a Legislative Council study. This last took five months, cost taxpayers $100,000, and resulted in a rare decision to not introduce legislation following such a study and the recognition that changes to the homeschooling law were unnecessary. WPA also has put out many brush fires, as school districts around the state at first tried to require more of homeschoolers than the law allows and more recently to entice them into the public schools. Several unwise and apparently self-serving actions by a national homeschooling organization have required action. All this work continues.

WPA works hard to prevent problems and prepare members to counter them when they arise. Among the many issues WPA has researched and written about are standardized testing, preschool screening, collaboration among government agencies, mental health screening, family privacy, and government regulation of homeschooling.

What are WPA's main activities today?

- **Help for individuals:** WPA responds to homeschoolers' calls and letters, whether they need help getting started, dealing with school officials, or meeting everyday challenges of homeschooling. WPA gives homeschoolers the information and resources they need to make the best decisions for their families.
- **Information:** Through newsletters, fact sheets, emails, a website, this handbook, annual conferences, and responses to individual inquiries, WPA gives homeschoolers the information and support they need to homeschool and to respond intelligently to threats to homeschooling freedoms. Background information from WPA prepares people to make good decisions and respond reasonably in a crisis.
- **Tracking and analysis:** Members and allies of WPA send information they have collected from their local communities and other sources, and share experiences they have had homeschooling and dealing with officials, legislators, and others. WPA gathers, organizes, and analyzes an enormous amount of information, much of which has been distilled into this book. The information is then given to members and others who need it so they can make decisions and take action.
- **Conferences:** Since 1984, WPA's annual spring conference has provided information, inspiration, and opportunities to meet other homeschoolers.
- **Freedom:** Wisconsin's current homeschooling freedoms are in large part due to the work of homeschoolers involved in WPA. Over and over again, WPA members have taken specific action that has maintained Wisconsin's reasonable homeschooling law.
- **Making connections:** WPA works with local support groups to help homeschoolers meet and support one another.
- **Self-representation:** Parents work together through WPA to represent themselves and their own best interests when action is needed, rather than relying on individuals or groups, however well-intentioned, who present themselves as experts or representatives of homeschoolers.

WPA Membership

Consider joining WPA, if you are not already a member. Members receive a quarterly newsletter, special bulletins and emails as needed, and discounts on conferences and handbooks. More importantly, members support WPA, which receives no state or federal funding. Without faithful and committed members, WPA could not continue to be an effective means for families to work together. In turn, WPA members have the satisfaction of knowing they are part of an organization of families committed to reclaiming and maintaining their rights and responsibilities.

How To Contact WPA and its Regional Coordinators

To contact WPA, call the Voice Mail at 608-283-3131, go to www.homeschooling-wpa.org or write to WPA, P O Box 2502, Madison WI 53701-2502.

WPA also has a network of Regional Coordinators who answer questions, help homeschoolers find support groups and connect with other homeschoolers, and provide a link to WPA and its resources. For the name and phone number of the Regional Coordinator nearest you, see the WPA newsletter or website, call the WPA Voice Mail, or write to WPA.

Appendix C

WPA Resolutions Adopted at Annual Meetings

TOPICS OF RESOLUTIONS

1. WPA and Choice in Education 4/88 *
2. Wisconsin's Home Schooling Law 4/88
3. State-Mandated Standardized Testing 4/88 *
4. Home Schooling, Private Education, and the DPI 4/88 *
5. State Review and Approval of a Home-Based Private Educational Program's Calendar and Curriculum 4/89
6. Teacher Certification of Home Schooling Parents 4/89
7. Entry and Re-entry Into Public Schools 4/90
8. Home Schoolers Taking Courses in Public Schools 4/90
9. Unity Among Home Schoolers 4/90 *
10. The Primary Role of Parents in Education 4/91
11. Opposition to State Control of Education and the Family 4/91
12. State goals in education 4/92
13. America 2000 and Wisconsin 2000 4/92
14. Education Vouchers 4/92 *
15. Outcome-Based Education 4/93
16. Government Collaboration 4/93
17. Maintain the Distinction Between Public and Private Schools 4/93
18. Screening, Evaluating, and Labeling Children 4/94 *
19. The Federal Government and Homeschooling 4/94 *
20. Privacy and Homeschooling 4/94
21. The Independence of the Homeschooling Movement 4/95
22. Families First 4/95
23. Homeschooling, Educational Reform, Freedoms, and Money 4/95
24. Maintaining Wisconsin's Homeschooling Law 5/96
25. Maintaining the Fundamental Foundation of Parental Rights and Responsibilities 5/96
26. Attempts by the State to Determine Eligibility to Homeschool 4/97
27. School-To-Work Programs 4/97
28. Day-Time Curfews, Truancy Sweeps, and ID Cards for Homeschoolers 5/98
29. The Real Cost of Tax Credits for Homeschoolers' Educational Expenses 5/98
30. Impact on Homeschooling Freedoms of Homeschoolers' Qualifying for Public School Sports Teams 5/98 *
31. High Schools' Mock Trial Involving a Homeschooler 5/98
32. Graduation Test 5/99
33. Legislation That Undermines Homeschooling Freedoms 5/99 *
34. Laws Designed to Prevent Certain Families from Homeschooling 5/00
35. Survey Research on Homeschooling 5/00 *
36. Standardized Testing Required by the Federal or State Government 5/01
37. Homeschools Defined by Law as One Family Unit 5/01
38. Public E-Schools 5/02
39. Government Imposed Immunizations 5/02
40. Education Vouchers, Educational Investment Accounts, and Tax Credits and Deductions for Education 5/03 *
41. Maintaining the Distinction Between Public Schools and Homeschools (and Other Private Schools) 5/03
42. The Media and Homeschooling 5/04
43. Student Identification Database Systems 5/04
44. Mental Health Screening 5/05 *
45. No Child Left Behind 5/05

*SELECTED RESOLUTIONS
(For all, see WPA's website)

1. WPA and Choice in Education

Whereas the Wisconsin Parents Association (WPA) is a state-wide association that watches, promotes, and defends the rights of parents, families, and children; and

Whereas WPA recognizes that there is no one best way to educate children since their talents and abilities are so varied; and

Whereas home schoolers are a very diverse group with widely varying income levels, approaches to education, religious and philosophical beliefs; and

Whereas the one thing home schoolers have in common is their commitment to establishing and maintaining their parental rights to educate their children according to their beliefs and principles;

Be it resolved that WPA and its members will support parents in their choice in education. **4/88**

3. State-Mandated Standardized Testing

Whereas standardized tests are only one way of measuring the mastery of a specific set of facts; and

Whereas standardized tests can become a means of determining and controlling the curriculum, teaching methods, and structure of a school or program; and

Whereas there is increasing evidence that standardized tests do not measure what they claim to measure; and

Whereas standardized tests can be used to label children, to justify additional testing, and to require child placement out of the home; and

Whereas state-mandated standardized testing provides that the state rather than the parent would decide when children are ready for tests, what tests will be used, how and where tests will be administered, and what to do about the results;

Be it resolved by members of the Wisconsin Parents Association (WPA) that WPA is opposed to state-mandated standardized testing and will work to prevent it from being mandated for Home-Based Private Educational Programs. 4/88

4. Home Schooling, Private Education, and the DPI

Whereas the United States by its constitution, tradition, and custom has long recognized, practiced, and provided for the parent to have the primary right in and responsibility for a child's education; and

Whereas the distinction between public and private education, including home-based private education, is established by custom, tradition, and statute and is fundamental to the exercise of choice in education and to the avoidance of a state monopoly in education; and

Whereas Article X of the Wisconsin Constitution grants the State Superintendent of Public Instruction authority over public, not private, education; and

Whereas the Wisconsin legislature has passed a law (1983 Act 512) that requires Home-Based Private Educational Programs to meet educational requirements and be in compliance with the compulsory school attendance law, a law that balances the state's, parent's, and children's rights and responsibilities in education;

Be it resolved by members of the Wisconsin Parents Association (WPA) that WPA views the Department of Public Instruction (DPI) to have no authority to regulate private education, including Home-Based Private Educational Programs.

Be it further resolved that the WPA will not initiate or propose matters to the DPI that would recognize, foster, or grant such regulatory authority by the DPI over private education. 4/88

9. Unity Among Home Schoolers

Whereas home schoolers come from all walks of life; they home school for a number of different reasons; and they use a variety of curriculums and approaches to education; however, they all have one thing in common, namely, their determination to preserve the right to choose for their children an education consistent with their beliefs and principles; and

Whereas the Wisconsin statutes defining private schools (including home schools) resulted from the hard work of the full range of home schoolers and people involved in other small private schools in this state; and

Whereas home schoolers have organized themselves as Wisconsin Parents Association (WPA) to watch and protect their parental rights in education, especially home schooling rights and responsibilities; and

Whereas WPA has steadfastly refused to take any position on approaches to education, religion, moral values, and has fought for the rights of its members and others to make their own decisions in these matters; and

Whereas it is not necessary for home schoolers to agree on educational approaches or religious and moral beliefs and principles in order to work together to secure and preserve the rights and freedoms all home schoolers need in order to make choices; and

Whereas home schoolers are a small minority and are opposed by powerful political interest groups and organizations; and

Whereas Wisconsin has a reasonable home schooling law; and

Whereas the unity of home schoolers on home schooling legislative issues has earned home schoolers respect in the Wisconsin Legislature and has worked to prevent unnecessary regulation of home schoolers; and

Whereas WPA is a grassroots organization which relies on the strength of its own local members rather than "experts," especially out-of-state experts who become involved in state legislative matters;

Be it resolved by members of Wisconsin Parents Association (WPA) that WPA affirms its goal of assuring reasonable home schooling laws by working together as a united group that is open to all home schoolers; and

Be it further resolved that WPA opposes any state or national efforts that would split home schoolers into factions and thus weaken the ability of home schoolers to ensure reasonable home schooling laws. 4/90

14. Education Vouchers

Whereas education vouchers being proposed at the federal and state levels of government would allow the government to define education and impose its values, judgments, and often its testing on people; and

Whereas such education vouchers would not be available to the family but only to the institutions that the family selects and which the state certifies as eligible to receive voucher moneys from the state; and

Whereas such education vouchers can easily lead to state control of education similar to a state religion and further control of families; and

Whereas there are better and more direct ways for the state and federal governments to assist families in funding private education, including home schooling, such as reducing taxes to families, increasing tax deductions for dependents, and providing tax credits;

Be it resolved by the Wisconsin Parents Association (WPA) that WPA and its members oppose education vouchers that would require the surrender of educational freedom, and, instead, WPA supports measures that would strengthen families by decreasing their tax burdens and thus leaving them money to use for private education or by returning money directly to the family, thus allowing the family true choice in how moneys are spent for education. 4/92

18. Screening, Evaluating, and Labeling Children

Whereas a growing number of government programs screen, evaluate, and label children at earlier and earlier ages; and

Whereas the power of these programs is growing and spreading because they often involve a number of different public and private agencies, organizations, and professionals now working together through new programs to promote collaboration among government agencies; and

Whereas the definition of "children with special needs" has been broadened so that many children who are following their own unique timetables but are well within the range of normal development are now being labeled as "developmentally delayed," or "learning disabled," or some such label; and

Whereas these labels are very destructive because they undermine the confidence of children and parents and become self-fulfilling prophecies; and

Whereas these programs are technically voluntary and require parental permission for children to participate and be evaluated, BUT increasingly parents who allow their children to be evaluated and placed in such programs are unable to get their children out of the programs unless they enroll in a private program or a private school (including homeschools); and

Whereas pressure is being put on parents and the general public to believe that institutions and so-called experts know how to evaluate, label, and train very young children; and

Whereas requiring children to participate in programs and/or schools at early ages is not generally good for children or their families; in fact, there is growing evidence that these programs are detrimental to children and their families; and

Whereas requiring young children to participate in such programs could lead to including younger children in the compulsory school attendance law; and

Whereas requiring participation in such programs could expand the authority of these programs, of the schools in general, and of "professional experts" and further reduce the role and respect given to parents and the family;

Be it resolved by the members of the Wisconsin Parents Association (WPA) that WPA and its members will work to inform parents about their rights and responsibilities in education; to inform parents about the problems associated with screening, evaluating, and labeling of children, including very young children; and inform parents about how they can get their children out of such programs. 4/94

19. The Federal Government and Homeschooling

Whereas the U. S. Constitution gives no authority to the federal or state governments in the area of education; and

Whereas rights and powers not granted to the state are reserved for the people; and

Whereas section 432 of the federal statute General Education Provisions Act of 1970 states that the federal government may not control education; and

Whereas the states have the authority to control schooling through compulsory school attendance laws based on the policing powers granted to the states by the U. S. Constitution; and

Whereas the federal government acquires its power in the area of education by providing money and services to people through public schools in exchange for their compliance with the federal government's regulations; and

Whereas if people request exemptions from federal education programs, they give authority to the federal government that it would not otherwise have, lose part of their freedom, and gain little if anything in return since the states rather than the federal government directly control public schools; and

Whereas once homeschools are named in federal education statutes there is the strong possibility that federal regulations will be written that define and establish criteria for what a homeschool needs to be in order to qualify for participation in programs and services; and

Whereas states might use such federal definitions and regulations to justify changing state homeschooling laws in order to be eligible to receive federal moneys;

Be it resolved by the members of the Wisconsin Parents Association (WPA) that WPA and its members oppose seeking funding or participation in federal education programs for homeschooling and oppose asking the federal government to protect or exempt homeschoolers from federal education programs. 4/94

30. Impact on Homeschooling Freedoms of Homeschoolers' Qualifying for Public School Sports Teams

Whereas homeschoolers have regained significant freedom of thought and belief by working to establish and maintain ourselves as private schools independent of public schools; and

Whereas Wisconsin has a reasonable homeschooling law that homeschoolers have worked hard to get passed and to maintain; and

Whereas homeschoolers are a very small minority but large and powerful interest groups are pressing for increased state regulation of homeschooling; and

Whereas, in order for Wisconsin Interscholastic Athletic Association (WIAA) rules to be changed so that homeschoolers could participate on public school sports teams, homeschools would have to comply with the Department of Public Instruction (DPI)'s policies and regulations, including the DPI's definition of a full-time student, standards for acceptable curriculum, determinations of scholastic standing in terms of grades and credits through testing, and other demonstrations of qualifications that are consistent with public school standards and approaches to education; and

Whereas if just a few homeschoolers convinced the WIAA to change its rules to allow homeschoolers to play on public school teams, this would result in state oversight and intrusion into homeschools; and

Whereas, once in place, such state regulation of homeschools could easily spread to other areas of homeschooling and over time to all homeschoolers; and

Whereas young people who want to play sports can either choose from among opportunities available outside public schools or can enroll in public schools, but families who want to homeschool can only do so under the laws and regulations of the state of Wisconsin (which would be less favorable to homeschoolers if WIAA rules were changed to allow homeschoolers to play on public school sports teams);

Be it resolved by members of the Wisconsin Parents Association (WPA) that WPA will continue to work through its members to maintain Wisconsin's reasonable homeschooling law and will oppose initiatives that would increase state regulation of homeschooling in exchange for the opportunity for a few homeschoolers (who were interested and judged to be qualified) to play on public school sports teams; and

Be it further resolved that WPA will work through its members to inform parents and the general public and legislators of the unacceptability and risks of such initiatives. 5/98

33. Legislation That Undermines Homeschooling Freedoms

Whereas homeschoolers are a small minority that has regained its rightful educational freedoms in Wisconsin through hard work and maintained them through constant vigilance; and

Whereas our approach to education is generally not understood or shared by the majority of people in our society; and

Whereas our elected representatives are accustomed to providing state programs in education in exchange for state regulation of schools by means of state goals, state educational standards, state-mandated tests, state audits of educational institutions, and state prescriptions of who is qualified to teach and/or receive benefits; and

Whereas most homeschoolers value their homeschooling freedoms more than they value receiving conventional state schooling benefits such as tax credits for educational expenses or educational vouchers; and

Whereas legislation supposedly designed to ensure that homeschoolers can participate in public school programs is unnecessary (because the few homeschoolers who want to participate can make the necessary arrangements with their local school districts) and would undermine our homeschooling freedoms; and

Whereas legislators may hear from a few homeschoolers who want some of the supposed benefits even though they undermine our homeschooling freedoms; and

Whereas legislators are accustomed to introducing bills when constituents ask for legislation that would give them government money; and

Whereas legislation that would undermine our homeschooling freedoms is likely to be adopted unless a significant number of homeschoolers actively communicate with their legislators both before such legislation is introduced and, if necessary, after it has been introduced;

Be it resolved by members of the Wisconsin Parents Association (WPA) that WPA and its members will work to ensure that their legislators understand that homeschoolers value their freedom more than they value legislation that would cost them their freedom, including legislation that at first may seem to provide benefits. 5/99

35. Survey Research on Homeschooling

Whereas survey research on homeschooling undermines our homeschooling freedoms in several ways, including the following:

- Survey research is generally designed to compare homeschoolers to students in conventional schools, using the standards of conventional schools, which implies that homeschools should adopt the standards, practices, and values of conventional schools and assumes that these are the only correct ones.
- People who feel homeschoolers should be required to take state-mandated tests can point to survey research that includes homeschoolers' scores on standardized tests as evidence that homeschoolers are willing to take such tests.
- Research that indicates that even a very small number of homeschoolers are not complying with their state's homeschooling law could be used by critics of homeschooling to claim that increased regulation of homeschooling is necessary.
- Research that shows that many homeschooling parents have a certain educational background, income level, etc. could be used to argue that all homeschooling parents should be required to have similar education, income level, etc.; and

Whereas it is very difficult to draw a representative sample of homeschoolers because some states do not require homeschoolers to register and states such as Wisconsin that require that parents file a form with the state fortunately are not willing to supply the names of homeschoolers to researchers. Therefore, when evaluated by the standards used by social scientists, survey research on homeschoolers is inaccurate and misleading; and

Whereas many families feel that the questions asked by researchers do not cover the most important reasons that they have chosen to homeschool; and

Whereas assurances of confidentiality of information do not mean much when the practice is that many people have access to this data in the name of research and increasingly government agencies can use and exchange data in the best interests of the state and/or child; and

Whereas more accurate information about what homeschooling is really like comes from cases studies of current and grown up homeschoolers and adequate evidence that homeschooling is working well comes from the lack of reports of homeschoolers having difficulty when they enter school, college, or the workforce, despite the fact that opponents of homeschooling look for such problems; and

Whereas researchers continue to probe deeper and deeper, claiming that each survey research report demonstrates the need for more research;

Be it resolved by members of the Wisconsin Parents Association (WPA) that WPA will work through its members to educate people about the problems connected with survey research, especially on homeschoolers; to encourage homeschoolers not to participate in survey research on homeschooling; and to oppose the use of the results of survey research to justify increased regulation of homeschooling. 5/00

40. Education Vouchers, Educational Investment Accounts, and Tax Credits and Deductions for Education

Whereas education vouchers, educational investment accounts, and tax credits and deductions for education that are being proposed at the federal and state levels of government would allow the government to define education and impose its values, judgments, and often its testing on people; and

Whereas such education vouchers would not be given to families but only to the institutions that families select from among those the state has certified as eligible to receive money from the state through vouchers; and

Whereas such education vouchers can easily lead to state control of education and further control of families; and

Whereas legislation providing for educational investment accounts and tax credits and deductions tied to educational expenses sets the terms of who, what, and under what conditions one qualifies for such tax breaks, including defining key terms such as teacher, educator, homeschool, private school, educational expense, etc.; and

Whereas defining, interpreting, and applying such key terms provides federal and state governments with the authority to further regulate private schooling including homeschools; and

Whereas monitoring (including auditing) the use of such tax breaks, credits, and deductions can further define and regulate homeschools; and

Whereas there are other publicly funded services that we as citizens pay taxes for (such as fire departments and prisons) but hope we will not use their services for ourselves; and

Whereas there are better and more direct ways for the state and federal governments to assist families in funding private education (including home schooling), such as reducing taxes to families and increasing tax deductions and credits for dependents;

Be it resolved that members of Wisconsin Parents Association (WPA) that WPA opposes education vouchers, educational investment accounts, and tax credits and deductions for education that would require the surrender of educational freedom, and, instead, WPA supports measures that would strengthen families either by decreasing their tax burdens and thus leaving them money to use for private education or by returning money directly to families, thus allowing families true choice in how moneys are spent for education. 5/03

44. Mental Health Screening

Whereas an increasing number of federal and state mental health screening programs are being established to screen preschool and school children as well as young children, teens, and adults; and

Whereas the questions asked during the screenings are so general and ambiguous that nearly anyone could be identified as mentally ill or in need of further testing; and

Whereas doctors, workers in health clinics, school personnel, social service workers, juvenile justice authorities, etc. are all being encouraged to conduct such screenings, and people may not realize that they are being screened; and

Whereas screenings are especially targeted at groups considered marginal to the mainstream of our society because of their practices, small numbers, and/or anti-social behavior (categories in which homeschoolers could easily be included); and

Whereas certain institutions and professionals are either suspicious or critical of homeschooling or have vested interests in stopping people from homeschooling; and

Whereas mental health screenings could be used as an effective way to curtail homeschooling; and

Whereas the pharmaceutical industry is spending large sums of money to encourage professionals and legislators to promote mental health screening; and

Whereas the drugs that are being administered through these programs to people who are diagnosed as "mentally ill" through these screenings have been shown to be harmful to people;

Be it resolved by members of Wisconsin Parents Association (WPA) that WPA will work to inform its members, homeschoolers throughout the state, and the general public about the importance of recognizing mental health screenings in whatever setting they occur, to inform them of their rights and responsibilities as parents and as patients, to question and/or refuse such screenings, and to oppose legislation that encourages or requires mental health screening that leads to highly subjective identification of mental illness and use of drugs for treatment. 5/05

Bibliography

Here is bibliographical information for resources cited in this book. Also, see the list of curriculum providers and correspondence schools in Chapter 7.

Homeschooling and Learning Resources

Beasant, Pam. *Introduction to Electronics* (Usborne Introduction to). E. D. C. Publishing, 1985.

Beechick, Ruth. *The Three R's: Grades K-3* and *You Can Teach Your Child Successfully: Grades 4-8.* Arrow Press, 1992.

Coates, Grace Davila. *Family Math for Young Children.* University of California at Berkeley: Lawrence Hall of Science.

________. and Virginia Thompson. *Family Math II.* University of California at Berkeley: Lawrence Hall of Science.

Dobson, Linda. *The Homeschooling Book of Answers: The 88 Most Important Questions Answered by Homeschooling's Most Respected Voices.* Rocklin, CA: Prima Publishing, 1998.

Griffith, Mary. *The Unschooling Handbook: How to Use the Whole World As Your Child's Classroom.* Prima Publishing, 1998.

Hakim, Joy. *The History of US.* Oxford University Press.

Healy, Jane M. *Endangered Minds: Why Children Don't Think and What We Can Do about It.* Simon and Schuster, 1990.

________. *Failure to Connect: How Computers Affect Our Children's Minds--For Better and Worse.* Simon and Schuster, 1998.

Hegener, Mark and Helen, ed. *Home School Reader: Collected Articles from Home Education Magazine 1984-1994.* Tonasket, WA: Home Education Press.

Heuer, Loretta. *The Homeschooler's Guide to Portfolios and Transcripts.* Foster City, CA: Arco/IDG Books Worldwide, 2000.

Hirsch, E. D., ed. *What Your First Grader Needs to Know: Fundamentals of a Good First Grade Education.* (Series goes through Sixth Grade) Doubleday.

Holt, John. *How Children Learn.* Revised Edition. Delacorte Press, 1983.

________. Learning All the Time. Redding, MA: Addison-Wesley, 1989.

________ and Patrick Farenga. *Teach Your Own: The John Holt Book of Homeschooling.* Perseus Publishing, 2003.

Home Education Magazine, P.O. Box 1083, Tonasket, WA 98855; 509-486-1351. www.home-ed-magazine.com.

Jones, Claudia. *More Parents Are Teachers, Too: Encouraging Your 6- to 12-Year-Old.* Williamson Publishing, 1990.

________. *Parents Are Teachers, Too: Enriching Your Child's First Six Years.* Williamson Publishing, 1988.

Kealoha, Anna. *Trust the Children: An Activity Guide for Homeschooling and Alternative Learning.* Celestial Arts, 1995.

Macaulay, Susan Schaeffer. *For the Children's Sake.* Crossway, 1984.

Mander, Jerry. *Four Arguments for the Elimination of Television.* Morrow, 1978.

McKee, Alison. *Homeschooling Our Children, Unschooling Ourselves.* Bittersweet House, 2002.

Milstein, Sarah. *Google: The Missing Manual.* Pogue Press/O'Reilly, 2006.

Moore, Raymond and Dorothy. *The Successful Homeschool Family Handbook.* The Moore Foundation.

Reed, Jean and Donn. *The Home School Source Book.* Third edition. Brook Farm Books, 2000.

Rivero, Lisa. *Creative Homeschooling for Gifted Children: A Resource Guide.* Scottsdale, AZ: Great Potential Press, 2002

Rupp, Rebecca. *Home Learning Year by Year: How to Design a Homeschool Curriculum from Preschool Through High School.* NY: Three Rivers Press, 2000.

________. *The Complete Home Learning Source Book.* NY: Three Rivers Press, 1998.

Russell, William F. *Family Learning: How to Help Your Children Succeed in School by Learning at Home.* St. Charles, Illinois: First Word Learning Systems, Inc., 1997.

Stenmark, Jean Kerr, Virginia H. Thompson, and Ruth Cossey. *Family Math.* University of California at Berkeley: Lawrence Hall of Science.

Tolan, Stephanie S. *Surviving the Applewhites.* HarperTrophy, 2004.

Wade, Theodore E., Jr., ed. *Home School Manual: For Parents Who Teach Their Own Children.* Berrien Springs, MI: Gazelle, 1998.

Winn, Marie. *The Plug-In Drug.* Revised edition. Viking, 1985.

Wise, Jessie and Susan Wise Bauer. *The Well-Trained Mind: A Guide to Classical Education at Home.* WW Norton, 1999.

World Book. *Typical Courses of Study, Kindergarten through Grade 12.* Available at www.worldbook.com/wc/browse?id=pa/tcs

Resources for High School and After

Note: Many of the resources listed above include high school.

Bear, John and Mariah P. Bear.. *Bears' Guide to College Degrees by Mail and Internet.* Ten Speed Press.

________. *Bears' Guide to Earning Degrees by Distance Learning.* Berkeley, CA: Ten Speed Press.

Bolles, Richard. *What Color Is Your Parachute? A Practical Manual for Job-Hunters and Career Changers.* Berkeley, CA: Ten Speed Press.

Career Development Manual of the University of Waterloo in Canada. www.adm.uwaterloo.ca/infocecs/CRC/manual-home.html

CLEP Official Study Guide. College Board

Cohen, Cafi. *Homeschoolers' College Admissions Handbook.* Rocklin, CA: Prima, 2000.

The College Board. *Ten SATs*.

Curry, Boykin, Brian Kasbar, and Emily Angel Baer. *Essays That Worked for College Applications: 50 Essays That Helped Students Get Into the Nation's Top Colleges.* Ballantine Books.

Fiore, Neil and Susan C. Pescar. *Conquering Test Anxiety: or How To Psyche Up for the SAT, GRE, GMAT, LSAT, MCAT, or Any Other Standardized Test.* NY: Warner Books, 1987.

Hayes, Charles D. *Proving You're Qualified: Strategies for Competent People without College Degrees.* Wasilla, AK: Autodidactic Press, 1995.

Internships: The Guide To On The Job Training For College Students. Peterson's Guides. (updated annually-not just for college students)

Kohl, Herbert. *The Question is College: Guiding Your Child to the Right Choices After High School.* NY: Times Books/Random House, 1989.

Llewellyn, Grace. *The Teenage Liberation Handbook: How to Quit School and Get a Real Life and Education.* Eugene, OR: Lowry House, 1991, 1998.

Meltzer, Tom and Paul Foglino. *Cracking the CLEP.* Princeton Review.

Naftali, Lee and Joel Naftali. *You're Certifiable: The Alternative Career Guide to More Than 700 Certificate Programs, Trade Schools, and Job Opportunities.* New York: Simon and Schuster, 1999.

Peterson's Independent Study Catalog. Peterson's.

Robinson, Adam, and John Katzman. *Cracking the System: The SAT.* NY: Villard Books.

Sher, Barbara with Annie Gottlieb. *Wishcraft: How to Get What You Really Want.* NY: Viking Press, 1979.

Simosko, Susan. *Earn College Credit For What You Know.* Washington, D. C.: Acropolis Books, Ltd., 1985.

Wisconsin Department of Workforce Development. *A Guide to Apprenticeship in Wisconsin: Geared for Progress,* available from Wisconsin Department of Workforce Development, Bureau of Apprenticeship Standards, 201 E. Washington Ave, PO Box 7972, Madison, WI 53707. 608-266-3332.

The Whole Work Catalog. The New Careers Center, Inc., PO Box 339, Boulder, CO 80306. 800-634-9024.

"Learning Disabilities" and Special Education

Armstrong, Thomas. *In Their Own Way: Discovering and Encouraging Your Child's Personal Learning Style.* Los Angeles: Jeremy P. Tarcher, 1987.

Coles, Gerald S. *The Learning Mystique: A Critical Look at "Learning Disabilities."* NY: Pantheon Books, 1987.

Granger, Lori and Bill. *The Magic Feather: The Truth about "Special Education."* NY: Dutton, 1986.

Smith, Frank. *Insult to Intelligence: The Bureaucratic Invasion of Our Classrooms.* NY: Arbor House, 1986.

__________. *Reading Without Nonsense.* Third Edition. Teachers College Press, 1996.

Legal Information

Elias, Stephen. *Legal Research: How to Find and Understand the Law.* Berkeley, CA: Nolo Press, 1982.

Henkel, Jane R. *Recent Court Cases Examining the Constitutionality of Other States' Laws Regulating Home Schools.* Copies are available at no charge from the Wisconsin Legislative Council, Post Office Box 2536, Madison, WI 53701-2536; 608-266-1304.

Holt, John. *Teach Your Own: A Hopeful Path for Education.* NY: Delacorte, 1981.

Using a Law Library, published by HALT, Inc., An Organization of Americans for Legal Reform, 1319 F Street NW, Washington, DC 20004.

Whitehead, John W., and Wendell R. Bird. *Home Education and Constitutional Liberties: The Historical and Constitutional Arguments in Support of Home Instruction.* Westchester, IL: Crossway, 1984.

Index

H

I

K

L

U

V

W

Y